THE GREAT TREKS

TURNING POINTS

General Editor: Keith Robbins

David Loades	England's Maritime Empire
Robert Tombs	The Paris Commune 1871
Andrew Shennan	The Fall of France 1940
A. L. Macfie	The End of the Ottoman Empire, 1908-1923
D. B. G. Heuser	The Bomb

THE GREAT TREKS

The Transformation of Southern Africa,
1815- 1854

NORMAN ETHERINGTON

Longman

An imprint of **Pearson Education**

Harlow, England · London · New York · Reading, Massachusetts · San Francisco
Toronto · Don Mills, Ontario · Sydney · Tokyo · Singapore · Hong Kong · Seoul
Taipei · Cape Town · Madrid · Mexico City · Amsterdam · Munich · Paris · Milan

Pearson Education Limited
Head Office:
Edinburgh Gate
Harlow CM20 2JE
Tel: +44 (0)1279 623623
Fax: +44 (0)1279 431059

London Office:
128 Long Acre
London WC2E 9AN
Tel: +44 (0)20 7447 2000
Fax: +44 (0)20 7240 5771
Website: *www.history-minds.com*

First published in Great Britain in 2001

© Pearson Education Limited 2001

The right of Norman Etherington to be identified as Author
of this Work has been asserted by him in accordance
with the Copyright, Designs and Patents Act 1988.

ISBN 0 582 31567 0

British Library Cataloguing in Publication Data
A CIP catalogue record for this book can be obtained from the British Library

Library of Congress Cataloging in Publication Data
A CIP catalog record for this book can be obtained from the Library of Congress

10 9 8 7 6 5 4 3 2 1

Typeset in 11/13pt Baskerville MT by Graphicraft Limited, Hong Kong
Printed in Malaysia,VVP

The Publishers' policy is to use paper manufactured from sustainable forests.

CONTENTS

CONTENTS

DEDICATION

To my friends who have travelled along with me on my long odyssey through Southern African history: Julian Cobbing, Jeff Guy, Pen Hetherington, Shula Marks, Christopher Saunders, John Wright, - and to the memory of John Omer-Cooper.

MAPS

PREFACE

Aspirations

This book began with a publisher's invitation to write about the Great Trek as a 'turning point in history'. I rejected the invitation, pointing out that the so-called Great Trek is no longer regarded, as it once was, as the central event of South African history. Furthermore, I argued that the end of apartheid has removed most of the audience for such a book. If any new book were to be written, it would have to deal with all the movements of people and their leaders which occurred during the early nineteenth century. Ideally, it would treat each of these movements with equal attention and integrate them into a single narrative. To my surprise, the publisher invited me to try writing a new history along these lines. After a great deal of hesitation, and with considerable trepidation, I accepted the brief, moved by several considerations.

If historians do not set about writing new narrative histories of South Africa, the old ones will survive. That would be a shame. Most standard South African histories are woven around a few simple stories that are well past their use-by dates: the story of European exploration and the foundation of colonial society at the Cape; the Great Trek, whether conceived as a flight from British rule or the planting of civilization in the interior; the rise of the Zulu, whether seen as a tremendous African achievement or the root cause of tribal warfare and general mayhem; the Boer War, whether seen as the brutal suppression of the Afrikaners as a people or as a great betrayal of African hopes that a liberal British Empire would stand against the rising tide of racism. None of these stories has much relevance to post-apartheid South Africa. Many of them plainly serve the interests of formerly dominant social formations whose day will not come again. Much of the best South African historical writing was motivated by a burning desire to chronicle the injustices of racial oppression. The result was work suggesting that the course of history was downhill all the way. Now that democracy has so unexpectedly arrived, it is time to put aside these gloomy volumes. We need histories which are less determined, more aware of multiple possibilities, histories which suggest life beyond the struggle against apartheid.

Some of the worst old histories tell the best stories and have reached a mass audience that academic historians can only dream about. The only way to compete is to try to tell equally compelling stories. In addition, I believe that history offers insights that other disciplines cannot deliver. We do not have many special tools of our own, but those we do have are very powerful. The ability of historical research to falsify assertions is the foundation of the modern profession, beginning with the exposure of the fraudulent Donation of Constantine. Chronology is a much underrated tool, enabling us to see a number of disparate forces working in different arenas at the same time. No history can be resolutely linear in its treatment of time, but I have attempted to come as close as I can. For this reason I have rejected the regional approach taken by most previous histories of this era. I think there is much to be gained by noticing that the frontier war of 1834- 5, the onset of the trekking movement, Andrew Smith's secret commission to survey the interior, and the drive to acquire firearms by Moshweshwe, Dingane and Mzilikazi were events all happening at the same time. That helps us to see the linkages. Above all, the historian has a powerful question to ask of all phenomena: how did this come to be? That question draws attention to the quirky alignment of forces which bring the world around us into existence. It is a question quite as analytically incisive as the engineer's question: how does this work?

The second overarching consideration that moved me was the hope that South African history might provide a counterpart to the Truth and Reconciliation Commission of the late 1990s. It is difficult to think of anything quite like that commission in all the annals of human experience. The victorious American revolutionaries seized the estates of the defeated loyalists. In the aftermath of the French Revolution, the enemies of the new regime lost their properties and often lost their lives. After the American Civil War, all who had served with the Confederate army were excluded from the political process. In the Soviet Union the pursuit of bourgeois enemies of the Revolution was a witch-hunt that never ended. South Africa has undergone comparable revolutionary change but so far no one has gone to the scaffold or to the Gulag. Instead a general invitation has been issued to people of all racial and ethnic affiliations to come forward and confess their involvement in illegal or immoral activities motivated by either the desire to prolong the life of the apartheid regime or to overthrow it. Those who tell their stories honestly walk free.

I like both parts of the Commission's title: Reconciliation *and* Truth. I very much admire the Commission's recognition that in great struggles excesses and evil deeds are committed on all sides. To suppose that the most lasting kind of reconciliation might result from trying to tell true stories about the past strikes me as a grand aspiration (even if advanced philosophical opinion tells us it is epistemologically impossible).

About a century ago, a Canadian named George McCall Theal set out
to write history which would reconcile Boer and Briton following a generation of conflict. For sixty years or so Theal's fat books underpinned the
House of History in South Africa. Looking back on them today most
scholars would agree that Theal pursued reconciliation at the cost of truth.
He claimed most of the land for the descendants of the first Dutch colonists
on the premise that they arrived about the same time that the first Bantu-
speaking African groups had begun to arrive on their migrations from
north of the Limpopo - a proposition that could be easily falsified even
before the advent of such archaeological tools as radio-carbon dating. Though
African farmers had plainly occupied extensive territories in the interior
long before the ox wagons of the white pioneers arrived, Theal argued on
the basis of fragmentary evidence that, by a wonderful coincidence, a series
of brutal African wars sparked off by Zulu aggression had 'depopulated'
those lands just prior to the Great Trek; thus white farmers could occupy
them without feeling guilty of the crime of dispossession. He hoped that
whites of both Afrikaner and British descent could be brought together by
learning to loath a common enemy - the hypocritical, 'negrophile' busy-
bodies who had pressured succeeding British governments into misguided
schemes to undermine white supremacy in South Africa. There is perhaps
a useful lesson here. Reconciliation is a dubious goal if it is pursued at
someone else's expense.

How might the project of writing 'truth and reconciliation history' be
expressed in a revisionist account of early nineteenth-century South Africa?
That question has been on my mind. It has led me to reject some ways of
looking at history that are deeply ingrained in my profession. Here are
some that are particularly troublesome.

The search for origins

History as a discipline betrays its nineteenth-century roots through an excessive concentration on origins. The organic model of national growth is
based on an unconscious assumption that every nation-state begins as an
embryo, progresses through formative experiences of infancy on the way to
finally achieving a mature identity through decisive crises or challenges.
This leads the writers of general history to dwell at length on beginnings.
German historians of the last century strove to find vital insights into their
own national character in a handful of lines by Tacitus on the northern tribes
of Europe. English historians swept away legends of original foundations by
Aeneas or King Arthur and put in their place a notion of a national character
deriving from Anglo-Saxons. Yankee historians tried to obliterate the obvious

evidence of colonial origins based on southern plantation slavery with a history tracing the lineaments of truly American culture to Puritans who arrived on the *Mayflower*. Australian historians strove to find keys to the national character in the experience of convict society in early New South Wales.

South African historians keep going back to the early colonial history of the Cape Colony in search of clues to the development of a racially stratified society. This is not entirely unreasonable. Peculiar and persistent forms of agricultural organisation based on captive black labour did make their first appearance there. However, the emphasis on Cape origins perpetuates a pernicious tradition of viewing South African history through the eyes of white colonists. Now that everyone acknowledges that the ancestors of most South Africans were present in the landscape by the fifth century or earlier, we should either seek another point of origin to work from - or throw the whole organic model overboard.[1] A major problem for those who want to create indigenous rivals for embryonic white settlements such as Plymouth Rock, Botany Bay and Cape Town is that there are no written records to work from. The temptation in such cases is to substitute archaeological, linguistic or anthropological data for written archives. The unfortunate result, all too often, is to reproduce by other means the Us/Them binary opposition typical of colonial encounters. We, the colonizers, read with interest the journal of Jan van Riebeeck who stepped ashore at Cape Town in 1652. They, the indigenous Others, are traced back to Neolithic and iron-age, cattle-complex populations whose appearance can be roughly dated from bones, pots, cattle dung and other rubbish found at scattered sites along the Mfolozi River. We have events, They have ways of life. We have history, They have culture.

Another problem caused by excessive concern with origins is that the historian tends to fall into the habit of viewing colonial expansion from behind the lines of an advancing frontier - and consequently from the point of view of the colonizer. In South Africa that point of view is deeply embedded in the language of place. We write unthinkingly about the Eastern Cape frontier, Transorangia, the Transkei, the Transvaal: terms that explicitly incorporate a reference back to Cape Town where history began. Historians who write in the era of Nelson Mandela should not be drawn into metaphorically riding with the army officers, officials, missionaries and travellers on whose evidence they must inevitably rely for accounts of events in the early nineteenth century. They have to strive to do more than simply set out to 'the other side of the frontier'. They and their readers need to be able to position themselves imaginatively in a landscape where the agents of colonialism appear first as specks on a distant horizon.

This is not easy when the contents of the archives continually drag the historian back toward the record makers' points of view. The seat of British colonial government remained at Cape Town until 1910. Nineteenth-century Cape Town was a very long way from the districts where most people lived. It is connected to the well-watered districts of south-eastern Africa by a 1000-kilometre-long narrow panhandle of arable land. From the verandah of Government House the rest of South Africa resembled the famous cartoon view of America from New York where Central Park looms larger than Texas. Maps compiled in Cape Town in the 1820s, 30s and 40s make some African groups (the Zulu for instance) appear the masters of huge territorial empires. Other important groups do not appear at all.

It is not only the record keepers at Government House who pester historians by insisting that we view things from their perspective. Missionaries generally identified with the people who lived around them and the leaders who were receptive to their message. Groups without missionaries tended to be vilified or ignored. Even anti-clerical historians have been sucked into adopting the characteristic points of view of missionaries who left big piles of records.

My strategy has been to strive for an alternative perspective by imaginatively situating myself at the centre of the territory occupied by the great majority of the people who fed themselves by farming and keeping herds of sheep and cattle. I call this huge area the heartland, a word of my own invention. I call the long rectangular pastoral region stretching from Grahamstown to Cape Town the panhandle. I have struggled, not entirely successfully, to avoid standard geographical terms which embed a colonizer's point of view, such as Transvaal, Transkei, Transorangia and Cape Colony. My most audacious innovation has been to call Britain's first South African Colony the British Zone rather than the Cape Colony. This attempts to decentre the colonizers in the same way that the use of the term Danelaw decentres the zone of Viking occupation in histories of early medieval England.

The tyranny of language

Language is a big problem for the would-be writer of truth and reconciliation history. I am not thinking here so much of the problem of translation. For the period that directly concerns me very few documents survive in African languages. I am thinking more about maddening questions of word choice that crop up in practically every paragraph. There are dozens of phrases routinely used in writing about the South African past which are reminiscent of the notorious example of Attila's 'hordes' facing the Christians' 'mighty host'. The British had soldiers, the Xhosa had warriors. The Natal colonists sent troops into battle against Zulu impis. Boers 'trekked' to escape the control of the Cape Government while Africans invariably 'fled' from

King Shaka's rule. White settlers 'colonized' new territories; black tribes 'drifted', or 'wandered', or 'streamed' or 'cut their way' into them. Constant vigilance is required to avoid perpetuating the double standards inscribed in old texts. I have tried to use a stripped-down, rather austere vocabulary, avoiding allusions to European texts. For example, I would not resort to Shakespeare and pronounce 'a plague on both houses' because that privileges the colonizer's cultural heritage. Occasionally I have referred to biblical texts, because these are now part of the shared culture of most South Africans. I cannot avoid the more deeply embedded distortions of the English language. I have not attempted to approximate a political scientist's abstract terminology for social groupings. While I know that the words chief, king, chiefdom, kingdom and state do not precisely convey the meaning of terms used by Shaka, Mzilikazi or Hintsa, I use them as a strategy for resisting exoticism and binary oppositions. European historians know that what the Romans called a kingdom and what the Saxons called a king differ in both scale and kind from the monarchies of Louis XIV and Victoria, but that does not cause them to reject those terms in favour of words such as 'polity' and 'second-order state'.

There are other equally perplexing problems of vocabulary. *Assegai*, meaning spear, is a word borrowed from the now defunct Khoikhoi language of the Western Cape. It is commonly employed in writings about Africans living thousands of kilometres from that region. Should it be dropped in favour of *umkonto* - a word still in common use by living people - when we write about Zululand? Or should we avoid all such exoticisms by confining ourselves to English?

While in the United States place names of Native American origin abound, in South Africa the Afrikaans language has swept across the land like a gigantic linguistic scouring pad, obliterating African names and multiplying Plaatbergs, Mooi Rivers, Modder Rivers and Driefonteins. A genuine reconciliation history might insist on restoring the old nomenclature, but would thereby run the risk of confusing everyone.

Educated opinion generally holds that social groups should be designated by the names and spellings preferred by living members of those groups. It is common practice for historians to extend the courtesy to members of extinct social groupings when we are confident of the way they referred to themselves. So South African historians have written Afrikaner instead of Boer, and San instead of Bushman. But getting things exactly right is simply impossible. The subjects of King Mzilikazi liked to be called Zulus; their Sotho-Tswana enemies called them Matabele (a word that seems to have been applied generally to alien invaders). Modern historians do not, however, respect the wishes of the dead in this case. Instead they use an invented word, Ndebele, which is the way the word Matabele might be rendered in Zulu, if such a word existed in that language![2] It so happens that in this case present-day descendants of those people have given in to the historians and now call themselves Ndebele. And, because they relish association with such successful conquerors, so do other, totally unrelated groups who used to be called Matabele by their Sotho neighbours. If we applied the same principle to English and Afrikaner people we might call them *amaLungu* and *amaBuna* (the designations employed by Zulu-speakers of the last century), or possibly Anglicize them as lungus and bunas.

Historians are still divided about the word to be applied to the hunter-gatherers of the south-western regions. Some still use Bushman, an English variant of the Dutch Bosjeman. Others use San, which is a word that may have been used by some of their neighbours who spoke a language which has since disappeared. Still others have accepted the theory that the only significant difference between those called Khoikhoi and the San was that the former kept sheep and cattle and the latter did not. This leads them to write of the 'Khoisan' people. Most of the people who believe themselves descended from those groups were classified as 'Coloured' by the apartheid regime. They have mostly followed the lead of English-speaking historians and insist that their forbears be called either Khoi or Khoisan. The word used by speakers of Bantu languages to designate hunter-gathers without cattle from Zululand to Rwanda is Twa, but the preferences of that vast population are ignored in all texts, again, probably because of the dominance of Cape-centred history. Some of the Khoisan of the early nineteenth century liked to be known as the Bastards. This so embarrassed a visiting missionary that in 1813 he convinced a number of them to call themselves Griqua, a name drawn from a former chief whose historical existence is still in question.[3] However, other people scorned the missionaries and continued to call themselves Bastards right through the 1850s. Whose wishes will be respected in the search for truth and reconciliation?

Even spelling becomes an issue. Some historians spell plural forms as they would be written today: for example amaNgwane. Those who prefer the first form often justify it as a mark of deference to African sensibilities. However, in almost all cases, the orthography of African languages was determined not by the speakers of those languages but by the European missionaries or linguists who first reduced them to writing. In conforming to present orthographical practice we are, in almost all cases, conforming to the linguistic theories of white scholars, not to the wishes of African people. The historian Leonard Thompson wrote a fine biography of the man who created the nation we now call Lesotho. He confronted a major spelling problem. His subject's name is properly pronounced more or less as Muh-shwee-shwee. English writers used to render it as Moshesh. The orthographical standard for the Sesuthu language adopted by Lesotho decreed that the man's name should be spelled Moshoeshoe (which a French speaker would pronounce correctly because the form derives from grammars devised by French missionaries). Across the border in South Africa, the standard Sesuthu spelling is Moshweshwe. Eventually Thompson decided that the official Lesotho spelling should prevail in a book about that country's founding father. The unfortunate result is that almost all English-speaking students now mispronounce the name as Mo-shoe-shoe.

With such examples before me as I begin to write, I can be confident that whatever words I choose, I am bound to offend someone. In general I have tried to make my spelling conform to the forms used by the most recent historians. For modern Zulu forms I have consulted the latest published volume of the *James Stuart Archive*, edited by John Wright. I have used the term Boer more than I have used Afrikaner in an attempt to jettison the cultural nationalism embodied in the latter term. More controversially, I have avoided racial terminology wherever possible because I believe that in the future race will disappear as a way of categorizing people. To my great surprise I found that it was seldom necessary to speak of black and white or even Africans and settlers. My meaning could be made plain without those words. This does not mean I have ignored issues of race, any more than I ignore issues of class. When historians argue that we must take account of 'race and class', they do not mean that they actually believe in racial difference. They only mean that we must take account of the effects of *beliefs* about racial difference held by people in this and previous eras.

Who may speak for the dead?

These vexatious questions of naming and spelling arise in South Africa, as elsewhere in the world, from present-day inter-group politics. Historians who want to be listened to cannot afford the journalist's or politician's ploy of pronouncing a general anathema on political correctness. We have to take the clearly-expressed wishes of living people into account. With one exception. There is a persistent undercurrent of opinion which holds that only group members are truly able to represent their own past. To give in to that demand is to make all history impossible. If only the Zulu can properly understand Zulu history, it follows that only a Zulu can write Zulu history, and only a Zulu reader will understand the historical texts so produced. For obvious reasons the perils of this approach are better understood in South Africa than in many other countries. It was the foundation stone of the apartheid regime's policy of providing fenced-off 'homelands' for every cultural group. It is fortunate that the political movement headed by Nelson Mandela came to power committed to the ideal of one South Africa and opposed to all claims of racial or ethnic particularism. The Truth and Reconciliation Commission paid no heed to those who would justify evil deeds on the ground that they were necessary to group survival. Nor did it admit that outsiders are incapable of judging the acts of government insiders. Its objective was to achieve an understanding of the past that all South Africans can share. Pursuing such a goal will not, of course, produce a single agreed version of history. There will always be many points of view, many stories to be told. What I am arguing here is that historians will tell their stories better if they hold the ideal of a shared history constantly in mind.

Of course I have to admit to a personal stake in this issue. In many ways I am the ultimate outsider: a white man, born in America, now an Australian citizen whose experience of South Africa is drawn entirely from research trips over the last thirty years and the books I have read. But I do not, for all that, feel disqualified from the task. I would not claim to speak with authority about the *experience* of being black in South Africa. Or an Afrikaner female in South Africa. Or a Zulu. Or an English migrant. The experience of being any of these things is beyond me, however much I might strive for empathy.

But the past *is* another country. There is no passport of colour, nationality or ethnicity which admits anyone to the fast lane through the border crossing. And that is a good thing. The task of writing new histories of South Africa - histories that all South Africans can share, histories that will sweep away the texts dedicated to emphasizing the superiority of this or that race or culture - is too big to be undertaken by insiders. And it has lessons worth teaching all the world.

Dealing with absences and silences

To my considerable consternation I have not achieved the democratic inclusion which I sought when I began to work on this book. The sources tell us much about some groups and very little about others - in some cases so little that a judicious historian must either speculate or remain silent. At every point in my research I tried to be specially alert to gender but once again was hampered (but, I hope, not defeated) by my sources. Where women appear as named individuals in sources, I have tried to draw them into the story through a strategy I call 'significant anecdote'. Much of the story I have to tell is about chiefdoms and kingdoms, but that does not mean that it solely concerns men. As I emphasize in Chapter 2, although chieftainship was gendered, it was a family affair, sustained as much by females as males.

It has been even more difficult to write the history of common people of both sexes. They are a constant presence but we can seldom find sources to illuminate their agency and change over time in the heartland regions before 1850. My strategy here has also been to use 'significant anecdote' to bring them on the stage from time to time, as I do in Chapter 10 with Dina and her children and the courageous, unnamed Zulu horseman who stabbed himself in the heart rather than being captured by the Boers.

In contrast, it is all too easy to over-emphasize the role of the British government, the Zulu kingdom and Moshweshwe's BaSotho because they are so fulsomely represented in the sources. I did not have much difficulty cutting the British government down to size; all that was required was to minimize discussion of personalities and to omit everything that specifically appertained to British rather than to Southern African history. My strategy for dealing with Moshweshwe was to bring his rivals in the Caledon Valley to the fore. The Zulu kingdom posed the most difficult problem because the magnificent *James Stuart Archive* provides such a tempting mother lode of historical information told by Zulu people in their own words. It would have been foolhardy to neglect it, but I have tried to use it sparingly, lest the Zulu overshadow all other groups in this history as they have in others.

Revisions

This history relies for the most part on published sources, because attempting to read all available unpublished archival resources would have taken me another ten years of full-time research, maybe more. Fortunately, as early as the 1840s people were busily publishing documents which historians regard as primary sources. One of the most valuable collections of printed primary sources has only emerged in recent years: B. J. T. Leverton's four volumes of *Records of Natal*, which includes many items previously unseen and unused by historians. (The title is misleading; much more than Natal is included.) My practice throughout the text has been to rely on the earliest printed primary sources because these are least likely to have been contaminated by the prejudices of subsequent generations of history writers.

My theoretical stance as a historian is incorrigibly materialist, tempered by a tendency to attend to the importance of language and representations in historical sources. Although I set out to write about South African history from an unusual vantage point, I did not plan to be otherwise original. Nonetheless, when I contemplate the finished work, I find that I have arrived at some conclusions which depart from the conventional wisdom.

For the benefit of practising historians who have learned the art of scanning texts quickly in search of revisionist interpretations, I will list mine at the beginning.

Rejecting the *mfecane*

Without the work of Julian Cobbing, this book would never have been contemplated or written. I consider Cobbing's criticism of the concept of the *mfecane* to be irrefutable. No reputable historian can now argue, as most historians used to argue, that the Zulu kingdom was a novel political formation whose appearance set off a chain reaction of violence, conflict and mass migration. After Cobbing, very few would argue, as many used to imply, that the history of the Zulu, Ndwandwe, BaSotho, Ndebele and other states in the early nineteenth century belongs to 'pre-colonial history' uncontaminated by influences emanating from Britain's Cape Colony or expanding networks of trade linked to overseas markets. Cobbing's published and unpublished writings have been controversial, not because of his critique of the *mfecane*, but because of his secondary argument that the fundamental causes of increased conflict in south-eastern Africa were the slave trade and other forms of violently seizing labour to serve colonial requirements. I believe that Cobbing was right to reject the concept of the *mfecane*, so I have dropped the term. Like many other historians I accept his argument about the importance of Griqua/Kora raiding as an incredibly disruptive force on the highveld beginning in the late eighteenth century. However, I cannot follow Cobbing in attributing the rise of large states in the coastal regions to accelerating demand for slaves. Nor do I believe that more than a relative handful of people from the highveld were seized by slavers operating out of Inhambane or Delagoa Bay. In part, I reach this conclusion for the reasons advanced by Elizabeth Eldredge; the evidence is too thin and inconclusive.

Did large states appear in the late eighteenth and early nineteenth centuries?

As I reread the sources, I unexpectedly arrived at a revisionist view that even Cobbing did not advance. I cannot find evidence that large states emerged for the first time in the late eighteenth century. Undoubtedly the Zulu kingdom was a new state, but I cannot find evidence that convinces me that it was a new kind of state, or necessarily larger than any that existed before. The much older states of Mapungubwe and Zimbabwe bear witness to the ability of large southern African chieftaincies to sustain themselves mainly on a surplus extracted from control of cattle and cultivators, supplemented by a trickle of trade. As Malyn Newitt has pointed out, large states undoubtedly existed in the southern Mozambique coastal regions at the time Europeans first landed there in the sixteenth century. As Martin Hall observes, multitudinous stone ruins in the uplands of KwaZulu-Natal attest to the existence of large, dense settlement over several centuries. It therefore seems to me more than likely that through long-established methods of controlling production and reproduction, states comparable to Shaka's Zulu kingdom existed in a much earlier era. The so-called Mbo grouping cannot be an invention of Shakan times because the word Mbo was written on maps centuries before oral traditions about it were recorded. This is supported by the long genealogies A. T. Bryant recorded for the Ndwandwe and related chieftaincies, which form a marked contrast to the very short genealogies of the chieftaincies headed by Dingiswayo and Shaka. I believe that the old view that iron-age farmers only reached South Africa in the fifteenth or sixteenth century unconsciously predisposed historians to view late eighteenth-century chieftaincies as new developments. The romantic, unsubstantiated pictures Bryant drew of life in 'olden times' reflected the missionary's tendency to look for ancient Edens. The influence of Henry Fynn's and Nathaniel Isaacs's eye-witness account of Shaka's recently founded paramountcy caused historians to jump to the unwarranted conclusion that there had been none like it before.

If the Zulu, Swazi, Pedi, BaSotho and other similar states were built on old lines, it is unnecessary to look for new factors responsible for their rise. For this reason, I do not expend much effort evaluating the relative merits of the population pressure theory or the drought theory or the trade theory or the slaving theory or any other theory put forward to account for the rise of the new states. Before I did, I would want to be convinced that they were new. The old view cannot be allowed to stand simply because of its longevity. It beggars belief that the elaborate institutions of those states were evolved during a few decades of constant conflict.

The scale of violent conflict in early nineteenth-century south-east Africa has been hugely exaggerated

Early settler historiography grossly exaggerated the scale of conflict in order to advance the colonists' claims as bringers of peace and occupiers of an empty land. Missionaries exaggerated the scale of violence as evidence that their preaching of the gospel of peace achieved quick results. There are no body counts for wars fought prior to the involvement of colonial commandos and armies. The fact that so many of the leaders most intimately involved in the conflicts of the early nineteenth century were still living in the 1840s and 1850s predisposes me to accept Eldredge's argument that losses of life on the battlefield were relatively small. The large number of people who thronged the Caledon Valley in the 1830s and whom the French naturalist/hunter Adulphe Delegorgue found living in the Magaliesberg is *prima facie* evidence disproving the missionary/settler story of mass killing, starvation and cannibalism. Everyone agrees that the years 1820-5 were marked by much higher degrees of conflict and disruption in the north-western, central and southern highveld, but estimates of people killed are highly speculative. Those years, by themselves, do not justify the use of *mfecane*, *lifaqane* or *difaqane* as aids to understanding historical processes at work.

Although Cobbing may have been wrong about the influence of slaving to supply Indian Ocean markets before 1820, he is certainly right in what he says about its influence after that date. It is not enough to say that the conflicts associated with the rise of the Zulu, Gasa and other states produced captives which could be sold at Inhambane and Delagoa Bay. The historian must go on to investigate how the slaves got there, who sold them and the effects of the trade on adjacent regions. I argue that Sobhuza, Soshangane, Nxaba, Zwangendaba and the other chiefs who moved northeast after Shaka's defeat of Zwide were not aimlessly in flight from Zulu power. They were seeking to gain power and influence by seizing the opportunities presented to supply a burgeoning market in slaves.

The open grasslands of the highveld were not depopulated by warfare; they had probably always been sparsely settled

That extensive unpopulated grasslands lay open for occupation when the Boer trekkers streamed onto the highveld is probably true, but it was not because those lands had been emptied by warfare. Chiefs whose power was based on control of people through cattle had always avoided the open plains because it was hard to defend their herds. Before irrigation, the plains were also avoided because agriculture was too risky except around springs. Tim Maggs's work uses convincing archaeological and historical evidence to show why chiefs and people preferred to establish their settlements on the sides of hills in districts of reliable rainfall. Other archaeological research has shown that movements to settle on hillsides for defensive purposes date back to at least the seventeenth century.[4]

I have formed the conviction that the reason for the horseshoe-shaped configuration of South Africa's twentieth-century 'Bantustans' is that these form the residue of the ecological districts preferred by people over several centuries. These were for the most part not lands they were reluctantly pushed into, but lands which - through their determined resistance - they managed to defend against the invading colonists.

Trekkers and British authorities were allied forces

I follow and to a slight degree extend a trend among historians of the present generation to reject the idea of a 'Great Trek' motivated by hostility to the British government of the Cape Colony. That idea originated in the writings of colonial propagandists bent on blaming the exodus of 1836 on the policies of the British Secretary for Colonies, Lord Glenelg. Those propagandists included Governor Benjamin D'Urban, high-ranking British officers, newspaper proprietors and land speculators. These people did not deplore the trekking movement. They cheered it on at every step, hoping that the home government would eventually come round to their view that the interior regions should be annexed. Many of the first trekkers, including the influential Piet Uys, claimed to be loyal subjects.

The idea of the trek as anti-British gained support later in the nineteenth century with the awakening of Afrikaner nationalism. If the nationalists had been correct in their exaltation of the trek as an expression of general Boer resentment, then the trekkers would have been drawn in large numbers from every part of the Cape Colony. In fact, as historians have always known, the trekkers were drawn almost exclusively from the less well-off farmers of the eastern districts.

The first and second Anglo-Boer wars sparked a reassessment of the trek among elements of the English-speaking population, who were attracted to the idea that the trekking movement represented a misguided revolt of backward 'seventeenth-century people' against the irresistible forces of modernity. Later writers of liberal and progressive sentiments blamed the trek for extending the rule of an outmoded system of racial domination over the most populous districts of South Africa, thereby paving the way for the triumph of white supremacy. Revisionist historians of the 1970s and 1980s comprehensively demolished that interpretation by showing how other major economic interests and the British imperial government advanced the cause of racial domination.

The 'official mind on the spot'

Historians of the British Empire have a long tradition of contrasting the policies dictated by the 'official mind' of the home government to the actions carried out by the 'man on the spot' - who is generally the governor of a distant province. I contend that over the course of time an 'official mind on the spot' develops out of the shared perceptions and bureaucratic institutions which bind the upper echelons of provincial government together. In early nineteenth-century South Africa, a set of local perceptions about military affairs developed into an official mind which can clearly be seen in operation over many decades. It was remarkably resilient in its resistance to directives from home. The idea that Boers were necessary allies who needed to be conciliated was one important axiom of the official mind. Another was that peoples across the border had to be continually and forcibly reminded of British military strength lest they be tempted to rise in arms. The revolt against 'philanthropic negrophilia' in 1836 was at least as much a revolt of Cape officialdom as a revolt of those who trekked off to the highveld.

Chieftainship

I began my research still believing that the old 'tribal' names such as Basuto, Swazi, Ndwandwe, Zulu, Ndebele had some utility as signifiers of ethnic units. I no longer hold that belief. I think that 'mfecane maps' which use arrows to show the movements of 'peoples' convey a misleading and even dangerous impression. The important movements discussed in this book were movements of chiefs whose followings could and did include people from all sorts of backgrounds. There is no evidence to show that such aggregations were a unique feature of the early nineteenth century. The near universality of the phenomenon across the region suggests that it was based on practices dating from a much earlier period. I think that the historical study of chieftainship as an institution before 1850 should be high on the agenda for research. The indications are that ethnicity was non-existent and chieftainship was an ancient institution of the utmost importance.

Notes

1   William F. Lye and Colin Murray, *Transformations on the Highveld: The Tswana and Southern Sotho* (Cape Town, 1980), p. 25.

2   R. Kent Rasmussen, *Migrant Kingdom: Mzilikazi's Ndebele in South Africa* (Cape Town, 1978), p. 161.

3   Robert Ross, *Adam Kok's Griquas: A Study in the Development of Stratification in History* (Cambridge, 1976), p. 12.

4   Simon Hall, 'Archaeological Indicators for Stress in the Western Transvaal Region between the Seventeenth and Nineteenth Centuries' in Carolyn Hamilton, ed., *The Mfecane Aftermath: Reconstructive Debates in Southern African History* (Johannesburg, 1995), pp. 309-11.

ACKNOWLEDGMENTS

It has been my privilege to be assisted at every step of my research and writing by friends and colleagues in the historical profession. Julian Cobbing shook my faith in the *mfecane* and later extended his hospitality to me during my period of research. Johannes Du Bruyn was the first person to encourage me to venture into print with my speculations on the Great Trek, dispelling my fear that only Afrikaners could tread that ground with confidence. Carolyn Hamilton invited me to the ground-breaking symposium she convened on the '*Mfecane* Aftermath' in 1991 and gave me a place in the book which came out of that event. The Australian Research Council generously supported my research. Christopher Saunders and Jeff Guy offered hospitality and critical comments at vital stages of my work. Jeff and Julian Cobbing lent me several volumes from their own libraries to accompany me on the 14,000-kilometre journey I took in 1997 in an attempt to make out-of-the-way places like Mosega, Sekukuniland and the wilder parts of the Caledon Valley live in my visual imagination.

During the later stages of my research Petra Fogarty helped me avoid mistakes in my use of Afrikaans sources. I am also very grateful to the production team at the Longman division of Pearson Education for their enthusiasm and help in turning my typescript into a book. In addition to those who read my draft chapters as a labour of love, I want especially to thank Jeff Guy, John Wright and Julian Cobbing for tough-minded comments, which steered me away from many rocks. Though they find it as difficult to agree with each other as with me, they are, to use our Australian vernacular, a great bunch of bastards.

ABBREVIATIONS

JSA   Colin de B. Webb and John B. Wright, eds, *The James Stuart Archive of Recorded Oral Evidence Relating to the History of the Zulu and Neighbouring Peoples*, 4 vols (Pietermaritzburg, 1976- 86).

Records of Natal   B. J. T. Leverton, ed., *South African Archival Records, Important Cape Documents, Volumes 4–7 Records of Natal*. These particular volumes are numbered 1- 4. (Pretoria, 1984- 1991).

Natal Papers   John Centilvres Chase, ed., *The Natal Papers: A Reprint of all Notices and Public Documents Connected with that Territory*, 2 vols in one (Grahamstown, 1843; reprinted Cape Town, 1968).

Basutoland Records   George M. Theal, ed., *Basutoland Records, Volume I, 1833– 1852* (Cape Town, 1883; reprinted Cape Town, 1964).

CHAPTER ONE

Introduction

In the first half of the nineteenth century many people anticipated that a movement of frontiersmen from the Cape Colony into south-east Africa would repeat the experience of the United States and Australia. They expected a flood of 'pioneers' to sweep away the indigenous people and replace them with white men's crops and herds. The story turned out very differently. Thin columns of farmers and ox wagons did push north onto the grassed plains known as the highveld and down into the lush semi-tropical lands of Natal. But African people stood much of their ground against the advancing legions of white settlement. They resisted the invaders' diseases. They expanded trade in ivory, hides and cereal crops. They formed new groupings, reorganized old chiefdoms and joined kingdoms which succeeded in holding some of the best agricultural land. They learned new fighting skills, often adopting the invaders' way of fighting with horses and guns. Where they did lose ground they inflicted significant casualties on the invaders and seized large herds of animals. They held most of the valuable coastal lands between East London and Delagoa Bay. They laid the foundations of the future independent African states of Botswana, Swaziland and Lesotho. They narrowly missed creating other states which might have been known as Zululand, Pediland and Gaza. By avoiding the fate of the Native Americans and the Aboriginal people of Australia, they entrenched their position as a permanent majority throughout the region. Thus, after many trials and setbacks, when democracy finally came to South Africa at the end of the twentieth century, Africans filled most of the elected positions in government.

All things considered, the period 1815 to 1854 can fairly claim to be a turning point in history.[1] That is one of the reasons so many historians have tried to tell its story. Many have concentrated on the movement of white farmers and their dependants which became known as the 'Great Trek'. Others have chronicled the bitter 'hundred years' war between the Xhosa and their enemies in the series of conflicts that used be known as 'the Kaffir wars'. Some of the finest historians and anthropologists of the twentieth century tried their hands at explaining the emergence and rapid expansion of the Zulu kingdom under the legendary Shaka. The story of Moshweshwe's creation and stalwart defence of Lesotho has been told many times. The Tswana, Swazi and Pedi likewise found their eloquent historians. However, there are no comprehensive treatments of this turbulent period, except in textbooks. There is no obvious model to copy, no obvious place to begin.

This book, which seeks to view developments as part of a unified story that all South Africans can share, needs an appropriate vantage point. For various reasons it makes sense to choose one up on the highveld.

An impressive mountain looms over the town of Harrismith in South Africa. Once the home of lions, it is still a gathering place for eagles who ride rising columns of air, up and up. On a good day the updraughts will carry a soaring bird far above the summit, which itself stands more than 2000 metres above sea level. It is no great feat for an eagle to rise above the highest mountains in the nearby ranges. If the eagle could see 500 kilometres in every direction, it would see as far as Delagoa Bay in the east, across the Maloti mountains to East London in the south, to Kimberley in the west and to the headwaters of the Limpopo in the north-west. A circle drawn that big takes in all the people of Swaziland and Lesotho, most of the population of the Republic of South Africa, and the capital cities of Botswana and Mozambique. Within the same circle lie the gold and diamond mines which have so largely shaped the modern history of southern Africa – and most of the battle sites of the region's bloody wars. In this history this region will figure as the heartland of southern Africa. In an attempt to hold onto this vantage point, it will deliberately be called *the heartland*.

A legend says the first men and women on earth emerged from the cave of Ntsuanatsatsi, only a little distance to the north of Harrismith.[2] As far as history is concerned the legend might as well be fact. Evidence dug out of the earth confirms that people with cattle have lived south of the Limpopo River since the third century of the present era.[3] That is to say, since the century that saw the break-up of the Han Dynasty in China and the birth of the future Emperor Constantine in Rome – before the Anglo-Saxons arrived in Britain; before the Mayans, Incas and Aztecs built empires in Central and South America; before the first people stepped ashore in New Zealand. A very long time ago.

Why not, then, view the unfolding history of southern Africa with the eyes of the eagle soaring above Harrismith? The old histories started with

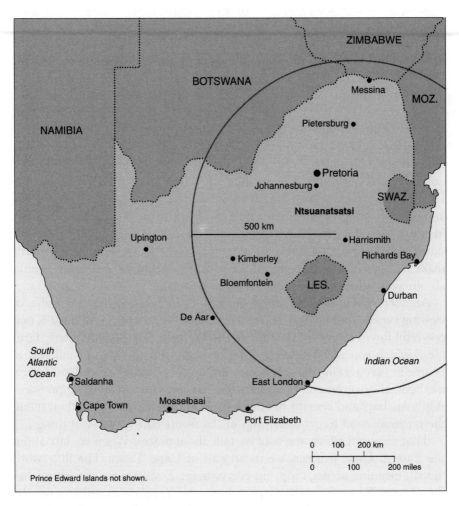

Map 1   With the eyes of an eagle

European explorers cruising along the coast – on their way to somewhere else. The story continued with the Dutch planting a station at Cape Town to supply their passing ships with fresh food. Then it followed the fortunes of the descendants of the Cape Town settlers as they expanded their 'frontier' eastwards. Even more recent histories, which admit that African peoples occupied the land in ancient times, soon get drawn into viewing events from behind the line of the Cape's expanding frontier of white settlement. Why? One reason is that people who lived in southern Africa during the centuries before the Dutch arrived left no records that speak to us with human voices. We know them only through the bones, tools and rubbish they left behind. When we talk about them we tend to use the language of archaeologists. They become the 'Leonard's Kopje people', 'cattle-complex populations', 'Neolithic' or 'iron-age' people. Above all they are *they*; not *us*, not like us – even if they are our own ancestors! Jan van Riebeeck and the Dutch men who came with him in 1652 left letters, journals, wills, title deeds and all sorts of other documents that speak with voices with which we can identify, even if we first have to translate them into English. They say 'we sailed', 'we landed', 'we trekked', 'we were attacked', 'we won'. The records make it easy to slip into seeing Africa with the eyes of the colonizer, even if all our sympathies lie with the colonized people.

Another reason why twentieth-century historians got into the habit of viewing events from behind the advancing frontier of white settlement is that powerful forces forged ways of life in the Western Cape – particularly farm life – which spread far into the interior and ruled the lives of millions of people in very recent times. It is very important to understand those forces: methods of government, land seizures, slavery, child-stealing, apprenticeship, pass laws and systems of inheritance. But the more we dwell on them, the more we tend to get caught up in the frontiersmen's view of things.

That view still affects the way we talk about places. When we talk about the Eastern Cape frontier, we mean east of Cape Town. The little word 'trans', meaning across, crops up everywhere: *Trans*orangia, meaning *across* the Orange River from the Cape colony; the *Trans*kei, meaning *across* the Kei River, beyond the line of white settlement; the *Trans*vaal, meaning on the far side of the Vaal River from where most white people used to live. Many other words similarly entrench the Cape settlers' view. One is *kraal*, a word which probably comes from the Portuguese language and was long used to indicate the place where individual Africans lived with their families and animals (places that Africans north of the Kei River called *umuzi*). Another is the word *assegai*, a word used by the indigenous people of the Western Cape to refer to a spear (which elsewhere would be called an *umkonto*). So long as we use the old words, we are unconsciously referring back to Cape Town, as though all life began there.

This is the twenty-first century. South Africa is free. The descendants of the colonizers are no longer in charge of the government. Today's historians must struggle against the temptation to ride in their imaginations beside the army officers, officials, missionaries and travellers on whose evidence they must inevitably rely. We have to strive to do more than simply see out to the 'other side of the frontier'. We need to be able to imagine ourselves in a place where the agents of colonialism appear first as specks on a distant horizon. We can get a better view if we soar with the eagles above Harrismith. From that great height all people look the same. In a fair and democratic history all people would count the same. Thus the 'great trek' of the Rolong from Plaatberg to Thaba Nchu and the epic journey of the Griqua over the mountains to Kokstad deserve notice alongside the more celebrated 'great trek' of the Afrikaner farmers and their dependants onto the highveld.

In an attempt to struggle against the old ways of thinking, this history will not use the words Transkei or Transvaal. Nor will it refer more than occasionally to 'the Cape' or the 'the Cape Colony'. Since, for most of the period covered in this book, Britain claimed the territory it called the Cape Colony, that district will be called the *British Zone*.

It is often difficult to write democratic history because many people who lived in previous centuries left no trace of their existence. In oral traditions chiefs count more than commoners. In colonial written records officials and generals count more than subjects and soldiers. In almost all records men are more visible than women. Southern African social history in the last quarter of the twentieth century tried to counter these built-in biases and blinkers by consciously writing 'history from below'. There will be little room for social history in this book, which by its very nature takes an Olympian perspective. How then to include those who have traditionally been excluded? One solution to the problem is suggested by the eagle who from time to time swoops down to seize a single mouse. By the use of significant anecdotes it is possible to bring the stories of women, children, forgotten peoples and outcasts sharply into focus.

Even on the clearest day, the eagle sees no national borders. The neat lines on maps which mark Lesotho off like an island in a South African sea were drawn by politicians. They also drew the long boundary which separates Mozambique from its neighbours. There was nothing natural or inevitable about the way these borders developed. They emerged as the result of life-and-death struggles for wealth and power. Change one or two events and today's maps would show an independent kingdom of Zululand. Change other things and most of what we think of as southern Mozambique, Zimbabwe and Botswana would be part of South Africa. That would have profoundly changed the way histories of South Africa are written, because the state would have included different people. Historians who think in terms of organic development of pre-destined nation-states include everyone inside the borders as part of 'our history'. People on the other side of the fence tend to get left out. When we write about people who lived in the early nineteenth century to the east of the Drakensberg and near the western headwaters of the Limpopo, we should imitate the eagle and ignore the boundary lines on modern maps. The inhabitants of those regions were constantly interacting – grouping and regrouping. Nobody thought of themselves as Zimbabweans, Botswanans, Mozambiquans, Swazi or South Africans. In the course of this century those imaginary lines will become less and less important. As the regional economy develops, people, products, ideas and money will move freely back and forth between Swaziland and South Africa, between Zimbabwe and Botswana, between KwaZulu-Natal and southern Mozambique – just as they do within the North American Free Trade Area and the European Union. So the future will resemble the time two hundred years ago when there were no national borders.

The soaring eagle sees people but not tribes or cultures or ethnic groups. Many of the differences in language and culture which distinguish people today arose very recently. They came about through complicated interactions between individual communities and various conquerors, politicians, missionaries and scholars. In 1800 there was no Ndebele, no Swazi, no 'Bhaca' or 'Shangaan' (though of course there were people living who were the ancestors of those who later came to think of themselves as belonging to such groups). During the twentieth century powerful political and intellectual forces pushed the idea that South African history must be written as group history. At the time of the second Anglo-Boer war, journalists wrote of the conflict as a 'race war' between English and Afrikaner. Officials in charge of 'Bantu affairs' divided up the African population into a patchwork quilt of 'tribes', and commissioned anthropologists to write separate ethnographies for them. Gold mine bosses split their migrant work forces into teams based on ethnic affiliations and promoted 'tribal' dance and musical competitions. After 1948 the apartheid regime tried to convince the world that the overcrowded and degraded old Native Reserves were really 'Homelands' of distinct nations who would, in the fullness of time, be granted independence. People who could not be squeezed into racial or cultural pigeonholes got shoehorned into boxes marked 'Coloured' and 'Asian'.

Less obviously political movements in religion, anthropology and linguistics unwittingly reinforced the idea of South Africa as a simmering cauldron of distinct cultural ingredients. Early missionaries were often the first to put African languages into writing. Their linguistic work sometimes produced new groupings. For example, in the 1830s people living near the headwaters of the Limpopo spoke virtually the same language as people living along the Caledon River. However, because different missionary societies wrote their speech down in grammars and Bibles, the world of scholarship came to accept Sesuthu and Tswana as distinct languages. Along the south-eastern coast missionaries turned what had been a continuous spectrum of closely related dialects into distinct Zulu and Xhosa languages. In the twentieth century it was not missionaries but anthropologists who emerged as the pre-eminent scholarly manufacturers of cultural difference.[4] Amazingly, scholars – who were mostly white people and whose first language was English or Afrikaans – told other people what tribe or culture they belonged to, how they thought, even how to write their own names.

Historians of Africa today seldom use the word 'tribe'. It has misled too many outsiders into thinking of Africans as primitive. The word 'people' is the generally accepted substitute. Thus we do not write about the Zulu tribe or the Mpondo tribe, we say the Zulu people or the Mpondo people. It is important to notice some hidden dangers in this practice. The word people used in this way is a straightforward translation of the German concept of the *volk*. It carries the full weight of the nineteenth-century German nationalist assumption that every *volk* has a distinct origin in a distant past and that members of the *volk* share common characteristics, common perceptions and a common destiny that others cannot share. This does not fit the evidence we have about the southern African past where social and political alignments were in a constant state of flux. Talking of 'peoples in conflict' or 'cultures in conflict' conceals a heritage of racist theory under a cloak of cultural relativism. The difference between immutable racial identities and immutable cultural identities is no thicker than a sheet of paper. This history will avoid explaining anyone's behaviour or thoughts on the basis of their culture.

European control over knowledge about culture and language has made a huge impact on the writing about southern Africa.[5] No historian would begin a book on nineteenth-century Britain with a description of the origins of the English people, speculations as to the origins of the Picts, and an account of the migrations of the Norsemen and Saxons. In contrast, most historians who have written about nineteenth-century South Africa start by describing the principal divisions of language, culture and physical appearance. Then they make guesses about when the distant ancestors of various African people might have appeared on the scene. White people stand out clearly on the page, with unquestioned personal and cultural identities. Other people's identities often get lost in clouds of debate about culture, language and spelling. Should we write 'Bushmen' or 'San'? Khoikhoi or Khoisan? Koranna or Kora? Was the founder of Lesotho named Moshesh, Moshweshwe or Moshoeshoe? Were his people Suthu, BaSotho or Basuto? Was the king of the Zulu (or amaZulu) named Chaka, Tshaka or Shaka? Did his subjects live near the Tugela, Tukela or Thukela River? It would be wonderful if some government commission could decide on definite rules for spelling. (It has been done in other places.) But most likely these problems of naming and spelling are insoluble. The important point to remember is that when we choose this way or that way of writing an African king's name we are not respecting his wishes or even those of his subjects. We are simply conforming to a scholarly convention recommended by some obscure academic linguist. King Mzilikazi called his people the Zulu. His enemies and conquerors called them Matabele. Anthropologists and historians decided they should be called Ndebele – a word that did not exist in any African language – and that is the name that stuck. In this history people will need names. But there is no reason to claim bogus authenticity for them.

The first people to make written records of what happened in the interior of southern Africa after 1800 were Europeans. Many of them were missionaries, who tended to think about history in terms of concepts suggested by their Bible. Finding the places where they settled torn by war and strife, they imagined an earlier time when peace had reigned, a time like that described in the book of Genesis, when Adam and Eve lived happily in an African Garden of Eden. The wars raging around them seemed the result of some Satanic force stalking the land. Having no concept of how long human beings had lived in this part of Africa, they looked for reasons why this Eden had fallen into the hands of the devil. Some blamed the faraway Zulu king Shaka. Others blamed a female chief, MaNthatisi, for unleashing a reign of terror. When something like law and order returned, many missionaries congratulated themselves for bringing peace to the land with their teachings. Later historians transformed the idea of the 'time of troubles' into the concept of the '*mfecane*' – a period of general conflict supposed to have begun with the emergence of the Zulu kingdom in the second decade of the nineteenth century and lasting well into the 1830s. Whether this is still a useful way of thinking about that time is one of the big questions taken up in later chapters. But at the outset we should dismiss the idea of the South African Eden. There is no evidence it ever existed. On the contrary, the oral traditions collected from every part of the region recount the mighty deeds of fighting men and women. One reason that the wars of the early nineteenth century seem to stand out as a period of exceptional violence is that the peaceful character of previous centuries has been exaggerated. As far as anyone can tell, the eagles had plenty of human bones to pick over in earlier times.

Just as people had learned to live with threats of attack, they had undoubtedly also learned to live with drought and famine. Ingenious arguments have been made which attribute widespread conflict and the emergence of new states around the turn of the nineteenth century to a crisis of food supply caused by a dramatic decline in rainfall. These have been answered by the equally plausible argument that after more than a thousand years' experience of recurring droughts in this region, Africans had found ways of surviving. If drought and famine were responsible for war and state-building in the nineteenth century, why, ask the critics, had they not produced similar results in earlier times?[6] Perhaps they had. Many kingdoms may have arisen and fallen due to failures of rain and food. On the basis of the evidence we have, we do not know.

We do have plenty of evidence to indicate that as far as the soaring eagle's eye could see, the eighteenth century in south-eastern Africa was marked by human movement, communication, change and conflict. That will be as good a place as any to begin.

Notes

1　The starting date is picked because the settlement ending Britain's long war with France ended any possibility of the Cape Colony reverting to Dutch ownership and because it predates the accession to power of Shaka, Moshweshwe and many other leaders who would play prominent roles in the years ahead. The ending date marks the Bloemfontein Convention which ended Britain's first attempt to control the highveld.

2　William F. Lye and Colin Murray, *Transformations on the Highveld: the Tswana and Southern Sotho* (Cape Town, 1980), p. 24; D. Fred. Ellenberger, *History of the Basuto, Ancient and Modern* (London, 1912), p. 18. Similar stories of the origins of human beings are told throughout southern Africa, and other places have been cited as Ntsuanatsatsi.

3　T. M. O'C. Maggs, *Iron Age Communities of the Southern Highveld* (Pietermaritzburg, 1976), p. 294.

4　No one is quicker to admit this than South Africa's home-grown fraternity of anthropologists; see W. D. Hammond-Tooke, *Imperfect Interpreters: South Africa's Anthropologists, 1920–1990* (Johannesburg, 1997).

5　And other places; see Edward Said, *Orientalism* (London, 1978).

6　Carolyn Hamilton, 'Ideology, Oral Traditions and the Struggle for Power in the early Zulu Kingdom' (MA thesis, University of the Witwatersrand, 1985), pp. 4–5.

CHAPTER TWO

Life in the heartland in the late eighteenth century

The old stories say that at the beginning of time, when the first men and women emerged from a cave, cattle came out with them. Archaeological evidence indicates that in the eastern regions of southern Africa, people and cattle have been living with each other for a thousand years and more. Judging from the evidence available about the opening decades of the nineteenth century this partnership had proved its worth in countless ways. People protected cattle from lions and other predators. Milk and meat gave people a healthy diet. Crops such as sorghum, millet and maize provided the most important food source for most people, but they were not always reliable. When crops failed due to drought or disease, cattle could make the difference between living and dying. By performing the daily miracle of turning grass into edible meat, cattle extended the range of places where people could live comfortably. As meat on the hoof, cattle were food people could take with them when they moved from one region to another. Cattle manure was useful as fertilizer and as fuel. Mixed with earth it made a handsome hard-wearing floor for human homes. Cattle hides could be used as clothing to protect people against the cold and also cover huts. Stretched and dried, those same hides could be made into shields to deflect the blows of enemies. All these advantages made cattle the most prized of all possessions. Wherever people lived together in large concentrations, places to keep cattle occupied a central position. In many places the ruins of stone walls people built long ago to control and protect their cattle are often the only visible testimony that those people ever existed.[1]

Life revolved around the cows. Tiny boys learned to know them as individuals, to call them by name, recognize the distinctive shape of their horns, the patterns of their hides – even the individual voices with which they mooed. When herdboys grew to manhood, no part of their homesteads enjoyed 'more consideration than their cattle and scarcely . . . [did] their wives or their children enjoy such a share of soft words and friendly caresses'. They were 'associated with as if they were human beings' and milked 'under a feeling that the occupation of milking is honourable'. Men talked to their cattle as if they 'understood every observation which man was able to make'; they taught them to 'understand to an extraordinary degree the language and signals employed by their owners'. When the cows went out to graze in the morning elders of the village told them 'to seek a luxuriant pasturage, to fill themselves well that they may afford abundance of milk' and to take care 'that the thief does not separate them from the hearts which sigh at home for their return'.[2]

Power over people

For as far back as historical records permit us to see, owning cattle meant wealth and power. Crops were a vitally important food supply but open fields could never be as tightly controlled as cattle. While plentiful evidence exists to show that growing crops could be men's work as well as women's work, care of cattle was mostly confined to males, because through owner-ship of cattle, males controlled the productive and reproductive power of females.

Exchanges of cattle cemented marriages between important families. A man who aspired to wed the daughter of an important family presented cattle to the father of the bride. The more significant the family, the more cattle were expected. Wealthy men gave their sons the cattle they needed to marry the daughters of other wealthy men. Every woman who bore a daughter dreamed that she might grow up with enough intelligence, grace and charm to win the love of a wealthy man. The marriage would bring more cattle to the family. In good times these alliances and exchanges helped the rich get richer. As cattle bred and multiplied, their owners prospered. With more cows a man could marry more wives. This meant more sons to revere him and look to him for the cattle they would need to give to the fathers of their chosen brides. In some places rich men loaned cows to poor people to look after. The borrowers could milk the cows to feed their families, but when calves were born, they were claimed by the original owner who thus grew even richer.[3] Looking after vast herds required a lot of manpower but this was not a problem for the rich and powerful. They could recruit followers by promising cattle in return for faithful service. With a bit of luck, in the course of two or three generations a personal following might become an army who called their leader 'Chief'.

Luck seldom held so long in this part of the world. Without warning an epidemic of cattle disease might decimate the herds. When the locusts stripped the fields bare, people had to consume the wealth they had stored up in their cattle. Likewise, when the rain failed for a season or two, the crops died and people had to eat their cattle to survive. Sometimes a drought could go on for three, four, even five years – enough to reduce everyone to the same dead level of poverty.[4]

Maintaining a good mix of crops as well as cattle was the best defence against starvation. This meant seeking out the areas of most reliable rainfall, springs or permanent rivers. Seventy-eight per cent of modern South Africa is too dry to support sustained agriculture.[5] The remaining 22 per cent is concentrated in coastal regions and near the eastern mountain regions. That is where most people lived in the past and where most people live today. Even within those regions, there are marked variations in rainfall. A few coastal areas can expect both winter and summer rains. Other areas depend on summer rainfall alone. This is especially important on the highveld. In an ordinary year great clouds of moisture are swept up from the Indian Ocean and carried in a lazy arc over Zimbabwe and Botswana until they eventually fall as summer rain near the Drakensberg and Maloti mountains.[6] If the clouds do not come, a year may pass before rain again sends water coursing down the dry creek beds to make the pastures green. Even in the single small region of KwaZulu there are considerable variations in patterns of drought and rainfall.[7] Soils matter almost as much as rainfall to cattle and agriculture. Some soils will support grazing but not planting. Some pastures nourish cattle at certain times of the year but are worthless in other months.[8] In lowlands with high annual or seasonal rainfall the bite of the tse-tse fly was an additional menace to cattle, communicating the deadly disease trypanosomiasis.

Over the course of centuries people learned ways of coping with these threats.[9] They tried to make sure of good crops and pastures for animals by avoiding regions where average annual rainfall was less than 500mm.[10] Many areas of low or unreliable rainfall were left to the wild animals.[11] Keeping pigs, goats, sheep and chickens helped stave off the dreaded time when cattle would have to be killed to ward off starvation. Hunting and fishing provided alternative sources of animal protein.[12] Instead of relying on a single crop such as maize, which quickly died if rain failed at a crucial time of year, several different grains and vegetables were planted. Storage pits in some places could keep emergency grain supplies in an edible condition for as long as a year. Cattle could be moved to greener pastures as the seasons changed. Burning off vegetation, clearing and other measures helped keep the tse-tse fly at bay in infested areas.[13] Men and women renowned for their skills in driving off locusts, curing sick cattle and bringing the rain

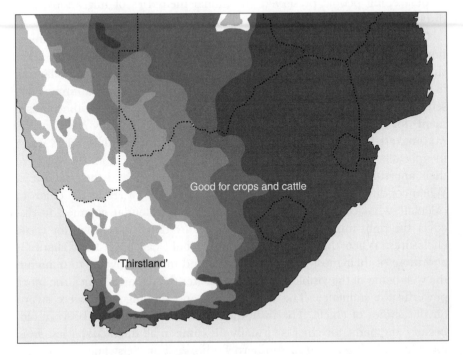

Map 2   Distribution of rainfall in an average year: darker areas receive more rain

never lacked clients. When it seemed a drought would never end, whole groups might abandon the graves of their ancestors and move to a new territory. This experience must have been common because most of the cattle-keeping people preserved communal memories of migrations from distant places.[14]

Co-ordinating all these activities required a high level of social organization. Chiefs had to earn their privileged positions through effective leadership. They allocated grazing areas. They told people when to begin planting in the spring and when the harvest could be gathered in autumn. They settled boundary disputes between neighbours. They decreed the punishments for theft, assault, trespass, adultery and murder. They called in the rain-makers when drought threatened, summoned the witch-finders when inexplicable ailments appeared, and implored assistance from the spirits of their ancestors to advance the interests of themselves and their followers. When conditions required a move to new territories, it fell to the chiefs to calculate what constituted a safe distance from potential enemies, to discover the right mix of pasturage and to secure defensible places for cattle enclosures. When they died, descendants would call upon their shades – and those of their most important female and male relatives – to maintain the well-being of the visible world. The greater the departed chief, the more powerful the influence. The most solemn and binding oaths were sworn on the names of chiefs. The institution of chieftainship must be very old, because the name for chief is virtually the same in all the dictionaries: *inkosi* in Zulu and Xhosa, *kosi* in southern Sotho, *kgosi* in Setswana.[15] Although only one person in each community bore the title, the institution itself was very much a family affair. The most honoured persons were chiefs' mothers, whose words were taken very seriously, even when they contradicted their sons.[16] Chiefs' wives worked and politicked throughout their marriages in the hope that their eldest sons might succeed to the title. It was not unknown for women to act as chiefs or regents for lengthy periods. The death of a chief's mother was honoured by solemn, elaborate and lengthy rites of mourning. The chiefs we know about from historical records did not depend on kin alone but surrounded themselves with other advisers – generally drawn from among the other important cattle-owners. They also held meetings or assemblies of the wider community which celebrated social cohesion with dance competitions, musical performances, poetry and oratory.

Life without cattle was difficult but possible. There was always the hope that cattle might be the reward for distinguished service to chiefs, a fortunate marriage or the unexpected death of a relative. Poor people were known, in various places, to attach themselves to cattle-owners by executing designated tasks, such as guarding cattle, chasing birds away from the fields, helping with harvests or performing household duties.[17] Historical literature sometimes designates these people as 'clients', but their status was so lowly that in many records they are simply called slaves.[18]

Those who preferred liberty to servitude or debt sought out the inhospitable regions where a precarious living could be made by hunting wild game and foraging for edible wild plants. The common names for such people in the historical records are 'Bosjeman' in Dutch, 'Bushman' in English, 'Thwa' in Zulu and Xhosa, 'Morwa' in Tswana. Some local legends of the creation say that Bushmen were overlooked in the first distribution of cattle.[19] These stories emphasize the important point that before the twentieth century the terms Bushman/Thwa/Morwa designated a way of life rather than a particular physical appearance or language. These words were not just applied to those known today as 'San' in the south-western regions of South Africa. They described anyone who lived primarily by hunting, gathering and occasional daring raids against the cattle-keepers. People who spoke the Tswana language but had no cattle were called 'barwa' or 'bushmen'.[20] Their abject appearance was, according to one report, 'solely the result of misery'. In all other respects they resembled their cattle-owning neighbours.[21] Zulu-speaking people who mainly lived by hunting were likewise known as Thwa.[22] Sometimes the term was used in a dismissive or derogatory sense to indicate people regarded as wild or uncivilized. Thus peoples in southern Mozambique called their Zulu-speaking neighbours to the South 'Vatwa' (= BaThwa). Mistaking this vague characterization for a group identity, old Portuguese map-makers wrote the name Vatwa over the territory later known as KwaZulu-Natal.[23]

There were many obvious hardships for the people called Bushmen, but as someone once remarked, as 'they could not exist elsewhere without becoming the servants, if not the absolute slaves, of others', they chose freedom.[24] The number of those who actively chose freedom in this way was probably never very large. Precisely because they made their homes away from prying eyes, they were not counted. One of the tragedies of the nineteenth century would be their virtual extermination and the disappearance of their ways of life.

The vast majority of people contented themselves with life in communities where possession of cattle underpinned and maintained class distinctions. Chiefs occupied the top positions but invariably depended on the co-operation of other well-off men and women.[25] This top layer of society consciously worked to maintain its privileged position by promoting the marriage of their sons and daughters to people of similar social status. Such marriages required the exchange of significant numbers of cattle, which normally ensured that marriage partners were drawn from the same class. The children of those marriages grew up confidently expecting that when they married the older generation would find them the required presentations of cattle. People devised ingenious and often extremely complicated arrangements for borrowing and repaying debts incurred as the result of the marriage system.[26] While these gave rise to endless disputes, they created networks of mutual obligation which bound members of the ruling class together. Because men (but not women) were permitted to multiply their marriages, they could multiply the number of high-status dependants. Over time these groupings, which scholars call lineages, could grow quite large. Naturally, they celebrated their superiority in song and story. 'Praise poems' elegantly and wittily recounted the achievements of distinguished ancestors and their most important living descendants.[27] They made class distinctions seem normal.

The significance for historians of these biased recountings of times past can hardly be exaggerated. It is vital to recognize that the praise poems for ancestors are about forgetting as much as they are about remembering. Winners got deliberately remembered. Losers got deliberately forgotten. There are many recorded instances of successful chiefs promoting the belief that all their people shared descent from their own revered ancestors – whether or not it was true.[28] Manipulation of memory could also be used to designate certain groups as outsiders and denigrate their ancestors as people of no account.[29] Such practices systematically erased the memory of defeated and impoverished ruling groups. They shut off knowledge of people and groups that may once have been extremely important. They make it appear as though the successful large chieftaincies which emerged in the nineteenth century were without historical precedent. That seems very unlikely.[30] All the conditions required for building large followings based on control of cattle and reproduction had been present in earlier centuries. It is just that control of historical memory practised by winning groups makes it very difficult to find out about them.

Despite the various techniques employed to keep power concentrated in existing chieftaincies and ruling classes, power could be lost or severely diminished through the operations of chance and human agency. The ravages of nature could wipe out herds and crops, instantly reducing everyone to a frantic scramble for survival. The inheritors of power could quarrel among themselves. When this happened the only alternative to civil war was for one group to move away.[31] Another danger was invasion by armed forces seeking to take cattle by force. Admirers of a certain Sotho chief sang frankly about his reasons for going to war:

Whither went Saole with plumes on his head?
Hi hi hi! Hi hi hi!
He went to seize cattle with which he might wed.
Ho ho ho! Ho ho ho![32]

In south-eastern, as in central and eastern Africa, 'the best response to raiding . . . [was] to move one's animals out of harm's way. Mobility . . . [was] the key to survival, not only in times of raiding but also to take advantage of seasonal fluctuations in the availability of grazing and water.'[33]

Political ideology tried to counter internal and external threats by condemning brothers who quarrelled about inheritance, children who defied their parents, and warriors who went about stealing other people's cattle. When southern Tswana chiefs went to war, they called specialists in to consecrate and safeguard the cattle:

> By this ceremony these animals . . . [were] secured against the enchantments of the enemy, and even against all danger of being forcibly carried away by him. This consecration consists in the priests taking each animal individually, as it is brought to him, and painting a particular mark upon its hind leg, with a jackal's tail dipped in a kind of black paint. This he performs kneeling, pronouncing at the same time certain mysterious words, during which, another person, kneeling behind him, repeats the same mark with a little brush upon his back or arms.[34]

When people spoke of losing cattle unfairly they spoke of having been 'eaten up'. If order generally broke down and people were 'eating others up' on all sides, it was said that cannibals ruled the land. This evocation of the most powerful taboo in human society should not be taken literally. So great was the horror of the very idea that people avoided the flesh of sacred animals 'for fear of eating an ancestor'.[35] Eye-witness accounts of people eating people are extremely rare in the historical record, and there are good reasons for doubting the few that do exist. It is often said that cannibalism was a new horror brought by widespread violence in the nineteenth century. However, rumours and tales about cannibals had been circulating decades, if not centuries earlier.[36] The best way to understand these tales is to read cannibalism as a metaphor for disorder.[37] Ferocious warriors were described colourfully as 'eaters of men'.[38] Fear of cannibals and cannibalism was instilled at a very early age. Mothers warned disobedient children that the cannibals might get them.[39] If you fell into their hands, they would cut off your third finger and keep the blood flowing until you died. They would tear off your hands and feet. They would make a drinking cup of your skull. They would cut out your bladder, blow it up and wear it as a trophy. The moral? Stick together. Do not venture into dangerous places. Uphold the established order of things.

For a small percentage of the population, arts, crafts and trade offered a way to survive – even to grow wealthy – without directly depending on cattle. Internal trade routes criss-crossing the land served traders who dealt in metal goods. The arts of mining and smelting such metals as iron, copper and gold had been known for centuries, but metal goods were not produced on a mass scale until late in the nineteenth century. Those who knew the craft always had ready markets for their products. Animal hides and carved woods were likewise traded actively throughout the region.[40] After AD 1500 there were markets for ivory, animal hides, meat and slaves on the eastern and south-eastern coast where foreign merchants occasionally came to do business. However valuable they might be, these crafts and trading systems were not in themselves a means of acquiring power over other people. In order to become tools of power they had to be exchanged for cattle, or as one historian aptly puts it, they had to be 'converted into cattle'.[41] Of all craftsmen, the most likely to attain power in this way were the iron smiths because they made hoes and spears. In order to ward off the threat they posed, some chiefs in some places forbade them to exchange iron goods for cattle.[42] Drawing a dependable income year after year from trade was difficult except in places where it was possible to control access to a trade route. In a land where there were so many different ways for traders to walk their way around obstacles, these favoured situations were rare.[43]

War and conflict

In general, the only way for ambitious people to speed up the long, tedious process of accumulating cattle – and the power over people that ownership of cattle brought – was to seize them by force. The historical record tells of no period when universal peace ruled the land. On the contrary, all the oral traditions tell of war and fighting. While these wars bore little or no resemblance to modern wars – which can go on for several years and aim at inflicting maximum casualties on opposing forces – they were no less serious in the minds of the protagonists. The wars of the heartland were often very brief affairs, marked by a single encounter and little loss of life. Everywhere the principal object was to take the enemy's herds.

The constant dangers of theft and war demanded eternal vigilance. Cattle needed to be penned up or watched through the night. The design of cattle enclosures, whether built of stone or sticks, helped direct the movement of beasts and frustrate thieves.[44] The enclosures generally stood at the centre of settlements. Where the terrain permitted, villages were built in elevated positions which commanded sweeping views of the landscape. Ruins of centuries-old stonewalled cattle enclosures and huts on the middle slopes of hills show that this practice originated long ago. While definite inconveniences were associated with these locations – it could be a long walk for those who tilled the fields, carried water and gathered firewood – the defensive advantages outweighed the problems.[45] In mountainous regions such as the upper Caledon Valley, the landscape provided thousands of natural terraces formed by nearly vertical cliffs. These offered very effective defences against attack from below, and had been favoured situations for settlements for a very long time.[46] Evidence for substantial settlements of the same type is also found in the upland areas of KwaZulu-Natal near the upper Thukela and White Mfolozi Rivers; archaeological dating suggests periods of construction ranging from the eleventh century up to the late eighteenth century.[47] In flatter areas, such as the western highveld regions stretching north of the place where the Vaal and Orange Rivers join, complex systems of tortuous winding passages made of brushwork used to be built on the perimeters of towns and villages as an alternative way of protecting cattle on the inside from any sudden rush of enemies.[48]

Before guns, winning battles depended on mobilizing fighting forces equipped with bows and arrows, spears, shields, battle axes and clubs. Sometimes fire was also used to burn the huts and crops of enemies. This limited array of weapons meant that the most important tools of war were strategy, leadership and the ability to send superior forces into battle. Women as well as men maintained a high degree of physical fitness until well into middle age through dancing. Skill in dancing ranked with skill in song-making and recitation as a mark of cultural attainment. Days of practice preceded dance competitions. When groups competed against each other the contests lasted hours, arousing all the emotion of modern rivalries in sport. On one recorded occasion a dance competition sparked off a bloody civil war.[49]

Hunting honed both the fitness and strategic skills needed in times of war. Killing large game such as elephant, rhinoceros and hippopotamus whose tough hides were not easily pierced by weapons required the mobilization of large groups of people.[50] Trackers located the game. Beaters drove the animals into pre-arranged traps, where they fell into concealed pits or were subjected to concerted attacks with spears. Hurling long throwing spears weakened animals, then a single daring hunter went in for the kill with a single short stabbing spear. The hunter's kit of long and short spears is known to have been in use in KwaZulu-Natal in the late seventeenth century. Most likely it originated at a much earlier time.[51] Organizing and leading hunts taught chiefs how to lead companies into battle. It taught their followers co-operation and bravery in the face of danger. It has been suggested that one of the key elements in military organization, the regiment, was itself a product of organized hunting.[52]

When or where regiments originated, no one can say. They existed throughout south-eastern Africa at least by the middle of the eighteenth century. In many areas, ceremonies marked the induction of teenage boys into regiments at a certain age. Sometimes these ceremonies were associated with circumcision of the penis as a mark of the transition from boyhood to manhood. In other places they were not. One historian has speculated that the practice of organizing regiments according to age began on the highveld, and was later adopted by peoples living on the south-eastern coast.[53] There were certainly regiments on the coast in the mid-eighteenth century.[54] Eighteenth-century regiments dating to the same era are also recalled in traditions of the Pedi on the eastern highveld.[55] Age-set regiments effectively mobilized manpower (and, in some instances, womanpower) on a principle that transcended kinship. For this reason they could be of great assistance to chiefs seeking to build up large followings. They may have existed long before they were recorded in documents or oral traditions. The same process of systematic forgetting that obliterated the memories of defeated chiefs and disintegrated political groupings would also have operated to erase the memory of ancient regiments. The important thing is that no evidence supports the proposition that regiments were the invention of any particular individual or group.

On the contrary, evidence does testify to the presence of formidable large-scale fighting organizations in the sixteenth and seventeenth centuries. A group of shipwrecked Portuguese, who arrived at Delagoa Bay armed with muskets in 1552, were confronted by a powerful African chief who was able to force them to hand over their weapons,[56] In 1686 a Dutch ship, the *Stavenisse*, ran aground on the Natal coast. The survivors could not prevent the local chief from breaking up the ship and salvaging its iron, because he commanded a force of '*fully 1,000 armed men*'.[57] Anyone able to marshal that many soldiers must have been a powerful regional ruler. Other reports by shipwrecked sailors 'show that some chiefdoms were better at fighting than others, that their armies sometimes used large shields covering their bodies and a variety of weaponry, including the single assegai [spear]; nor did hunters or fighters seem to wear the sandals they carried'.[58]

How deadly the wars may have been before the nineteenth century is hard to say.[59] As one observer noted, cattle rather than men were the objective:

> they are not very anxious about apprehending the man; to seize his cattle is their chief object. Should they get possession of them, they are certain the owner will follow; and if not, the cattle will be theirs, and the man sufficiently punished by being reduced to a state of poverty.[60]

On the other hand, men did die. An aged chief living near Kuruman in 1820 counted eight of his sons dead as the result of various battles in previous years.[61] A traveller among the Tlhaping in 1805 got into a heated discussion about the relative merits of polygamy and monogamy. The chief explained that 'a number of wives forms part of his riches'. It 'was perfectly incomprehensible to him' that 'a whole nation could submit voluntarily' to laws limiting men to one wife. When the traveller appealed to the chief's wives to back him up, one of the women remarked 'very judiciously' that laws enforcing monogamy would not suit them 'because there were so great a number of women, and the male population suffered such diminutions from the wars'.[62]

Few people desire to live in a state of constant war. Some widespread social practices worked to counter the temptation to acquire wealth through conflict. Marriage alliances between powerful chiefs created bonds of kinship and settled women of potential enemies at the heart of important homesteads. Many sons of chiefs spent part of their childhood living away from home among neighbouring peoples.[63] As a young man chief Matiwane attempted to cement a pact of friendship with Sobhuza, founder of the Swazi kingdom, by promising to send his son to reside with him and asking at a future date to take one of Sobhuza's daughters in marriage.[64] To ensure that good communications kept possible enemies in diplomatic conduct, the lives of messengers were protected by the most sacred conventions. Thus, negotiation was nearly always available as an alternative to war.

War began with formal declarations of grievances. The chivalrous customs which governed warfare in most places followed the procedures described in this early nineteenth-century account of conflict among the Xhosa-speaking people:

> The army is now put into motion, taking with it as many oxen for slaughter as are deemed necessary for its support. When it approaches the habitation of the enemy, ambassadors are again sent to give notice of the intended attack, and repeat the declaration of the motives which have given occasion to the war. If the enemy declares that he has not yet collected all his people together, and is not prepared to fight, the attacking army waits with patience till he notifies that he is ready . . . . If one of the armies has taken to flight, the commander alone is to blame: everything depends upon his personal bravery, and his falling back is the signal for the whole body to do the same. A flying enemy is immediately pursued, and, above all things, the conquerors seek to possess themselves of their women and children, and cattle: of the latter a great part are immediately killed and eaten. If the vanquished party agrees to submit, his submission is accepted, on condition that he acknowledges his conqueror from that time forward as his sovereign, and solemnly promises obedience to him. When this is done, the women and children are sent back: the victors also return some of the cattle taken, though perhaps but a small part, dividing the rest among themselves. This claim of the conquered to the return of some part of the booty rests upon a principle . . . 'that we must not let even our enemies die with hunger'.[65]

Continuity and change in social groupings before 1800

Where power over people was based on ownership of cattle, it was difficult for particular chiefdoms and lineages to endure for long periods. Drought, disease, war, and internal struggles over power and inheritance militated against continuity. Splitting, moving, regrouping, 'fission' and 'fusion' went on all the time. No mountains were high enough, no river was wide enough to inhibit interaction between groups. While today we tend to think of Zulu, Xhosa, SeSothu and SeTswana as quite distinctive languages, in former times they shaded into each other. Along the coast all the way from Delagoa Bay to Algoa Bay people spoke dialects of basically the same language. Each group along the way had no trouble understanding its neighbours on either side. That is why scholars group them together as Nguni speakers. Likewise on the highveld people spoke variations on the same language throughout the region. The distinction between Sotho and Tswana largely derives from different methods used by French- and English-speaking linguists who first tried to write down the language. Although there is a good case for calling all the people who speak the language BaTswana (a word which probably originally meant 'us'), modern scholars tend to refer to Sotho/Tswana speakers. While someone on the coast would have had difficulty understanding the speech of someone in the far interior, by learning a few simple rules it was not difficult to learn to communicate. Historians have conventionally treated the divide between Nguni and Sotho-Tswana as a great cultural as well as linguistic divide. There is, however, clear evidence of interaction between them over a long period of time.

People who moved from the coast to the highveld were known as strangers or marauders (Matabele, later rendered as Ndebele) or Bakoni (singular Nkoni=Nguni). The survival of these names for people whose ancestors moved to the highveld several centuries ago provides evidence of their origins even though they now all speak SeSothu or SeTswana.[66] The ancestors of the people of the eastern highveld known in the twentieth century as the 'Transvaal Ndebele' settled in that area in or possibly before the seventeenth century.[67] No traditions tell exactly when or why they moved from the coastal area, but many tales record their military exploits.[68] Later movements from south-east Africa from the coast to the highveld are better remembered. People known as Zizi in the upper Caledon Valley may have moved up in the early seventeenth century.[69] By the late eighteenth century, several other groups had followed in their footsteps.[70] Because their new home was only about seven days' walk from their old one, it was easy to keep in touch with relatives and neighbours left behind.[71] Archaeologists point to the ruins of stone cattle enclosures in the highlands of KwaZulu-Natal as evidence of continuous communication with peoples of the highveld. Those old structures, some of which appear to have been in use as late as the eighteenth century, are virtually identical in form to stone ruins found in the eastern sections of the southern highveld.[72] We can only guess at the character of relations between people living in the lowlands and those in the highlands before the eighteenth century. Most likely, they were marked by the same mix of peace and conflict that we find recorded in later periods throughout the region.

In the coastal regions, solid evidence attests to long-standing stability of several groups. The multitude of deep river valleys which run between the mountains and the sea may have reinforced regional identities. For many months of each year, torrents of water would have inhibited communications. These regions also were less prone to drought than the highveld. Whatever the reason, group identities persisted. Survivors of shipwreck on those shores in 1686 who travelled widely in the region reported 'five kingdoms, namely, the Magoses, Makriggas, the Matimbas, Mapontes and Emboas'.[73] The 'Magoses' may confidently be assumed to be the modern Xhosa, the 'Matimbas' are the Thembu, the Makriggas (in other reports, Mageryga) may possibly be Griqua and the 'Mapontes' are the Mpondo. The 'Eboas' (in another report, the Semboes) are the Mbo, the only one of these five groupings which does not survive in some form into the nineteenth century. Mpondo and Xhosa used to refer to people to the north of them in Natal as Mbo. They appear in a Portuguese account of 1589 as Vambe (=abaMbo).[74] Old English maps record their presence in large letters as 'Hambonaas'. North of the Mbo lived the people variously called Ronga, Tsonga or Tonga.

Of all these coastal groupings the most fascinating is the Mbo; while the other large groupings persist into the nineteenth century, the Mbo disappear. Who were they? One account says there were once 250,000 of them but that they were broken up about the turn of the nineteenth century.[75] A. T. Bryant, who spent many years collecting and collating genealogical information from Zulu people in the early twentieth century, came to believe that a single individual, Langa, was leader of the Mbo about 1700 and that his descendants split into the separate large clans known as the Hlubi, Dhlamini, Ngwane, Ndwandwe and Mkize – all of whom recalled a Langa in their family trees.[76] Bryant found this splitting unremarkable because he believed that the Mbo had migrated from the far north in the fifteenth century into a largely empty land. From his point of view it made sense to see these colonizers splitting into many sections as they occupied new lands. Now that archaeological evidence has demolished all such myths of recent migration, the Mbo need reconsideration. It is quite conceivable – though ultimately unprovable – that a large chieftaincy or kingdom under a real person named Langa did exist in the late seventeenth century, but that his kingdom fell apart. Following this line of speculation, it could be that the ferocious struggles for power which are recorded in the late 1700s were to some extent struggles to reconstitute a kingdom that had been lost. This may also have been the reason for the sudden desertion of the stonewalled settlements whose ruins mark the upland regions. The Ndwandwe of King Zwide, who figure as the chief antagonists of the Zulu (see Chapter 4) in the early nineteenth century may well have regarded themselves as defenders of the Mbo legacy. Admittedly, this is very difficult to prove because of the gaping holes in the historical record. As one scholar has guardedly written, 'although there is no reason to suppose that the chiefdoms known to have existed in northern Zululand in the sixteenth century disappeared in the seventeenth, there is no way of relating the earlier political structure to that dominated by the Ndwandwe in the late eighteenth century'.[77]

Up on the highveld, there are no such longstanding traditions of settled life and descent. On the contrary, everywhere evidence points to frequent shifts of location, leadership and group identification. This mobility was no doubt the reason why everyone spoke dialects of a single language. Mobility helped people cope with the uncertainties of the climate. When the rain did not come or springs dried up, people moved on, leaving the ruins of their old homes and cattle enclosures behind. It was quite normal for chiefs to move substantial towns to new locations.[78] A nineteenth-century observer reported that the Tswana,

> When they leave any of their little towns to go and found another in some
> new situation, better adapted to the support of their cattle, they carry with
> them the materials of which their cabins are built, their clothes, their
> utensils, and their weapons. If they be attacked by an enemy more
> powerful than themselves they flee before him, taking with them what they
> can of their goods. . . . In either of these cases of migration, nothing but
> the walls for the cattle of the village remain, and for these they have no
> peculiar designation; they call them simply *lerako*, – wall.[79]

After centuries of occupation so many of these ruined walls and towns existed that ignorant newcomers jumped to the mistaken conclusion that some great catastrophe had caused them to be suddenly deserted.

Relationships among the people who came to be known in the nineteenth century as the Rolong, Pedi, BaSotho, Harutshe, Fokeng, Taung, Ngwato and Ngwaketse were very close.[80] They shared clan names. They remembered old times when they had lived together in distant places. They were in continual communication with each other. They were, for all practical purposes, a single ethnic group. The eighteenth-century southern Sotho chief Mohlomi won a reputation as a great traveller. His journeys are said to have taken him as far afield as modern Botswana, Swaziland and the territories of the Venda and Pedi near the Limpopo River.[81] Nowhere did he have trouble making himself understood. The lines of communication which criss-crossed the region enabled people to have knowledge of distant places they had never seen. In the early nineteenth century people living in Lesotho knew about Lake Malawi and the river which fed it – a region located about 2000 kilometres to the north-east of them.[82]

It is impossible to state confidently what the total population of the entire region bounded by the Kalahari, the Limpopo and the Indian Ocean might have been by the eighteenth century. Based on estimates made in the nineteenth century, the distribution of population in important centres might have been roughly:

Central highveld/Swaziland region	100,000
Xhosa/Thembu/Mpondo region	100,000
North-western region	100,000
Eastern highveld	50,000
Delagoa Bay region	50,000
KwaZulu-Natal region	150,000
Total	550,000

That would suggest a total population of less than one million altogether, but this is only the roughest of guesses.

Because of the absence of entrenched ethnic differences, the universal heartland practice was for people to identify their groups by the name of their chiefs. Even so-called 'totemic names' were impermanent; there are many instances of people changing them after joining a new chief.[83] In many instances the group label endured long after the chief named had passed away. This practice helps us to know something about the lives of important eighteenth-century leaders. The narrative history of modern times begins with their remembered battles and conquests.

Warfare and leadership in the eighteenth century: a bird's-eye view

Rather than being spread evenly across the land, great chiefs and states concentrated on particular areas where reliable supplies of water, good soils, defensible locations and trading networks were present. This meant that some zones were much more densely settled and politically contested

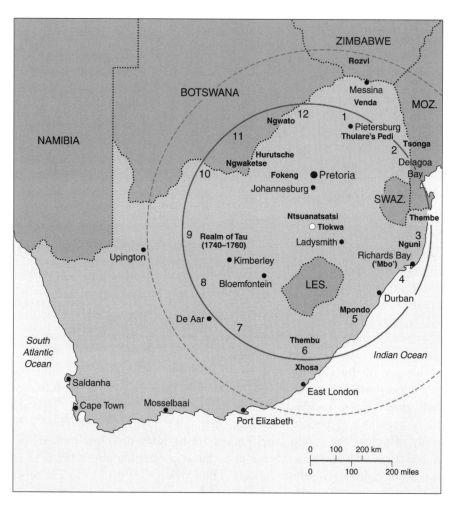

Map 3   Eighteenth century south-eastern Africa

than others. To simplify an extremely complicated picture, imagine the heartland of eighteenth-century south-eastern Africa as a clock face with 12 pointing due north.

Ntsuanatsatsi, legendary home of the human race, lies very near the centre of this imaginary clock. This, in the eighteenth century, was the realm of very closely related SeSothu-speaking people loosely identified as the Sia and the Tlokwa whose settlements were scattered along the Wilge River Valley. They had many well-remembered links to Sotho/Tswana-speaking peoples living in the north-western, northern and north-eastern highveld.[84] Well-to-do Sia and Tlokwa families intermarried.[85] Geography positioned them near the easiest point of descent into the coastal regions dominated by the Nguni-speakers. For as far back as anyone could remember people of Nguni origin had been using this route to move up to the highveld. This region thus was a site of cultural fusion rather than sharp divisions between Sotho/Tswana and Nguni. A little to the south-west lay the beautiful Caledon River Valley – steep-sided in its upper reaches, broadening out so wide as to be hardly identifiable as a valley as the river flows towards its confluence with the Orange. This was likewise a region where incoming Nguni-speaking and SeSothu-speaking people had long been settling and blending. Conflict and struggles to build great herds of cattle were endemic so the level of military skills was high.[86] Oral tradition recounts many instances of chiefs raiding south over the mountains in efforts to replenish lost stock.[87] As the eighteenth century closed the Tlokwa were the strongest power but certainly not the masters of the central region.

Between Lesotho's high mountains and the sea – at about 6 on the imaginary clock face – lived speakers of the Xhosa dialects of the Nguni language groups. Local people recognized four major divisions – the Xhosa, the Thembu, the Mpondo and the Mpondomise – distinguished by chief-tainship rather than any important differences in ways of life. It was the practice for chiefs of these groups to marry the daughters of great chiefs of the other groups. In this way, bonds of reciprocal obligation were created which helped to minimize inter-group conflict.[88] The principal conflicts which mark the eighteenth century were caused by dissension within chiefly families. The most notable chiefs were Gcaleka and Rharhabe, sons of the western Xhosa chief Phalo (d. 1775). When these brothers quarrelled, they permanently split their father's house into 'Gcaleka Xhosa' and 'Rharhabe Xhosa', according to their allegiance to one or the other of these notable chiefs. Rharhabe made a name for himself as a warrior. His campaigns in the west resulted in defeat for Khoi pastoralists, who were then incorpor-ated into the Rharhabe Xhosa kingdom, as earlier Khoi groups had been absorbed through Xhosa conquests dating back to at least the beginning of the eighteenth century.[89] The rugged Amatola mountain region fell to

Rharhabe's forces in about 1750. However, when he attempted an attack on the Thembu to his north he met defeat and lost his own life in 1778. The mantle of leadership fell then upon the shoulders of his son Ndlambe, whose fate it would be to lead his people into battle against formidable new foes.

At about 9 on our imaginary clock face was the realm of King Tau (or Taung; tau=the lion), most of whose people were later to be known as the Rolong.[90] His territory lay in a low rainfall region but it contains numbers of very substantial springs spread at irregular intervals on a line extending north of the place where the Vaal River meets the Orange. In good seasons the Harts River Valley also offered good pasturage. Between about 1740 until his death in battle about 1760, Tau imposed his authority on a region stretching from the springs of the Kuruman right up to the Molopo River. In the process he gained a fearsome reputation as a warrior-king, 'conquering, dispersing, destroying and subjugating, until his name was a terror for miles around'.[91] He is the earliest chief in all southern Africa to be remembered for 'hurling the victims of his justice over a precipice'.[92] His capital stood near the junction of the Harts and Vaal Rivers, but his military campaigns carried his troops all the way to the upper reaches of the Limpopo. Ruins of many large towns which once had acknowledged Tau's authority were still notable features of the region in the 1830s.[93]

Tau's northern campaigns brought him into conflict with the powerful Hurutshe kingdom whose stronghold lay in the region north-west of modern Rustenburg – at about 11 o'clock on the imaginary clock face. This was a region much fought over in the eighteenth century. Here, where the sources of the Limpopo rise from undulating hills, were good water, defensible positions and the intersection of at least two important trade routes, one running north–south and the other east–west. Not far away were extensive plains abounding in wild game which could be killed for ivory, hides and meat. Iron, copper and tin deposits supported a flourishing local industry in metalwork. Hurutshe traditions recalled leaders living as early as the sixteenth century who laid the foundation for later glory by allying themselves to Nguni-speaking mercenaries and clans allied to the Pedi-Venda cluster of people living in the middle regions of the Limpopo River.[94] This single example, with its recollections of interaction and shifting alliances with faraway peoples, testifies to the fluidity of social groupings over a long period of time.

To the west of the Hurutshe lay the lands of the Ngwaketse, a group that grew mighty during the chieftainship of Makaba II beginning in the last decade of the eighteenth century. From his fortified stronghold of Kanye hill, he pursued a highly successful career in cattle-raiding. Eventually his irritated neighbours formed a grand alliance to challenge him in a campaign remembered as the 'war of Moabi'.[95] One incident in this struggle under-lines the importance of personal leadership. Outnumbered and besieged upon his hill by thousands of opposing forces, Makaba dared not risk a battle. On the other hand, he realized that with no supplies of water, his enemies must soon retreat. He had a goat skinned alive, then drove the wretched animal, with its skin tied on its head, down the hill into the ranks of the opposing forces. Terrified by this apparition, they fled in panic and the siege was lifted.[96] For decades to come the Ngwaketse were a practically invincible regional military power.[97]

Well to the north of the Hurutshe, across the Limpopo on the plateau of what is now Zimbabwe, lay a formidable military power, the Rozvi.[98] Mystery enshrouds our knowledge of the relations that may have existed between the Rozvi and their southern neighbours, but from what we know about long-distance networks of communications, the existence of such a large state must have been known. It may have been the conduit by which trade goods were directed south. Early in the nineteenth century a traveller to Makaba's country was told by a man who had once accompanied a military expedition north of the Hurutshe that 'there was no end to nations in that direction' and that 'they had nothing else to do but to kill one another'. Another told the traveller that he had been going on raiding parties 'all his life'.[99]

A little to the east of the Hurutshe on the northerly slopes of what are known as the Magaliesberg mountains were smaller groupings remembered as the Fokeng, Kwena and Po.[100] It was one of the Po chiefs, Mogale – well-known in the 1820s as 'king of the blue cattle' – whose name is commemor-ated in the word Magaliesberg. These groups lived in large towns surrounded by large stone walls. Raiding and counter-raiding sucked all the chiefdoms of this district into an escalating whirlpool of violence toward the end of the eighteenth century.

To sum up the situation in this region, the borders of South Africa, Botswana and Zimbabwe today divide what was, in the eighteenth century, a single region where Tswana-speaking armed chieftaincies jostled against one another in competition for cattle and favourable trading positions. A traveller passing through in the year 1820 remarked that 'all the nations in this land of *strife and blood* watch for each other, and seize the first opportun-ity that may occur to attack and carry off cattle'.[101] In the early nineteenth century this competition would result in significant realignments of power and movements of people.

Moving on around our imaginary clock face, at about 1 o'clock lay the lands of peoples later to be known as the Pedi, the Venda and the 'Trans-vaal Ndebele'. The strongest power in this region in the eighteenth century was the Pedi state built of diverse social elements under the leadership of

Mampuru and Thulare (died 1820).[102] Its strongholds skirted the edge of the Drakensberg escarpment above the lowlands which now form the Kruger National Park.[103] Although the Pedi were located on an important trade route running down to the Indian Ocean, the foundation of chiefly power here, as elsewhere, was ownership of cattle. As his power grew, Thulare consolidated power through cattle-raiding which eventually extended far to the west as the territory of the Fokeng north-west of modern Rustenburg in the Magaliesberg mountains.[104]

Trade routes ran down the Drakensberg to the south-east towards Delagoa Bay at about 2 on the clock face. People speaking dialects of the Tsonga language dominated the lowlands of what is now Mozambique from south of Delagoa Bay all the way up to the Inhambane region. At the southern end of the Tsonga territory the language shaded gradually into dialects readily understood by the neighbouring Nguni speakers. The environment of this region poses many difficulties. Deadly fevers kill people who have not acquired some childhood immunity. The tse-tse fly kills domestic animals. Drought and locust plagues bring intermittent famines. Heavy rains can produce simultaneous flooding of both the Limpopo and Zambezi plains in Mozambique.[105] Historical records running back several centuries tell of the rise and fall of many different powers in this region. While in other parts of the country the oral traditions of successful chieftainships operated to obliterate the memory of their predecessors, in these low-lying coastal areas written records were kept by traders who visited from time to time. Traders from far to the north and from across the Indian Ocean had been visiting the Mozambique coast for many centuries. They had spread the Islamic religion to settlements well south of the Zambezi River. Whether the cultural influence of this trading system had ever touched the region immediately adjacent to Delagoa Bay is not known.

The first traders from outside Africa to leave records of their visits to the Bay came from the distant kingdom of Portugal in Europe. Beginning in the early sixteenth century Portuguese forces attacked the Islamic trading cities, hoping to establish their own power on the entire East African coast. One of their maps from 1502 clearly shows Delagoa Bay. By the 1540s they were starting to make regular visits to that place to trade for ivory.[106] With limited resistance to the local diseases – and no rumours of gold to lure them into the interior as was the case farther north – the Portuguese had little incentive to establish any permanent presence south of Inhambane. However, people living along the coast soon acquired a limited knowledge of the aliens' ways of life when trading ships dropped anchor or when survivors of a shipwreck sought help. According to some stories, coastal peoples surmised that each vessel contained a separate family who fished in the sea for the beads they used to trade, and who lived on salt water and ivory.[107] Their guns were a potentially deadly novelty. If the Portuguese had made them an item of trade, the nature of warfare would have altered dramatically. As early as 1552, a chief at Delagoa Bay forced a shipwrecked party to hand over their muskets and gunpowder.[108] The Portuguese made a deliberate decision not to trade guns for fear of equipping their trading partners with weapons which could be used to drive harder bargains. Only when rival traders from other countries arrived in the eighteenth century did guns begin to be an important item of trade. Otherwise trading was a source of luxuries rather than necessities: coloured beads, cloth and metal-ware.

The appearance of the foreigners presented a political opportunity to chiefs. They could exchange the goods they acquired by trade for cattle brought from the interior, and thus gain all the advantages that cattle ownership conferred. The emergence of a single powerful kingdom based on this trading advantage was prevented by local rivalries. In the early seventeenth century the Portuguese first favoured one and then another of the local rulers.[109] Frequent wars, marked by shifts of power allegiance, became a permanent feature of the Delagoa Bay area.[110] This makes the important point that there is no automatic linkage between trade and the growth of kingdoms. The growth of trade can operate to fragment as well as to centralize power.

Competition accelerated in the eighteenth century both among Africans and traders from Europe. In 1721 the Dutch East India Company tried the experiment of planting a permanent trading post on the site of the present city of Maputo. Over the course of the nine years they maintained their fort, they found that their presence attracted not only local people but traders from the interior regions above the Drakensberg – people whose speech the Tsonga of the Delagoa Bay area found very difficult to understand. By the 1770s the sea trade had expanded to include visitors from England, France and Austria, as well as Muslim traders from farther north on the east African coast. Other ships came to the oceans off southern Africa to hunt for whales. They frequently called at Delagoa Bay where they could trade for fresh food. Rivalries among these foreigners, who were often at war with each other, made it impossible to maintain the former Portuguese ban on trade in guns.[111] In addition deserters from these ships sometimes offered their services – and their firearms – to chiefs on the coast. A deadly new element was thus gradually introduced into warfare on the land. Local chiefs tried to play the competing foreigners off against one another. The foreigners in their turn attempted to capitalize on the rivalries of the chiefs.

Another new feature of eighteenth-century competition was a growing trade in slaves. Chiefs whose power was based on cattle had previously had little reason to acquire people by trading or raiding. Captives seized in wars were often kept in a state of abject servitude, but they were not traded away as slaves. The arrival of foreigners wanting to buy people changed the situation. Now people could be traded for goods which could either be consumed or 'converted into cattle'. Many found that temptation hard to resist. An English ship cruising the Mozambique coast in the late 1680s bought slaves. Another English ship trading to Natal in 1719 exchanged brass collars and other goods for seventy-four boys and girls.[112] As the century progressed, a demand for slaves to work on plantations on islands in the Indian Ocean caused the sinister trade to rise to new heights on the East African coast. Tsonga chiefs in southern Mozambique funnelled supplies of slaves to Delagoa Bay and Inhambane. A desire to capture a larger share of the traffic in both ivory and slaves may have fuelled the expansion of Tsonga war bands up the coast towards Inhambane which continued for most of the eighteenth century.[113]

In the seventeenth century the most important kingdom based immediately to the south Delagoa Bay was the Thembe (named for an early chief). By the late eighteenth century another powerful kingdom under chief Mabhudu had developed a military organization based on regiments, had thrown off Thembe domination and was seeking to control a trade in cattle coming up to Delagoa Bay from the Nguni regions lying to the south.[114] Under Makhasane, who ruled from the 1790s until 1854, this so-called Mabhudu kingdom successfully maintained its independence against challenges from many directions. In the north-western hinterland of the bay, a chief named Moamba likewise made extensive conquests in the last decade of the century.[115]

The impact of these eighteenth-century coastal developments on the interior regions is hard to measure. Long-distance trading routes must have been stimulated because, by the opening of the nineteenth century, information about activities of people on the coast could be found on many parts of the highveld. People living near modern Mafeking knew what settlements lay on the road to Delagoa Bay and approximately how long the journey took. They had learned about inoculation for smallpox from 'white men who lived to the N.E.'. They had acquired unusual metal-ware from the same source. They knew of people on the coast who used bows and arrows in warfare rather than spears.[116] Reports also circulated of contact and conflict with people with long straight hair and light complexions who carried long thin rifles.[117] Some of these, described as wearing long white gowns, were almost certainly Muslim trader/slavers. Others may have been deserters from European ships and forts who joined coast-based chiefs. Taken together, these reports indicate that there were many routes by which news and goods travelled back and forth between the interior and the coast.

South of Mozambique, across the Lebombo (uBombo) mountain range which roughly marked the limit of endemic malaria and tse-tse fly, there were other impacts. Here, at about 4 on the imaginary clock face, it has been argued that influences emanating from Delagoa Bay stimulated conflict and the militarization of society. In other parts of Africa fairly clear cause-and-effect relationships link trading networks to the creation and maintenance of large states. For example, the empires which rose and fell in the West African grasslands are known to have drawn revenue from trade moving back and forth on the reliable caravan routes across the Sahara Desert. In the eastern regions of Zimbabwe large states also appear to have levied tribute on a passing trade in gold destined for East African ports. Surplus revenue drawn from such trading networks can be a valuable resource for rulers who need to pay the military and civilian officials required to sustain the state. Although it is more difficult to find examples of this practice in the southernmost parts of Africa before 1800, one influential historian argues there were three distinct impacts on Nguni-speaking people living south and south-west of Delagoa Bay.[118] First, the expansion of Mabhudu may have pushed Nguni groups inland, thus provoking struggles over control of territory in what would later become Zululand and Swaziland. Second, the growth of the ivory trade stimulated the organization of large hunting parties to trap and kill the huge beasts; this, in turn, could have stimulated the development of regimental organizations which could also function as military regiments. Third, chiefs who sent cattle for eventual sale to ships calling at Delagoa Bay may have sought to replenish their stocks by attacking neighbours, thus setting off a chain reaction of warfare. This was the region which had previously been reported to have been dominated by the Mbo, whose apparent disappearance has been noted above (pp. 23–4). This too, was the region where foreigners who survived a shipwreck in 1686 found a chief who could marshal 1000·armed men (above, p. 20).

There is a startling contradiction here. The shipwreck survivors testify that at least one large kingdom existed in this region in the seventeenth century. Ruins of stone cattle enclosures in the uplands of KwaZulu-Natal likewise indicate communities living in very sizeable settlements into the eighteenth century. On the other hand, a venerable scholarly tradition maintains that large kingdoms only appeared during a period of consolidation in the late eighteenth century – a period in which regimental organization and new fighting methods evolved stimulated by increased trade and other developments in the Delagoa Bay region. In the absence of new evidence it is difficult to resolve the contradiction. But a possible solution can be suggested.

Suppose that one or more kingdoms did exist in the region, as the evidence clearly indicates.[119] Suppose that the strongest was the Mbo. Suppose that in the course of the early eighteenth century it fell apart for reasons unknown, but very possibly connected with pressures emanating from the Delagoa Bay area. Perhaps there was a disastrous war, a secession, a famine. In succeeding decades, splinter groups of the old kingdom strove to rebuild a single authority. In addition, new groups may have pushed in, attempting to impose their hegemony. Prominent among them might have been the Mthethwa, a group whose dialect contained forms of speech associated with the Tsonga of the North, but who acknowledged social links with the Mbo.[120] Among the clan/lineage groups later to claim descent from the Mbo were the Ndwandwe, the Dhlamini, the Hlubi and the Ngwane.[121] These happen to be precisely the groups involved in well-remembered regional struggles for power in the late eighteenth and early nineteenth centuries.

Although the hypothesis is, at present, difficult to prove, it has many attractions. The evidence for primordial fragmentation is non-existent. Evidence does exist indicating previous experience with large-scale social and political organization. The alternative theory, which imagines that the nineteenth-century Zulu kingdom established by Shaka was the culmination of a very brief period of experimentation, must carry a heavy burden of explanation. How, during a period of more or less continuous armed struggle, could all the colourful paraphernalia of the Zulu and neighbouring Swazi kingdoms have been invented? Kingship in these states occupied centre stage in an ongoing pageant of dance, costume, oratory, design and architecture. Is it credible that the central institutions – regimental loyalty, the *isigodhlo* (the assembly of unmarried women quartered at the capital), the layout of the king's headquarters, ceremonial forms of speech, courtesy, rites of passage and mourning – all developed in a brief period of thirty to forty years with war raging on all sides? The feature of Zulu life which most impressed foreign visitors was the stoical willingness of individual men and women not merely to die for their king, but to die at a single word from their king. A very powerful edifice of ideology is required to sustain such practices. Can it be credibly supposed that this ideology was forged within the lifetime of a single individual? The old school of thought held that the Zulu kingdom invented a host of practices which were then adopted by neighbouring peoples. Is it not easier to believe that the new states which emerged in the early nineteenth century clothed themselves in the garments of time-honoured tradition? The hypothesis will at least be worth bearing in mind as the story of Zulu and Swazi power unfolds in subsequent chapters.

What is beyond doubt is that in the last decades of the eighteenth century, all the northern Nguni were being drawn into struggles among the leading chieftaincies. All of them had organized *amabutho*, that is, regiments of tough fighting men, who could be called away from their homesteads at short notice.[122] In the main, their object was the old one of acquiring cattle, the foundation of power over people. Which might emerge victorious – the Ndwandwe, the Qwabe, the Dlamini, Hlubi or Mthethwa – remained unclear as the new century dawned.

Summing up

For a thousand years and more in the Bantu-speaking heartland of southern Africa south of the Limpopo River power over people had been connected with the ownership of cattle. Through effective leadership, military prowess, judicious marriages, loaning cattle to clients, and skilful diplomacy, chiefs in many parts of the region could build large followings. There is no reason to suppose they had not been doing so for centuries. However, the uncertainties of rainfall, disease and warfare operated to limit the ability of any single kingdom to sustain a dominant role in any region for any length of time. In addition to external threats, there was always the danger that internal strife would flare into civil war. Marrying many wives built alliances and power, but it also produced many children to quarrel about who should succeed to the chieftainship.

By the middle of the eighteenth century notable struggles for power were in progress in key regional centres. Rharhabe's Xhosa had made successful forays against their Khoi neighbours to the south. Tau of the Rolong had built a large kingdom on the western highveld. In the north-west there were continuing struggles among chiefs of the Hurutshe, Ngwaketse, Ngwato and Fokeng. On the eastern highveld the Pedi under Thulare had emerged as the chief regional power. The situation was more confused in the Delagoa Bay region where the introduction of foreign trade in food, slaves and ivory complicated struggles for power among the Thembe, Mabhudu and Moamba kingdoms. To the south of them, where the Mbo had formerly been reputed to be the strongest kingdom, various Nguni chiefs had been building regimental followings in a bid for local supremacy: the Ndwandwe, the Qwabe, the Dlamini, Hlubi and Mthethwa. Near the centre of the region, only the Tlokwa stood apart from other groups as a major power whose influences stretched from modern day Harrismith to the upper Caledon Valley, and whose chiefs were well aware of the contests under way in areas to the south, north-west and north of their territory. Everywhere there was movement and struggle.

Notes

1   T. M. O'C. Maggs, *Iron Age Communities of the Southern Highveld* (Pietermaritzburg, 1976), pp. 1–3.

2   W. F. Lye, ed., *Andrew Smith's Journal of his Expedition into the Interior of South Africa/1834–36* (Cape Town, 1975), p. 68.

3   This was called the *ukusisa* system in Zulu and the *mafisa* system in Southern Sotho. See: David Hedges, 'Trade and Politics in Southern Mozambique and Zululand in the Eighteenth and Early Nineteenth Centuries' (PhD thesis, University of London, 1978), pp. 69–71; William F. Lye and Colin Murray, *Transformations on the Highveld: the Tswana and Southern Sotho* (Cape Town, 1980), p. 48.

4   In 1647 it was reported that a drought afflicting coastal regions was in its fifth year and in 1705 the same region was suffering its fourth year of drought; Graham Mackeurtan, *The Cradle Days of Natal (1497–1845)* (London, 1930), pp. 50, 73. Other great droughts struck in the 1760s, the late 1790s and 1820s; Malyn Newitt, *A History of Mozambique* (London, 1995), pp. 252–4. Old men of the Caledon Valley region spoke of the great 'Sekoboto' drought of 1803 as the worst ever seen; D. Fred. Ellenberger, *History of the Basuto, Ancient and Modern* (London, 1912), p. 42.

5   William F. Lye, 'The Sotho Wars in the Interior of South Africa, 1822–1837' (PhD thesis, UCLA, 1970), p. 18.

6   The Drakensberg range is part of a long system that stretches right up the Great Rift Valley in East Africa. Parts of this long range have been given different African names by local people. For example, in KwaZulu-Natal the range was called Kahlamba (sometimes spelled Kathlamba and Qathlamba). I have chosen to use the Afrikaner word Drakensberg (='Dragon mountain') because it was the first to be applied to describe the whole south-eastern mountain chain.

7   Hedges, 'Trade and Politics', pp. 32, 35.

8   Jeff Guy, 'Ecological Factors in the Rise of Shaka and the Zulu Kingdom' in S. Marks and A. Atmore, eds, *Economy and Society in Pre-industrial South Africa* (London, 1980), pp. 102–19; Hedges, 'Trade and Politics', p. 31.

9   For discussion of a range of strategies, see Hedges, 'Trade and Politics', pp. 27–52.

10 This appears to have been true for many centuries. Ruins of old cattle enclosures are extremely rare beyond the 500mm line; see Maggs, *Iron Age Communities*, p. 16.

11 As late as the 1820s great stretches of the western highveld were reported to be populated mainly by herds of wild animals. See John Moffat, *Missionary Labours* (London, 1842), p. 515.

12 Hedges, 'Trade and Politics', p. 58.

13 Helge Kjekshus, *Ecology Control and Economic Development in East African History* (London, 1977), pp. 51–6.

14 Hedges, 'Trade and Politics', p. 28; C. Ballard, 'Drought and Economic Distress: South Africa in the 1800s', *Journal of Interdisciplinary History* 17 (1986), p. 370. Nineteenth- and early twentieth-century historians misunderstood these memories of migration, supposing them to refer to movements from the northern and eastern regions of Africa. Accurate dating of ancient settlements has completely discredited the idea that the arrival of the cattle-keeping, metal-working, farming people happened in the last four or five centuries.

15 The word was certainly in use by the sixteenth century when it first appears in printed records; Monica Wilson and Leonard Thompson, eds, *Oxford History of South Africa*, 2 vols (Oxford, 1969–71), I, p. 118.

16 N. J. Van Warmelo, ed., *History of Matiwane and the Amangwane Tribe, as told by Msebenzi to his Kinsman Albert Hlongwane* (Pretoria, 1938), pp. 235–6.

17 See for example, Martin Legassick, 'The Griqua, the Sotho-Tswana and the Missionaries, 1780–1840' (PhD thesis, UCLA, 1969), pp. 52–3; John Campbell, *Travels in South Africa (2nd Journey)* (London, 1922, reprinted New York, 1967), p. 282.

18 There is no evidence of any internal trade or sales of such people for money before the advent of European slave dealers; see Newitt, *History of Mozambique*, p. 252. Whether destitute people who were kept but not sold should be called slaves is a question of semantics endlessly debated by historians. The indeterminacy of language is illustrated by a traveller passing through Kuruman in 1820 who noted the existence of 'many people . . . considered as servants'. Their 'captains' could 'claim their service at any time when they can afford to give them food; but in general these dependants are not regarded, but are permitted to go where they like, and to do what they please': Campbell, *Travels*, p. 167. Children of clients and 'servants' in most places were released from involuntary servitude when they reached adulthood; see, for example, Campbell, *Travels*, p. 138.

19 Lye, ed., *Andrew Smith's Journal*, p. 178–9.

20 Campbell, *Travels*, p. 140; Lye, ed., *Andrew Smith's Journal*, p. 185.

21 Eugene Casalis, *The Basutos or Twenty-Three Years in South Africa* (London, 1861, reprinted Cape Town, 1965), p. xv. For an alternative view, see Legassick, 'The Griqua, the Sotho-Tswana and the Missionaries', p. 45.

22 Mackeurtan, *Cradle Days of Natal*, p. 157.

23 A. T. Bryant, *Olden Times in Zululand and Natal* (London, 1929; reprinted Cape Town, 1965), p. 286.

24　Lye, ed., *Andrew Smith's Journal*, pp. 182–4.

25　See, for example: Legassick, 'The Griqua, the Sotho-Tswana and the Missionaries', p. 42; T. Arbousset and F. Daumas, *Narrative of an Exploratory Tour to the North-East of the Colony of the Cape of Good Hope*, translated from French by John C. Brown (first published 1846, reprinted Cape Town, 1968), pp. 273–4.

26　For an extensive discussion of the complex ways in which dominant lineages acted to maintain and enhance their power, see Hedges, 'Trade and Politics', pp. 160, 166, 171, 179, 188, 192–224.

27　Leroy Vail and Landeg White, *Power and the Praise Poem: Southern African Voices in History* (Charlottesville, 1991).

28　Hedges, 'Trade and Politics', pp. 23, 67–8, 79.

29　Carolyn Hamilton, 'Ideology, Oral Traditions and the Struggle for Power in the Early Zulu Kingdom' (MA thesis, University of the Witwatersrand, 1985), pp. 474–86; C. A. Hamilton and J. Wright, 'The Making of the AmaLala: Ethnicity, Ideology and Relations of Subordination in a Precolonial Context', *South African Historical Journal* 22 (1990), pp. 3–23.

30　Hedges, 'Trade and Politics', p. 9.

31　In discussing these movements of secession, John Wright points out that they were balanced by a 'converse process . . . by which chiefdoms incorporated groups of outsiders which came to give their allegiance'; 'The Dynamics of Power and Conflict in the Thukela-Mzimkulu Region in the late 18th and early 19th Centuries' (PhD, thesis, University of the Witwatersrand, 1989), pp. 24–5.

32　D. Fred. Ellenberger, *History of the Basuto, Ancient and Modern* (London, 1912), p. 82.

33　Peter Robertshaw and David Taylor, 'The Rise of Political Complexity in Western Uganda', *Journal of African History* 41 (2000), p. 18.

34　H. Lichtenstein, *Travels in Southern Africa, in the Years 1803, 1804, 1805, and 1806*, translated from German by A. Plumptre, 2 vols (London, 1812–15; reprinted Cape Town, 1928–30), I, pp. 416–17.

35　Ibid., pp. 242–4.

36　H. O. Mönnig, *The Pedi* (Pretoria, 1967), p. 20 recounts a tale of roving bands of cannibals dating back to before the middle of the eighteenth century. See Campbell, *Travels*, p. 368, for tales of cannibals among the Tswana. When missionaries from Europe arrived in South Africa they made the mistake of taking these tales literally instead of metaphorically. Then, when they noticed an absence of cannibalism around them, they congratulated themselves for having eradicated the evil practice through their Christian teachings! (See especially, Arbousset and Daumas, *Narrative*, p. 54.) The contradictions in the missionary histories are often blatant. For example in one sentence D. Fred Ellenberger tells his reader that cannibalism was an idea that had originated among the Venda of the north-eastern regions. In the next he said that it was the principal result of misery provoked by warfare in the Caledon River valley of Lesotho during the 1820s; Ellenberger, *History of the Basuto*, p. 217.

37 Carolyn Hamilton, *Terrific Majesty, The Powers of Shaka Zulu and the Limits of Historical Invention* (Cape Town, 1998), pp. 211–12.

38 Arbousset and Daumas, *Narrative*, p. 144.

39 Ibid., pp. 56–69.

40 Legassick, 'The Griqua, the Sotho-Tswana and the Missionaries', p. 56; Lye, 'The Sotho Wars', p. 38.

41 Hedges, 'Trade and Politics', pp. 86–7.

42 Ibid., pp. 88–9.

43 Ibid., p. 93; Maggs, *Iron Age Communities*, p. 280.

44 Maggs, *Iron Age Communities*, pp. 23, 30; Lye, ed., *Andrew Smith's Journal*, pp. 173–4.

45 Campbell, *Travels*, pp. 231–2. Makaba II of the Ngwaketse stated that in his region settlements were built on hills 'because of enemies' but that his people 'found it very inconvenient, being so far from wood and water'.

46 Ibid., p. 193. Although mid-slope settlements had the advantage of being warmer than either hilltop or valley locations, there is evidence that on occasion the even more easily defensible flat mesas were occupied well before the nineteenth century; Maggs, *Iron Age Communities*, pp. 13, 16.

47 Martin Hall, 'The Myth of the Zulu Homestead: Archaeology and Ethnography', *Africa* 54 (1984), pp. 68, 70, 72.

48 Lye, ed., *Andrew Smith's Journal*, pp. 173–4.

49 A. T. Bryant, *Olden Times*, p. 191; Colin Webb and John Wright, eds, *A Zulu King Speaks* (Pietermaritzburg, 1978), p. 15.

50 It was not until the middle of the nineteenth century that guns capable of felling elephant with a single shot were developed. An English hunter of the 1830s described an occasion on which fifty wounds had to be inflicted before a particular bull elephant dropped; John Mackenzie, *The Empire of Nature: Hunting, Conservation and British Imperialism* (Manchester, 1988), p. 95.

51 Hedges, 'Trade and Politics', pp. 73–4. Many books incorrectly ascribe the invention of the short stabbing spear to the Zulu king Shaka. See Chapter 4, note 45.

52 Wright, 'Dynamics of Power and Conflict', pp. 31–2.

53 Lye, 'The Sotho Wars', pp. 48, 51. A visitor to the Tlhaping town of Latakoo in 1820 saw companies of soldiers 'marching two and two as regularly as any trained regiment. Most of them were armed with four assagais or spears, and had also battle-axes, and shields made of the hide of an ox'; Campbell, *Travels*, p. 258.

54 Bryant, *Olden Times*, pp. 317, 641–2; Wright, 'The Dynamics of Power', pp. 33, 35, 164, 168; Hedges, 'Trade and Politics', p. 153.

55 Mönnig, *The Pedi*, pp. 19–20.

56 Mackeurtan, *Cradle Days of Natal*, p. 18.

57 *Natal Papers*, I, p. 5. My italics.

58 Hedges, 'Trade and Politics', pp. 106–7.

59 Elizabeth Eldredge in 'Migration, Conflict and Leadership in Early 19th Century South Africa. The Case of Matiwane' (seminar paper, Dept of History, University of Natal, Durban, 3 August 1994), argues that Europeans vastly exaggerated the mortality rate in African battles. She notes that very few deaths were recorded in some famous battles of the early nineteenth century. John Wright, in 'The Dynamics of Power', p. 270, argues a similar case.

60 Campbell, *Travels*, p. 127.

61 Ibid.

62 Lichtenstein, *Travels in Southern Africa*, I, pp. 385, 392.

63 This was most famously true of Shaka the future Zulu king. Other recorded instances include: Sekonyela of the Tlokwa, who, like his father before him, was brought up by the BaSia, his mother's people (Ellenberger, *History of the Basuto*, p. 42); Sekwati of the Pedi who spent a period of residence among the Ramapulana (Mönnig, *The Pedi*, p. 19); and Mnini of the Thuli who lived as a child with the Cele.

64 Eldredge, 'Migration, Conflict and Leadership', p. 12.

65 Lichtenstein, *Travels in Southern Africa*, I, pp. 342–3.

66 Arbousset and Daumas, *Narrative*, p. 421; Bryant, *Olden Times*, pp. 308–9; Mönnig, *The Pedi*, p. 17; Lye and Murray, *Transformations on the Highveld*, p. 14; Neil Parsons, 'Prelude to *Difaqane* in the Interior *c.* 1600–*c.* 1822', in Carolyn Hamilton, ed., *The Mfecane Aftermath, Reconstructive Debates in Southern African History* (Johannesburg, 1995), p. 332.

67 Peter Delius, 'The Ndzundza Ndebele: Indenture and the Making of Ethnic Identity, 1883–1914', in P. Bonner, I. Hofmeyr, D. James and T. Lodge, eds, *Holding their Ground, Class, Locality and Culture in 19th and 20th Century South Africa* (Johannesburg, 1989), pp. 228–9.

68 Parsons, 'Prelude to *Difaqane*', pp. 331–5.

69 Ellenberger, *History of the Basuto*, p. 21.

70 Named in old records as Hlubi, Makholoko, Makakana and Matlapatlapa. See: Ellenberger, *History of the Basuto*, pp. 29, 128, 200; Arbousset and Daumas, *Narrative*, p. 77; Lye, 'The Sotho Wars', p. 28. In addition, A. T. Bryant, in *Olden Times*, p. 136, records that Masumpa, father of Matiwane, whose appearance in the Caledon Valley in the 1820s caused a great upheaval, had been raiding onto the highveld in previous decades.

71 Theal, *Basutoland Records*, I, p. 45.

72 Hall, 'The Myth of the Zulu Homestead', pp. 68, 70, 72.

73 *Natal Papers*, I, p. 8; Bryant, *Olden Times*, p. 290. See also Casalis, *The Basutos*, p. xvi.

74 Bryant, *Olden Times*, p. 403; Wright, 'Dynamics of Power', p. 313.

75 John Ayliff and Joseph Whiteside, *History of the Abambo, generally known as Fingos* (Butterworth, South Africa, 1912). The estimate of the population can only be fanciful, but that oral traditions remembered them as very numerous is significant.

76 Bryant, *Olden Times*, pp. 313–14, 335, 354, 403.

77 Hedges, 'Trade and Politics', p. 155. See also Wright, 'Dynamics of Power', pp. 313–16.

78 These towns could amount to 16,000 or more people. See Campbell, *Travels*, p. 277.

79 Arbousset and Daumas, *Narrative*, pp. 122–3.

80 Ellenberger, *History of the Basuto*, pp. 37–9, 52; Campbell, *Travels*, pp. 126, 197, 299; Lye and Murray, *Transformations*, pp. 26–7; Maggs, *Iron Age Communities*, p. 4.

81 Arbousset and Daumas, *Narrative*, p. 273; Leonard Thompson, *Survival in Two Worlds: Moshoeshoe of Lesotho, 1786–1870* (Oxford, 1975), p. 25.

82 Arbousset and Daumas, *Narrative*, p. 183.

83 Ellenberger, *History of the Basuto*, p. 244.

84 M. Wilson and L. Thompson, eds, *Oxford History of South Africa*, 2 vols (London, 1969–71), I, pp. 135–9.

85 Thompson, *Survival in Two Worlds*, pp. 33–4.

86 Ellenberger, *History of the Basuto*, p. 38.

87 Arbousset and Daumas, *Narrative*, pp. 92–3.

88 J. B. Peires, *The House of Phalo: A History of the Xhosa People in the Days of their Independence* (Johannesburg, 1981), pp. 18–19, 46–7.

89 Ibid., pp. 22–3, 48–50.

90 Rolong is another catch-all name, which by 1850 was applied to people called in other accounts Hurutshe, Kwena, Fokeng and Po.

91 S. M. Molema, *Chief Moroka* (Cape Town, n.d.), pp. 1–2.

92 William Lye, 'The Sotho Paramount Chief and the Difaqane', paper presented to the 14th meeting of the African Studies Association, Denver, 1971, p. 8.

93 J. P. R. Wallis, ed., *The Matabele Journals of Robert Moffat, 1829–1860*, 2 vols (London, 1945) I, p. 57.

94 Parsons, 'Prelude to *Difaqane*', p. 332.

95 Andrew Manson, 'Conflict in the Western Highveld/Southern Kalahari *c.* 1750–1820' in Carolyn Hamilton, ed., *The Mfecane Aftermath*, p. 354; Campbell, *Travels*, pp. 141–2, 310, 314.

96 Wallis, *The Matabele Journals of Robert Moffat*, I, pp. 152–3.

97 R. Kent Rasmussen, *Migrant Kingdom: Mzilikazi's Ndebele in South Africa* (Cape Town, 1978), pp. 106–7.

98 Historians calculate that the Rozvi extended its control to the south-western Zambezi plateau in the 1680s; Parsons, 'Prelude to *Difaqane*', p. 327.

99 Campbell, *Travels*, pp. 121, 151, 233, 303.

100 To name only the strongest. A Hurutshe chief in 1820 named some 'twenty nations' in his vicinity; Campbell, *Travels*, pp. 271–2. See also Ellenberger, *History of the Basuto*, p. 68. The terms Kwena and Kgatla, which denominate totemic lineages, are often used to describe chiefly groups in various parts of the highveld. The scattered use of these names in old records can easily lead to confusion, so I have avoided them as much as possible – preferring instead to identify groups in relation to known chiefs.

101 Campbell, *Travels*, p. 174.

102 Peter Delius, *The Land Belongs to Us: The Pedi Polity, the Boers and the British in the Nineteenth-century Transvaal* (London, 1984), pp. 12–13.

103 Mönnig, *The Pedi*, pp. 19–20; Lye, 'The Sotho Paramount Chief', pp. 8–9.

104 Manson, 'Conflict in the Western Highveld', pp. 352–3.

105 The devastation can be measured in the 'once in 50 years' drought of the 1980s and the 'once in 50 years' floods of 2000.

106 Newitt, *History of Mozambique*, pp. 152–4.

107   Mackeurtan, *Cradle Days of Natal*, p. 104.

108   Ibid., p. 18.

109   Newitt, *History of Mozambique*, pp. 155–7.

110   Hedges, 'Trade and Politics', p. 123.

111   Newitt, *History of Mozambique*, pp. 247–8. The Dutch were told in 1721 that the only thing nearby chiefs would accept in exchange for slaves were guns; Alan Smith, 'The Struggle for Control of Southern Mocambique' (PhD thesis, UCLA, 1970), p. 68. Between 1780 and 1780 the price paid for ivory at Delagoa Bay doubled due to increased competition among the buyers; Hedges, 'Trade and Politics', p. 131.

112   Mackeurtan, *Cradle Days of Natal*, pp. 55–6, 74; *Natal Papers*, I, p. 13.

113   Newitt, *History of Mozambique*, pp. 156, 257.

114   Smith, 'The Struggle for Control of Southern Mocambique', p. 223; Hedges, 'Trade and Politics', pp. 127, 141–2.

115   Smith, 'The Struggle for Control of Southern Mocambique', pp. 218–20. Bryant, *Olden Times*, pp. 293, 304–5, reckons Makhasane's reign to have begun in 1800.

116   Campbell, *Travels*, pp. 165, 179, 241.

117   Mönnig, *The Pedi*, p. 19.

118   Hedges, 'Trade and Politics', pp. 26, 138–9, 195–9; see also Newitt, *History of Mozambique*, p. 257.

119   The original proponent of the hypothesis of primordial fragmentation, A. T. Bryant, was himself of two minds on the subject. In some places he writes of KwaZulu-Natal as an Eden, where 'dotting every hillside were "quaint human habitations" belonging to some fifty or more independent clans' – a land where 'Zulu daily life of a hundred, perhaps a thousand years ago was precisely that which it is today' (*Olden Times*, pp. 72, 74). On the other hand he writes on p. 403: 'We have already related how in 1589 the early Portuguese found the abaMbo folk dwelling southward of Delagoa Bay and northward of the St. Lucia Bay; how a century or more later, the tribe broke up and a considerable portion of it marched away inland, there in the lapse of centuries, to grow into the Hlubi, Dlamini and Mkize clans.'

120   Bryant, *Olden Times*, p. 83. As Hedges points out in 'Trade and Politics', p. 25, there 'were several intermediate dialects between northern Nguni and southern Tsonga languages' which 'suggests the absence of any marked barrier to communication'.

121   Bryant, *Olden Times*, pp. 158–9; Wright, 'The Dynamics of Power', pp. 26–7.

122 Even A. T. Bryant (*Olden Times*, pp. 641–2), the authority most widely relied
on by twentieth-century historians of this region, stated clearly that 'The
Zulu regimental system is often erroneously supposed to have been an invention of Shaka; by others, of Dingiswayo. In reality, military regiments were
the universal Nguni custom before either of them was king.'

CHAPTER THREE

Foreign invaders advance along the western panhandle

Environment and ecology of the panhandle

In the previous chapter the human heartland of southern Africa was pictured as a clock centred on Ntsuanatsatsi. Now imagine the same circle as a frying pan. Its long handle, about 200 kilometres wide, stretches westward for about 1000 kilometres from East London to Cape Town. The handle shows up clearly on relief maps as a series of mountain ranges running in parallel lines from east to west. From the northernmost line of mountains all the way up to the thin, life-sustaining ribbon of the Orange River, the land is dry, a virtual desert. It has been aptly called 'the thirstland' – no good for farming and not much better for sheep or cattle. But in the panhandle itself there is water enough to support man and beast. Agriculture thrives only in the extreme west, in small pockets of freakishly abnormal rainfall or abundant underground water. The land was not, for that reason, suitable to the way of life developed in the heartland, which depended on agriculture as well as cattle-keeping. The people of the panhandle region had their own distinctive culture, evidently a long-established one because they spoke distinctive languages. Historians and anthropologists have agreed, for not entirely convincing reasons, to call them by an invented compound name: Khoisan. Those who specialized in hunting are generally known to historians as the San. Others, who specialized in herding domestic animals, are called the Khoi. It should not be supposed that these names derive from the people themselves or that they describe hard and fast divisions. In one district, for example, the cattleless people known to aliens as Baroa or Bushmen called each other Khoi.[1] The population of the entire panhandle region can never have been great. By 1800 it was estimated to number about 60,000.[2] This is tiny compared with the areas of

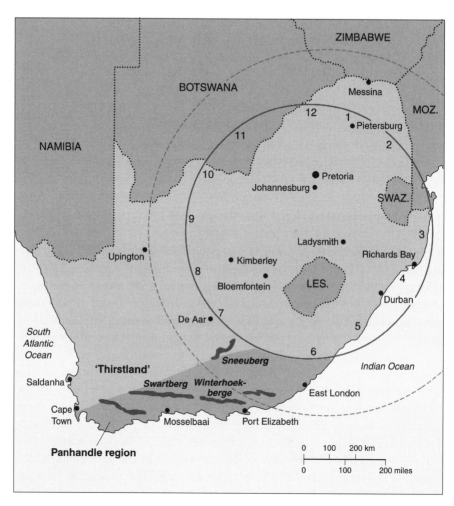

Map 4   The narrow 'Panhandle' region of adequate rainfall
After Maclennan, B. (1986)

mixed farming. However, the region has been historically very important. Up this corridor and along the Orange River came waves of invaders bringing conflict and different ways of life.

The headquarters of change were located at Table Bay, which nestles beneath imposing mountains on the south-easternmost tip of the African continent. It provides some shelter against stormy weather and for that reason attracted the attention of European companies involved in long-distance seaborne trade with India and South-east Asia. One of these trading groups, the Dutch East India Company, founded a station at the Cape in 1652 as a stopping place and a source of fresh food for passing ships. From Holland and Asia the company brought soldiers, slaves and free settlers to Cape Town.

Nearby people viewed this development with justifiable apprehension. The newcomers had guns which they used with deadly effect in a series of early wars. They also used their firepower to steal livestock and take land. While the Dutch East India Company expressed no desire to expand its domain beyond the immediate hinterland of Cape Town, it tolerated the spread of its people into whatever territory they might successfully invade and hold. In return for a small annual charge, the Company issued title deeds to land seized by these raiders. This was something quite new. Previously the source of political power had been the ability to control people and the distribution of animals. The newcomers distributed power by inscribing records of land ownership. This protected the land against competing claims. Title holders could exchange it for money or will it to children. Courts based in Cape Town settled disputes about ownership.

Of course, the Khoisan people cared nothing for title deeds or courts. They fought for their country with every weapon at their disposal.[3] The newcomers retaliated with a new kind of warfare called the *commando*. Like the regiments used in warfare in the heartland, the commando may possibly have originated as a way of organizing hunting parties.[4] When war was to be waged men were 'commanded' to assemble with their horses and guns. They would seek out their enemy and attack in series of charges. At each charge they would fire their weapons, then gallop back to a safe distance, reload, then charge again. In open country the commando proved to be practically invincible. The animals kept by Khoi herders proved to be especially vulnerable to commando raids. Those who could, saved their herds by retreating. Others accepted defeat and went to work for the victors.

Over time this pattern of conquest evolved into a social system. The first Europeans who came to the Cape called themselves burghers, that is, townsmen. Their descendants, who later came east over the mountains with their commandos, were more often called boers, a Dutch word meaning farmers. The way of life they evolved eventually made them so distinctive that the word is now usually written with a capital B. The Boers used heavy wagons hauled by oxen to move themselves and their belongings. At the end of each day's travel they let the animals loose to graze. In the morning, they yoked them up again and the wagon driver shouted in Dutch the command to pull: '*Trek!*' This ritual gave the name 'trekboers' to those whose slow but relentless advance threatened the settled ways of all who stood in their path. The trekboers lived simple lives, but their needs for guns, metal, spare parts for their wagons and other household goods kept them technologically dependent on supplies from Cape Town.[5] Holding on to the land they seized required title deeds registered in Cape Town. Marriage was the best way to guarantee the right of children to inherit property and these marriages, too, had to be registered in Cape Town. So back and forth the Boers trekked with their ox wagons, driving flocks of short-haired, fat-tailed sheep and a few cattle to sell in town. They also moved their flocks at certain seasons to seek better pastures or avoid drought. However, it would be wrong to think that, because they were called trekboers, they were nomadic. Most aspired to stay put and make a modest living. But the land could not support a dense population. Moreover, the Dutch regulations would not allow registered parcels of land to be subdivided when a landholder died. Regulations also decreed that property had to be divided equally among children. This inheritance system concentrated significant power in the hands of wealthy widows. It also forced the sale of estates so that children could get their share. Since the average trekboer family in the eighteenth century had seven children – most of whom lived long enough to found families of their own – there was constant pressure to expand the system into new lands.[6]

However poor in material goods, the typical trekboer establishment contained a wealth of human capital. Like the cattle-keepers of the heartland, they sought help to safeguard their herds and to move them from place to place in accordance with seasonal changes in pastures. Few had the money to buy slaves in the Cape Town markets. Their main sources of new farmhands were the indigenous people of the panhandle region. Many defeated and impoverished folk actively sought work with the trekboers; the commando system generated a steady stream of additional recruits. The invaders waged war without mercy.[7] Even when their main objective was cattle-raiding, they shot to kill – especially men.[8] Adult males knew their country well and would know where to go if they could escape. Women, too, might escape, but they at least could produce children: farm workers of the future. Most valuable of all were young children. They were least likely to run away and would grow up knowing no other world than the farm. In most respects their condition approximated slavery. The only significant difference was that they could not be sold on the open market. Modern historians write of *inboekstelsel*, the practice of keeping captured or purchased children as farm labourers as a fundamental 'form of indigenous slavery that originated in the Cape and was transferred inland in the nineteenth century'.[9]

Complex social relations developed on the Boer estates. Ultimate power lay with the landholding married couple and the children born to the wife. They alone would inherit and accumulate property. Female servants often lived in the main house, where they were easy prey for the sexual desires of the landholder and his sons. Male servants lived on the perimeter, excluded by the most stringent conventions from any sexual contact with female members of the landholding family. In the course of several generations this one-way pattern of sexual relations produced a population of mixed descent destined to be forever farm workers, never landholders. Often when a farm was sold, the work force stayed on, an unregistered part of the assets. Sometimes the whole establishment might trek off together to new farms. The divide between landholders and their dependant work force was social and economic rather than cultural. A variant of the Dutch language evolved among the farm workers and was eventually spoken by the whole establishment, including the landholding family: the language known now as Afrikaans. Daily interaction bred a pattern of socializing marked by informality rather than rigid conventions of domination and servility. It could happen that a poor son of a trekboer family would fail to achieve a landholding of his own, and would join another farm's work force as a hired hand or overseer. Others without much property lived as *bywohners*, tenants of the title holders. These poorer males sometimes married servants and produced children, thus promoting further mixing of the rural working class.[10] For outcasts and adventurous spirits, hunting offered a way to break the tedium of farm life. From the beginning of the eighteenth century armed parties pushed inland looking for animals to shoot and people to trade with for ivory tusks and teeth.[11]

A poet once fancifully described the trekboer as someone who loathed the sight of his neighbour's chimney lest his 'neighbours' smoke shall vex his eyes, their voices break his rest'.[12] In reality, the Boers depended absolutely on contact and co-operation with neighbours. Holding and expanding their territory required the organized force of the commando. However widely scattered they might be, they needed to respond instantly to the call to assemble, generally at the summons of a semi-military appointed official (the *veldkornet*). In the early 1820s one official in a desolate and isolated region boasted that he 'could call out in six hours upwards of 1000' men, 'armed and mounted'.[13] Landholders made up only a part of the commando; most of the men came from the farm work force.[14] For this reason commando service was generally an unwelcome disruption to the routine of rural life. Military objectives had to be achieved quickly, or the force would disperse.

Quick victories could often be scored in raids on Khoi herders, who found the commando a fearsome enemy. Defeat took away the beasts whose possession meant wealth and power. Rather than risk losing everything in pitched battle, they would seek out new places to live.

The San hunters put up a more effective resistance to the invaders who stole their children and killed off the wild game they depended on for meat. Having no domestic animals to protect was actually an advantage for them.[15] The long mountain ranges running from east to west offered them places to live and rugged terrains where horsemen were at a disadvantage. They also had a weapon which terrified foes: the poison arrow. In those days there was no known antidote to its toxin. Once an enemy felt the sting of the arrow, agonizing death swiftly followed. By about 1776 the San had effectively organized a line of defence in the mountains around Graaf Reinet and for the next quarter of a century they more than held their own.[16] They beat back the enemy and reclaimed lands which had been marked out as Boer farms. By 1800 the people had muskets as well as arrows in their armoury.[17] Their rock paintings recorded the fortunes of war. One depicted 'a great fat Dutch farmer thrashing his Bushman, and also Bushmen surrounding a farmer to kill him'.[18] But never in this long war of attrition did the joys of battle outweigh the miseries of daily life. A combatant described

the condition of his countrymen as truly deplorable . . . for several months in the year, when the frost and snow prevented them from making their excursions against the farmers, their sufferings from cold and want of food were indescribable: that they frequently beheld their wives and children perishing with hunger, without being able to give them any relief. The good season brought little alleviation to their misery. They knew themselves to be hated by all mankind, and that every nation around them was an enemy planning their destruction.[19]

One Boer recalled seeing over 3000 San killed on the commandos he attended between 1803 and 1809.[20] In one region the name for 'white man' was the same as the word for gun.[21] As more land and game were lost, people's relations with each other grew strained. Early in the nineteenth century an old man recalled that in the past the San co-operated for mutual advantage in times of drought and hunger. Now they crowded in upon each other and 'every community found it necessary to guard each district with jealous care'.[22] Thus the struggle for individual survival gradually sapped the collective will to co-operate in the larger struggle for the survival of a way of life. Few fighters in all the annals of South African heroism displayed such courage against overwhelming odds. Their struggle deserves to be better known and honoured. Today the 'bushmen' are misrepresented as 'harmless little people' of the desert lands. Their disappearance from other places was not a choice but a forced retreat. People of the heartland should remember them as brave men and women whose lonely struggle for a time held the line against the advance of the invaders.

Kora and other raiders begin to infiltrate the heartland

A cruel twist of fate turned some of their cousins, the Khoi herders, into an advance guard of the slow-moving trekboer army. As they lost land to the Boers, many of the Khoi retreated to the north and east.[23] Some of these had adopted the technology of their enemies: horses and guns. These they used to hunt wild animals, capture cattle and kidnap people. They went by many names – Griqua, Koranna or Kora, Oorlams, Bastards – which spoke of their diverse origins. Although there was a fair sprinkling of runaway slaves and outcasts from Cape colonial society, most were descended wholly or in part from the ancient inhabitants of the western regions. The names of former chiefs may well have been the source of the names Griqua and Koranna.[24] One of their number, Hendrik Hendriks, has left us a brief and poignant account of their historical experience:

> The [Boer] Farmers say the Griquas now occupy the Bushmen's land, who was it that drove us there? Let the names Kaapstad, Stellenbosch, Tulbagh [towns founded by the Dutch], give the answer; it was the Dutch people who sent us forward.[25]

Newcomers from many places swelled their ranks. They first seem to have threatened peoples of the heartland in the middle decades of the eighteenth century.[26] By the end of century they begin to emerge in the historical record as individuals with names and personalities.

Cornelius Kok had once held a Dutch appointment as a captain of a group of Khoi, and had briefly owned a farm in the Western Cape, which he sold before moving to the Orange River Valley with relatives. His son Adam would found a notable Griqua dynasty.[27]

Jan Bloem, according to some accounts, was a German sailor who deserted his ship in 1780 and later murdered his wife.[28] By joining the Khoi adventurers of the interior he escaped punishment and found new wives. In time he married some eight or ten drawn from different places, thereby cementing alliances which eventually enabled him to found a substantial chiefdom – the Springbok Kora led by his son, Jan Bloem, Jr – whose diverse following included people drawn from Sotho, Tswana, Khoi and San groups.

Klaas Barends is said to have been the son of a Cape burgher named Barents.[29] After his father rejected his mother so he could marry a Boer woman, young Klaas was thrown upon his own resources. In 1760 he accompanied a Company expedition to the Orange River. Over the course of the next twenty years he accompanied other expeditions and established friendly relations with Kora people in the Orange Valley. His son Barend Barends became a famous commando leader.

Joseph Arend, who had been held as a slave by a Boer in the Sneuwberg area, escaped, and established himself as an itinerant trader. By 1820 his travels had taken him to the headwaters of the Limpopo and eastward nearly as far as Delagoa Bay.[30]

The man known widely as Afrikander had once been employed, along with his two sons, by a Boer named Piet Pienaar. He had from time to time accompanied his master and Jan Bloem on commandos against southern Tswana villages. When Pienaar and his brother raped his sons' wives, the offended husbands ambushed and killed Pienaar, before escaping north with their father and the rest of their family.[31]

The Kok family stemmed from a freed slave, Adam Kok, who married a Khoi woman and acquired grazing rights to a farm about 170 kilometres north of Cape Town in the middle decades of the eighteenth century.[32] His son Cornelis moved to the Orange River and fathered Solomon who moved east with his family, followers and herds into the area later known as Griqualand West.[33] By the 1820s Adam Kok II had acquired a large following who called him their 'Captain'. Other captains of importance in the early nineteenth century included Andries Waterboer, Hendrik Hendriks and Gert Taaibosch.

In their own eyes these leaders were persecuted people who had used the Orange River as a corridor to escape the expanding zone of Boer influence. In the eyes of those whose territory they invaded, they looked very much like trekboers – especially those who could afford horses and guns. Their armed commandos ruthlessly seized cattle and people. A San hunter compelled to join one of Jan Bloem's raids in the early 1790s recalled attacking a large Tswana town near what is today the site of Kuruman. The people

> were attacked, many of them shot, and all their cattle, sheep and goats taken. . . . Before leaving the country of the Bushmen, Bloom left a few cattle among them as a reward for the services he had compelled them to afford. The Corannas, who formed a very considerable proportion of this plundering band, with the small share of the booty which was ceded to them, preferred seeking a new abode to returning to the one they had left. . . .[34]

After a similar raid, an entire Tswana group lost all its cattle and survived only by living on 'roots, wild berries, gum, locusts, white ants, and other insects'.[35] The incoming raiders attacked Bushmen groups with the same merciless fury that had characterized the trekboer wars in the south-west.[36]

Many of these invading raiders spoke the Afrikaans language. Occasionally they offered their services as guides to expeditions sent from Cape Town.[37] They depended on trade with Boer farmers south of the Orange for supplies of vital materials such as firearms and gunpowder.[38] To get these goods they sold captured children.[39] Their own homesteads included large retinues of captive labour. The principal wives of the 'captains' commanded a variety of household servants.[40] Only in one respect did they differ dramatically from the advancing tide of trekboers: they had no government to record and defend written titles to land.[41] What they won with muskets had to be held with muskets.

Confronting the Griqua and Kora raiders

The raiders presented a grave challenge to the western Tswana. Whether it was for this or some other reason, the large realm carved out by 'Tau the Lion' in the mid-eighteenth century (see Chapter 2) did not long survive the death of its creator.[42] (One story attributes the death of Tau to Tlhaping chiefs who allied themselves with Kora.)[43] The availability of ground and underground water sources had determined the pattern of western Tswana settlement. Between the isolated springs and waterholes lay uninhabited open plains. These created wonderful opportunities for the raiders who could swoop upon their prey as if from nowhere – and depart as mysteriously as they had arrived. The old method of defence had been a maze of thorns and branches interlacing and surrounding the town. Fire and bullets rendered this shield useless. The invaders acknowledged no mutual code of honour, no shared belief in sanctions inflicted by an unseen world. One raid could strip away a heritage of cattle holdings built up over decades. One raid could plunge a generation of mothers into bitter tears for their stolen children. Two kinds of response were obvious strategies for dealing with the unprecedented threat. Chiefs could either fall back before the invaders or they could attempt to negotiate with them.

The Rolong who had been united under Tau retreated northwards. In the process they split into at least five separate communities.[44] The most numerous group was probably that headed by Mashow (Masweu or Mashaw) and settled around the headwaters of Molopo.[45] Although glad to be free of Rolong overlordship, the closely related Tlhaping people of the Langeberg mountains could not hold their territory in the face of repeated attacks from the southern invaders, so they retreated to a more defensible position on the Kuruman River. Later they joined forces with Jan Bloem and a section of the Taaibosch Koranna in an attack on Makaba's Ngwaketse.[46] Some Tlhaping chiefs attempted to create alliances with the Koranna through marriage.[47] This continued for some decades until many Koranna 'had Sotho-Tswana living as subordinates in their communities and vice versa'.[48] Trade flourished, as manufactures, tobacco and pack animals from the south-west were exchanged for the ivory, hides, high-quality iron ware and ochre of the Tswana.[49] In this way a trading network developed, extending all the way from Cape Town to the Zambezi. Chiefs plied the newcomers with questions about the Europeans. Who was their king and where did he live? Did the glass beads they traded come from the sea? How large were their towns? Did people in Europe wear skin cloaks?[50]

The main adaptation required to deal with the newcomers was to learn to address them as 'Mynheer' or 'Vrou' and to acquire a smattering of other Afrikaans words.[51] As these dealings and interminglings increased, there was a growing temptation for ambitious Tswana chiefs to use the horses and guns of the invaders against old rivals and enemies. Many cattle raids in the late eighteenth century involved allied forces of Tswana and Kora. So, surprising as it may seem, the first effect of the encounter between the Tswana and the newcomers was to divide and fragment the old chiefdoms – not to bring them together in a united effort at defence.

A time-honoured method of repairing losses inflicted by cattle raids was to organize raids on other people. This practice set off an advancing wave of raiding and counter-raiding which gradually affected the whole region east of the Kalahari Desert from the Orange River to the headwaters of the Limpopo. The names Kok, Barends, Bloem, Links and Taaibosch evoked terror everywhere. Any man with a horse and gun could find employment in these troubled times. Take for example the career of the Afrikaner raider from trekboer territory, Coenraad de Buys. By early 1815 he

> had left the Colony and was apparently living on the Harts River. . . . In the second half of 1816, he and the Hartenaars raided a Rolong or Ghoya community to the east of the Tlhaping at Dithakong. After this Buys appears to have separated from the Hartenaars, and joined the Tlhaping (with whom he had had some contact) on a battle against the Fokeng-Motlala. The Tlhaping had been invited to join this expedition by the Rolong-Seleka, but were so disgusted by their defeat by the well-defended Fokeng that they raided the Rolong-Seleka on their return, but were again defeated as a result of Buys warning the Rolong. Shortly after this commando . . . Buys joined the Rolong-Seleka. He was accepted by the community on the condition that his herds (large in number despite his

occasional trips to the Colony for cattle) 'should remain his if he continued to live with them, but if he left, they should remain.' Although Buys seems to have built a house at the Rolong-Seleka settlement of Thabeng, he was still restless, and within the next two years had lived among, or raided in the company of, the Hurutshe, the Ngwaketse, the Kwena-Modimosana, and the Kwena of Sechele. After 1820, he travelled northwards, was among the Ngwato in 1821, and later vanished even further in the north. . . . he is reputed to have had 51 children apart from those by his Dutch wife.[52]

Raiding paid Coenraad de Buys in the traditional currency of the heart-land: wives and cattle.

New enemies on the Xhosa western frontier

For an indeterminate length of time sovereignty over land in the coastal region between the present-day Port Elizabeth and East London had been disputed between the Xhosa mixed farmers and Khoi pastoralists (see Chapter 2). Historians used to regard this conflict as the product of a Xhosa drive down the coast during a long process of migration. The discovery of very ancient iron-age archaeological sites on the coast casts doubt on this migration hypothesis.[53] More likely, the divide between the mixed farmers and the purely pastoral peoples swayed backwards and forwards in line with long-term variations in rainfall and politics. The presence of many 'click' consonants in the Xhosa language argues for a very long period of interaction with the Khoi. This must have involved much intermarriage. On the western Xhosa frontier the distinction between peoples blurred, being more a matter of economics than culture.

New reasons for conflict appeared in the eighteenth century as trekboer expansion pressured the Khoi from the rear. Soon the Xhosa met the Boer face to face. The first arrivals were hunters who had shot the elephant, rhino and hippo of the panhandle region to virtual extinction and lusted after new sources of ivory. As early as 1702 an armed party of Xhosa clashed with a group of the plundering newcomers.[54] In 1736 two Boer expeditions reached the very heart of Xhosa and Thembu territory, seeking to hunt and trade. One of these parties caused trouble, provoking some Xhosa to attack and kill several hunters. It was an ill-omened start to what would prove to be a terrible relationship. It showed people the deadly potential of horses and guns, while at the same time demonstrating the invaders to be mortal men as vulnerable as themselves. The attractions of trade, at least in the short run, appeared to outweigh the hazards of conflict.

On the heels of the hunter came the farmer. By 1770 trekboer farms had been marked out in districts lying a little to the northwest of Algoa Bay. By 1786 a company official resided in the district of Graaf-Reinet.[55] The smash-and-grab commando tactics used so effectively to steal cattle and children from the Khoi did not have the same devastating effect on Xhosa people, whose crops enabled them to survive big cattle raids. Moreover, they heavily outnumbered the invaders. Cattle-raiding was an old game which they could play as well as the advancing foe. Potential for war was present from the beginning, not just because there were causes for conflict, but also because there was no agreement on ways to keep the peace.

Xhosa and Thembu chiefs had managed conflict by creating webs of marriage alliances. It proved impossible to achieve security by making such alliances with the newcomers – except those whose word carried no weight with the principal authorities. Various escaped slaves, Khoi and Boer hunter/traders were allowed to settle as refugees. Some made themselves useful. Coenraad de Buys turned up with a gang of gun-toting companions after fleeing the Cape colony in 1799. Ngqika – who had succeeded to the chieftainship of the Rharhabe Xhosa – treated him as a chief of some importance. His powerful, widowed mother, Yese, took de Buys as her lover. As a mark of reciprocal regard de Buys promised his own fifteen-year-old daughter to Ngqika.[56] However, as we have seen, he soon absconded to pursue life as a hired gun beyond the Orange. The real chief of the Boers was the governor who lived beyond the horizon in his distant Cape Town home. And there the law did not allow men more than one registered wife. When a Cape governor did arrive in 1778 to talk to Xhosa chiefs about ways to keep the peace, he offered a completely different solution. He set boundary markers in the ground and proposed that no Boers should go east of his line and no Xhosa should travel west of it. However, in the absence of border police, people from both groups ignored the line. Its only effect was to delay legal recognition of any Boer farms established on the further side. Trading and raiding went on as before. Full-scale war flared for the first time in 1779 and continued intermittently for the next century, in a conflict which has been justly termed South Africa's Hundred Years' War.[57]

Inevitably, some people on the Xhosa side of the line began to acquire guns and horses, a development whose unsettling consequences soon spread north over the mountains and beyond the Orange River. Small groups of Xhosa were encountered north of the Orange by travellers as early as 1801.[58] The chiefs of these groups soon began to accumulate their own mixed followings of San, Kora and assorted renegades. By 1805 there may have been as many as 500 Xhosa living in that region, some with firearms which they had acquired by working for farmers. There were important men among them, two nephews of chief Ndlambe and a son of Rharhabe.[59] Born Nzwane, but more commonly known by the name of Danster, he had entered the territory about 1797 and gradually acquired a fearsome reputation as a war leader.[60] Later he moved his field of operations down to Boer territory, from which he was deported to his Xhosa homeland. In 1814 he was associated with Coenraad de Buys in raiding enterprises north of the Orange. Incredibly, he was still alive as late as 1852, living in the Caledon Valley with a following of 200–300 people – remembered with awe as the first man to bring a gun into that territory.[61]

The appearance of Xhosa raiders in the company of Kora and Griqua matters, not so much because of the numbers involved, but because it exposes the fundamental interconnection between violence on the Xhosa western frontier and violence in the lands of the Sotho and Tswana to the north. The ability of small groups of armed, mounted raiders to create havoc should not be under-estimated. A single Kora raid on the Tlhaping which captured 'the whole of their cattle' reduced them to 'living upon roots and whatever game they could occasionally kill'.[62] When a mass of people as numerous as the Rolong desert whole towns in a headlong retreat northward there must be a good reason. And the raids they in turn mounted to repair their losses of cattle exemplify the chain-reaction set in motion by violence in the south.

The British succeed the Dutch East India Company as masters of the western panhandle

Violence on a much grander scale erupted in Europe and India during the last decade of the eighteenth century as powerful empires clashed in titanic struggles for mastery. Early in the struggle, the Netherlands fell into the hands of Britain's chief enemy, France. In an earlier war the French had occupied Cape Town in a bid to challenge British naval supremacy in the Indian Ocean. To counter the strategic threat to maritime supply lines which the French might pose if they returned, the British sent a force to attack and occupy the region in 1795. The peace settlement which finally ended the great war in 1815 left Britain permanently ensconced as imperial master of the entire panhandle region. By this time they occupied a pre-eminent position as a world-wide military and naval power. The war which broke out in the 1790s was merely the last in a series of conflicts in which Britain had been engaged for more or less the whole of the eighteenth century. The state itself was little more than a war machine. Between 1700 and 1815, the government spent more than 85 per cent of annual revenue paying for the army, the navy and the debts incurred as the result of planning and conducting wars.[63] The king and his courtiers, as well as all the great families of the realm, were personally involved in the war machine. Their sons filled most of the top positions in the army and navy. Their fortunes were invested in the bonds used to finance wars. They also drew profits from plantations in the West Indies – where slaves transported from Africa toiled in the sugar cane and tobacco fields – and from India where the British East India Company had transformed itself from a trading enterprise into a territorial empire drawing most of its revenue from taxes levied on the peasants. Capital generated from these and other sources was simultaneously helping to finance an industrial revolution which would further enhance Britain's dominant position among nations. Britain thus came to South Africa backed by huge resources of money and weapons.

Another Britain of somewhat different character was emerging from within the bosom of the 'military fiscal state' at the time British government came to the Cape. The development of better ships, guns and financial institutions had stimulated advances in scientific knowledge. The state needed more and more literate, educated people. It was difficult to spread education without at the same time giving ordinary people the ability to question the existing order of things. Some demanded more say in government. Some questioned the morality of slavery and the slave trade. Some even questioned the rightness of war. The advent of British rule brought some of these questioning spirits to South Africa. It also paved the way for people who believed that their God had sent them on a 'mission' to convert Africans to their Christian religion. Some of the very first of these so-called 'missionaries' to be sent abroad by British religious groups went to South Africa – beginning with agents of the London Missionary Society in 1799.[64] Adventurous souls, imbued with the belief that death in the service of their God would speed them on the way to eternal life, they moved quickly to establish contact with the Xhosa and communities living north of the Orange River.

Most of the first missionaries were humble men and women with no links to the military and aristocratic classes. They preached love and peace. It was an essential part of their business to seek out and converse with the people they meant to convert. That meant they had to learn Southern African languages. They believed that fundamental truths about God, the universe and moral conduct were written in their Bible. They believed that converts to their religion should learn to read the Bible either in English or in local languages. Thus, education for literacy was an indispensable element in their mission. Poor though they were, they constituted a profoundly subversive force. On the one hand their ideas threatened to undermine entrenched ideas which supported the power of all chiefs, fathers, rain-makers and every other practitioner of supernatural arts. They preached against exchanges of cattle at marriage, denounced polygamy and denied the efficacy of sorcery and divination. On the other hand, their educational programme threatened to give their converts ideas and technologies which could be turned against the advance of British power and the institutions devised to supply forced labour to farmers and other employers. Many of them frankly denounced the institution of slavery. They, along with the soldiers, traders and bankers which British rule brought to South Africa, gave the new order in the western regions a more complex, contradictory character than the Dutch regime which a faraway war had swept away for ever.

John Barrow, the Englishman who undertook to survey the economic resources of the Cape at the time of the initial British occupation, found few causes for enthusiasm.[65] The trekboers' short-haired, fat-tailed sheep were useless as a source of wool. Grape vines did not flourish beyond the Cape Town region. Whaling, along with trade in hides and ivory, offered about the only expanding possibilities for profit. Still, it was a place which, if properly managed, might pay its own way. A man who had risen from humble origins through education and intellectual endeavour, Barrow belonged to that growing class of thinkers who measured the world by the light of science rather than the yardstick of tradition. He empathized with the extreme poverty of the trekboers and ridiculed missionaries for a credulous faith in Providence, but ranked the Xhosa people he met with the ancient Greek and Roman heroes of European history. For all his science, Barrow was very ignorant of Africa. Wherever he went, he asked who had seen the unicorn. He held out great hopes that the fabled animal might be found somewhere north of the Orange River.[66] Barrow embodied the most charming as well as the most dangerous characteristics of the new regime. He was a measurer, a mapper, a keen observer of plants and animals, bent on maximizing the economic potential of this and all the territories in Britain's expanding empire. He soon left the Cape and put his questing intellect at the service of the Admiralty Office in London – the very engine room of the world-wide war machine.

Those who stayed to rule the zone which the British called the Cape Colony were cast in a different mould. Almost all the governors in the first half of the nineteenth century were high-ranking officers, professional warriors with minds and bodies forged in the decades of war against the French. Their subordinate staff were likewise drawn from the officer corps. They smelled of polished leather, canvas and steel bayonets. Hating liberty and equality because these were the doctrines of their European enemies, their fraternity was the officers' mess. When the great war was over, they looked for new military adventures to satisfy their cravings for battle, glory and advancement. As one historian has written, 'hundreds of bored and discontented British officers, the under-employed detritus of the Waterloo generation, demanded action'.[67] By 1808, the size of the British garrison had grown to more than three times the size of the old Dutch establishment at Cape Town. The economic burden of supporting the expanded military and naval establishment put a further burden on the slaves and Khoi workers who were subjected to new labour laws. The military ruling caste looked with disdain on the little band of British journalists and merchants who asked for votes and rights of free speech. There would be no votes and precious few rights granted during the period covered by this history. Nor did the military governors demonstrate much sympathy for the missionaries, whose lowly origins they despised and whose preaching they believed to be dangerous. They only reluctantly agreed to lift a decree which made it illegal for missionaries to teach writing.[68] The military governors recognized the Boers as their natural allies and looked upon the commando system as a cheap and efficient adjunct to the garrison of regular soldiers. Although they were under orders after 1815 to cut military expenditure, their own ingrained habit was to seek military solutions to the problems which arose along the border they inherited from their Dutch predecessors. Like the Dutch, they held the questionable belief that fixed territorial boundaries helped quell conflicts. Realizing that they were heavily outnumbered by peoples to their east, they tried – with only limited success – to ban trade in guns and ammunition.[69]

First Xhosa encounters with the British on the western frontier

Political divisions among the Xhosa chiefs bedevilled all their dealings with the new power across the frontier and prevented them from ever presenting a united front. The most important of these divisions continued to be that inaugurated by the sons of Phalo: Rharhabe and Gcaleka (see Chapter 2, p. 27). Their heirs, Ndlambe and Khawuta, carried on an inconclusive struggle until Khawuta's death (1794) left a five-year-old child, Hintsa, the anointed heir to the house of Gcaleka. Thereafter, Ndlambe advanced from strength to strength, using every means at his disposal to build his power in the western regions until a coup engineered by his nephew, Ngqika, made him a virtual prisoner in his own homestead.[70] In this history the names Hintsa and Ngqika will figure most prominently among chiefs of the Xhosa, along with Ngqika's talented son, Maqoma.

The Boer advance presented opportunities as well as dangers to contenders in the endless, ultimately futile, struggle to establish a single kingship.[71]

In the closing decades of the eighteenth century various chiefs had struck bargains with Boer commanders who offered support against their internal enemies. Now the British government offered an even stronger potential ally. As chiefs competed for favours, they undermined each other. Tragically, some offered military support in campaigns against the bushmen defenders of the Sneuwberg mountains.[72] One of these was Chungwa, chief of the Gqunukhwebe group from 1793 to 1812. His territory between the Fish and Sundays Rivers constituted the front line of Xhosa defence against the oncoming colonists. The strains caused by two decades of delicate diplomacy made enemies of Ngqika and other chiefs to his rear without converting British officials into reliable friends. That was partly because neither he nor any other chief was in a position to deliver what the British officials demanded: an ironclad guarantee that no Xhosa men would attempt to take cattle from Boer farmers.

The advent of the farmers presented common people with opportunities to acquire stock and thus raise their standing in society. They could work for farmers as they had previously worked for chiefs – but in a profoundly different economic system, where money was the medium of exchange. Chiefs were powerless to prevent their movements across the ill-defined, unpatrolled frontier.[73] When any of them made off with Boer cattle, however, blame fell on the nearest chief. Punishment generally took the form of a commando raid. Adding to the misery of chiefs were other commando raids whose object was the theft of Xhosa cattle from innocent people under the pretext of retribution for thefts. On one occasion Boer farmers in one district reported 65,327 cattle as stolen by the Xhosa, an amount eight times greater than all the cattle they had previously declared for tax purposes![74] While the British government did little or nothing to investigate or punish such criminal commandos, they held Xhosa chiefs responsible for any thefts on their own side of the frontier.

If the chiefs could not prevent or punish thefts, then, decreed the British commanders, they must give up their land and accept a new frontier line. As early as 1799 a British general had tried to compel chief Chungwa to retreat to the eastern side of the Great Fish River, but disorganization on the side of the Boer/British alliance foiled the scheme.[75] A decade later a more determined effort was made to 'clear' the territory which the Boers – in anticipation of conquest – called by a Dutch word, the Zuurveld ('sour grasslands'). This was a beautiful tract of coastal countryside roughly bounded on the north and east by the Great Fish River, on the west by the Sundays River. Chungwa and Ndlambe both made claims to this territory. Ndlambe had even tried to confirm his title in the eyes of the Dutch by sending herds of oxen as 'payment'.[76] The British took no trouble to investigate these claims, because they were obsessed by the idea that a stable frontier could

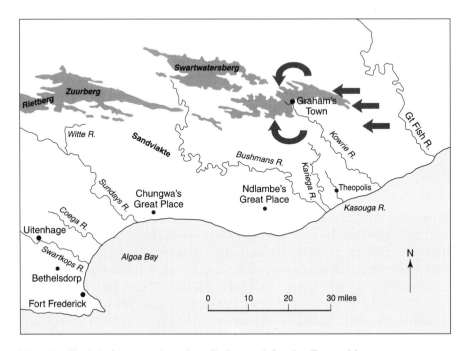

Map 5   Nxele's forces make a last-ditch stand for the Zuurveld
After Maclennan, B. (1986)

be established along the Fish River. In pursuit of this objective they were prepared to ignore legal niceties and use whatever force was required.

In 1809, the British Governor, Lord Caledon, decreed that all Xhosa labourers working for Boers should immediately return to 'their own country'. Many protested that they had already been living and working on farms for up to twenty years and had 'no other country'.[77] By the end of the year several thousand had been brutally rounded up and expelled. To ensure that Boer farmers retained an adequate supply of labour, the British subjected Khoi workers to harsh new labour laws (the so-called Caledon Code) which forbade them from moving from place to place without official 'passes'. In the same year the governor's special commissioner recommended that all Xhosa should be driven out of the Zuurveld and replaced by farmers from Europe whose presence would act as 'a formidable barrier' against any attempt to retake the territory. Two years later, Colonel John Graham took the first step in implementing the plan late in the year 1811. He commanded forces larger than any hitherto confronted by the Xhosa chiefs, including cannons, riflemen, cavalry, a recently formed Khoi regiment and a commando of 450 men called up from the Boers – in all, more than a thousand men.[78]

This was no ordinary commando of civilians bent on defending or acquiring property – who would withdraw rather than risk death in a pitched battle. Graham's attacking force of regular soldiers and officers adhered to a stern military ethic. Like the Xhosa defenders, they were ready to fight and die for the glory of their king and their regiment. Ndlambe and Chungwa between them could muster, at best, perhaps 5000 able-bodied soldiers. Ndlambe bravely shouted defiance, 'This country is mine; I won it in war, and shall maintain it.'[79] Chungwa was too old and sick to put up an effective fight. A commando patrol tracked him down at night and shot him as he slept.[80] Both sides suffered grievous losses, but in the end the superior firepower of the attackers compelled Ndlambe to withdraw behind the Fish River. Many of his followers now deserted him and recognized his nephew Ngqika as their chief. Meanwhile, as the British/Boer forces advanced through the Zuurveld they systematically burnt the huts and destroyed the crops they found along their march. As Colonel Graham explained, 'We chose the season of corn being on the ground' so that 'we might the more severely punish them for their many crimes by destroying it'.[81] Perhaps as many as 20,000 retreated into Ngqika's territory. Landless and hungry, they placed a heavy burden on the hospitality of their compatriots and chiefs. The sound of cannon and the stink of gunpowder haunted them along with the remembrance of the way an implacable foe had indiscriminately killed men, women and children. At the same time they had learned that in rough country and thick bush, the British could be as vulnerable as the Boers.

From one point of view, Ngqika had won a great victory without losing a soldier. Most people acknowledged him as paramount chief of all the Rharhabe Xhosa. His uncle, at least for the time being, posed no threat. From another point of view, Ngqika had many reasons to worry. Land and food supplies must be found for his 20,000-odd new subjects. While the British government recognized his pre-eminent position and claimed him as an ally, its governor announced that they would henceforth hold him responsible for all breaches of peace along the long boundary. In fact, Ngqika could no more stop people travelling across the Fish River to work, trade or raid, than he could prevent water passing through a sieve. Living now on the front line, he could expect the next British advance to come at his expense. Soon there emerged in his own neighbourhood a fiery prophet, Nxele, preaching a new and frightening analysis of Xhosa relations with the British.

Nxele gained a first-hand knowledge of life on the other side of the frontier, growing up as the son of a Xhosa commoner on a Boer farm.[82] There he learned Dutch and experienced the peculiar colonial pattern of human relationships. As a young adult, he sought out his ancestral home where he won recognition as a powerful *inyanga* (diviner). Soon he had moved beyond divination to preaching and prophecy. Early in his career he had actively cultivated the company of Christian ministers and missionaries whom he regarded as specially gifted people like himself. Later, finding his overtures rejected, his powers despised and the British enemy ever on the march, Nxele hardened his heart. His new message was that the world was divided between forces of good and evil. Thixo, God of the white people, had banished the Boers and British to South Africa for the crime of killing his son, Jesus. Before long, Mdalidiphu, the God of the black people, would drive the invaders back into the sea from whence they had come.

A fateful moment. The division of humankind according to skin colour – an idea common enough among the Boers and British – was now preached among the Xhosa.[83] Following Nxele's logic, there could be no permanent alliances, no peaceful intermingling of peoples according to the immemorial custom of the country. For all anyone knew, the next war might be the prophesied final conflict. That idea gave those who believed his message a special zeal and determination to win. His herds and following of people enabled the charismatic commoner to claim *de facto* recognition alongside Ngqika and Ndlambe as one of the three great chiefs of the western region.

The special object of his wrath was the Zuurveld, symbol of lost herds and pastures. There stood a British fort named Grahamstown in honour of the region's destroyer. There, in accordance with Caledon's original scheme, plans were well advanced to divide the land into farms for settlers from England. However, before a concerted effort could be mounted to reconquer the land, Britain's nominated ally, Ngqika, must be neutralized. A grand coalition, including not only Nxele's and Ndlambe's forces, but also troops commanded by young King Hintsa of the Gcaleka-Xhosa, met and over-whelmed Ngqika at the battle of Amalinde (October 1818), the most fero-cious contest known to have been fought among the Xhosa. Ngqika then made things worse by invoking the aid of the British, telling them that he had been attacked for the crime of punishing cattle thieves. Without inves-tigating the truth of Ngqika's claims, a British commando swept across the Fish River, carrying off an estimated 23,000 cattle. The effects, as one of Nxele's councillors told the British, were devastating.

> You sent a commando – you took our last cow – you left only a few calves
> which died for want, along with our children. You gave half the spoil to
> Gaika [Ngqika]; half you kept yourselves. Without milk – our corn
> destroyed – we saw that we must ourselves perish; we followed, therefore,
> the tracks of our cattle into the colony.[84]

Enough of them followed the tracks into the Zuurveld to create panic among farmers. Many Boers fled, leaving the Xhosa in possession of much of their lost territory. British commanders called for reinforcements from Cape Town and braced themselves for an attack, which came the day after Nxele, in accordance with the chivalrous conventions of warfare, sent a messenger to announce that next morning he would 'breakfast' with the commandant at Grahamstown.[85] It is said that Nxele stirred his soldiers with an appeal to national unity.

> There they come! They have crossed the Qagqiwa and they have crossed
> the Nqweba; only one river more, the Nxuba [Great Fish] and they will be
> in our land. What will become of you then? Let us combine, and be one
> powerful nation, that we may drive the Umlungu [white people] into the
> sea.[86]

On the appointed morning, 22 April 1819, a force of about 6000 men ringed the hills above the fort. Behind them stood several thousand women and children carrying mats and cooking pots, ready to reoccupy their lost land after the expected victory.

It was not to be.

With grim courage they pushed forward into the face of concentrated British cannon and rifle fire, breaking their throwing lances into short stab-bing spears as they charged. Finally, however, as the numbers of their dead and wounded grew, the patriotic forces wavered, and then retreated, leav-ing several hundred of their comrades on the field of battle. One of the defenders of Grahamstown, Captain Harding, who had fought the French in Egypt, Italy and Spain, recalled in later years that 'he had never seen a more spirited little action'. Had the Xhosa possessed better arms, he reflected, they surely must have triumphed.[87]

Ngqika exulted as the British moved implacably to follow up their victory. They captured Nxele and banished him to the far-off prison of Robben Island in Table Bay. They swept through the territories of Hintsa and Ndlambe, killing many people and carrying off cattle. Yet, in the end, Ngqika's joy turned to dust. The British governor, Major-General Charles Somerset, announced that still more territory must be taken for the usual reason of 'securing the frontier'. To that end Ngqika must give up about 10,000 square kilometres of his own fine pastureland between the Kat and Keiskamma Rivers which would be constituted as a neutral buffer zone to prevent future conflict. This would be called, with unconscious irony, 'The Ceded Territory'. With such an ally, Ngqika had no need of enemies. Yet, isolated and weakened as he was following the battle of Amalinde, he could not resist. Henceforth the British would be remembered among his people with a proverb coined on that occasion: '*omasiza mbulala* (they who came to help came to kill)'.[88] The next year the British landed their first contingent of '1820 settlers' to occupy farms in the Zuurveld.

Conclusion

Over the course of 170 years, European immigrants had extended their power throughout the panhandle region from Table Mountain to the Keiskamma River. Their systems of landholding, inheritance, forced labour and war had subjugated the Khoisan peoples and spread trekboer farms across the land. Some dispossessed people joined forces with renegades and adventurers to form raiding parties with headquarters north of the Orange River. Though they lacked certified titles to the lands they seized, in many other respects their lifestyle resembled that of the trekboers. In the course of time they were joined by parties of Xhosa-speaking people also mounted on horses and armed with guns. The scattered pattern of settlements along springs and water holes made Tswana towns extremely vulnerable to attack by the incoming raiders. To save the herds on which their political power rested, many Tswana chiefs retreated northward. Instead of presenting a united front to the threat, they quarrelled with each other. Whereas in the eighteenth century Tau the Lion held sway over much of the region, political power now fragmented.

The British seized the Cape territories of the Dutch East India Company for strategic reasons connected with the world-wide war they were waging against the French. Not surprisingly, their government had an autocratic, military character. Though some British individuals expressed humanitarian feelings and others came as missionaries with the intention of converting people to their Christian religion, such persons were very much a minority. The British governors needed the support of the Boer farmers. They found nothing to object to in the prevailing system of forced labour and reinforced that system with new laws. They relied on commandos raised from among the Boers and their farm labourers to safeguard their distant borders.

By 1780 Xhosa farmers were experiencing regular contact and conflict with Boers in the western zones of their territory. Contact offered advantages as well as dangers. The newcomers could be recruited as allies in wars with rival chiefs. Trade presented new ways to accumulate cattle. Those daring enough to raid Boer farms could likewise increase their wealth, though there was always the danger that commandos would wreak revenge on the innocent as well as the guilty. Like the Tswana chiefs to the north, they displayed a tendency to fragment rather than to unite as contact with the newcomers developed. These divisions contributed to disastrous losses of land in the war for the Zuurveld in 1812 and the aftermath of the war of 1819. In the course of these contests, new ideologies made their appearance which recast the struggle with the invaders as a titanic battle between colour-coded forces of white and black. At the dawn of the 1820s, as Xhosa chiefs were struggling to cope with their losses, they watched apprehensively as new waves of British settlers poured into the Zuurveld. With their forces depleted and demoralized, the way was open to potential invaders.

Notes

1   T. Arbousset and F. Daumas, *Narrative of an Exploratory Tour to the North-East of the Colony of the Cape of Good Hope*, translated by John C. Brown (first published 1846, reprinted Cape Town, 1968) p. 242; in this text the word is rendered 'Khuai'.

2   John Barrow, *Travels into the Interior of Southern Africa*, 2 vols (London, 1806), II, p. 2. In 1806, 26,000 of these were counted as 'Burghers', claiming descent from European ancestors; see Eric Walker, *The Frontier Tradition in South Africa: A Lecture Delivered before the University of Oxford* (Oxford, 1930), p. 6.

3   Richard Elphick, *Kraal and Castle: Khoikhoi and the Founding of White South Africa* (New Haven, 1977), pp. 131–2; Shula Marks, 'Khoisan Resistance to the Dutch in the Seventeenth and Eighteenth Centuries', *Journal of African History* 13 (1972), pp. 55–80.

4　John MacKenzie, *The Empire of Nature: Hunting, Conservation and British Imperialism* (Manchester, 1988), p. 89.

5　Timothy Keegan, *Colonial South Africa and the Origins of the Racial Order* (London, 1996), pp. 26–9; Robert Ross, *Adam Kok's Griquas: A Study in the Development of Stratification in History* (Cambridge, 1976), p. 29.

6　The best discussion of the development of this system is to be found in Robert Ross, *Beyond the Pale, Essays on the History of Colonial South Africa* (Johannesburg, 1994).

7　Nigel Penn, 'The Orange River Frontier Zone, *c.* 1700–1805', in Andrew B. Smith, ed., *Einiqualand, Studies of the Orange River Frontier* (Cape Town, 1995), p. 48.

8　On one commando in the early 1820s, a Boer recollected that of 32 San killed, 22 were men, 2 were women and 2 were children – the presumption being that the rest of the women and children were taken as labour captives; George Thompson, *Travels and Adventures in Southern Africa*, ed. V. S. Forbes, 2 vols (Cape Town, 1967), I, p. 134.

9　Elizabeth A. Eldredge and Fred Morton, *Slavery in South Africa, Captive Labor on the Dutch Frontier* (Pietermaritzburg, 1994), p. 266.

10　Ross, *Beyond the Pale*, p. 137.

11　Mackenzie, *The Empire of Nature*, p. 87.

12　Rudyard Kipling, 'The Voortrekker' in *Rudyard Kipling's Verse* (London, 1969), p. 555. Kipling's fancy was taken to be fact by some historians after it was quoted (without attribution) in Walker, *Frontier Tradition*, p. 13. The best statement of the opposing point of view was made by a South African governor: 'From the scattered state of the population, when one farmer makes up his mind to remove, his neighbour, who probably depends upon him and his family for society, and does not like the idea of being lonely, immediately determines to follow, and so from one farmer to another the desire to emigrate increases and spreads far and wide'; Napier to Glenelg, 18 May 1838, in *Records of Natal*, III. pp. 291–5.

13　Thompson, *Travels and Adventures*, I, p. 37, quoting Captain Harding of Cradock.

14　Keegan, *Colonial South Africa*, pp. 30–1.

15　W. F. Lye, ed., *Andrew Smith's Journal of his Expedition into the Interior of South Africa/1834–36* (Cape Town, 1975), pp. 178–9.

16　Ibid., 21; Thompson, *Travels and Adventures*, I, p. 37.

17　John Barrow, *Travels into the Interior of Southern Africa*, I, p. 190.

18　Arbousset and Daumas, *Narrative*, p. 252.

19　Barrow, *Travels into the Interior of Southern Africa*, I, p. 195.

20 Alan C. Webster, 'Land Expropriation and Labour Extraction under Cape Colonial Rule: The War of 1835 and the "Emancipation of the Fingo"' (MA thesis, Rhodes University, 1991), p. 40.

21 Arbousset and Daumas, *Narrative*, p. 229.

22 Lye, ed., *Andrew Smith's Journal*, p. 180.

23 They had long possessed knowledge about people to their east. The first Dutch commander at Cape Town noted in his journal of 1662 that a Khoi man told him about people living beyond 'the great river'; T. M. O'C. Maggs, *Iron Age Communities of the Southern Highveld* (Pietermaritzburg, 1976), p. 287. Archaeological evidence dating back to the seventeenth century supports the hypothesis of gradual movement up the Orange River Valley by Khoi people; Maggs, *Iron Age Communities*, p. 42ff. See also, Andrew B. Smith, ed., *Einiqualand*, p. xix.

24 Arbousset and Daumas, *Narrative*, p. 25; D. Fred. Ellenberger, *History of the Basuto, Ancient and Modern* (London, 1912), p. 212; R. L. Cope, ed., *The Journals of the Rev. T. L. Hodgson* (Johannesburg, 1977), pp. 66n, 70n.

25 *Natal Papers*, II, p. 270.

26 Martin Legassick, 'The Griqua, the Sotho-Tswana and the Missionaries, 1780–1840' (PhD thesis, UCLA, 1969), p. 63.

27 John Campbell, *Travels in South Africa (2nd Journey)* (first published 1922, reprinted New York, 1967), pp. 159–70.

28 Ibid., pp. 133, 139.

29 Ibid., pp. 112–13. The surname is sometimes written Berends.

30 Ibid., pp. 130, 356–9. The name often appears simply as Aaron or Arend.

31 W. F. Lye, ed., *Andrew Smith's Journal*, p. 148.

32 Ross, *Adam Kok's Griquas*, p. 14.

33 The detailed story of transitions in societies along the lower Orange River Valley is told in a series of studies in Smith, ed., *Einiqualand*.

34 Lye, ed., *Andrew Smith's Journal*, p. 178. This recollection was written down in 1835. Whether this was Jan Bloem or Jan Bloem, Jr is uncertain. According to some accounts Jan Bloem died in 1789, according to others some time between 1802 and 1804; Legassick, 'The Griqua', p. 135.

35 Campbell, *Travels*, pp. 171, 180, 188–92.

36 S. M. Molema, *Chief Moroka: His Life, His Times, His Country and His People* (Cape Town, n.d.), p. 43; Ross, *Adam Kok's Griquas*, p. 24.

37 Legassick, 'The Griqua', p. 148.

38 Ibid., p. 132.

39 Something of the extent of the informal and formal internal slave market among the farmers is indicated in Eldredge and Morton, *Slavery in South Africa*, passim.

40 Arbousset and Daumas, *Narrative*, pp. 12–13.

41 Cope, ed., *The Journals of the Rev. T. L. Hodgson*, p. 70n.

42 Some have speculated that land north of the Orange was growing gradually more arid during the late eighteenth and early nineteenth centuries; this could have contributed to decisions to move farther north. See Maggs, *Iron Age Communities*, p. 18.

43 William Lye and Colin Murray, *Transformations on the Highveld: the Tswana and Southern Sotho* (Cape Town, 1980), p. 29.

44 Campbell, *Travels*, pp. 80, 222. Legassick, 'The Griqua', p. 67. The five most prominent groups were the Rolong-Mariba, the Rolong-Ratlou, the Rolong-Tshidi, the Rolong-Seleka, and the Rolong-Rapulana – all names indicating their sometime chiefs.

45 M. Wilson and L. Thompson, *Oxford History of South Africa*, 2 vols (Oxford, 1969–71), I, p. 153. M. H. K. Lichtenstein, *Travels in Southern Africa, in the Years 1803, 1804, 1805, and 1806*, translated from German by A. Plumptre (first published 1812–15; reprinted Cape Town, 1928–30), I, p. 385.

46 Campbell, *Travels*, pp. 80, 171; Legassick, 'The Griqua', pp. 71, 135, 251.

47 Legassick, 'The Griqua', pp. 68–9.

48 Ibid., pp. 68–9.

49 Ibid., pp. 227–8.

50 Campbell, *Travels*, p. 285.

51 Ibid., pp. 213–14, 283–4.

52 Ibid., pp. 244–6.

53 Johan Binneman, 'Preliminary Report on the Investigations at Kulubele, an Early Iron Age Farming Settlement in the Great Kei River Valley, Eastern Cape', *South African Field Archaeology* 5 (1996), pp. 28–35. Radio-carbon dates for materials excavated from a site on the Kei River range from the eighth to the thirteenth century, including plentiful evidence of iron-working.

54 Wilson and Thompson, *Oxford History of South Africa*, I, p. 234; MacKenzie, *Empire of Nature*, p. 87.

55 Wilson and Thompson, *Oxford History of South Africa*, I, pp. 213, 237.

56 J. B. Peires, *The House of Phalo: A History of the Xhosa People in the Days of their Independence* (Johannesburg, 1981), p. 54.

57 Ibid., pp. 52, 56.

58 Wilson and Thompson, *Oxford History*, I, p. 236.

59 Noël Mostert, *Frontiers, the Epic of South Africa's Creation and the Tragedy of the Xhosa People* (London, 1992), p. 417.

60 Legassick, 'The Griqua', pp. 248–9. Peires, *House of Phalo*, pp. 49, 117–18

61 George M. Theal, ed., *Basutoland Records, Vol. 1. 1833–1852* (first published 1883; reprinted Cape Town, 1964), p. 541.

62 Campbell, *Travels*, p. 171.

63 See Philip Harling and Peter Mandler, 'From "Fiscal-Military" State to Laissez-faire State, 1760–1850', *Journal of British Studies* 32 (1993), pp. 44–70; John Brewer, *The Sinews of Power: War, Money and the English State, 1688–1783* (London, 1989), especially pp. 29–37.

64 A small number of German-speaking Moravian missionaries preceded the British society, but their small, self-contained communities were all located in the extreme western region, close to Cape Town. An early experiment failed in 1743, but in 1792 the Moravians returned to stay.

65 See John Barrow, *Travels into the Interior of Southern Africa*, 2 vols (London, 1806), especially volume 2.

66 Ibid., I, pp. 158–9, 201–2, 272–3, 277–8.

67 Christopher Bayly, 'The First Age of Global Imperialism, *c.* 1760–1830', *Journal of Commonwealth and Imperial History* 26 (1998), pp. 34–5.

68 Legassick, 'The Griqua', pp. 156–7.

69 Ibid., p. 131.

70 Peires, *House of Phalo*, pp. 46–53.

71 Peires sees the struggles as an attempt to reunite 'the house of Phalo', though no one appears to have formulated the situation in precisely these terms.

72 Ibid., pp. 56, 138.

73 Ibid., pp. 53–4.

74 Ben Maclennan, *A Proper Degree of Terror: John Graham and the Cape's Eastern Frontier* (Johannesburg, 1986), p. 70.

75 Mostert, *Frontiers*, pp. 295–302.

76 C. W. Hutton, ed., *The Autobiography of Sir Andries Stockenstrom* (first published 1887; reprinted Cape Town, 1964), p. 58. Many of Ndlambe's followers swore on oath as to the descriptions and number of the cattle, but there is no record on the Dutch side of the cattle ever having been received. Most likely they were fraudulently appropriated by frontier Boers.

77 Maclennan, *A Proper Degree of Terror*, pp. 60–1. It appears that with the conniv-ance of their employers many evaded the order.

78 Ibid., p. 81.

79 Mostert, *Frontiers*, p. 382.

80 Maclennan, *A Proper Degree of Terror*, p. 212.

81 Peires, *House of Phalo*, p. 65.

82 Ibid., pp. 69–71.

83 Clifton Crais, *White Supremacy and Black Resistance in Pre-Industrial South Africa: The Making of the Colonial Order in the Eastern Cape, 1770–1865* (Cambridge, 1992), p. 105. On the way the colonial experience altered and enhanced European concepts of race, see pp. 127–33.

84 Quoted in Peires, *House of Phalo*, p. 71.

85 Mostert, *Frontiers*, p. 472.

86 Quoted in Maclennan, *A Proper Degree of Terror*, p. 188.

87 Thompson, *Travels and Adventures*, I, p. 36.

88 Peires, *House of Phalo*, p. 79.

CHAPTER FOUR

The emergence of new leaders and state-builders

History mostly remembers the names of people who emerged victorious in the complex events of the 1820s and 1830s: Shaka, Dingane, Moshweshwe and a handful of others. It is important that their names should not be allowed to obscure those of other people who played important parts. The historian must apologize for introducing many other names and running the risk of sowing confusion in the ranks of readers. At the same time, readers should be assured that gradually the dust will settle, a few notable individuals will stand out from the crowd and the main forces of political change will be identified, just as they are in histories of other complicated struggles in other places, for example, the wars of the Mughals in India, the Wars of the Roses in medieval England, the Thirty Years War in Europe and the Civil War fought in the United States.

MaNthatisi becomes a chief

It was once the custom for Sotho/Tswana women to take a new title at the birth of their first child. The woman would henceforth be known by a name formed by adding the prefix Ma- to the name of her first-born. This is how a young woman who married Mokotcho, king of some of the people who called themselves by the totemic name Tlokwa at about the turn of the nineteenth century, became known as MaNthatisi – because her first child was Nthatisi. Under this name she figures prominently in just about every history ever written about the turbulent times in which she lived. She grew up a little to the south of Ntsuanatsatsi, the legendary home of humankind – not far, in fact, from the modern town of Harrismith, which we took as the original vantage point of this history. For a decade after her husband died, she had the task of safeguarding her chieftainship during a landmark period in South African history.

Because her home stood so near the centre of the heartland, it makes a good starting point for Chapters 4, 5 and 6, which will attempt to chart some momentous shifts of political power which occurred between 1815 and 1828. As we have seen, to the south-west, across the mountains of Lesotho, Xhosa chiefs were being pushed back by British aggression. To the west Griqua/Kora raids were spreading ever farther into the grasslands and north towards the thickly populated lands around the headwaters of the Marico and Limpopo Rivers. In those regions themselves fierce contests were already under way which would further fragment the so-called Rolong people whom Tau had once united. Another, somewhat surprising, loser during the coming decade would be the Hurutshe whose capital occupied everybody's favourite valley district in the region of present-day Rustenburg. Some of the problems of the Hurutshe stemmed from external enemies, others from a bitter succession dispute among rival claimants to the para-mountcy. The internal weakness of the Hurutshe opened opportunities for King Makaba II of Ngwaketse to the west of them and for the rising power of the Pedi king, Thulare, to the east of them. From time to time, Griqua/Kora leaders lent support to one and another of the regional contenders for power.

Looking east from MaNthatisi's capital across the mountains to the Mozambique lowlands, the slave-traders were flooding the coast with un-precedented demands for their dark cargoes of human misery. Before long, Delagoa Bay would rank with Inhambane and Quelimane as a slave-exporting centre.[1] Increases in trade, which in previous decades had enriched the Tembe chiefs around the Bay, would now lead to the disintegration of many of those chieftaincies. As they broke apart, aggressive newcomers allied to the ancient Ndwandwe kingdom – part of the old Mbo grouping – would make an explosive entry into the slaving business. At the same time a new power would arise to the south of the Ndwandwe, uniting small coastal lineages into the extraordinary Zulu kingdom.

Finally, in MaNthatisi's immediate vicinity, a three-year period of drought would initiate conflict between chieftaincies and desperate struggles to find well-watered, defensible positions to safeguard people and cattle. Many people would straggle down the depleted waterways of the Vaal River system, their bodies growing emaciated as their cattle died round them. Some would wander straight into musket range of the Griqua/Kora raiders. But while some perished, others grew in strength. Young new leaders would find opportunities to gather people round them: notably Moletsane and Sebetwane from the Sand River region. Another was Moshweshwe, who staked out an unassailable position on his mountain-top fortress of Thaba Bosiu on the south side of the Caledon River. For a few short years, two lowland Nguni chiefs, Mpangazitha of the Hlubi and Matiwane of the Ngwane, would try to find secure positions in that same Caledon River Valley. So would MaNthatisi. As the drought retreated, all the chiefs of the Caledon would attempt to rebuild their cattle holdings by raiding across the Lesotho mountains – stealing from Thembu and Xhosa chieftaincies who had the good luck to inhabit a fairly drought-proof region.

Many early histories of southern Africa tried to write this period off as too confusing for analysis. One wrote simply that 'pandemonium reigned'. Many others tried to simplify matters by blaming everything on a single leader, Shaka of the Zulu. This history cannot be certain of success in the difficult task of trying to make sense of the complex movements of this time. But the pages cannot be left blank without doing a profound injustice to the common people who lived through them, and to some of their extraordinary leaders whose names deserve to be remembered in generations to come: Shaka, Soshangane, Zwide, Zwangendaba, Barend Barends, Adam Kok, Mzilikazi, Makhasane, Sobhuza, Moshweshwe, Hintsa, Matiwane, Sebetwane, Sekwati, Sekonyela, and – not least among them – MaNthatisi.

MaNthatisi and Sekonyela

MaNthatisi's people preserved memories of common descent from another legendary mother, MaThulare. So did people spread right across the highveld. All that was long past. MaNthatisi's folk claimed to have occupied the district for upwards of two hundred years.[2] The Tlokwa were their neighbours. Their roots connected them to peoples scattered right across the highveld, while their strategic location near the Drakensberg passes gave them a window onto the Nguni-speaking communities of the lowlands.

MaNthatisi's ancestors must have had much to do with the people who left behind the multitude of ruined stone settlements stretching in the uplands of KwaZulu-Natal all the way from Bushman's River to the White Mfolozi. (They may even, as we shall see, have been among the builders of some of those stone settlements near modern Estcourt.) Over the centuries they would have witnessed a procession of different Nguni groups moving past them on the way to new homes on the highveld – people called by the Sotho names for intrusive elements who came that way: Matabele, Zizi or Nkoni.[3] The language of the Tlokwa recorded in the early nineteenth century includes many borrowings from Zulu.[4] The historian must regret that no chronicles of interactions between the Nguni and the Tlokwa survived

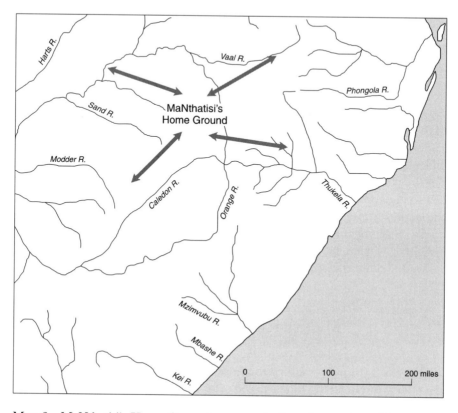

Map 6 MaNthatisi's Home Ground – arrows indicate interaction with
neighbouring chiefdoms

long enough to be written down. They would have illuminated vital changes among the Nguni which appear to have occurred in the seventeenth and eighteenth centuries but whose details are now shrouded in an impenetrable darkness. It is tempting to surmise that the ruling Tlokwa lineage derived from Sotho/Tswana ancestors but that over time it came to rule over a considerable number of commoners of Nguni origin.[5]

Some time soon after 1815, MaNthatisi's husband died. As her son, Sekonyela, was too young to become chief, she assumed power as queen-regent, as many other women in the same situation had done in times past. She proved to be a more than capable leader in peace and war. During her regency, she may have ruled over as many as 40,000 people, a considerable presence on the land. People who met her later in life remarked on her 'great intelligence' as well as her 'sweet and agreeable expression of countenance'.[6] Though not all Tlokwa chiefs acknowledged her pre-eminence, MaNthatisi had every right to feel confident in her strength.[7] Before long her subjects (and enemies) had accorded her the usual tribute accorded to powerful chiefs. Instead of saying they were Tlokwa, they said they were 'MaNthatisis'.[8]

About 1817 she launched her troops on an audacious expedition into the lowlands. Some accounts indicate the target was Zwide, king of the Nwandwe, reputedly the most formidable power between the Drakensberg and Maputo. But it seems more likely that her target was a Hlubi chief. Either way, she won a famous victory. Her forces captured vast herds of cattle.[9] How long MaNthatisi's troops were engaged on the further side of the Drakensberg is hard to say. Two independently recorded accounts, based on statements of Tlokwa people dating from the late 1830s, state that some or all of the Tlokwa actually moved down into the highlands of what is today KwaZulu-Natal. One says vaguely that they 'resided for some time upon the territory of the Matabele tribe' (the Nguni; see Chapter 2, pp. 22–3).[10] The other states that the Tlokwa ancestors came from the upper Vaal River area, and later went through a long period of warfare 'with the adjacent Zulu tribes, who, as they became conquered, blended with their conquerors, and thus changed their language by mixing the Zulu with the purer Sechuana (i.e. Tswana)'. This account goes on to say 'they next removed towards Natal', nearly as far as the present-day village of Weenen.[11]

This success is said to have attracted the attention of a Hlubi petty chief Motsholi,[12] who was at that time embroiled in a dispute with the Hlubi paramount, Mthimkulu, and his brother, Mpangazitha. Motsholi and an estimated two thousand followers arrived at MaNthatisi's capital (wherever that may have been) about the middle of 1818, begging for a place to live. The queen-regent, delighted at this unexpected accession of strength, found them an appropriate valley.

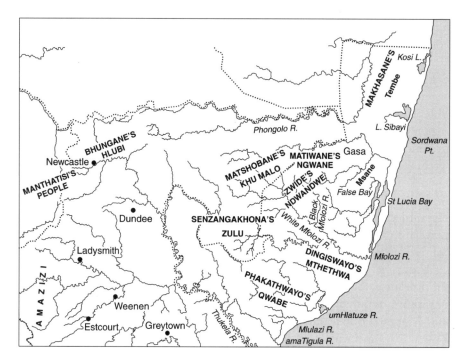

Map 7   Relative situation of major chiefs in the south-east *circa* 1815
After A. T. Bryant, *Olden Times in Zululand and Natal* (Longman, 1929)

Before long, however, her son, Sekonyela, had picked a fight with the newcomers. It was understandable that the adolescent on the verge of manhood should try asserting the authority that was his by right of inheritance. Tall like his mother, but utterly lacking her charm and tact, Sekonyela relied on his impressively muscular physique to intimidate foes. In a stand-up fight he killed Motsholi and provoked the flight of many Hlubi. The dead chief's widow happened to be the sister of Chief Mpangazitha, who made her grievance his own.[13] When the time was ripe, he launched a retaliatory attack whose consequences spread ripples of violence in all directions.

As with all such tales, there is more to the story than a personal vendetta.

Power struggles in the south-east

Mpangazitha had for some years been caught up in a complex power struggle involving the dominant chiefs of the coast lands between Delagoa Bay and the Thukela River. By the last decades of the eighteenth century the principal players all commanded formidable regiments (*amabutho*) of dedicated soldiers. Whether, as suggested in Chapter 2, these chiefs were striving to fill the vacuum left after an older regime fell apart; or whether they offered competing versions of an entirely new order cannot be known. The most obvious unsettling force in the south-eastern region was Delagoa Bay, where aliens came to trade for ivory, cattle and slaves. For this reason historians have devoted much discussion to its possible political effects (see Chapter 2, pp. 30–1).

Although the European state of Portugal had been sending ships to the Bay since the early sixteenth century, it had not maintained a permanent presence. For much of the eighteenth century, there was no resident Portuguese official. Vessels of many different foreign countries called in from time to time. Whether growing trade favoured fragmentation or consolidation is debatable. However, there appears to be good reason to suppose it stimulated military conflict. Cattle traded to passing ships needed to be replaced. The time-honoured method of getting them quickly was to raid. Raiding in turn generated counter-raiding. One plausible argument, based on fragmentary evidence, is that an alliance aimed at controlling and supplying demands for trade developed between the Mabhudu Tembe on the southern side of Delagoa Bay and the rising power of the adjacent Mthethwa chief Dingiswayo at the turn of the nineteenth century.[14] A Portuguese report of 1803 cited the Bay as the most important of their trading centres on the Indian Ocean coast.[15] Popular memory associates Dingiswayo with a horse and a gun; this may be a metaphorical comment on his connections to the east.[16]

More deserves to be written about the man said to have been Dingiswayo's Tembe ally. His name was Makhasane. Born about 1764, he succeeded to the chieftainship in the late 1790s. By the time of his death in 1854 only a few of the great figures of his era were still alive.[17] He had known many of them. While states rose and fell around him and the ravages of the Indian Ocean slave trade devastated the hinterland of Delagoa Bay, Makhasane held his ground, proud and independent to the last. Too bad no one interviewed him about his life and times. His people profited by trading metal and cloth bought at Delagoa Bay south and east to northern Nguni groups, in return for which they acquired cattle, sheep, mats and shields.[18] When Makhasane formed his alliance with Dingiswayo, he was a considerable regional military power with a number of *amabutho* under his command.[19] Some said he possessed magical powers which could send plagues of locusts down upon his enemies.[20] According to other accounts it was the growth of Mabhudu power which pushed the important Dhlamini and Khumalo lineage chiefs to move west.[21] Geography as well as manpower played a role in safeguarding Makhasane's independence. His lands (lying north of Lake Sibayi and east of the Lebombo mountains) were endemically infested with both malarial mosquitoes and sleeping sickness spread by the tse-tse fly. During the bad seasons, special doctors were employed on the western slopes of the Lebombo to ward off the deadly fevers of the east.[22] Elephant, rhino and lions roamed other parts of Makhasane's domain where cattle could not flourish.

With the Tembe alliance securing the coastal region to his north, Dingiswayo set about building up the power of his Mthethwa lineage. His power base lay between the lower Mfolozi and Mhlatuze Rivers. Military success brought him new recruits and allies, whose loyalty he bought through distributions of captured cattle. Dingiswayo's allies were mostly chiefs concentrated in his immediate vicinity.[23] Some he had fought and conquered; others he cajoled into co-operation. His early campaigns, most likely fought between 1810 and 1815, subjugated neighbours located within a roughly 60-kilometre radius of his own Mthethwa stronghold.[24] Oral traditions remember Dingiswayo as imposing a light yoke. The chieftaincies he absorbed were required to recognize his paramountcy, pay tribute in cattle or agricultural produce and to give up their performance of certain important public rituals.[25] Dingiswayo's most promising and celebrated commander was Shaka, a young man of the Zulu chiefly lineage, whose birth is customarily dated at 1787. As a reward for his military services, Shaka was permitted to keep a portion of the booty taken in successful campaigns. This he used to acquire clients, thus building up an independent power base. When Shaka's father died in about 1816, Dingiswayo connived to promote the young man's installation as chief of the Zulu.[26]

All authorities agree that the most determined of Dingiswayo's foes was Zwide, the Ndwandwe king. Few could boast a more distinguished pedigree. The names of twenty-two chiefs preceded his in a direct line of descent. The graves of his ancestors occupied sacred, secluded groves in the MaGudu hills just south of the Phongolo River – near what is today the Swazi border.[27] Zwide headed the most powerful branch of the related lineages who claimed the name Mbo. How long they had been a power in the land is hard to say. The conclusion of one historian who has carefully sifted through the evidence is that 'the emergence of Ndwandwe chiefly power in northern Zululand cannot be precisely dated to the period 1780–1810, and that a much earlier date is probable'.[28] Many traditions attest to fights between Zwide and his near neighbours, the chiefs of the uplands who traced their line back to Langa of the Mbo. Though his daughter became the chief wife of Sobhuza (founder of the Swazi nation), that chief was not immune to Zwide's raids.[29] Zwide claimed paramountcy over – and tribute from – the Ncwangeni, Msane and Mzimeleni groups who were closely related to the Nwandwe.[30] One tradition recounts that after an attack on Zwangendaba of the Ncwangeni, Zwide was first captured, and then magnanimously released with a present of cattle, in recognition of his superior status. Chief Matiwane of the Ngwane likewise clashed with Zwide.[31] So did the related Ngwane of the Phongolo River region. The traditions recording these contests do not include estimates of lives lost or cattle captured. For all anyone knows they may have been minor affrays. Zwide married many daughters of the chiefs with whom he fought. He also gave his own daughters to them in marriage. This would seem to indicate that inter-group relations were being conducted in accordance with time-honoured rules of diplomacy.

To simplify a complex situation, it appears that by about 1816 the rival ambitions of Zwide and Dingiswayo dominated political affairs north of the Thukela River. Zwide may well have been aiming at establishing his paramountcy over all the chiefs who traced their descent back to Langa and the Mbo. Dingiswayo had built his rival Mthethwa bloc by incorporating a disparate collection of chiefdoms in his immediate vicinity. Zwide and his allies stood for a glorious past. In social if not economic terms Dingiswayo stood for change, cobbling together a coalition of small and medium-size lineage groups who had previously been independent.

Historians do not agree about who initiated the clash between the Mthethwa and the Ndwandwe. One hypothesis casts the Ndwandwe in the aggressive role, pushing south to capture cattle – and possibly people – to sell to the slave and ivory traders at Delagoa Bay.[32] Another hypothesis casts Dingiswayo as the aggressor, striving to drive a wedge between the Ndwandwe and Delagoa Bay, in order to monopolize trade to that marketplace.[33] Another sees Dingiswayo's 'Mthethwa Confederacy' as a defensive alliance aimed at preventing Zwide's drive to conquer south. A third notes that the direction of Dingiswayo's conquests was upland away from elephant country and toward the best cattle country; this may have been a response to an increased demand for cattle at Delagoa Bay. All these conjectures are ultimately unprovable. There is, however, good reason to believe that at least one momentous confrontation did take place in 1818, because it brought about Dingiswayo's death.

One tale recounts that Zwide sent his sister Ntombozana to seduce Dingiswayo with the object of stealing his semen.[34] This was duly obtained and then used to concoct a magical potion. Soon after Dingiswayo came north with his troops, he was induced by the spell to leave his bodyguard and walk straight into the hands of an Ndwandwe regiment. The story goes on to say that Zwide accorded Dingiswayo all the honour and courtesy due a royal prisoner, until, goaded by his mother's taunts, he acceded to her demand that he be executed and beheaded. Following the execution, elaborate rituals of purification were performed and oxen slaughtered in honour of the departed chief. Meanwhile, deprived of their leader, the Mthethwa forces had turned and fled south to safety, apparently without offering battle.

Three features of this strange story merit comment. First, the tale portrays Zwide as a reluctant executioner, the tool of his vengeful mother, Ntombazi. This underscores the point made at the beginning of this chapter about MaNthatisi: in this era women played central roles in chiefly politics. Second, Ntombazi's fury is said to have been fuelled by Dingiswayo's rejection of her daughter as a wife (notwithstanding the alleged semen-stealing plot). Another story tells of Zwide being thwarted by Shaka in his efforts to wed three royal daughters of the Zulu clan.[35] Taken together the stories suggest that Zwide had been trying to normalize relations with his enemies through the usual strategy of marriage alliances. Third, the emphasis on ritual purification and funeral rites for the murdered king draws attention to the way chiefly classes maintained an element of ideological solidarity, even in times of all-out war.

Upon the death of Dingiswayo, Shaka killed the legitimate Mthethwa heir and seized power in a military coup. The usurper's first urgent task was to carry on the resistance to Zwide. In one version of the story, Shaka's forces took their stand at kwaGqokli hill, a little to the south of the White Mfolozi River. When the battle was over, neither side could claim victory. Shaka's *amabutho* held their ground, killing five of Zwide's sons, including the heir-apparent. On the other hand, they lost most of their cattle. Given the importance of cattle as a source of power over people, this loss would have at least counter-balanced the deaths of the Ndwandwe princes.[36] Badly shaken, though by no means destroyed, Zwide now withdrew to the north-east, while Shaka took advantage of the breathing space to bring new chieftaincies into his orbit.

The most important of these was the Qwabe, a lineage which may have been distantly related to the Zulu but had for a long time constituted an independent power. By the late eighteenth century its disciplined *amabutho* had made the Qwabe masters of the territory between the Mhlatuze and Thukela Rivers.[37] Their success had caused two other sizeable chieftaincies, the Thuli and the Cele, to move their herds and people south of the Thukela before 1800.[38] Although older histories tended to view these moves as desperate flights, it seems just as likely that the Thuli and Cele leaders made calculated decisions to keep their wealth intact by distancing themselves from a rising power. In their new homes they set about incorporating previously independent chieftaincies.

Shaka's confrontation with the Qwabe was brief, decisive and, it would appear, relatively bloodless. Oral tradition recounts that a dance meeting laid the grounds for a quarrel. Shaka arranged with Phakathwayo, the Qwabe paramount, that their young men and women should adorn themselves for this most cherished of social occasions. At the end of the day, it is said that the Qwabe dancers shamed the Zulu with their accomplishments. Soon afterwards Shaka sent messengers to ask Phakathwayo to join his forces in the fight against Zwide, whom he designated by a calculated insult. Phakathwayo replied that Shaka had no right to insult such a venerable ruler in this fashion, and he should seek allies elsewhere. Shaka's reply was to challenge Phakathwayo to meet him on the field of battle.[39] After night fell on a day of inconclusive manoeuvring, Shaka's forces managed, after a brief skirmish, to capture the Qwabe king. When Phakathwayo died from his injuries the next day, some of his heirs moved away – one to join Zwide – while the bulk of the dead chief's people acknowledged Shaka's supremacy. Subsequently, Qwabe *amabutho* accompanied Zulu regiments on campaigns but were permitted to maintain their own identity. Although the Qwabe can only be accorded a little space in this history, their experience underlines an important point about the growth of Shaka's kingdom. It was not built on an inflexible plan. Some lineage chiefs were hounded to extinction. Others were allowed to assume an honoured place in the Zulu political structure. In no case were 'whole peoples' hunted down, killed or expelled. Nor did they flee before Shaka in terror. Shaka's quarry were chiefs and their cattle, not commoners. He welcomed accessions of ordinary people. Many came to join him, some from hundreds of kilometres away, as his fame and wealth increased.[40]

Early in 1819 – about the same time that Nxele's Xhosa alliance was launching its desperate assault upon the British fort at Grahamstown –

Zwide renewed his campaign against Shaka.[41] Instead of confronting the onslaught directly, Shaka withdrew his regiments and cattle to the south-west, destroying crops and grain storage pits as he went. By the time the Ndwandwe regiments caught up with Shaka's forces near the Thukela River, hunger and exhaustion stalked their camps. Now Shaka suddenly turned the tables. The hunted became the hunters. In a series of engagements, Shaka drove the Ndwandwe back to the Mhlatuze River where he hit them so hard that they fled homeward in a disorderly rout. Meanwhile Shaka dispatched two of his *amabutho* on a lightning raid upon Zwide's capital. It is said that they advanced at night singing the Ndwandwe victory song (*iHubo*) to trick the enemy into believing they were soldiers returning in triumph.[42] By the time the hapless people discovered the stratagem, the Zulu spearmen were among them. In the ensuing confusion, Zwide himself and his remaining sons escaped. Now they retreated north of the Phongolo where they nursed their wounds and attempted to rally the fragments of their regiments. They had suffered a reversal of fortune but were by no means a spent force. Still, Zwide's drive to unite the old Mbo aristocratic lineages had clearly failed. Many of them sought new opportunities in other places. Sobhuza's Dlamini concentrated their power in what is now Swaziland. Zwide's allies, Zwangendaba and Soshangane, had moved toward Delagoa Bay. Zwide pulled his remaining forces to a new stronghold a little north of the Phongolo River. The Hlubi lineage chiefs sheltered under the Drakensberg near the sources of the Thukela River. Of all the old Mbo groups, only the Mkhize lineage threw its lot in with Shaka; they were rewarded by perpetual recognition as the only Mbo in the kingdom. As will presently be seen, the Mbo Diaspora would eventually affect southern African history more profoundly than the celebrated conquests of Shaka.

Making the Zulu

After 1819, Shaka made no further significant territorial conquests. Never again would he lead his troops in battle. He devoted most of his energies to consolidating his hold on the people already under his rule and to the large numbers of recruits who joined him as his fame and wealth increased. Some came from 'far inland'.[43] Like all lineage chiefs, he employed praise singers to exalt his name and to erase the achievements of his enemies. Within a few years, white men would enter his service and advertise him to the world as 'the Black Napoleon', implying by that title that Shaka had been both a great general and a social innovator. In the course of time popular writers would credit him with the invention of *amabutho*, new techniques of military training, new strategies for victory and a new weapon: the long-bladed, short stabbing spear. Twentieth-century scholars would treat the Zulu kingdom as a new kind of social formation and endlessly debate the reasons for its emergence. More recently, however, the work of industrious historians has proved that most of the social and technical innovations credited to Shaka existed long before he was born.[44] (See Chapter 2, pp. 19–20). Wherever chiefs allied to the Ndwandwe went in the years after Zwide's downfall, they carried similar institutions and fighting methods with them. Given the length of their lineages, it seems unlikely that they copied Shaka's ideas and tactics. More likely he, the upstart, copied theirs. The description of basic institutions sketched below should not be taken as a profile of a new kind of state; it describes one particularly well-documented state of a type to be found in many places.

If Shaka contributed anything new to the conduct of war, it was a heightened ruthlessness. The short stabbing spear had been in use in many parts of southern Africa for decades, if not centuries. In most places it was employed in conjunction with a kit of other spears. All reports agree that Shaka insisted that his soldiers carry only the short spear into battle.[45] Those who failed to return with their spears were branded cowards or incompetents who deserved execution. Another atypical practice was Shaka's use of the surprise attack, often at night, without giving the conventional, chivalrous, prior warning. When attacking settlements, his troops set huts on fire, simultaneously blinding and confusing the enemy. Before carrying off the enemy cattle, they would destroy crops and spoil grain supplies to deter counter-attacks. Survivors of such raids bore witness to their frightful terror.

It is more difficult to appraise Shaka's role in the construction of the government he commanded. The basic structure of political life had evolved over centuries. Similar social institutions permeated all the organized states of the highveld and the coastal districts. People everywhere basically agreed about the honour owed to chiefs, the chiefs' obligations to their subjects, the respect due to ancestors, the hospitality accorded to strangers, public ethics, court etiquette, the conventions of oratory and the dance. The organization of *amabutho* based on the induction of young men soon after the age of puberty was likewise similar from region to region. However, in societies where longstanding chiefly lineages held sway, members of each regiment were relatively homogeneous. Shaka faced the problem of fusing young men from different lineage backgrounds into a like-minded, patriotic force utterly devoted to his person and his state. If too many lineage groups were – like the Qwabe – allowed to maintain a separate identity, the state might be in perpetual danger of falling apart. The institution of the age-set regiment provided an instrument for transcending old divisions. When young men of different lineages were inducted together, fought together and worked together over a period of years, they acquired a powerful sense of a common identity.

Shaka built his state on the economic foundation of the *amabutho*. Instead of levying taxes or tribute on his subjects, he commandeered the labour of young, unmarried men. Those men served both as an army and the police force. Shaka quartered them along with significant numbers of women in what amounted to barracks (*amakhanda*) in different parts of the land where they fed themselves by milking the royal herds and growing their own crops.[46] For the most part Shaka appointed members of Zulu and closely related lineages to command these outposts – including a number of unmarried women of his own royal lineage who ranked as queen-commanders.[47] A second available source of exploitable labour were the *umndlunkulu*, young women who had been presented to him by his subjects and who performed a variety of domestic and agricultural duties.[48] Of course, more than patriotism and *esprit de corps* was required to command the continued loyalty of the *amabutho*. From time to time, Shaka rewarded veteran regiments by releasing them from active service and pensioning them off with presents of cattle, with which they acquired wives. Thus, military service was the route to achieving the age-old young man's goal of forming his own prosperous homestead. Of course, this system demanded the replacement of those cattle through the capture of new ones. This made Shaka's kingdom a perpetual cattle-raiding machine. This need, rather than a lust for territorial conquest, motivated most of the military expeditions he sent into neighbouring regions.[49] The army, which had been called into existence by the threat of invasion, now demanded new campaigns to keep itself alive.

Shaka also worked to promote an ideology which would bind minds to him as the *amabutho* bound bodies. A central element of this campaign was promotion of a common identity. A primary task was to give a sense of cohesion to the disparate chieftaincies he had brought under his control. Unlike Zwide, he could not build on a common Mbo identity built on beliefs in common descent from Langa and other shared ancestors. Instead, he tried to foster a belief that the geographically closely situated lineages who first constituted the kingdom shared a special destiny. They were the *amantungwa*, the old comrades in arms, whose status towered over the so-called *amalala*, the more oppressed and recently conquered lineages on the periphery of the new state.[50] Though they shared no obvious common ancestry, they specially embodied 'Zuluness'.

Many scholars simply treat the word Zulu as another example of the way people took on the name of an honoured chief to designate the group to which they belonged. According to the collectors of genealogical records, a chief named Zulu does figure in Shaka's family tree. Why he should be specially honoured no one can say, for no traditions recall his life and deeds. It might be thought that Shaka would have wanted to obliterate the memory of his devious succession by invoking the name of his father, and calling his people Senzangakhonas. Or celebrated his own achievements by calling them the Shakas (amaShaka).[51] One reason for preferring the name Zulu is that in common parlance it carried a heavy load of meaning. Among all the Nguni-speakers it was the word for the sky or 'the heavens above us'. In another context, it refers to lightning. The spirit-queen who rides the storm clouds when the thunder rolls is *Inkozikasi phezulu*. A praise name for the king was *izulu eliphezulu*: he who is the heavens. A man who knew Shaka pointed out that in battle 'they generally commence by setting fire to the houses and making a great noise, hence they derive the name of Zoolahs (sic), meaning thunder and lightning'.[52] Here was a word with which many might proudly associate, though they had nothing to do with Shaka's lineage. When people on the highveld first heard of a people who called themselves Zulu, they assumed they were calling themselves the 'heaven-sent' or 'the Celestials'.[53] Mzilikazi of the Khumalo lineage, who in the later 1820s was to carve out a kingdom for himself on the highveld, took the title 'Zulu' as one of his praise names. This is inexplicable if one accepts that the word simply referred to one of Shaka's ancestors. Mzilikazi's people told outsiders they wished to be called Zulu, not Matabele, the generic term for strangers.[54] And when the followers of Soshangane's Gasa branch of the Ndwandwe – certainly no friends of Shaka – remembered their old country in later years they sighed '*Woza sibuyele kwaZulu lapho abantu befa bekhuluphele*': 'Come let us return to Zululand where people die fat.'[55] From an ideological point of view, Zulu was an awe-inspiring name which would echo down the centuries.

All chiefs had ritual and supernatural functions to carry out. Shaka took these very seriously. He claimed, in his dreams, to have communicated with the dead. He interpreted omens. He took an interest in the doings of doctors, diviners, rain-makers and witch-finders. Once the struggle against Zwide had been won, Shaka also took a personal interest in the layout of his capital and military outposts. He made his capital the stage on which the spectacle of his kingship ran seven days a week. It was the place of rituals, dances, executions, mourning and celebration. The huts of the soldiers occupied the perimeter of a perfect circle, some of which measured five kilometres in circumference. At the centre stood the outward and visible symbol of earthly power: the cattle enclosure. The cattle themselves were disposed in herds in accordance with their colours and the shapes of their horns. At Bulawayo – a word which means 'the place of execution' – Shaka would utter the phrase used to pronounce the death sentence on convicted wrong-doers: 'kill the wizards'.[56] Here, too, he held great dances and competitions. On these occasions he generally led the dance himself. He designed costumes and composed songs. He decreed what this year's fashions would be at his court. For example, there was a period in which he insisted that he and his retinue would lie on their stomachs when taking their meals. The telling of praises and the lyrics of songs were continually updated to reflect this year's understanding of political realities. It was 'considered disgraceful to sing the songs of the previous year'.[57]

There appear to have been real constraints on the size of the Zulu kingdom. Messengers and military patrols ran on foot. Amazingly, they might cover up to 80 kilometres in a day. Beyond this distance it was difficult to keep rebellious subjects in line, because they generally had the opportunity to run away. Thus the kingdom never took in much more than a circle with a diameter of 160 kilometres. Shaka could *project power* beyond this range by dispatching troops accompanied by cattle to feed them on the march. But he could not really *govern* beyond this range. According to a man who fought with Shaka's army, the maximum military strength of the kingdom was about 40,000 men, though it is doubtful that anything more than a third of this figure ever assembled together.[58] It makes sense to see this as a fundamentally defensive formation from which occasional long-distance raids could be launched. Statements made in some histories to the effect that Shaka ruled from Delagoa Bay to the Mzimkhulu River are gross exaggerations.[59] The purpose of his long-distance raids was, as one eye-witness noted, to take 'booty in cattle', not to kill people.[60] Consequently, chiefs who wished to keep their cattle safe from Shaka's raids wisely kept their distance. The withdrawal of the Mbo chiefs and their retinues must have substantially reduced the population in the upland regions. That is not to say that the regions were depopulated.[61] But lineage chiefs with large cattle holdings were scarce on the ground. It was once thought that Shaka aimed at maintaining a belt of unpopulated 'scorched earth' around his kingdom to deter invaders.[62] However, there was no such unpopulated zone on the northern frontier where protection would have been most welcome. It appears more likely that he prevented people from spreading themselves into lands vacated by the departed chiefs so as to maintain a tighter grip on his own government.[63]

Now is time to resume MaNthatisi's story.

MaNthatisi's advance and retreat

Against the background of the great contests grinding on below her to the east, MaNthatisi's foray into KwaZulu-Natal makes sense. With Zwide's eye fixed on Dingiswayo, his Ndwandwe were less likely to notice raids mounted from a nearly opposite direction. There is no indication of just how much time intervened between MaNthatisi's invasion in 1817 and the conclusion of her temporary alliance with Motsholi's Hlubi (another name taken from an ancestral chief). Nor is it possible to say exactly when Sekonyela attacked that chief and provoked the flight of his people. If, as one source indicates, Sekonyela was born in 1804, his circumcision ceremony could hardly have been held much before 1820.[64] In order to make some chronological sense of events, it will be useful to learn more about the Hlubi.

According to their own recorded remembrance, a great many of them were living in relative peace and contentment in the vicinity of present-day Newcastle under the paramount, Bhungane, in the early years of the nineteenth century.[65] By marriage and tradition they were closely linked both to Sobhuza's people to the north and to the southern Sotho people. (As one of them remarked in the late nineteenth century, 'we are one with the Swazis as well as the Basuto'.) Their customs closely resembled those of people on the western side of the Drakensberg: men wore their hair in plaits, not in head rings like the Zulu; boys were circumcised at puberty; they covered their genitals with a tied loincloth; their speech was related to the tongues of people on the other side of the mountains. In fact, the Zulu and other people of the lowlands referred to the Hlubi as 'abeSutu'. In Bhungane's time they had not formed regiments. It was said they were so numerous and powerful that they had no need of such things. Dingiswayo lived among them as a young man. (In afteryears they believed that he had come to learn the secrets of good rulership – and they regretted he had learned so well.) After Bhungane's death, his sons came to blows over the question of the succession.[66] Most Hlubi acknowledged Mthimkulu, but a significant number joined the party of his rival Mpangazitha.

While the succession dispute continued, their neighbourhood was disturbed by the arrival of Matiwane, chief of the people called after one of his ancestors, Ngwane. They had previously made their home not far from the sources of the Black Mfolozi River. Matiwane's father, Masumpa, was remembered as a military adventurer whose raiders had once made a successful attack on Fokeng people beyond the Drakensberg.[67] Now his son found himself caught between the grinding wheels of Dingiswayo and Zwide. In an attempt to safeguard some of his herds from possible attack, he sent them away for safekeeping. Not long after this, Zwide attacked him. This must have been in the year 1817 or 1818 because by all accounts it was prior to the death of Dingiswayo. Matiwane then moved west with his followers and attacked Mthimkulu's Hlubi with the clear intention of recovering his cattle. Within a very short space of time, one of Matiwane's patrols had succeeded in trapping and killing Mthimkulu, probably in 1818.[68]

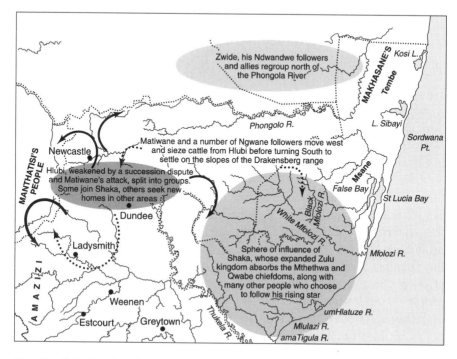

Map 8   Relative situation of major chiefs in the south-east *circa* 1819
After A. T. Bryant, *Olden Times in Zululand and Natal* (Longman, 1929)

The Hlubi people refused to believe that military strength alone had enabled the smaller forces of their enemy to triumph. They reckoned that Mthimkulu had been bewitched and entrapped by an Ngwane girl – much as Dingiswayo was to be fatally entrapped the following year.[69]

It is extremely difficult to say what happened next. According to some accounts, Matiwane did not linger long in the Mzinyathi River area, but moved in the same year with his people south-west along the slopes of the Drakensberg. There he attacked the Bhele folk, close relations of the Hlubi, whose territory stretched from the upper Thugela sources to the picturesque region of Champagne Castle. Having arrived here, Matiwane incorporated many of the Bhele into his own chieftaincy and settled down for three or four years.[70] The most detailed account of these events from a Hlubi point of view was told in 1909 by Mabonsa, who was then a very old man.[71] Mabonsa remembered the strife between Mthimkulu and his brother Mpangazitha as merely a disturbing force. The real disaster, he claimed, was the death of Mthimkulu, after which the Hlubi kingdom built by Bhungane shattered 'like the breaking of a bottle into a thousand fragments'. Three of Mthimkulu's sons went off with a sizeable following and pledged their allegiance to Shaka, who formed them into the *Iziyendane* regiment under the special patronage of his mother, Nandi. Mpangazitha took his following over the Drakensberg briefly before returning to the Estcourt district of KwaZulu-Natal. Another brother, Maranqa, first ran north to his mother's people in western Swaziland where, after a battle with a local chief, he turned west and descended the upper Vaal (Liqwa) River, before turning up the Namahari (Wilge) River toward MaNthatisi's country. Yet another brother, Ngalonkulu, made his way west toward the vicinity of modern Bloemfontein. And another, Sondezi, made his way down to the middle reaches of the Vaal River. All in all, it was a terrible time. So the Hlubi gave it a terrible name: *izwekufa*, whose literal meaning is 'country of death'.[72]

If we take this account at face value, these Hlubi bands did not enter southern Sotho territory as a united fighting force. Nor did they all come by the same routes. Most of them must have appeared as pathetic refugees. Some of them may well have been in touch with, and have sought out, the Hlubi groups who had migrated to the Caledon River area in former times.[73] Their knowledge of Sotho life and customs should have enabled some of them to strike bargains and win protection. This fits well with the story that MaNthatisi welcomed Hlubi refugees.[74] On the other hand, the appearance of ragtag bands of desperate people on the lookout for cattle was a worry. Matiwane's appearance with organized regiments just over the mountains to the south must also have been troubling. And a little way to the south-west of the Tlokwa, a new power was just beginning to rise on the upper reaches of the Caledon.

Moshweshwe, the cattle razor

The lovely Caledon River Valley sheltered a wide variety of people. This is not surprising in view of the good supplies of water and many natural defensive positions. Some people living there, as we have seen, had come up from coastal regions and treasured their Nguni origins.[75] Others had moved in from the central highveld and remained in touch with relations scattered as far afield as the Magaliesberg mountains and the Olifants River. Chapter 2 described the way Mohlomi used his network of acquaintances to travel from his Caledon Valley home all over the highveld. His people sometimes called themselves BaKwena (or crocodile people), after a totemic name common in many regions of the highveld. At other times they called themselves BaMonaheng, after Mohlomi's great grandfather, a celebrated chief.[76] In the ordinary course of events, succession to the paramount chieftainship at Mohlomi's death (c. 1816[77]) would probably have passed without much controversy to his brother, Makhetha. A challenger appeared on the scene, however. Lepoqo, son of Mokhachane, and cousin to Makhetha, was born about 1786. (The date can be fixed with some certainty because it is remembered that his circumcision ceremony had to be delayed because of a devastating famine in 1803.) From his adolescence, he attracted attention for his strength and daring. One story says 'he killed five men in cold blood, some for having been dilatory in executing his orders, and others for having sucked milk from the cows. He brained them, it is said, with a club made of rhinoceros horn, which his father used in dancing.'[78] He also made a name for himself as a cattle-raider. With his friend and comrade in arms, Makoanyane, he achieved amazing success. They took

> first a herd of three hundred cattle at Maquai; then one of two hundred at Ntisane; then another of seven hundred at Molagilane. Crossing the Caledon he threw himself on the Lighoyas of Mabula, a town situated between Thaba Unchu and Mekuatling, put to the sword ten or twelve herdsmen, and carried off about a thousand head of cattle.[79]

For small-time raiders, these are big-time numbers. After another audacious expedition against a nearby chief, he acquired the nickname Moshweshwe, because he could steal cattle away as neatly and silently as a razor shaves hair.[80] Although in the modern orthography of Lesotho the word is spelled Moshoeshoe, in this history it will be printed in the fashion of South African Sotho orthography. This may help readers imagine the sound of the close shave: something akin to Muh-shwish-swish. The name stuck.

Moshweshwe did not just acquire and save cattle. He invested. Following the example of his relative Mohlomi, he lent cows to his faithful followers which they used to acquire wives. He lent cows to poor people on the understanding that while the milk belonged to them, any calves born would belong to him.[81] (See Chapter 2, p. 11.) He used other cows to marry widely and thus forge alliances with notable families of the district. Thus, by the time of Mohlomi's death, Moshweshwe was well on the way to becoming a significant chief – a remarkable feat in view of the fact that his own father still lived. He could not have foreseen that within a few years' time MaNthatisi would storm his stronghold at Butha Buthe.[82] Nor do any of the available sources indicate that he knew anything of the mounted gunmen whose raids were the terror of the grasslands less than 200 kilometres away.

Griqua and Kora praise the Lord – and pass the ammunition

Chapter 3 (pp. 51–3) described the infiltration of Kora and Griqua groups coming up the Orange and Vaal river systems. By 1800 a number of them had settled at the springs which stretch northward in a ragged line from the Vaal/Orange confluence to Kuruman – oases of reliable water in an otherwise barren landscape.[83] They gathered round them very mixed communities, including many people of San and Sotho origin, over whom they reigned as a would-be aristocracy.[84] From time to time other refugees from the land and labour laws of the British Zone joined them.[85] A few of the Griqua lived in a fashion virtually identical to the Boers and deeply resented the colonial prejudices which had forced them to become migrants. Take, for example, Dirk Boukes, living near the Orange River in 1823:

> He had large flocks and herds, and had cultivated a considerable quantity of land; and his establishment altogether was on a very respectable footing, excepting his dwelling, which was only a temporary hut, in the style of the Namaquas. . . . [his] father . . . occupies another place in the Kamiesberg, and he has seven or eight brothers, all of whom likewise possess property. This Griqua family may, therefore, be considered, as in circumstances, much superior to the generality of their caste. It is a great hardship, in regard to this class of people, that they have hitherto been systematically prevented from acquiring landed property in the [Cape] Colony. In consequence of this, they are generally driven entirely beyond the boundary, and tempted to become outlaws and robbers; for if any of them occupy and improve a vacant spot within the limit, they are always liable

to be dispossessed by some boor obtaining a grant of it from the Government, who thus reaps the fruit of all their improvements and industry.[86]

Most of the Griqua leaders spoke Afrikaans and had a reasonable knowledge of what went on among the Boers living in the south.[87] Most possessed horses and guns, which they acquired through illegal dealings with those same Boers, thereby circumventing the Cape government's prohibition on the arms trade beyond the Orange. Though their numbers were small, their mobility and firepower gave them the ability to wreak havoc on periodic raids. Like the Boer commandos, Griqua raids served several purposes, including cattle theft, extermination of San hunter-gatherers and the kidnapping of children. These children were then sold on to Boers in exchange for guns and gunpowder.[88]

Soon after the London Missionary Society (LMS) came to South Africa in 1799, Griqua families began to send messages asking for missionaries.[89] These pleas demonstrate the degree to which many of them had assimilated the Christian culture of the trekboers.[90] Missionaries gratefully answered the call, establishing stations at the more important springs and beginning their work of religious instruction. By the time John Campbell came from London in 1813 to inspect the operations, the Griqua mission shone as the brightest light in the London Missionary Society's African operations. The Society's underlying strategic goal was that the Griqua would turn missionaries themselves and spearhead the conversion of all southern Africa. The Society's agents mostly turned a blind eye to their brutal commandos – trusting that in time the gospel of peace would change hearts and minds. Campbell convinced most of the congregations that they should stop calling themselves Bastards in recognition of their mixed ancestry. The more decorous name Griqua emerged from a discussion of their distant origins and gradually spread among them.[91]

The missions gave the Griqua a direct line of communication to the British government in distant Cape Town. After 1816 a superintendent of LMS operations resided permanently at the capital and acted as a lobbyist for Griqua interests. For three decades this post was held by John Philip, a brilliant propagandist and fearless critic of injustices perpetrated by the British officials and the Boer farmers.[92] Philip never wavered in his support for the Griqua strategy, though it placed him in an embarrassingly false position. On the one hand, he condemned the Boers' commandos, sale of captured children and use of forced labour.[93] On the other, he ignored the Griqua's employment of the same policies, trusting that the gospel would eventually make them agents of peace and justice. While arguing strongly that the British government should prevent Boers from moving north of the Orange River and east of the Kei River, Philip looked benignly on Griqua expansion in all directions. At times he argued that his own society held the Griqua-occupied territory as a kind of trust territory of the British Empire.[94]

The early LMS missionaries knew next to nothing about the South African heartland and its history. When John Campbell travelled over the Orange River, he kept a watchful eye out for unicorns – and created a stir in Cape Town by displaying an authentic skull, pictured in his book as 'Head of a Unicorn, killed near the City of Mashow'.[95] In place of a real history of the heartland, the missionaries substituted an imaginary narrative of their own which went something like this: the land had once been a paradise of green pastures and peace; then Satan and wickedness entered the hearts of the people, unleashing an unending round of savage warfare that would only end when the missionaries had redeemed the land with Christian truth and the peace of God. Thus, when Campbell looked round in 1820, he saw everywhere a 'land of strife and blood'.[96] This unsubstantiated and mis-leading story was to have an enduring impact on the writing of southern African history; it still lives in many books.

Turning Griqua captains into messengers of peace proved more difficult than Philip and Campbell anticipated. In 1814 a group of them who were dissatisfied with missionary arrangements – and a British attempt to con-script them into military service – left Griqua Town and established them-selves near the more reliable waterholes of the generally dry Harts River. Soon these so-called *Hartenaars* acquired a fearsome reputation as ruthless murderers and plunderers of the western highveld.[97] When in 1822, the LMS backed Andries Waterboer as head of all the Griqua, another secession occurred. This group of dissidents became known as the *Bergenaars* (moun-taineers) because they based themselves in hilly territory, from which they too launched periodic commando raids. Both the Hartenaars and Bergenaars acquired followings of Kora.[98] Soon the words Kora and Koranna lost any ethnic or cultural meaning they might once have possessed. As one observer wrote perceptively, 'The name of Koranna designates . . . less a people than an association of brigands.'[99]

The missionary who disagreed most strongly with John Philip's Griqua strategy was a young man named Robert Moffat who joined the LMS in 1820. As he saw things from his station at the wellspring of the Kuruman River, Sotho-speaking people held the key to the evangelization of Africa. They vastly outnumbered the Griqua. Their settlements stretched far away to the north and east. The raids of the Griqua, Kora, Hartenaars and Bergenaars had frightened and antagonized these people. Moffat contended that so long as the missionaries continued to be viewed as the champions of the Griqua, the northern chiefs would view them with suspicion. Far

Map 9   Area subject to frequent Griqua and Kora raiding *circa* 1800–38 –
superimposed on a modern map of South Africa

from being the key to Africa, the Griqua alliance locked the door to further expansion. To a large extent, he was right.[100]

Trade wars in the north

Tswana chiefs displayed various degrees of misgiving and alarm when the ox wagons carrying John Campbell lumbered into their towns in 1820, en route to the sources of the Limpopo.[101] Previous ox wagons had carried traders seeking ivory and hides. Campbell told an unlikely story about preaching God's word. Again and again people asked Campbell if he had beads for sale. Every chief along the way told him that it would be dangerous to go further. The Thlaping chief Mothibi warned him against Makaba of the Ngwaketse whom he painted as the chief villain of the region. When the missionary reached his territory, Makaba absolutely denied the charge. His only purpose in fighting, he said, was 'to regain cattle that had been stolen from him'. Hurutshe chiefs told Moffat they had been forced to build their towns on the tops of hills in order to defend their herds. As Campbell pushed further, he heard more such conflicting advice. Much of it consisted of deliberate misinformation, designed to prevent the missionary from alerting rivals to their plans.[102]

In fact, the unsuspecting missionary had wandered into a battle zone where the major players were jockeying for favourable positions at the intersection of important trade routes. The extent of the regional trading networks was evident in the stories people told about distant places. Men wearing silver ornaments said they could be procured from white men in the north. Others had been taught to inoculate themselves against smallpox by 'white men who lived to the N.E.'.[103] One chief

> had heard of a nation to the N.E., called Mahalaseela, who use elephants as beasts of burden; beads came from them, and they lived near the Great Water. He had heard also of a people called Matteebeylai [the generic word for aliens] to the eastward, who also lived near the Great Water, and have long hair; and of another nation to the N.E., who bring beads to the Boquains, called Molloquam. . . . The Molloquam use only bows and arrows in war.[104]

Although it is impossible to be sure, these stories point to at least three different trading routes to the Indian Ocean: one running via the Zambezi, another via the Save (Sabi) River, and a third running overland to Delagoa Bay. Stories of 'white men' probably should not be taken at face value.

Map 10   North-western zone of competition for command of trade routes

Reports of people dressed in 'long chintz gowns' living to the north-east most likely refer to the so-called Prazos of the lower Zambezi Valley who were at this time vigorously promoting a growing slave trade. Further north along the coast there were also Swahili African and Arab slavers whose descriptions fit the reports filtering in to the Hurutshe.[105] By early 1822 the town of Quelimane at the Indian Ocean end of the Zambezi Valley was 'the greatest mart for slaves on the east coast' with annual exports of more than 10,000 slaves.[106] The trade was likewise growing at the port of Inhambane between the Limpopo and Save Rivers.

On his travels, Campbell met an escaped slave from the Cape named Arend (or Aaron) who had grown wealthy as a trader.[107] He gave a memorable account of the journey to Delagoa:

> Being in want of clothing for his wife and child, he set out with the intention of going to Delagoa Bay to purchase some, but when within about a day's journey of the Portuguese settlement, he procured the goods he wanted from the natives, and returned without going farther. He gave me a piece of chintz which he procured in this manner, and which is of Indian manufacture. On this excursion, which he computed to be about ten days' easy journey, he travelled through a fine country very thickly inhabited. . . . Arend added, that among these tribes, the chief danger to travellers arises from the suspicion of their being spies, of which there is great jealousy. On this account he considers it expedient for travellers to remain about ten days at the principal town of each tribe, in order to acquire the confidence of the chiefs and obtain their free permission to pass through their territories.[108]

Wealth accumulated through trade could be converted into cattle, whose possession here, as everywhere else, meant power over people.

War had been endemic in the region for decades and showed no signs of abating (see Chapter 2, pp. 28–9).[109] As of 1820, Hurutshe chiefs still occupied the most desirable territory, in the vicinity of modern Zeerust, where good grazing, plentiful water and defensible hills enabled them to build large towns. Campbell estimated the population at Karechuenya at 16,000, which would have given it a claim to be the largest town in southern Africa.[110] Already, however, the rising power of the Ngwaketse and Ngwato pressured the Hurutshe from the north and north-west. To the east, Fokeng chiefs had asserted their independence from Hurutshe hegemony and fought wars with the neighbouring Kgatla. Meanwhile, the ambitious Pedi king, Thulare,[111] was extending his power westward from his base on the Steelpoort River, gradually acquiring control of formerly independent Kwena chiefs beyond present-day Pretoria. He evidently intended to dominate longer stretches of the trade route from Delagoa Bay to the interior. As long ago as 1798–9, Griqua and Kora raiders led by Jan Bloem had begun to hammer the region.[112] And even as John Campbell attempted to interest people in the peace of God, old Coenraad de Buys was skulking somewhere nearby with his sons and guns and wives – still on the make.[113] Since leaving Xhosa territory he had at various times lent his support to the Tlhaping, the Rolong and the Ngwaketse. He had recently helped the Hurutshe to attack the Po people of the Magaliesberg, acquiring in the process a series of Hurutshe praise names. About a decade later, Robert Moffat would travel through the Magaliesberg, wondering at the impressive ruins of stone towns, and trying to pinpoint who was responsible for the devastation of the Po. His own opinion was that the ruins were the work of Mzilikazi (who only entered the region in about 1827). But some of the damage Moffat saw could just as well have been the result of the earlier attack.[114]

Hurutshe chiefs had many questions to put to John Campbell about prospects for trade in the south. Did beads come from beyond the sea? Did many people at the Cape keep slaves? Did the king of England live in a town as large as Karechuenya? Did the demand for hides and skins reflect an English preference for dressing in furs?[115] Campbell answered as best he could while pressing his own scheme for sending preachers. By the time he turned his wagon wheels once more towards the south, he had secured promises that any missionaries who might be sent would be received with kindness.

More Europeans arrive

Campbell made a bit of a splash in Cape Town with his unicorn skull, but British officials showed only passing interest in his other information. The big news of the moment was the arrival of several thousand immigrants from England. They would 'settle' in the Zuurveld, the region so recently and brutally wrested from its original owners. A year before, Nxele's 6000 soldiers had mounted their futile assault on Grahamstown, while their women and children waited behind them with their cooking pots and household belongings. Now ships unloaded some 4000 ill-prepared English immigrants with their cooking pots and household belongings. Never before had such a large group of Europeans been so suddenly catapulted onto South African shores. They knew virtually nothing about the country which they expected to 'farm'. In fact many of them came from English towns and knew nothing about farming. An impartial observer might wonder at the folly of planting such a population next to people who still seethed with anger at the theft of their land. Anyone who bothered to tell the Xhosa chiefs that these people had been sent to solve alleged population and unemployment problems in England would have been greeted with hollow laughter.[116] The '1820 settler' project sowed the seeds of future wars.

The other seeds sowed by the new arrivals sprang briefly into life, then withered and died: victims of 'rust' disease. As the threat of mass starvation loomed, profiteers moved in. A Boer speculator named Pieter Retief managed to buy up virtually all the available grain supplies and sold them at exorbitant prices.[117] Only the distribution of government rations warded off catastrophe. Unfortunately, the next year's planting also failed, and the one after that. Nature was about to teach southern Africa one of its periodic brutal lessons about drought and famine.

Notes

1   The rank of Delagoa Bay among coastal slaving centres before 1820 is difficult to calculate. A Portuguese report in 1803 implied that it was the most important of their ports on the Mozambique coast (see note 15 below), but we lack statistics to measure the slave component of that trade. The only fact on which most historians agree is that 'by the late 1820s the slave trade out of Delagoa Bay had reached its full proportions, and the effects were disastrous'; Elizabeth Eldredge, 'Sources of Conflict c. 1800–1830' in Carolyn Hamilton, ed., *The Mfecane Aftermath: Reconstructive Debates in Southern African History* (Johannesburg, 1995), p. 137.

2   D. Fred. Ellenberger, *History of the Basuto, Ancient and Modern* (London, 1912), pp. 31, 38.

3   There is room for confusion over the term Zizi. Although it is associated with a chief of a particular lineage, according to one source from the 1830s, the word AmaZaze as used among the Tlokwa meant '*those from down there*, the lowlanders, because they lived for a long time on the sea coast'; T. Arbousset and F. Daumas, *Narrative of an Exploratory Tour to the North-East of the Colony of the Cape of Good Hope*, translated from French by J. C. Brown (first published 1846; reprinted Cape Town, 1968), p. 134.

4   G. M. Theal, ed., *Basutoland Records*, Vol. I (first published 1883; reprinted Cape Town, 1964) pp. 33–4.

5   Alternatively it might be useful to view MaNthatisi's people as a product of their situation in a zone of interaction/transition. For them, the Sotho/Nguni divide (a product of nineteenth- and twentieth-century linguistic scholarship) may have seemed artificial or even non-existent.

6 Arbousset and Daumas, *Narrative*, p. 31.

7 The precise relationships among the Tlokwa and Sia chiefs have not been much explored by historians. For example, Arbousset and Daumas (Ibid., p. 33) wrote in the 1830s that the chief Enghaltla was by then, 'very much enfeebled, his name is none the less popular'; one of his daughter had married Sekonyela 'to whom he considers himself a tributary, but not a subject'.

8 See Andrew Smith's report of 1836 in Theal, ed., *Basutoland Records*, Vol. I, p. 13.

9 Ellenberger (*History of the Basuto*, p. 45) identifies the victim as 'Zwedi, of the Amahlubi'. The only chief known to have been so named in that era was Zwide of the Ndwandwe.

10 Arbousset and Daumas, *Narrative*, p. 32. Their observations were based on conversations recorded in 1836. The passage reads in full, 'After having resided for some time upon the territory of the Matebele tribe, they were driven before two formidable foes toward the west, where they committed fearful ravages.'

11 '. . . nearly to the place where Dingan lately attacked the Boers', i.e., the site of the battle of Bloukrans in 1838. This is the version recounted by the Wesleyan missionary, James Allison (at that time living among the Tlokwa) to the Quaker visitor James Backhouse, printed in Theal, ed., *Basutoland Records*, Vol. I, pp. 33–4. This account identifies the original Tlokwa home as the Donkin River, an ambiguous name. Stephen Kay's *Caffrarian Researches* of 1833 appears to afix the name Donkin to the Sand River. However James Wyld's map of 1842 gives the name Donkin to the extreme eastern end of the Vaal River. The latter location fits better with the text.

12 Given in other accounts as Mjoli or Motshodi.

13 Ellenberger, *History of the Basuto*, pp. 47–8. See also A. T. Bryant, *Olden Times in Zululand and Natal* (first published 1929; reprinted Cape Town, 1965), pp. 150–1.

14 John Wright, 'The Dynamics of Power and Conflict in the Thukela-Mzimkhulu Region in the late 18th and early 19th Centuries: A Critical Reconstruction' (PhD thesis, University of the Witwatersrand, 1989), pp. 31–2, 156–9. The Mabhudu Tembe took their name from chief Mabhudu, Makhasane's grandfather.

15 Mabel Jackson, *European Powers and South-east Africa* (London, 1942), p. 92.

16 David Hedges, 'Trade and Politics in Southern Mozambique and Zululand in the Eighteenth and Early Nineteenth Centuries' (PhD thesis, University of London, 1978), p. 183.

17 Bryant, *Olden Times*, pp. 293, 304–5. Another account puts his death at 1853; *JSA*, II, p. 142.

18 Hedges, 'Trade and Politics', p. 142.

19 Ibid., p. 153.

20 Bryant, *Olden Times*, pp. 210, 305. The last plague occurred in the year of his death; there was not another for some forty years.

21 Hedges, 'Trade and Politics', pp. 138–9.

22 *Records of Natal*, II, pp. 183–8.

23 For one conjectural map of group locations see Bryant's 'The Native Clans as located in Pre-Shakan times' in *Olden Times*, p. 698.

24 Including the Langeni, Buthelezi, Qungebini, Sibiya and the Zulu chieftaincies; see Bryant, *Olden Times*, pp. 162–3. For previous links through marriage between the Mthethwa and Zulu lineages, see Hedges, 'Trade and Politics', p. 189.

25 For a good summary of Carolyn Hamilton's interpretation of Dingiswayo's system, see Wright, 'Dynamics of Power', pp. 173–4.

26 This is why people in Shaka's own time dated his accession at 1817 because it was then that he first became a chief in his own right; P. R. Kirby, ed., *Andrew Smith and Natal* (Cape Town, 1955), p. 89. His displacement of Dingiswayo as head of the confederated chieftaincies did not occur until 1818. According to an alternative account of Shaka's accession, recorded in the late 1830s, Shaka himself arranged for the assassination of his chief rival; *Natal Papers*, I, p. 20.

27 Bryant, *Olden Times*, pp. 158–9, and genealogy facing p. 314.

28 Hedges, 'Trade and Politics', p. 158.

29 *JSA*, II, p. 7; testimony of Mabola. John Wright agrees that Zwide was attempting to claim 'suzerainty' over Sobhuza; 'Dynamics of Power', pp. 156–9.

30 Bryant, *Olden Times*, pp. 162, 276. It is important here to reiterate that these group names and others referred to in the KwaZulu-Natal region must not be read as indicators of ethnic, cultural or linguistic divisions – let alone what used to be called 'tribal' distinctions. Culture and language were shared across these lineages. These names will all be found on the family trees of important lineages, denoting chiefs of some distinction. The same chiefs' names crop up again and again on these lists, which were preserved in oral memory and began to be written down in the nineteenth century.

31 Authorities differ as to the outcome. Matiwane's people preserved a tradition that held they had never been defeated. A valuable, though confused, account recorded in 1828 that Matiwane had fought both Zwide and Mpangazitha's father, Bhungane; *Records of Natal*, II, pp. 88–91. Bryant, *Olden Times*, pp. 137–8, believed that Matiwane had fought both Dingiswayo and Zwide.

32 Wright, 'Dynamics of Power', p. 176. Julian Cobbing proposes a variation on the theme, classing both the Zulu and Ndwandwe as 'reactive' state formations called into existence by the threat of the accelerating slave trade at Delagoa Bay; 'The Mfecane as Alibi: Thoughts on Dithakong and Mbolompo', *Journal of African History* 29 (1988), pp. 487–519, especially p. 518.

33 First advanced by A. K. Smith in 'The Struggle for Control of Southern Mozambique 1720–1835' (PhD thesis, UCLA, 1970) and shrewdly appraised in Hedges, 'Trade and Politics', pp. 11–13.

34 Bryant, *Olden Times*, pp. 163–6. Bryant, as is often the case, cites no source. A substantially similar tale was related by James Stuart's Zulu informants, Makuza, Mandhlakazi and Ndukwana; *JSA*, II, pp. 170, 186; IV, p. 279.

35 Bryant, *Olden Times*, pp. 173–4.

36 Ibid., pp. 174–5.

37 Wright, 'Dynamics of Power', pp. 35, 164; Bryant, *Olden Times*, p. 185.

38 Wright, 'Dynamics of Power', pp. 39, 41–5, 53.

39 Bryant, *Olden Times*, pp. 190–2.

40 Wright, 'Dynamics of Power', p. 183.

41 Bryant, *Olden Times*, pp. 204–8. Many histories describe this as a 'disastrous' defeat from which the Ndwandwe never recovered. See, for example, Monica Wilson and Leonard Thompson, eds, *The Oxford History of South Africa*, 2 vols (Oxford, 1969–72), I, p. 344; and Malyn Newitt, *A History of Mozambique* (London, 1995), p. 258.

42 N. J. Van Warmelo, ed., *History of Matiwane and the Amangwane Tribe, as told by Msebenzi to his kinsman Albert Hlongwane* (Pretoria, 1938), p. 18; Bryant, *Olden Times*, p. 208.

43 N. Isaacs to the Governor of the Cape, n.d. (but before Dec. 1832) in *Records of Natal*, II, pp. 226–31.

44 Hedges, 'Trade and Politics', pp. 73–4.

45 There is no point in which popular writing about Shaka is so filled with romantic nonsense as on this issue of the long-bladed, short stabbing *umkonto*. Careful attention to the original sources generally cited on this question shows that no one credits Shaka with the invention of the weapon itself. An early report (1825) of F. G. Farewell stated that the Zulu 'charge with a single *umconto*, or spear, and each man must return with it from the field, or bring that of his enemy, otherwise he is sure to be put to death'; *Natal Papers*, I, p. 21. Andrew Smith was told in 1832, that 'Chaka was the first that introduced one hassegay [spear]. One day he sent for all his people about the kraal and called in all their hassegays. He put all, excepting one for each,

into the fire and gave each one' (Kirby, ed., *Andrew Smith and Natal*, p. 46). Nathaniel Isaacs, who knew Shaka, reported that he 'proceeded to introduce a new system of warfare. It had hitherto been the practice to carry several iron spears, and throw them at the enemy, besides the assegai or common spear . . . which he forbade under penalty of death'; *Travels and Adventure in Eastern Africa*, newly revised and edited, in one volume, by Luis Herman and Percival R. Kirby (Cape Town, 1970), p. 150. John Wright, 'Dynamics of Power', p. 41, who places the Thuli migration to the southern side of the Thukela well before the beginning of the nineteenth century, cites Maziyana's recollection that 'as the Thuli fought their way along, . . . they stabbed their opponents at close quarters rather than throwing assegais at them as was the practice in more restrained forms of warfare'. It does not appear that Shaka's dictum was adopted by the chiefs who moved away to other parts of Africa. When Captain Owen encountered the Ndwandwe chief Soshangane at Delagoa Bay in 1822, he noted that attached to his shield were 'his assagayes and spear; the only difference in these weapons is that the former is narrow in the blade and small for throwing, the later broad and long, with a stronger staff for the thrust' (Bryant copied this account into *Olden Times*, p. 450). W. C. Harris reported that in 1836 Mzilikazi's soldiers rushed upon their foes, 'stabbing with their short spears, of which a sheaf or bundle of five or six is taken when going to war' (*The Wild Sports of Southern Africa*, first published 1837; reprinted Cape Town, 1963, p. 150). The use of the stabbing spear for warfare was widespread, even on the western slopes of the Drakensberg. A picture of a 'typical' Tswana man drawn to illustrate Arbousset and Daumas's *Narrative*, p. 147, shows him carrying the short-handled spear. According to James Backhouse 'the chief weapon of war among the Basuto is an assagai with a short handle, but they generally carry long ones with them'; *Basutoland Records*, I, p. 28.

46 Jeff Guy, 'Production and Exchange in the Zulu Kingdom', *Mohlomi, Journal of Southern African Historical Studies* 2 (1978), pp. 101–2.

47 Carolyn Hamilton, 'Ideology, Oral Traditions and the Struggle for Power in the Early Zulu Kingdom' (MA thesis, University of the Witwatersrand, 1986), pp. 366–7.

48 Historians take divergent views of this labour, some regarding it as vital, others as peripheral; for an informed discussion see Sean Hanretta, 'Women, Marginality and the Zulu State: Women's Institutions and Power in the Early Nineteenth Century', *Journal of African History* 39 (1998), pp. 389–415, especially pp. 400–3.

49 Guy, 'Production and Exchange', p. 102.

50 Though Bryant and James Stuart recognized the existence of the *amantungwa-amalala*, Carolyn Hamilton first pointed out the potential significance of this distinction in 'Ideology, Oral Traditions and the Struggle for Power in the Early Zulu Kingdom', especially pp. 277–97, 465–510.

51 Apparently that name was applied to the Zulu by their Sotho neighbours in the early days; see Arbousset and Daumas, *Narrative*, p. 76.

52 Statement of John Cane, 13 Nov. 1828 in *Records of Natal*, II, p. 33.

53 Arbousset and Daumas, *Narrative*, p. 134n.

54 J. P. R. Wallis, ed., *The Matabele Journals of Robert Moffat, 1829–1860*, 2 vols (London, 1945), I, p. 89; R. Kent Rasmussen, *Migrant Kingdom: Mzilikazi's Ndebele in South Africa* (Cape Town, 1978), p. 62. The early French missionaries of Lesotho likewise called Mzilikazi's people Zulu. See, for example, E. Casalis, *The Basutos or Twenty-Three Years in South Africa* (first published 1861; reprinted Cape Town, 1965), pp. 23–24.

55 C. M. Doke *et al.*, *English-Zulu, Zulu-English Dictionary* (Johannesburg, 1990), p. 900.

56 The phrase was in use long before it condemned Boers to death in 1838. See Isaacs, *Travels and Adventures*, p. 150. That the word 'tagati' in this context was applied to any criminal, not just one suspected of having practised witchcraft, is made evident in Adulphe Delegorgue, *Voyage dans l'Afrique Australe*, 2 vols (Paris, 1847), II, pp. 51–2.

57 Isaacs, *Travels and Adventures*, pp. 155, 157–8.

58 Statement of John Cane, 13 Nov. 1828, in *Records of Natal*, II, p. 33.

59 Or even, 'from the Phongolo to the Thukela'; see Wright, 'Dynamics of Power', p. 187.

60 Isaacs, 'Travels and Adventures', p. 100.

61 As Wright puts it, ibid., p. 273, 'political re-aggregation was accompanied by demographic concentration'. As people attached themselves to the stronger and more stable chiefdoms, other areas 'became relatively denuded of inhabitants'.

62 Wilson and Thompson, eds, *Oxford History of South Africa*, I, p. 346; William F. Lye and Colin Murray, *Transformations on the Highveld: The Tswana and Southern Sotho* (Cape Town, 1980), p. 31.

63 Wright, 'Dynamics of Power', pp. 279, 294.

64 Ellenberger, *History of the Basuto*, p. 42.

65 This paragraph is based on an interview conducted in 1909 with Mabonsa, a Hlubi man then aged about 80; *JSA*, II, pp. 11–35. His recollection was that Bhungane had dominated virtually all of what later became known as the Klip River and Utrecht districts of Natal.

66 The date of Bhungane's death cannot be fixed with confidence. Bryant, *Olden Times*, p. 148 gives the date 1810; on p. 157, he gives the date 1800. G. M. Theal's *History of South Africa: 1795–1834* (London, 1891), pp. 300–1,

stated that Bhungane and Mthimkulu both died in the Ngwane attack, which he dated at 1820. But as Theal did not cite his sources, there is no reason to accept his account.

67 Ellenberger, *History of the Basuto*, p. 122; Bryant, *Olden Times*, pp. 136–7.

68 The dates cited in this paragraph accord with: Bryant, *Olden Times*, pp. 138–9; Wright, 'Dynamics of Power', p. 178; and Hedges, 'Trade and Politics', pp. 189, 193. They do not accord with Ellenberger, *History of the Basuto*, who based his reckoning on Lesotho traditions. John Omer-Cooper, in *The Zulu Aftermath* (London, 1966), p. 86, chose to follow Ellenberger and date Mthimkulu's death to 1821. By ignoring the Zulu-based sources, Omer-Cooper could preserve the notion of a rapid-fire invasion of the highveld by both Hlubi and Ngwane, caused by the rise of Shaka.

69 *JSA*, II, pp. 13–14.

70 Bryant, *Olden Times*, p. 139; Elizabeth Eldredge, 'Migration, Conflict and Leadership in Early 19th Century South Africa: The Case of Matiwane' (seminar paper, Dept of History, University of Natal, Durban, 3 August 1994), p. 1; Wright, 'Dynamics of Power', p. 266.

71 *JSA*, II, pp. 11–35.

72 Ibid., II, pp. 18, 38n.

73 Ellenberger, *History of the Basuto*, p. 128.

74 So does the date, 1818; Ellenberger, *History of the Basuto*, p. 45.

75 See also Lye, 'The Sotho Wars in the Interior of South Africa, 1822–1837' (PhD thesis, UCLA, 1970), p. 28.

76 Moshweshwe told Andrew Smith in 1834 that his people 'were originally Baquaina, and that they left the country of their forefathers in consequence of oppression and poverty', but that for some time they had 'conformed to the custom of their immediate neighbours', MaNthatisi's Tlokwa; Theal, *Basutoland Records*, I, p. 9. Arbousset and Daumas, *Narrative*, p. 273, say that 'before the Basutos called themselves Basuto, they called themselves Bamonahins', after their chief.

77 The source closest to the event (Arbousset and Daumas, *Narrative*, p. 284) gives the date as 1818 or 1819. J. P. Orpen, in his pioneering *History of the Basutus* (Cape Town, 1857), p. 4, gives the date as 'about 1815'. Leonard Thompson, who made a close biographical study of Moshweshwe, consulted many sources before choosing the date 1816; see Wilson and Thompson, *Oxford History of South Africa*, I, p. 399.

78 Ellenberger, *History of the Basuto*, pp. 106–7.

79 Arbousset and Daumas, *Narrative*, pp. 292–3.

80 Ellenberger, *History of the Basuto*, p. 106; William Lye and Colin Murray, *Transformations*, p. 48.

81 Orpen, *History of the Basutus*, p. 4.

82 Though many sources suggest Moshweshwe only settled at Butha Buthe in 1820 and then made experiments with hilltop defensive strategies (for example, Ellenberger, *History of the Basuto*, p. 110, and Lye and Murray, *Transformations*, p. 48), Moshweshwe's own statement plainly asserts that Butha Buthe was his 'birthplace'. It had also, he said, been the home of his father, grandfather and great grandfather. See Theal, ed., *Basutoland Records*, I, pp. 82, 514.

83 John Edwards, *Reminiscences of the Early Life and Missionary Labours of the Rev. John Edwards*, ed. W. C. Holden (Grahamstown, 1883), pp. 46–7.

84 Robert Ross, *Adam Kok's Griquas: A Study in the Development of Stratification in History* (Cambridge, 1976), p. 24; Martin Legassick, 'The Griqua, the Sotho-Tswana and the Missionaries, 1780–1840' (PhD thesis, UCLA, 1969), pp. 175, 196.

85 Lye and Murray, *Transformations*, p. 40.

86 George Thompson, *Travels and Adventures in Southern Africa*, ed. V. S. Forbes, 2 vols (originally published London, 1827; reprinted Cape Town, 1967) II, p. 72.

87 Though for a time the Hartenaars pledged not to speak Dutch among them-selves, as a way of emphasizing their separate identities. See, Legassick, 'The Griqua', p. 207.

88 Ibid., pp. 132–3.

89 Ibid., p. 146.

90 Ibid., p. 185.

91 R. L. Cope, ed., *The Journals of the Rev. T. L. Hodgson* (Johannesburg, 1977), p. 70n.

92 The most appreciative study of Philip's life and work remains W. M. Macmillan's *Bantu, Boer and Briton: The Making of the South African Native Problem* (London, 1927).

93 Legassick, 'The Griqua', p. 354.

94 Ibid., pp. 313, 468.

95 John Campbell, *Travels in South Africa: Second Journey* (first published 1822; reprinted New York, 1967), pp. 294–5, 334. The name Mashow belonged to a Tswana chief of the group later generally called Rolong.

96 Campbell, *Travels*, p. 174. For a brilliant discussion of LMS narratives of paradise lost, see Richard Grove, 'Scottish Missionaries, Evangelical Discourse

and the Origins of Conservation Thinking in Southern Africa', *Journal of Southern African Studies* 15 (1989), pp. 163–87.

97 Lye and Murrary, *Transformations*, p. 40; Legassick, 'The Griqua', pp. 121, 200–4; Ross, *Adam Kok's Griquas*, p. 19. For a time the redoubtable Boer adventurer Coenraad de Buys threw in his lot with the Hartenaars.

98 Ross, *Adam Kok's Griquas*, pp. 25; Legassick, 'The Griqua', pp. 355–6.

99 E. Cassalis, quoted in Legassick, 'The Griqua', p. 649.

100 Legassick, 'The Griqua', p. 261; Cope, ed., *Journals of the Rev. T. L. Hodgson*, pp. 254–5.

101 Campbell, *Travels*, pp. 66, 74–5, 157, 231–2, 242–3, 249, 262–3.

102 T. M. O'C. Maggs, *Iron Age Communities of the Southern Highveld* (Pietermaritzburg, 1976) p. 280.

103 Campbell, *Travels*, pp. 165, 179.

104 Ibid., pp. 240–1. The so-called Molloquam would appear from this description to be people of the Save River region in Mozambique; see Newitt, *History of Mozambique*, p. 260.

105 Newitt, *History of Mozambique*, pp. 243, 291–2. The Prazos were people of partly Portuguese and partly African ancestry. By the early 1820s they had been sighted south of Delagoa Bay. Travellers in the early 1830s met a party of about forty 'bastard Portuguese' dressed in the long chintz gowns near the Black Mfolozi River; see Graham Mackeurtan, *The Cradle Days of Natal (1497–1845)* (London, 1930), p. 149.

106 Eldredge, 'Sources of Conflict', pp. 133–4.

107 Legassick, 'The Griqua', pp. 247–8.

108 Thompson, *Travels and Adventures*, I, pp. 99, 106. Campbell describes his meeting with Arend in *Travels*, p. 130; and gives another account of the eastern trade route on p. 241.

109 For excellent summaries see Neil Parsons, 'Prelude to *Difaqane* in the Interior' and Andrew Manson, 'Conflict in the Western Highveld/Southern Kalahari, *c.* 1750–1820', in Hamilton, ed., *Mfecane Aftermath*, pp. 323–61.

110 Campbell, *Travels*, p. 277.

111 See Chapter 2, p. 30.

112 Manson, 'Conflict in the Western Highveld', pp. 352–5.

113 Parsons, 'Prelude to *Difaqane* in the Interior', pp. 345–6.

114 Robert Moffat, *Missionary Labours* (London, 1842), pp. 523, 527–8. Another story recorded by Moffat, but not printed in *Missionary Labours*, attributed the

devastation to 'Mantatees' and 'other tribes' 1823; what this reveals is that Moffat had no direct knowledge of who was responsible for the ruins he saw; see Wallis, ed., *The Matabele Journals of Robert Moffat*, I, p. 9.

115 Campbell, *Travels*, p. 285.

116 Much of the history written about the nineteenth-century Cape Colony concerns the 1820 settlers. For a blow-by-blow account of their first years from a celebratory chronicler, see George Cory, *The Rise of South Africa*, 5 vols (originally published 1910–30; reprinted Cape Town, 1965), II, pp. 1–220. For a more clear-eyed appraisal, see Timothy Keegan, *Colonial South Africa and the Origins of the Racial Order* (London, 1996), pp. 61–5.

117 Cory, *Rise of South Africa*, II, pp. 75–6.

CHAPTER FIVE

Hardship, ambition and opportunity create new conflicts

Drought

On 14 March 1820, day briefly turned to night, as the earth's shadow eclipsed the sun. Only five total solar eclipses had been seen in the heartland during the previous hundred years.[1] Those with a gift for seeing the future prophesied disasters. The first catastrophe to arrive was drought. Many regions recorded failures of rain in the years 1820–2. Crops died at Grahamstown and the newly arrived English immigrants cursed their luck. Practically no rain fell there between December 1820 and October 1823.[2] Rain failed east of Kuruman in 1820 and Tlhaping chiefs blamed the missionaries.[3] This was unfair, for the drought gripped all the land north of the Orange.[4] The drought also appears to have affected parts of the Zulu kingdom, adding to the urgency with which King Shaka sought new sources of cattle for his *amabutho*.[5] Drought may have begun to affect the lower Maputo River region as early as 1817 and gradually extended northward through Mozambique. By 1823 (at the latest) drought stalked the Zambezi Valley.[6]

Drought, even on such a scale, affects different regions in different ways. Rarely does any drought in any region last more than three years.[7] There are coastal areas which have only once ever recorded annual rainfall below 660 millilitres. In contrast, half of the highveld plateau can expect drought one year out of every three.[8] Map 11 provides a broad overview of patterns of drought. It shows that some districts are virtually drought-proof and several others suffer only in exceptional circumstances. For centuries peoples of the heartland preferred the good areas and left the more drought-prone grasslands to wild animals.[9] When drought struck (see Chapter 2, pp. 12–14)

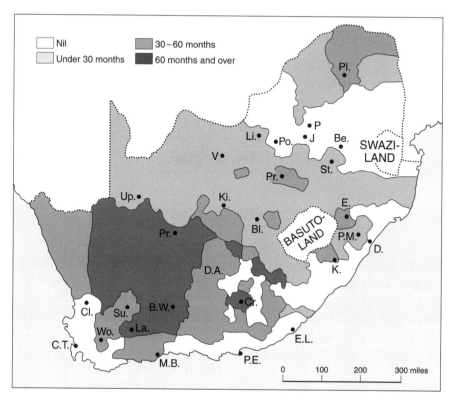

Map 11   Areas of South Africa declared 'drought-stricken', 1926–39
After Cole, M. (1966)

people pulled back to permanent springs, water holes and hills. If the worst came to the worst, they moved. When people under opposing chiefs competed for scarce resources, conflict followed.

Old histories of southern Africa imply that peoples of the heartland were continuously at war from the time of Shaka. This generalization ignores periods of relative tranquillity when the daily round of human life took its normal course. People took care of their animals, grew crops, raised their children, talked, danced and quarrelled with each other. It is remarkable how little open warfare is recorded for the years 1820 and 1821. There appear to have been no campaigns by Zwide, Sobhuza or any other northern Nguni chiefs in the region between the Phongolo and Olifants Rivers. Shaka, reputed terror of the land, does not seem to have launched a major attack on anyone during that period. If, as seems likely, Matiwane of the Ngwane and Mpangazitha of the Hlubi had found resting places between the upper Thukela and Bushman's Rivers in 1818–19, they appear to have lived there with a fair degree of harmony until 1822. Even the aggrieved Xhosa enjoyed something of a respite from Boer commandos on the southern frontier. As far as is known, MaNthatisi and Sekonyela launched no cattle raids on the scale of the 1817 expedition. They left their ambitious neighbour, Moshweshwe, free to pursue his promising career as a small-time cattle-lifter and canny lender of milch-cows. The only glaring exceptions to the general pattern were the continuing trade wars in the north-west and ceaseless predatory activity of the Griqua/Kora mounted gunmen for whom plunder had become a way of life. (See Chapter 3, pp. 51–5, Chapter 4, pp. 94–6). But even here there was room for hope. The Griqua faction headed by Andries Waterboer had solemnly pledged to keep the peace. To signal their good faith they accepted the appointment of a former LMS missionary as an official agent of the Cape government in Griqua Town.[10] In return, British authorities dropped a plan they had concocted to invade Griqualand.

In 1822, with drought taking hold of many different regions, conflicts broke out in many places. No single chief or group initiated the strife. There was no simple chain-reaction or domino effect at work. In another era, violence associated with competition for scarce resources might have been temporary. When the rains resumed, the overall political landscape would have looked much the same as before. After all, people had been living with their climate for 1700 years or more.[11] Historians dealing with this particular drought face the problem of explaining why fundamental and long-lasting changes in the regional power relationships followed. In climatological terms the drought was nothing special. Those who experienced it continued to look back to the terrible drought which climaxed in 1803 as absolutely the worst of all time. They called it by different names.

Among the northern Nguni it was the '*mahlatule*', among the Sotho, the '*sekoboto*'. Old men who went through it in their youth said 'that never before or since has there been such a famine'.[12] A few historians have flirted with the idea that the *mahlatule* set off the Mthethwa/Ndwandwe struggle and promoted consolidation of small chieftaincies into larger states.[13] The trouble with this hypothesis is that no one can pinpoint the mechanism by which such changes might have occurred.[14] In fact, from what we know of other regions, the opposite is common: famines – like increases in trade – are associated with fragmentation and break-up of states.[15]

Experiences with drought in late twentieth-century Africa provide some pointers to the circumstances in which drought can lead to famine and famine, in turn, can lead to fundamental political change. Failure of rain in itself need not lead to starvation if people can take preventative action. Drought brought famine to the Sudanic regions in the 1970s and 1980s because intensive, export-oriented agriculture had permanently degraded soils, blocking alternative food-supply strategies.[16] Efforts to get food to starving people ran into obstacles erected by political regimes. Some states refused to acknowledge rural famine because it might imperil their own existence. Demands that the world 'do something' about the threat of famine in the Horn of Africa led to a misconceived United Nations intervention in Somalia which fundamentally reshaped regional politics. The lesson of these more recent experiences is that drought cannot be treated in isolation from economics and politics.

Understanding the changes which followed the onset of drought in the 1820s requires study of the interaction between an old acquaintance – lack of rain – and new factors, including: a terrible increase in slaving and slave trading on the east coast; demands for wage labour among farmers south of the Orange River; the presence of marauding bands of mounted riflemen north of the Orange; a quantum jump in communications among people living in different regions due partly to trade and partly to the advent of missionaries; and the adventurous leadership shown by several gifted individuals.[17]

The times cast proud people down and lifted others up to undreamed of heights.

Soshangane, Zwangendaba and Nxaba in Mozambique, *c.* 1822–6

Some talented leaders emerged from the Ndwandwe/Mbo lineages. Though Shaka had forced Zwide and his allies to withdraw north of the Phongolo

River in 1819, he lacked either the force – or the fortitude – to launch follow-up campaigns. It does not appear that he sent any expedition in the direction of Delagoa Bay until 1828.[18] On the contrary, most of his cattle-raiding was done south of the Thukela River. This provided a long breathing space for Zwide and his former allies. Documentation of their activities for the period 1819 to 1822 is sparse, but some of Zwide's old comrades emerged sensationally from the shadows in 1821. In July the commander of the Portuguese fort at Delagoa Bay regretfully informed his superiors that a force of 'Olontones' had attacked the local Tembe chief 'Capella', forcing him to take refuge on an island. By mid-July the invaders had attacked another chief, 'Matoloa', and then threatened the Portuguese fort itself. Unable to defend his position, the commander gave presents to the invaders, and eventually persuaded them to lift their siege.[19] More information about the attacking forces comes from a British naval captain, W. F. W. Owen, who carried out a survey of the East African coast in the years 1822 and 1823. On his first visit in October 1822 Owen met a chief he called the young 'Chinchingany' dressed 'in full regalia'. This was none other than Soshangane, who had fought alongside Zwide in the 1819 war with Shaka. Owen penned a memorable description of an Ndwandwe leader at the height of his powers:[20]

> Round his head, just above the eyes, was a band of fur, somewhat resembling in size and colour a fox's tail, neatly trimmed and smoothed: underneath this his black woolly hair was hidden; but above it grew to its usual length, until at the top, where a circular space was shaved in the manner of the monks and Zoolos; round this circle was a thick ring of twisted hide, fixed in its position by the curling over of the surrounding hair, which was altogether sufficiently thick to resist a considerable blow. On one side of his head was a single feather of some large bird as an emblem of his rank, and just above his eyebrows a string of small white beads, and another across the nose; close under his chin he wore a quantity of long coarse hair, like the venerable beard of a patriarch hanging down on his breast; his ears had large slits in their lower lobes, and were made to fall three or four inches, but without any ornaments; these holes in the ears are often used to carry articles of value. Each arm was encircled by a quantity of hair like that tied on his chin, the ends reaching below his elbows. Round his body were tied two strings, with twisted strips of hide, with the hair on them, much resembling monkeys' tails; the upper row was fastened close under his arms, and hung down about twelve inches, the end of each tail being cut with much precision and regularity; the lower resembled the upper, and commenced exactly where the latter terminated, until they reached the knees. . . . On his ankles and wrists he had brass rings or bangles. His shield was of bullock's hide, about five feet long and three-and-a-half broad; down the middle was fixed

a long stick, tufted with hair, by means of holes cut for the purpose, and projecting above and below beyond the shield about five inches. To this stick were attached his assagayes and spears; the only difference in these weapons is that the former is narrow in the blade and small for throwing, the latter broad and long, with a stronger staff for the thrust.

He and his companions were 'tall, robust and warlike, in their persons, open, frank and pleasing in their manners, with a certain appearance of independence, infinitely above' other people Owen had met in this region. When the British captain impertinently asked if he could buy some of the weapons as souvenirs, the chiefs asked with lofty disdain whether he, in an enemy's country, would sell his arms? Soshangane was evidently less pleased with Owen's appearance, for the very next night he mounted a surprise attack with a force of 200–300 men, which very nearly succeeded in finishing off the naval survey party.

It is worth pausing for a moment to study this snapshot from 1822. Are these defeated, dejected or desperate men? Here they stand, resplendent in full battle costume, fresh from successful campaigns, prepared to dare the worst that Portuguese or British musketry might throw at them. They carry with them the full traditional pack of long and short spears – clearly they saw no advantage in copying the Zulu preference for a single stabbing spear. These are no refugees on the run from 'Shaka's fury'. After all, Shaka's headquarters lay only a little distance away to the south-west. Three years after the rout on the Mhlatuze River, in the midst of a terrible drought, they are still around, well fed, meticulously dressed, fully alert to the potential of doing business at the Bay.

The next year Owen returned and encountered another one of Zwide's former generals, a man whom he called 'Loon Kundava', properly spelled Zwangendaba, in charge of a force of about 5000 on the north side of Delagoa Bay.[21] He had for some time been raiding for cattle and people between the Bay and the Limpopo delta. His forces had resisted several Portuguese attempts to drive them back. Through all these struggles, however, the Portuguese commander and his garrison continued to buy Zwengendaba's 'spoil of cattle and slaves'. This was just the beginning. During the 1820s the slave and cattle export business swelled to horrendous proportions on the Mozambiquan coast, driven on by a grim partnership between increased demand and expanding supply. As one historian aptly comments,

> the slave trade and the drought played in dreadful harmony with each other. The desolation of famine filled the baracoons [holding places for slaves awaiting shipment] with the starving and the destitute. Whole communities were ruined by the drought and its economic consequences.

Agriculture and trade contracted, artisan communities were dispersed, and
the only form of commercial life was slaving. The violence and destruction
of slaving merely compounded the ecological disaster and prevented full
recovery. The ability of communities to defend themselves collapsed and
only the warlords and the militarised society of their followers were able to
survive in a world of increasing violence and endemic banditry.[22]

Increased demand was an ironic by-product of various conventions which
followed a British act of 1806 making slave trading illegal for British subjects. Other nations followed suit, until the Portuguese could only keep
supplies of slaves flowing to Brazil by drawing from their own African
colonies.[23] That is not to say that only Portuguese slaving ships called in at
East African ports. American freebooters came, defying their own country's
laws under the pretence that they dealt only in meat, cloth and metal-ware.
So did ships from France and other nations, surreptitiously feeding the
labour demands of plantations on various islands in the Indian Ocean. The
historian's debate over the extent of the coastal slave trade before 1820 has
diverted attention away from the slaving which unquestionably attained
boom proportions over the next two decades. It is important to ask, who
captured and sold the slaves?

All available evidence points to the chiefs of the old Ndwandwe coalition. They had turned their attention away from the unproductive business
of trying to swat down Shaka, in order to concentrate on the more lucrative
prospects of the export trade. Indeed, according to some interpretations,
Soshangane and Zwangendaba still remained active agents of Zwide.[24]
Soshangane established his headquarters in the lower Limpopo region
(only about 150 kilometres from the graves of his ancestors).[25] There could
have been no other reason for doing this than to participate in the trade.
Compared with the old homeland south of the Phongolo, the environment
was hostile. Malaria and other fevers found easy targets in people without
childhood immunity. Cattle – still the necessary underpinning of chiefly
power – had to be protected from the trypanosomiasis by keeping wild
game and the tse-tse fly at bay.[26] The Portuguese garrison had to be kept
in line. Soshangane managed all this and more. As his power grew, he
promoted a collective identity for his people in the time-honoured way by
incorporating them into his lineage memory. He took as one of his titles
Manukuza (sometimes written Manucusse) after one of his ancestors
reckoned to be the son of the legendary Mbo founding figure, Langa. His
kingdom began to be called by the name of his grandfather, Gasa.[27] In later
years, when his kingdom had grown to vast proportions – and outlasted the
Zulu monarchy – people would honour their founder by calling themselves
Soshanganes (or Shangaans).

Map 12   The Ndwandwe diaspora 1820

Soshangane's ascent came at the expense of the Tsonga and Tembe chiefs of the south. An early casualty was Maiett (or Mayett or Macetas), whose lands flanked the Maputo River mouth. Devastated by the recent invasions and the Portuguese inability to protect him, the young man purportedly signed a treaty with Captain Owen in March 1823 ceding his lands to King George IV, so that Britain might

> establish such a force in the lands of Temby as may protect my people not only from the incursions of the more warlike natives of the interior but also from the insults and continued oppressions which have hitherto been practised on us by European nations, and more particularly by the Portuguese, who are not only unable to afford us any protection themselves, but by a most despotic, enthralling and unreasonable interference prevent when they can our commerce with the people of any other nations, even instigating us to murder those of our subjects who may have had any such commerce and to all this in the late war with the outcast Olontones [Soshangane and Zwangendaba's forces], when our whole country was devastated and no family safe, the Portuguese factory on the North bank of the English river were not only at peace with our invaders but on such amicable terms as to buy their plunder of cattle and slaves and to carry on other peaceable traffic with them whilst my people were reduced to a famine by the effects of the said war.[28]

Britain turned the offer down and the Tembe were ruined. By early 1827, a visitor to the Bay reported, the entire country had 'nearly been depopulated in consequence of the slave trade being in active operation. Among one tribe near Delagoa Bay he found only women, the old men being killed and the young ones carried off and sold.'[29]

Zwangendaba chose to not merge his forces in Soshangane's rising kingdom. Instead he moved north of the Limpopo mouth and very quickly extended his operations towards Inhambane, at that time the most active slave mart south of Quelimane (see Chapter 4, p. 74).[30] A glance at the map will show that this is the unhappy low-lying region where – when drought does not reign – the floods of the Limpopo and Sabi (on some maps, Save) river systems desolate the land.[31] Some time later (it appears to be impossible to say precisely when[32]), Zwangendaba moved yet again, this time in an inland direction along the Sabi River Valley where low country (under 500 metres) extends well into present-day Zimbabwe.

Before Zwangendaba's departure, a third former Ndwandwe ally arrived in Mozambique.[33] Nxaba of the Msane lineage came in a roundabout way from the highveld. At some unspecifiable time following Zwide's defeat in 1819, the Msane group split. Some joined Shaka and rose to high positions in his kingdom.[34] Others moved off with Nxaba. Why Nxaba moved is difficult to say. One oral account recorded in 1905 said that he went to pay tribute to Shaka, but became frightened when he observed a man being executed for a trivial offence.[35] Another oral account dating from 1921 also implies that Nxaba had joined Shaka, but left to avoid punishment for the crime of keeping white cattle.[36] Another history places the date of Nxaba's departure at 1821, which would have coincided with the onset of drought.[37] Whatever the reasons and whatever the initial date, it appears that Nxaba and his following travelled north along the spine of the Drakensberg, crossed the Limpopo and then descended into Mozambique. The only date in this long progression which can be put down with some confidence is 1824, when Nxaba attacked Inhambane. By 1827 he had defeated two Tsonga chieftaincies north of the Sabi River. With each success he 'rounded up the cattle of the conquered people and seized young men and girls to boost their numbers still further'.[38]

The previous few brief paragraphs chronicle a sequence of events pieced together from fragmentary scraps of evidence. This bald narrative raises more questions than it answers. What precisely was going on? What was happening to ordinary people? The available documentation does not tell us, because it derives mainly from a handful of observations recorded by poorly informed outsiders present at different times at scattered coastal ports. The old story that Soshangane, Nxaba and Zwangendaba 'fled' to Delagoa Bay to get away from Shaka will not do. For one thing, the dates do not fit. Zwide's defeat at the Mhlatuze happened in 1819. Soshangane and Zwangendaba's first attacks on the Tembe chiefs and the Portuguese trading post occurred in 1821. It could not have taken two years to 'flee' 200 kilometres – a distance which *amabutho* in fighting trim could cover in a few days. Neither could it be convincingly argued that Nxaba accidentally took a right turn on the Zimbabwe plateau and wandered unknowingly down to the coast.[39] When first glimpsed at Delagoa Bay Soshangane's soldiers are fit and well, not haggard and drawn. The invading groups were evidently unfazed by the presence of Prazo slavers and Portuguese soldiers. They moved deliberately into an area where the slave trade was hotting up, not cooling down. The first reports say they traded both cattle and slaves. Where did the slaves come from? It beggars belief that they could have brought captives up from KwaZulu-Natal, a place they were said to be fleeing. Of course, slaves and cattle were not the only commodities in demand at Inhambane and Delagoa Bay. Ivory too was traded. But elephant hunters would have had no incentive to swarm over the coastal lowlands, which had been by that time pretty well hunted out.

The simplest explanation is that Soshangane, Nxaba and Zwangendaba made war on the Tembe to acquire the slaves they wished to sell. Anyone wishing to advance a different theory must first identify an alternative source of supply to the slaving ports, and then explain how those supplies could continue unhindered with such powerful armies operating from Delagoa Bay to Inhambane.[40] Cattle might likewise have been captured locally, but these *amabutho* would not have gone raiding anywhere without taking cattle along for food. For people whose hierarchical social structure depended on the possession of cattle, trading animals away was a losing business. Any animals sold would have to have been replaced by trading or raiding somewhere else. It is not beyond the realms of possibility to imagine Zwangendaba buying slaves and cattle in the Swaziland interior with goods acquired at Delagoa Bay. But who would have been selling those slaves? In the early 1820s the records are silent on this point. Moreover, it would have been out of character for such chiefs to turn themselves into itinerant traders. It is not inconceivable that they might have sold their own subjects into slavery. But that could not have gone on for long without causing a general flight of their people into the waiting arms of other, kinder and more sensible chiefs. No, it is more reasonable to assume that all three war leaders made a deliberate decision to move to Delagoa Bay and take up slaving. The terrible drought would have made peoples of the lowlands easy targets. The drought itself would have lessened the threats of mosquito- and fly-borne diseases which in normal times would have threatened the intruders and their herds. Although the drought did not make them slavers, it assisted their aggression.

These ruthless attackers would not have been tamely received by their intended victims. Some must have fled to safety. What became of the others? Many must have been sold, for by 1824 'the glut [of slaves for sale on the coast south of Quelimane] was such that the price of a slave had fallen to only a few shillings'.[41] Slave ships at Delagoa Bay wanted healthy young men. These were hard to come by during the drought. One account claims that only about one in three arrived alive after the voyage to Brazil. If the slavers had the good fortune to keep half their miserable cargo alive, they made profits good enough to encourage them 'to more extensive speculations'.[42] Many people with no market value would have joined the invaders. Young women may have been unwanted on the slave ships, but Soshangane, Zwangendaba and Nxaba would have looked on them as a valuable resource. They could be dragooned into agricultural labour. They could be married off to veteran soldiers. They could be added to the prestigious ranks of the *isigodhlo*, the kings' secluded assemblies of unmarried women who played a vital role in maintaining royal control over female production and reproduction.[43] How many women from lower Mozambique went with Zwangendaba up the Sabi River is impossible to say. For Soshangane, the incorporation of local women must have played a great part in his successful kingdom-building enterprise. Many of the lowland women would have acquired a childhood resistance to malaria, thus increasing their chances of survival relative to the core group of invaders from the highland regions. While at first there must have been invidious distinctions drawn between the conquerors and the conquered, over time, the children born of mixed Gasa/Tsonga marriages would have come to look upon themselves as part of a single community.

Three small groups maintained their identities intact following the advent of Soshangane's kingdom in southern Mozambique. One group comprised the men in long gowns – Prazo and Swahili – who acted as brokers and middle men in the slave trade.[44] Their knowledge of languages and the marketplace made them invaluable; references to their activities continue into the 1830s. The second group of survivors were based in the Portuguese forts. Although these places were several times sacked and burned and served no particular need for either the slave ships or the slave sellers, Portuguese authorities were determined to maintain their presence on this coast. They therefore continued to send new forces in to replace those who fell.[45] The third group of survivors were, surprisingly, the Tembe under Makhasane (see Chapter 4, p. 80) whose country lay between Delagoa Bay and the Zulu kingdom. Had Shaka been the all-devouring conqueror depicted in some histories, or had he aimed for commercial reasons to extend his domain to the Bay, Makhasane would surely have been crushed and his people incorporated into the Zulu kingdom. Yet Makhasane survived, despite reports that on two different occasions he had helped dissident chiefs escape from Shaka's grasp.[46] One plausible explanation is that Shaka found it in his interest to maintain the alliance forged between Makhasane and Dingiswayo for purposes of keeping a trading corridor open to Delagoa Bay – and therefore he protected Makhasane from the rising power of Soshangane. Another is that Shaka was satisfied with an occasional small gift signifying a tributary relationship. A third is that he valued Makhasane's people as skilled metal-workers. A fourth is that he did not have the power to crush Makhasane. And a fifth, perhaps, is that he feared that the 'king of the locusts' would send a plague upon anyone who attacked him. In the late 1830s Makhasane was still reportedly ruling as many as 10,000 subjects.[47] Whatever the reason, the long reign of Makhasane poses a continuing challenge to the legend of invincible Zulu expansionism and rapacity.[48]

Zwide and Sobhuza stand their ground

No person had better reasons for 'fleeing Shaka' after 1819 than Zwide, whose ambitions had suffered a huge setback. Yet it appears he hardly moved. In the following years he bided his time north of the Phongolo River, where he died in his hut from natural causes in 1824. That is to say, Shaka made no attempts to pursue or destroy his oldest enemy for five years. Old tales about Zwide 'fleeing' north to the Pedi country appear to have been based on a misapprehension.[49] The Pedi preserved memories of having fought with 'Matabele' and 'Ngoni'. These words, as we have seen, are profoundly ambiguous. In order to get to the Limpopo and on to the Zimbabwe plateau, Nxaba may very well have passed through the country of the Pedi and 'Transvaal Ndebele'. His forces may have been the 'Matabele' of Pedi traditions. Oral traditions collected in Swaziland indicate that Zwide undertook no great journey but settled down a little to the north of the Phongolo. From there Ndwandwe may have spread west into the eastern highveld or taken advantage of the drought to raid weaker peoples, but the available evidence is not conclusive. In about 1824, when Sikhunyana suc-ceeded Zwide as king, large numbers of the Ndwandwe still lived near their ancestral home, cultivating fields in the upper Phongolo region.[50] Although a succession dispute had followed Zwide's death and some Ndwandwe had defected to the Zulu, in 1825 Shaka still regarded them as the greatest threat to the security of his kingdom.[51]

The most significant Mbo lineage to have stood outside Zwide's anti-Zulu confederation was the Dlamini under King Sobhuza, who succeeded to the chieftaincy in about 1815. The relationship between the Dlamini and Ndwandwe lineages was extremely close; Sobhuza had taken as his chief wife Zwide's daughter, Tandile. Nonetheless, after a quarrel over agricul-tural land on the Phongolo, Zwide attacked his son-in-law, who then moved northward. Sobhuza took no part in the subsequent Ndwandwe–Zulu war, pursuing instead his own push to consolidate paramountcy over a number of so-called 'Sutu' chiefs. When the rains failed in so many places after 1821, his territories had the good fortune to fall within a relatively drought-proof zone. Instead of using the opportunity which arose to plunder unfor-tunate people in the famine-stricken west, Sobhuza concentrated his attention on the east. On several occasions he launched raids in the direction of Delagoa Bay, evidently with the intention of cashing in on the opportunities which had attracted Soshangane and Zwangendaba. It appears likely that Sobhuza pursued aggressive cattle-raiding not just for the ordinary purpose of increasing his power, but also in order to trade beef down to Delagoa Bay.[52] As his fame grew, his people became known to the highveld Sotho people as BaRaputsa – Raputsa being their rendering of the name Sobhuza. Only later, when Tandile's child succeeded to the throne, would they be called by his name, the people of Mswati, i.e. the Swazi. By the time the great drought receded, the creation of the Swazi nation was well under way. Shaka had virtually nothing to do with it.

Three bad years on the southern highveld, 1822–4, and the struggle for the Caledon River Valley

Many books of the nineteenth and twentieth centuries presented the history of the heartland in the first two decades of the nineteenth century as a chain of cause-and-effect reactions set off by the rise of the Zulu kingdom. In this cosmology of the South African universe, the appearance of Shaka is the 'Big Bang' that sets everything in motion. Here is one example:

> Eventually Shaka, king of the Zulu, coalesced all the people of the north coast into a great conquest state. Those who resisted either succumbed to the assegai [spear] or fled away. The refugees who escaped, thoroughly conversant with the new fighting strategies, burst upon their unsuspecting neighbours to precipitate a holocaust in every direction. Such was the *Difaqane*, as the Sotho victims named the wars, 'the Scattering'.
>
> The first major refugee from Shaka's fury was the great Hlubi chiefdom, possibly the largest among the Northern Nguni. . . . The majority followed a lesser chief of the 'right-hand house', Mpangazitha, up to the highveld.
>
> Their first encounter with the Southern Sotho community was against the Mokotleng branch of the Tlokwa, who lived near the Wilge River under a regentess named MaNthatisi. . . . Without warning the Hlubi band attacked the Tlokwa villages, driving out their hapless victims.[53]

In another version:

> the ripples spreading outwards from the explosive rise of Shaka's Zulu state had their effect on Transorangia. From the time, early in 1822, when Mpangazitha crossed the Drakensberg to fall upon the Tlokwa of MaNthatisi, the dislocating effects of southern frontier extension interacted with those of the *Difaqane*.[54]

The sources and even the language of the story can be traced back almost to the era of the original events. In 1857, J. M. Orpen wrote:

> After about 1818, convulsions produced by Chaka, which shook all South Africa, commenced, and dislodged the Amanguani [Ngwane] Zooloos under Matoana [Matiwane], the Amatluibi [Hlubi] Fingoes under Pacarita [Mpangazitha], from the district of Natal and the Mantatees from Harrismith; all these fell promiscuously upon the Basutus like a deluge, while they were disunited, attacking them and each other for years, without intermission, while Moselikatse, flying also from Dingaan [Dingane, who succeeded Shaka as Zulu king in 1828], ravaged the country to the north, and almost exterminated the Bataungs, Molitsane's tribe.[55]

Even earlier, in 1852, Moletsane, the chief of the last mentioned 'almost exterminated tribe', said in a sworn statement:

> Towards the years 1822–23 political commotions took place among the Zulus of Natal. Msilikazi was obliged to leave that country on account of the cruel proceedings of the Inkosi Tshaka [Shaka]. He passed the Quatlamba [Drakensberg] Mountains, devastating all before him. Other Chiefs, as Matiwana [Matiwane] and Pakalita [Mpangazitha], followed his example, and fell on the neighbouring tribes. The first who had to suffer from the invasion was Sikonyela's tribe, which was living on the Eland's River, near Harrismith. This people drove before them the Bamonaheng-Basuto and other tribes, so that the whole land was in a state of confusion and desolation.[56]

Careful reading will reveal significant variations in the detail and sequence of these accounts, but in every one of them, Shaka sets off the Big Bang and mayhem – if not a 'holocaust' – follows. Different authors put wildly different dates on the subsequent period of alleged chaos. Moletsane compresses the whole story to a period of two or three years. The French missionaries of Lesotho claimed that the chaos and killing did not stop until they arrived with their message of peace in 1833.[57] Other authors make the mayhem stretch to 1836 or even later. However tempting it might be to fall into line with precedent and shroud the southern highveld in a dust cloud of unknowable chaos in the early 1820s, the historian must try to pierce the clouds and identify the main forces and actors at work.

Drought cannot be substituted for Shaka as a first cause of regional violence because its effects were highly concentrated. Clearly, drought would have hit the KwaZulu-Natal highlands and the central highveld very hard, beginning in 1821. Although no meteorological observatories existed to measure rainfall in different places, Map 11 (based on early twentieth-century data) suggests that life must have been toughest in the highlands on the eastern slopes of the Drakensberg, and along the whole of the Vaal river system right down to its confluence with the Orange. The normal response of chiefs living in those regions would be to concentrate their cattle in defensible situations with enough water to sustain agriculture and the herds. If the followers of Hlubi chief Mpangazitha were at that time living – as one account suggests – near the sources of the Thukela River, their options would have been limited. Moving down the river would have required submission to Shaka. Moving south-west along the Drakensberg would have required an accommodation with their old enemy Matiwane. Their one remaining option was to move up over the Drakensberg, passing into MaNthatisi's territory. On the other hand, if Mpangazitha was already on the highveld in 1822 along with the other Hlubi remnants who had moved there after Mthimkulu's defeat and death in 1818, options for coping with the drought were equally limited. To the east stood Zwide's Ndwandwe, still eager to repair previous losses of cattle. To the north and north-west lay a long succession of parched plains. The best prospects lay in the direction of the Tlokwa. So, one way or another, the constraints on resources pointed to a likely clash between Mpangazitha and MaNthatisi. Whether something like the legendary quarrel between MaNthatisi's son, Sekonyela, and a minor Hlubi chief constituted the excuse for a fight (Chapter 4, p. 79), cannot be known. What is beyond doubt is that Mpangazitha attacked MaNthatisi in 1822, seizing many cattle, and that she set out to repair her losses by raiding in the direction of the Vaal River. The reason this can be taken as fairly certain is that all sources attest to the attack, and that by early in 1823 well-documented rumours began circulating in the lower Vaal region to the effect that MaNthatisi was terrorizing the land. There could not have been smoke in 1823 without fire in 1822. At the same time, it is important to notice evidence that sections of the Tlokwa, not under MaNthatisi's rule, stayed put and escaped attack by Mpangazitha's forces.[58]

Where MaNthatisi's followers went next is almost anyone's guess.[59] The only certainty is that they sought to rebuild their herds by raiding cattle, and to survive the loss of their fields by raiding other people's food. By this time MaNthatisi's forces had been joined by many people from her father's people, the BaSia. How many other groups may have been actively raiding in the upper and middle reaches of the Vaal and Sand river systems cannot be known. These districts were in striking distance of Zwide and Sobhuza to the east. Nxaba could not have been far away, passing through these regions sometime between 1821 and 1823 (see above, p. 119). Reports from Sotho-speaking people about invaders of the eastern and central highveld are complicated by vagueness of terminology. Any invader coming from the south-east could have been called by the generic terms Matabele or Nkone (or Nkoni). Those words could therefore have been indiscriminately applied to Zulu, Ndwandwe, Ngwane, Msane, Jele – the possibilities are huge. Someone unfamiliar with the Tlokwa queen-regent could easily have confused the terms Matabele and MaNthatisi. Nor when someone spoke about being attacked by 'Shakas' can it be confidently assumed that they meant the Zulu. In the Sotho/Tswana languages, the word *tshaka* means battle axe. Someone chased by Tshakas might therefore have been chased by any weapon-wielding enemy. The people who lost their cattle and saw their crops destroyed did not make fine distinctions. Following their chiefs they fled the drought and their attackers in the later part of 1822, making their way along the shrunken waterways of the Vaal system, where an occasional water hole could keep life going. The word spread that they had

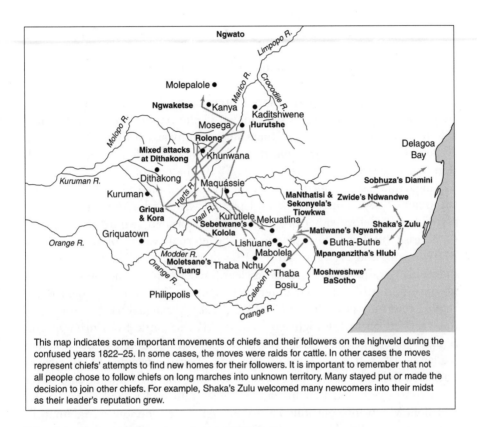

This map indicates some important movements of chiefs and their followers on the highveld during the confused years 1822–25. In some cases, the moves were raids for cattle. In other cases the moves represent chiefs' attempts to find new homes for their followers. It is important to remember that not all people chose to follow chiefs on long marches into unknown territory. Many stayed put or made the decision to join other chiefs. For example, Shaka's Zulu welcomed many newcomers into their midst as their leader's reputation grew.

Map 13   Some significant movements, 1822–5

been driven out by 'Mantatees' (i.e. MaNthatisi's people), 'Matabele' (i.e. aliens) and 'Tshakas' (meaning either Shaka's victims or battle axes). By early 1823 straggling groups of them calling themselves Fokeng, Taung, Hlakwana and Phuting began to appear west of the Vaal – the region that for so many decades had been the happy hunting ground of Griqua/Kora raiders.

Meanwhile, Mpangazitha and MaNthatisi had their own problems to deal with. Each longed to trounce the other in some decisive showdown, but the search for good pastures took precedence. Until the rains returned, there was no point trying to settle down in the parched districts they had ravished. Warily, they turned their steps southward toward the Caledon Valley, where their cattle could drink from mountain-fed streams that seldom failed, even in the worst droughts.[60] By the end of 1823, at the latest, Mpangazitha had grabbed territory on one side of the river, MaNthatisi on the other. They planted crops and plotted ways of building up their depleted herds. Before either group got well established, a third chief arrived to nourish his herds and people on the eternal waters of the Caledon: Matiwane of the Ngwane. How Mpangazitha's most feared enemy had made his way to these parts is unclear. According to one oral tradition he once had a friendly encounter with Sobhuza in the upper Vaal River region; that may have been in 1822–3.[61] Like Mpangazitha, he appears to have moved on to the highveld to safeguard his cattle from drought and Shaka's raiders in 1822.[62] He and his people were definitely in the Caledon Valley by 1823. It was a territory they knew because people of Hlubi origin had been living there for some time.[63] Boasting that his Ngwane had never been conquered, and that his father before him had raided as far as the Caledon, Matiwane constituted a real danger.[64] He soon found MaNthatisi's forces equal to the challenge. In his first assault, the Tlokwa forces turned the tide and pursued the Ngwane regiments so ferociously that, it was remembered in later years, many soldiers killed themselves 'with their own spears rather than return defeated to their chief'.[65]

Moshweshwe, the rising 'cattle razor', had been well on the way to making himself chief of the valley's Kwena people before these aliens arrived. The work of displacing Mohlomi's rightful heir, Makhetha, had to be interrupted while these troublesome new neighbours were dealt with. For a time, Moshweshwe managed to keep a firm grip on his father's lands at Butha Buthe, which lies across the river from the present-day village of Fouriesburg. Here the Tlokwa, heartened by their victory over Matiwane, for the first time tried to overcome Moshweshwe in the so-called 'Battle of the Pots'. After forty of his men had fallen, Moshweshwe staged a strategic retreat to the table-top of the adjoining mountain and successfully withstood a siege.

After consuming his crops, the Tlokwa forces moved south and attempted to follow up their recent victories with an attack on Mpangazitha. Their first assault was inconclusive for Mpangazitha was able within a short time to mount a surprise counter-attack. This set the scene for one of the most remarkable events in all the annals of southern African warfare. MaNthatisi's son, Sekonyela, and most of the young men were away when the Hlubi foes approached. In a flash of inspiration, the queen-regent summoned all the women from the cornfields and assembled them in a long line on a ridge with their hoes. When the Hlubi saw the glint of the sun reflected from the women's hoes, they mistook them for spearsmen. Fearing the results of an encounter with so numerous and well-prepared a foe, they turned away. When Sekonyela and the young men returned, they pursued the retreating Hlubi and hammered them.[66]

As MaNthatisi's forces advanced from victory to victory, Moshweshwe took stock of his situation. Though he had withstood a short siege at Butha Buthe by retreating to a mountain top, it was by no means certain that he could survive a long one. In 1824, he decided to move with his followers about 100 kilometres down the Caledon. There he attacked and put to flight chief None who occupied another flat-topped mountain, Thaba Bosiu. A spring on the mountain plateau promised a reliable source of water sufficient to withstand many a long siege.[67] Here Moshweshwe established the future capital of his nation. Proof of the wisdom of his move came when Matiwane failed in a first attempt to storm his position. Moshweshwe, ever the canny diplomat, sent a present of cattle after his departing foe.[68] This chivalrous (and calculated) gesture obviously stuck in Matiwane's mind, for in after years he ironically praised Moshweshwe for always speaking 'very humbly. He was like the antbear which puts its tongue into an antheap and then, when it is covered with ants, suddenly draws it out and lets it disappear into its stomach.'[69]

At about the same time, MaNthatisi and Sekonyela attacked and defeated the chief, Marabe, who occupied another highly desirable fortress between two adjoining flat-topped mountains. Quickly their people went to work to link the mountains with a well-built stone bulwark.[70] Located on the north side of the Caledon, near the present-day town of Ficksburg, the weary conquerors nurtured their own hopes that they too had laid the foundations of a future great nation's capital. Neither they nor Moshweshwe had any further reason to fear attack from Mpangazitha or Matiwane.

For a time those old enemies harassed each other in minor skirmishes. Finally, in March 1825, they met in a full-dress battle for the first time since 1818. As before, it was Mpangazitha who tasted the bitterness of defeat. As before, the death of a Hlubi chief signalled the break-up of the people as a cohesive unit. As before, they scattered to take refuge in various places.[71]

Many joined Matiwane, who welcomed the addition of their menfolk to his army. A great many others joined Sekonyela and Moshweshwe, including one of Mpangazitha's sons.[72] Others fled west and south, making their way to the country of the Xhosa and Thembu chiefs as individual refugees. Here they were also welcomed, and made to labour in subservient positions. The Xhosa called them AmaMfengu, meaning wanderers, or 'hungry people in search of work'.[73]

Little more than three years after the onset of the regional drought, the political landscape of the Caledon Valley had been transformed almost out of all recognition. The forces of Mpangazitha, Matiwane and MaNthatisi had been drawn to the valley by the age-old chiefly imperative of preserving power by preserving herds. The Caledon offered water, pasturage and defensible positions. Though some historians have misrepresented Mpangazitha and Matiwane as invincible commanders using the 'new fighting techniques of Shaka', MaNthatisi's people proved more than equal to the challenge. They won more battles, and won them more decisively than any other regional power. MaNthatisi's son, Sekonyela, was now a man. People who met him were less than impressed by his surly demeanour and taciturn manner of speaking. But though he lacked his mother's charm, he had shown himself to be a highly capable general. People flocked to join him. Moshweshwe, that other rising star, had been forced to move his power base down to Thaba Bosiu, but he had withstood every attempt to take away his cattle. His cousin Makhetha had also shown his ability to inflict defeat on the Ngwane.[74] Because of his legitimate hereditary claims as Mohlomi's successor, Makhetha was a bigger worry for Moshweshwe than any of his other powerful neighbours. In years to come, Moshweshwe would work assiduously to obliterate both his power and the memory of his line.

Meanwhile, the four surviving leaders needed to find ways of normalizing their relationships. Astonishingly, they had all established their headquarters within a day's walking distance of each other. Moshweshwe formally recognized Matiwane's supremacy with gifts marking his tributary status. Sekonyela sought alliances with first one and then another of his neighbours. Makhetha, too, sought to counter the power of his upstart junior relation by allying himself to a series of forces – including, for a time, Sekonyela.[75] Though there were some serious skirmishes among the four chiefs of the valley after 1825, there were no more do-or-die battles. Most ordinary people of the region joined one of the large groupings. As a result, the followings of each great chief were extremely heterogeneous. At any of their capitals could be met descendants of the old Nguni, Hlubi, Zizi and Kwena inhabitants of the valley, living peacefully alongside the mixed assemblages of people who had followed Matiwane, MaNthatisi and

Mpangazitha on their adventures of the previous three years. The mixed nature of their followings should be borne in mind even though it will be convenient from time to time to refer to them by the pseudo-ethnic names Ngwane, Tlokwa and Hlubi.

Each of the major chiefs faced Shaka's problem of finding an ideology which would make people loyal and – they hoped – forge a shared identity. They went about this in different ways. Matiwane insisted that people learn to speak his language – which was virtually identical to Zulu – and that they dress and build their huts in the lowland fashion. This they learned to do, though it meant shivering in cold weather. They also learned to pierce their ears and to sing the Ngwane war song: 'We strive for cattle only, and for land.'[76] Makhetha and Sekonyela emphasized recognition of their hereditary claims to chieftainship. Moshweshwe fostered a cult of his own superior leadership, diplomacy and generosity. At the same time, he pursued Mohlomi's time-tested formula of marrying widely to build alliances, while multiplying his cattle holdings through the *mafisa* loan system. In a strange turnabout of the usual process by which foreign intruders acquired the name Matabele, Moshweshwe accepted for his own people the name by which the Ngwane called people of the highveld: BaSutho (or BaSotho). It proved to be a workable and durable name for people of diverse origins.[77] Whatever chief people followed in these confusing times, they were discouraged from striking out on their own by widespread tales of cannibals roving the land. Such tales had always been around – an invaluable aid to mothers trying to keep errant children in line (Chapter 2, p. 17). Now they appear to have been actively promoted by chiefs as means of keeping their followers from drifting away.

Building *esprit de corps* was not enough to guarantee the allegiance of subjects. They needed to be rewarded with land to cultivate and gifts of cattle. The land question was serious and would involve Caledon Valley leaders in disputes that extended into an indefinite future (at the end of the twentieth century there were still unresolved land questions). The problem of finding cattle in the short run had to be addressed by raiding. If the great chiefs were not to engage in mutually self-destructive raids on each other, they would have find external sources of cattle. Drought and war had already reduced the pickings available on the highveld, so they began to focus their attention collectively on peoples over the mountains to the south: the Thembu and Xhosa whose pastures weathered practically every drought (Chapter 6, p. 152).

Some 'BaSutho', however, made the mistake of moving down the Caledon in search of better pasturage.[78] They ran straight into the guns of the Griqua and Kora mounted raiders. A poignant account survives of one such encounter:

This unfortunate man relates that his town was unexpectedly attacked by a large party of men on horseback; being a people they had never seen before, and not knowing the destructive nature of their weapons, the Bashootoos [BaSotho] attempted to defend themselves, but seeing great numbers of their people falling down dead, and the enemy, in spite of their utmost efforts, driving away their cattle, they at last gave way, running in all directions, leaving nearly all their cattle in the possession of the plunderers.

Some time after this, while removing to another part of the country where they hoped to be more secure, the same kind of people were discovered coming towards them. In a state of despair at the prospect before them, the chief desired his people to sit down, saying, 'We shall now all be killed.' The enemy approached within 30 yards, and halting, asked whether they would fight, to which the Bashootoos replied, 'No; come and take us all away with you.' They were then desired to put away all their spears, which they did, and the enemy dismounting came and selected such of the boys as were strong enough to accompany them. While thus employed, four white men, different from the rest of the plunderers, joined the party and having collected all the boys carried them off, when leaving a few of their people to take care of them, the rest of the party proceeded to attack another town in the neighbourhood, where they succeeded in taking a great many cattle, when they returned to the spot where the boys were and carried them off. On being asked whether the parents made any resistance, or cried when the children were taken from them, the king [chief] said they were all too much terrified to speak; one woman, however, resisted when one of the band attempted to drag her away, which so enraged the cruel wretch that he tore an infant from her back, and murdered it by dashing it against the ground. Having but a few cattle left to subsist on, many of them, rather than starve, resolved to follow the track of their plunderers in hopes of getting something to eat; others said they would not live with those who had reduced them to such misery. When those who followed the plunderers arrived near the residence of the Bergenaars, they were met by some people of the plundered tribes returning to their country, who said the Bergenaars would kill them if they proceeded; upon hearing this, many hundreds returned.[79]

A frightful, but familiar story: guns, horses, cattle theft, children taken by men who would sell them into a lifetime of servitude with Boers across the Orange (Chapter 3, pp. 48–52). The remains of this particular BaSotho group found refuge with the Christian Griqua captain, Andries Waterboer. Others found their way across the Orange and survived by getting wage labour with farmers in the British Zone.

For the Bergenaar and Kora raiders, an encounter with people who had never seen horses or guns meant new fields to plunder. Within a year or two of the Bergenaar secession from Griqua Town in 1822, opportunities were opening up on all sides.[80] From bases named for their captains in the west – Jagersfontein, Bloemfontein, and others – they began raiding up the Caledon Valley, injecting a deadly new ingredient into regional conflicts. Gradually the people of the valley came to know them by name – Barend Barends, Gert Taaibosch, Piet Witvoet, Abraham Kruger, Hendrik Hendriks – and to recognize their familiar costumes: 'white fustian jackets, leather pantaloons, striped waistcoats, white hats, with broad edges, shirts, neck-cloths, stockings and shoes'.[81] Inevitably, some Caledon chiefs began to enlist the mounted gunmen in their own local quarrels. Makhetha may have been the first to do so in the 1820s, but he would not be the last.[82]

Three bad years on the southern highveld, 1822–4: temporary displacement of many people scattered along the Vaal river system

It is more difficult to follow the fortunes of those refugees who made their way down the many branches of the Vaal river system at the height of the drought on the grasslands. Away from the dry river beds, the grasslands were what they had always been, the haunt of wild animals and occasional bands of hunter-gatherers.[83] The refugees moving west came from widely separated small communities and preserved no records of their adventures. Having lost their cattle and crops to various raiders, their situation was desperate. When asked who had attacked them, some said Mantatees (i.e. MaNthatisi) but others only gave the generic word for foreigner: Matabele, which could have been applied to Sobhuza, Zwide, Nxaba, Matiwane, to name but a few.[84] Many chiefs must have been among them, but only the names of a few survive. People closely related to MaNthatisi's and Moshweshwe's people were certainly among them. They all appear to have been SeSotho speakers. Two groups, whose names could not have been fabricated by the record-keepers, because they came from the distant eastern highveld, were the 'Phuthing' and the 'Hlakwana'. Others came from the Sand River Valley a little to the north of the Caledon. But so disparate were the streams of humanity making their way west that it would be misleading to lump them together under two or three dubious labels. Fabulous rumours preceded their appearance in the west. 'An immense horde, or nation . . . were said to be approaching from the north-east . . . laying waste the country, and destroying all who ventured to oppose them.' Some were 'white men, with long hair and beards, led on by a giantess, with one eye in her forehead'. Another report said 'that a mighty woman, of the name of Mantatee, was at the head of an invincible army, numerous as the locusts, marching onward among the interior nations, carrying devastation and ruin wherever she went; that she nourished the army with her own milk, sent out hornets before it, and, in one word, was laying the world desolate'.[85] Understandably, but wrongly, the rumour-mongers had confused the people doing the raiding in the upper Vaal regions with the people who had been raided. Neither MaNthatisi, nor Griquas nor bearded slave dealers in gowns led the straggling rabble on. Rather, the grim spectres of Hunger and Famine commanded their haggard legions. They streamed as best they could toward the places where there were cattle, crops and water.

The best prospects lay to the north-west beyond the Magaliesberg range where the Hurutshe occupied generally drought-proof lands. A large body of refugees left the Vaal in about January of 1823 and began moving toward the Hurutshe capital at Karechuenya (or Kaditshwene). Most people who found themselves in the path of this mass of human locusts simply abandoned their fields to be devoured. The wretched invaders scored no great victories in pitched battles. Indeed, wherever they did fight, they appear to have lost – most notably to King Makaba of the Ngwaketse.[86] Unable to seize control of Hurutshe or Rolong territories in April–May, 1823, they turned south towards Kuruman where pastures around the springs promised supplies of food. There at the height of the drought the Kuruman River was still 'gushing' forth.[87] Alarmed by the rumours which preceded them, the Tlhaping chief, Mothibi, set about organizing the defence of his capital, a town of about 8–10,000 inhabitants. When the young LMS missionary Robert Moffat heard the news, he was sufficiently alarmed to summon a contingent of Griqua horseman from Griqua Town. Given their own extensive record of marauding expeditions, this was like summoning foxes to defend rabbits. Though Mothibi and his father had suffered at the hands of Griqua raiders, his wife was the daughter of a Kora chief, so he knew what he was doing when he accepted the offer of assistance. Mothibi held his first *pitso*, or general meeting of men, women and children, on 14 June 1823. One speaker after another strode to the centre of the great walled meeting place to hurl defiance at the approaching enemy. On the 22nd about eighty Griqua horsemen arrived, including several notable war leaders: Adam and Cornelis Kok, Andries Waterboer, even the Bergenaar, Barend Barends. For Barends to be present, there must have been prospects of booty. At a second hurriedly assembled *pitso,* as one of the notable men was speaking, a woman darted forward to interrupt him. Addressing the Griqua, she declaimed 'with violent and indignant gestures: "Griquas! Should any of my countrymen turn their backs in the day of battle, shoot them, destroy them without mercy; such cowards deserve not to live."'[88]

What exactly took place when battle was at last joined near the Tlhaping town of Dithakong, on 24 June 1823, is unclear. The 'eye-witness' accounts of Moffat and the British government agent to the Griqua, John Melvill, are so garbled as to cast doubt on what they actually saw – or even whether they were there.[89] Estimates of the number of the attackers vary wildly – from 30,000 to 50,000 or more – and must therefore be discounted.[90] How many of this crowd were men in fighting condition is equally uncertain. Nobody was counting. It appears that the attackers had not previously encountered guns or horses, that their assault in a winged formation failed in its attempt to surround the Griqua, and that they finally fell back in a disorderly rout. By the time fighting ceased on 26 June, perhaps as many as 500 of the desperate attackers had been killed. Others, who had been abandoned on the field by the retreating mob, cried out for pity. Women bared their breasts, shouting, 'I am a woman! I am a woman.'[91] Little pity was shown, either by the Tlhaping or Griqua fighters. The Griqua, as was their custom, took off an estimated 1100 head of cattle, a very modest number considering the colossal estimates made of the opposing forces. In the days that followed, many people were found nearby, some dead from starvation, others emaciated from famine.[92] None of the survivors bore the slightest resemblance to the rumoured giants and bearded men. They all spoke dialects of the Sotho/Tswana language, and could, therefore, be readily understood. From the confused accounts taken down by Moffat, it appeared that two minor chiefs had perished in the battle: Tsowane and Nkarahanye, who were known in the neighbourhood. The migrating mass of people had grown over the previous months to include people from many different communities. Apparently the sole object of the movement toward Kuruman had been to capture sheep for food.[93] Nonetheless, Moffat was quick to jump to the mistaken conclusion that the root cause of their appearance was that they had been driven west by chiefs Chaka, 'Matabele' and some of the 'Mapootas' (by which is probably meant Sobhuza's or Zwide's people).[94]

As for the rest of the hungry horde, the record is practically silent after July 1823. We hear of no more battles they fought. Isolated reports from inexperienced travelling missionaries suggest by August many of them had turned back towards their own country and melted away into the grasslands of the central highveld.[95] A decade later, the survivors were reported living again in their old home districts.[96] From start to finish, the trek of the ludicrously misnamed 'Mantatee Horde' lasted just eight months, at the height of the drought in the year 1823. Tragic as it was, it was an anomalous event. Unfortunately, because Robert Moffat and John Melvill were there to record their impressions, it was inflated to grotesque proportions by later historians. Instead of being cited as a unique occurrence, it was treated as a typical example of highveld violence stretching over a dozen or more years. Readers of those old histories are left with the impression that large numbers of vaguely named '*Difaqane* raiders' continued to wander over the highveld as brigands, wreaking general havoc. The reality is that for most people by 1824, life in the western regions was back to business as usual, with the most feared raiders being the Bergenaars. In December of that year, Moffat told a fellow missionary that the London Missionary Society would probably have to abandon Kuruman and the southern Griqua missions. Due to murderous raids by 'the dreaded Bergenaars', he said, all the communities to the north had developed a loathing for men with horses, guns and light-coloured skins – including the missionaries.[97]

Even the worst of times create opportunities for enterprising individuals. The crisis of 1822–3 launched the careers of two remarkable young men from the southern highveld, Sebetwane and Moletsane. They are important for several reasons, not least of which that they contradict the stereotypical view of the Zulu as the invincible inventors of new fighting techniques. Neither of them owed anything to the Zulu, and began their adventurous conquests before the arrival of Matiwane and Mpangazitha on the highveld. In 1822 Sebetwane was perhaps nineteen or twenty when a group of MaNthatisi's raiders swept through the cluster of stone villages where he lived on the southern side of the Sand River.[98] Through his mother he claimed kinship with the famous traveller Mohlomi and his brother Makhetha (Moshweshwe's rival on the Caledon). Sebetwane's wife's sister married another extraordinary individual, Moletsane of the Taung, who lived not far away. Like others, they moved west to save what they could of their herds and their followings. As they moved, their own charismatic qualities attracted followers.[99] Some accounts say they were among the attacking forces defeated at Dithakong.[100] By 1824, Sebetwane had acquired a considerable following and felt confident enough to launch an audacious assault on the Ngwaketse, managing in the process to kill their venerable chief Makaba (Chapter 2, p. 28). It may have been about this time that his followers began to be known as Kololo, after a woman he captured and married – so easily were names acquired. In subsequent years he enjoyed great success as a raider in the north-west before moving north of the Zambezi to found a great kingdom in the 1830s, later known as Barotseland (after BaHarutshe?)

His young friend and ally, Moletsane, took another path, dreaming for a time of recreating the lost kingdom of Tau the Lion. He left his home on the Sand River in 1822, perhaps seeking respite from the drought, perhaps fearing an attack by MaNthatisi. His talents soon attracted followers from nearby communities. The fact that some were called Taung and some Lighoya should not be taken to mean they were separate peoples. The so-called Lighoya were Taung, who had previously taken the name of one of their admired chiefs.[101] Through intermarriage, the various groups of the southern highveld were virtually a single community though they went under the assorted totemic names of Tau, Kwena and Fokeng. In Moletsane they found an able champion at exactly the moment they needed one. Oral traditions relate that Moletsane's first plan was to lead his followers to the country of the Hurutshe, and there to offer their services to the Hurutshe chiefs – a reasonable strategy in a time of drought. When hostility rather than hospitality greeted him, Moletsane fought back with some success, for he wrote himself a praise poem to commemorate his capture of Hurutshe flocks.[102] Next he turned south to attack various Rolong chiefs, despite the fact that they were close relatives of his own people.

News of his fame reached halfway round the globe to the headquarters of the Wesleyan Methodist Missionary Society, when, in July 1824, he attacked the Rolong chief, Sefunela, who had recently been persuaded by missionaries to locate his people at Makwassie near the middle Vaal. Moletsane looted the house of the absent missionaries, in the course of which they found a quantity of gunpowder. An attempt to roast it inflicted severe injuries on several of his men.[103] Such were the times, that Sefunela sought out Barends' Bergenaar gunmen to help him retrieve his position.[104] Moletsane now found his own Kora ally, Moakabi. The balance of power in the region first swung this way then that, until late in 1825, Moletsane was able to return to his own homeland. He still cherished dreams of a wider empire, but for the moment it was time to plant. The drought had broken the year before.

Summing up so far

Readers trying to make sense of the swirling mass of names and places mentioned in this chapter will most likely have struggled to master material that has confused even the most experienced scholars. But if we once again try to soar above the fray with the far-seeing gaze of the eagle, several features stand out. Three short years had joined the destinies of peoples who had previously known little about each other. In the coastal lowlands from Delagoa Bay to Inhambane, new prospects for the export of slaves had drawn the attention of Zwide's old generals, Soshangane and Zwangendaba, as well as the independent adventurer Nxaba. On the highveld, by 1825, the names of Shaka, Sobhuza and Matiwane were known everywhere. In the southern and western districts, as new worlds of victims opened up for Griqua and Kora raiders, new leaders arose to challenge them. MaNthatisi and her son, Sekonyela, had shown themselves to be more than a match for the forces of Matiwane and Mpangazitha. Evidently their fighting methods compared favourably with those of the lowland Nguni. Moshweshwe had not just survived but prospered following his move from Butha Buthe to Thaba Bosiu.

The combination of localized drought and conflict caused large numbers of people to desert the upper Vaal and its tributaries. Their desperate search for food and grazing land in 1823 led them on a grotesque and deadly eight-month odyssey through the territory of north-western and southern Tswana communities. Though many of the survivors returned to reoccupy their old homelands in 1824, their passage had left lasting scars. Rolong communities at the sources of the Molopo system fractured into several fragments, each pursuing its own frantic search for security. Some had already begun to gather round English Methodist missionaries. Other victims of the crisis of 1822–3 succeeded in acquiring their own hetero-geneous body of fighting men, families and captives. Sebetwane managed to succeed where Hurutshe, Rolong and Bergenaar chiefs had all failed, inflicting a mortal defeat on Makaba of the Ngwaketse. Moletsane, calling himself by the historically potent name of MoTaung (the 'lion man'), em-barked on an ambitious attempt to restore the glory of that title. In days gone by, after a crisis such as the drought of 1822–3, chiefless men, women and orphans would have attached themselves to the victors, gradually merg-ing their identities and their fortunes with the successful lineages. The same phenomenon can be observed in this crisis. Soshangane, Sekonyela, Shaka, Moshweshwe, Moletsane, Sebetwane and many others demonstrated the peculiar genius of the lineage system and chieftainship for bringing different kinds of people together. However, many thousands of other people were not absorbed in this way. Instead they found themselves directed to the British Zone across the Orange – some having been forcibly seized by Griqua/Kora dealers in the illicit slave trade, others having discovered their own independent routes to wage labour on Boer farms.

A revolution in communications among peoples stretching all the way from Delagoa Bay to the Caledon Valley, and from the Caledon to the British Zone, placed new demands on chiefs, even as it opened opportun-ities for them. Clearly the winners would need guns and horses.[105] The problem was acquiring them. The winners would also have to learn new languages, manners and diplomatic protocols. Moletsane, who for a time, at least, numbered himself among the winners, did as well as any:

[He] adroitly assumes the dress, speech, tone, and manners of the tribes around him, as the chameleon is supposed to take the colour of the objects which are near it. Does he go to see the Barolongs [Rolong], he puts on, like them, a long and well fitted cloak of jackal skins, gaily anoints his body with yellow clay, and speaks serolong with a tone rather loud, it is true, but liked by those who know that dialect. With the Basutos, on the contrary, Molitsane [sic] appears in a costume more modest than the first, and not so well fitted, and he speaks sesuto.

He visits the Griquas in leathern or moleskin trousers, a vest of the same, a striped shirt, and with wretched shoes of the country on his feet, his head covered with a stuff hat, very much slouched; he arrives amongst them on horseback, a gun on his shoulder, and followed by a young *agter ruiter*, their kind of groom . . . he tries their dutch brogue. . . . For all this there is nothing to hinder Molitsane going to Entekoa (if he ever go there) accoutred in true lighoya fashion [i.e., in the fashion of his forefathers], that is to say, his loins covered with a jackal skin, a gnu skin thrown over his shoulders, sandals on his feet, carrying in his left hand, besides his little square shield, a javelin or two, and to complete the whole a good club in his right hand.[106]

Notes

1 Historical data on eclipses visible in southern Africa supplied by the website of the South African Astronomical Observatory, www.saao.ac.za. For the historically minded, total solar eclipses that have crossed continental southern Africa south of latitude −20 degrees in recent centuries have been:

1731 Jan. 08	1755 Sep. 06	1811 Mar. 24	1874 Apr. 16
1746 Sep. 15	1786 Jul. 25	1820 Mar. 14	1940 Oct. 01

The premonition is documented by T. Arbousset and F. Daumas, *Narrative of an Exploratory Tour to the North-East of the Colony of the Cape of Good Hope*, translated from French by J. C. Brown (first published 1846; reprinted Cape Town, 1968), p. 294.

2 George Cory, *The Rise of South Africa*, 5 vols (first published 1910–30; reprinted Cape Town, 1965), II, pp. 160–1.

3 Martin Legassick, 'The Griqua, the Sotho-Tswana and the Missionaries, 1780–1840' (PhD thesis, UCLA, 1969), pp. 276–7.

4 Julian Cobbing, 'The Mfecane as Alibi: Thoughts on Dithakong and Mbolompo', *Journal of African History* 29 (1988), p. 499; Elizabeth Eldredge, 'Migration, Conflict and Leadership in Early 19th Century South Africa. The Case of Matiwane' (seminar paper, Dept of History, University of Natal, Durban, 3 August 1994), pp. 30, 36.

5 John Wright, 'The Dynamics of Power and Conflict in the Thukela-Mzimkhulu Region in the late 18th and early 19th Centuries: A Critical

Reconstruction' (PhD thesis, University of the Witwatersrand, 1989), pp. 283–4; Charles Ballard, 'Drought and Economic Distress: South Africa in the 1800s', *Journal of Interdisciplinary History* 17 (1986), pp. 359–78; *JSA*, I, p. 201, testimony of Jantshi da Nongila.

6   Malyn Newitt, *A History of Mozambique* (London, 1995), pp. 252–7; David Hedges, 'Trade and Politics in Southern Mozambique and Zululand in the Eighteenth and Early Nineteenth Centuries' (PhD thesis, University of London, 1978), p. 27.

7   Monica Cole, *South Africa* (London, 1961), p. 58.

8   Hedges, 'Trade and Politics', p. 32; William F. Lye and Colin Murray, *Transformations on the Highveld: The Tswana and Southern Sotho* (Cape Town, 1980), p. 24.

9   In the 1830s lion, giraffe, zebra and buffalo could be found on the Vaal plains, when they had long since disappeared from the Caledon Valley; Arbousset and Daumas, *Narrative*, p. 218.

10   Legassick, 'The Griqua', pp. 291–6.

11   Carolyn Hamilton, 'Ideology, Oral Traditions and the Struggle for Power in the Early Zulu Kingdom' (MA thesis, University of the Witwatersrand, 1985), p. 5.

12   D. Fred. Ellenberger, *History of the Basuto, Ancient and Modern* (London, 1912), p. 42. In the absence of documentation, it is difficult to calculate the magnitude of this famine. Newitt, *History of Mozambique*, p. 254, extends its scope to cover the period 1794–1802.

13   Newitt, *History of Mozambique*, p. 257, advances a plausible scenario leading to increased conflict, but this in itself does not explain what he regards as a new level of political consolidation.

14   Another problem is the one previously noted; there is no evidence proving the absence of previous large states.

15   Newitt, *History of Mozambique*, p. 255. The association between increased trade and fragmentation accompanied by violence is marked, as we have seen, in the western and northern districts, as well in the Xhosa homeland.

16   See, for example: Amartya Sen, *Poverty and Famines: An Essay on Entitlement and Deprivation* (London, 1981); Dawitt Wolde Georgis, *Red Tears: War, Famine and Revolution in Ethiopia* (London, 1984), pp. 121–81. P. E. Lovejoy and S. Baier, 'The Desert-side Economy of the Western Sudan', *International Journal of African Historical Studies*, 7 (1975), pp. 557–81; E. Shindo, 'Hunger and Weapons: The Entropy of Militarization', *Review of African Political Economy* 33 (1985), pp. 6–22; Naomi Chazan and Tim Shaw, 'The Political Economy of Food in Africa', in Chazan and Shaw (eds), *Coping with Africa's Food Crisis* (London, 1988), pp. 1–21.

17   Credit for asking the critical questions about the interplay of these factors belongs entirely to Julian Cobbing, who, in a series of published and unpublished papers, uncovered fundamental flaws in the theoretical model of the '*mfecane*' which held the rise of the Zulu kingdom responsible for setting in train all the violence in south-eastern Africa from 1820 to 1833. The force of his critique led Carolyn Hamilton to convene a major conference on the subject in Johannesburg, 1991.

18   Patrick Harries, cited in Wright, 'Dynamics of Power', pp. 191–2.

19   John Omer-Cooper, *The Zulu Aftermath* (London, 1966), p. 57.

20   Capt. W. F. W. Owen, *Narrative of Voyages to Explore the Shores of Africa, Arabia and Madagascar*, 2 vols (London, 1833), I, pp. 93–4.

21   Ibid., I, pp. 448–50, 509. A. T. Bryant, *Olden Times in Zululand and Natal* (first published 1929; reprinted Cape Town, 1965), p. 459, unable to face this blatant contradiction of his narrative of Zulu supremacy and Ndwandwe flight, commented that the figure of 5000 should 'wisely be halved, if not quartered'.

22   Newitt, *History of Mozambique*, p. 244.

23   Wright, 'Dynamics of Power', p. 199.

24   C. Montez, 'As Invasoes dos Mangunis e dos Machanganas', *Mocambique* 9–10 (1937), pp. 25–55, cited in Omer-Cooper, *Zulu Aftermath*, p. 57n.

25   Hedges, 'Trade and Politics', p. 161.

26   This could be done by clearing, burning, hunting out wild game and other measures. See Hedges, 'Trade and Politics', pp. 48–9, 52.

27   Newitt, *History of Mozambique*, pp. 261–2; Bryant, *Olden Times*, pp. 161, 452; Wright, 'Dynamics of Power', pp. 188–9.

28   *Records of Natal*, I, pp. 14–15, G. M. Theal, *Records of South-Eastern Africa*, 9 vols (first published 1903; reprinted Cape Town, 1964), IX, pp. 23–4, 71–4.

29   Statement by John Cane, October 1828 in *Records of Natal*, II, pp. 17–18.

30   Newitt, *History of Mozambique*, pp. 291–2.

31   As happened, for example, in February 2000.

32   Bryant, *Olden Times*, p. 454, guesses 1826–7. Omer-Cooper, *Zulu Aftermath*, p. 64 skips from 1822 to 1831 without specifying what happened at dates in between. Newitt, *History of Mozambique*, p. 261, guesses that Zwangendaba left Soshangane 'sometime in the early 1820s to invade the Zimbabwe plateau'.

33   Hedges, 'Trade and Politics', p. 174.

34   Bryant, *Olden Times*, pp. 279–80.

35 *JSA*, II, p. 59, testimony of Madikane.

36 Ibid., II, p. 230. It is said that Shaka seized the cattle.

37 Newitt, *History of Mozambique*, p. 258.

38 Ibid.

39 A priceless example of A. T. Byrant's tendency to attribute everyone's movements to war for its own sake is his account of Nxaba, who, he says, lost a battle to Zwangendaba, after which: 'swerving abruptly round to the west, came into violent collision, about Pediland, with Mzilikazi and ricochetted again sharply off to the north-east, into Portuguese territory. Whether Nxaba or Zwangendaba arrived first in those northern parts is not clear. In any case, Nxaba hacked his way through the mass of intervening Tongas, and at last (1824–25), crossing the Sabi river, pitched his camp in the Busi region'; *Olden Times*, p. 461.

40 Julian Cobbing's important unpublished paper, 'Grasping the Nettle: The Slave Trade and the Early Zulu', presented at Workshop on Natal and Zululand in the Colonial and Precolonial Periods, University of Natal, Pietermaritzburg, September 1990, has been criticized for exaggerating the extent of the pre-1820 slave trade at Delagoa Bay. However, no one as yet has disputed his extensive evidence for the effects of the trade on the coast *after* that date.

41 Newitt, *History of Mozambique*, pp. 291–2.

42 Theal, *Records of South-Eastern Africa*, IX, p. 33.

43 Sean Hanretta, 'Women, Marginality and the Zulu State: Women's Institutions and Power in the Early Nineteenth Century', *Journal of African History* 39 (1998), pp. 397–8.

44 Graham Mackeurtan, *The Cradle Days of Natal (1497–1845)* (London, 1930), p. 149. The men in gowns were also remembered in Pedi oral traditions. See H. O. Mönnig, *The Pedi* (Pretoria, 1967), p. 19.

45 See, for example, Theal, *Records of South-Eastern Africa*, IX, p. 41, and Newitt, *History of Mozambique*, pp. 292–3.

46 Bryant, *Olden Times*, pp. 473–4, 593. These were by no means insignificant chiefs. One was Soveli, legitimate heir of Dingiswayo; the other was Sikhunyana, son of Zwide.

47 Arbousset and Daumas, *Narrative*, p. 165.

48 Wright, 'Dynamics of Power', pp. 191–2.

49 Bryant provides the classic statement in *Olden Times*, pp. 209–12, which not only identifies Zwidi with the 'Ngoni' who clashed with the Pedi some time in the early 1820s, but also appears to confuse the so-called Transvaal Ndebele with the Ndwandwe.

50 Wright, 'Dynamics of Power', pp. 186, 338–40, citing, among other sources, traditions collected by the eminent historian Philip Bonner.

51 *Natal Papers*, I, p. 21, quoting Francis Farewell who had spoken to Shaka:

> the only powerful enemy he has now to contend with is Esconyana, [Sikhunyana] whose territories lie N. W. of the Mapoota; he has gathered all his forces, with an intention of destroying Chaka. Several attempts have been made, but have always been repulsed.

52 Hedges, 'Trade and Politics', p. 26.

53 Lye and Murray, *Transformations*, p, 31.

54 Legassick, 'The Griqua', p. 326.

55 J. M. Orpen, *History of the Basutos of South Africa* (Cape Town, 1857), p. 6.

56 G. M. Theal, ed., *Basutoland Records*, Vol. I (first published 1883; reprinted Cape Town, 1964) p. 517.

57 Arbousset and Daumas, *Narrative*, p. 54.

58 Ellenberger, *History of the Basuto*, p. 39.

59 No historian has been brave enough to draw even a hypothetical map of the route taken.

60 MaNthatisi would have been familiar with the valley because of the longstanding trade her people had conducted there. Mpangazitha would almost certainly have known that groups of Hlubi had established themselves in the valley; see Ellenberger, *History of the Basuto*, p. 128.

61 N. J. Van Warmelo, ed., *History of Matiwane and the Amangwane Tribe, as told by Msebenzi to his kinsman Albert Hlongwane* (Pretoria, 1938), p. 80.

62 Wright, 'Dynamics of Power', p. 99. Eldredge, 'Migration, Conflict and Leadership', p. 11, dates Matiwane's advent in the Caledon at 1821; for reasons already made clear, I believe this is far too early.

63 Ellenberger, *History of the Basuto*, p. 128.

64 Matiwane's father, Masumpa, had been a highveld raider of the Fokeng, long before the rise of Shaka; Van Warmelo, ed., *History of Matiwane*, pp. 10–12.

65 Ellenberger, *History of the Basuto*, pp. 139–40.

66 Ibid., pp. 124–7; Lye and Murray, *Transformations*, p. 31.

67 Orpen, *History of the Basutus*, p. 6; David P. Ambrose, 'The Basotho Settlement at Griquatown, 1824–41', *Lesotho Notes & Records* 10 (1973–4), pp. 60–4; Statement of Moshweshwe, 15 May 1845 in Theal, ed., *Basutoland Records*, p. 82.

68 Ellenberger, *History of the Basuto*, p. 110.

69 Van Warmelo, ed., *History of Matiwane*, p. 26.

70 Ellenberger, *History of the Basuto*, pp. 149–50; William Lye, ed., *Andrew Smith's Journal of his Expedition into the Interior of South Africa, 1834–36* (Cape Town, 1975), pp. 89–90.

71 Lye and Murray, *Transformations*, p. 32. The decisive battle was fought near Lishuane at a site which for a long time was marked on maps as 'Mpangazitha'; see T. M. O'C. Maggs, *Iron Age Communities of the Southern Highveld* (Pietermaritzburg, 1976), p. 227. Elizabeth Eldredge, in 'Migration, Conflict and Leadership', p. 27, makes the astute observation that mortality in the battle itself was surprisingly small aside from the death of the chief.

72 James Backhouse met him in 1839; Theal, ed., *Basutoland Records*, p. 32; Arbousset and Daumas, *Narrative*, p. 298.

73 The word Fingo originally designated refugees, whatever their origin. It should never be taken as synonymous with either the Hlubi in particular or northern Nguni people in general. See: Alan C. Webster, 'Land Expropriation and Labour Extraction under Cape Colonial Rule: The War of 1835 and the "Emancipation of the Fingo" ' (MA thesis, Rhodes University, 1991), pp. 125–8; John Ayliff and Joseph Whiteside, *History of the Abambo, Generally Known as Fingos* (Butterworth, 1912), p. 15; Cowper Rose, *Four Years in Southern Africa* (London, 1829), p. 192.

74 Ellenberger, *History of the Basuto*, p. 151.

75 Ibid., p. 153.

76 Ibid., p. 170; Eldredge, 'Migration, Conflict and Leadership', p. 32; Van Warmelo, ed., *History of Matiwane*, p. 18.

77 James Backhouse, quoted in Theal, *Basutoland Records*, p. 24.

78 Arbousset and Daumas, *Narrative*, pp. 293–4.

79 Ambrose, 'The Basotho Settlement at Griquatown', pp. 63–4.

80 Robert Ross, *Adam Kok's Griquas: A Study in the Development of Stratification in History* (Cambridge, 1976), p. 20.

81 John Philip in 1825, quoted in Legassick, 'The Griqua', p. 358.

82 Arbousset and Daumas, *Narrative*, p. 310.

83 Ibid., p. 218; William Cornwallis Harris, *The Wild Sports of Southern Africa* (first published 1837; fifth ed. of 1852 reprinted Cape Town, 1963), p. 114.

84 Margaret Kinsman, ' "Hungry Wolves": The Impact of Violence on Rolong Life, 1823–1836', in Carolyn Hamilton, ed., *The Mfecane Aftermath: Reconstruction Debates in Southern African History* (Johannesburg, 1995), p. 367, identifies 'Matabele' as Matiwane's Ngwane, but the label is too vague to be so confidently pinned on a single suspect in the line-up.

85   George Thompson, *Travels and Adventures in Southern Africa*, ed. V. S. Forbes, 2 vols (first published 1827; edited and republished Cape Town, 1967), I, p. 79; see another garbled account in the same book on pp. 80–1. Robert Moffat, *Missionary Labours* (London, 1842), p. 340.

86   Margaret Kinsman in 'Hungry Wolves', pp. 365–7, makes a stab at mapping the movements of the 'refugee hordes'. See also Thompson, *Travels*, I, pp. 80–1.

87   Thompson, *Travels*, I, p. 83.

88   Ibid., I, pp. 115–16.

89   Julian Cobbing calls attention to difficulties with the reports in 'The Mfecane as Alibi: Thoughts on Dithakong and Mbolompo', *Journal of African History* 29 (1988), pp. 487–519. An alternative reading of the evidence is given by Elizabeth Eldredge, 'Sources of Conflict in Southern Africa *c*. 1800–1830', in Hamilton, ed., *Mfecane Aftermath*, pp. 141–50.

90   S. M. Molema, *Chief Moroka: His Times, his Country and his People* (Cape Town, n.d.), p. 16.

91   Thompson, *Travels and Adventures*, I, p. 147.

92   Ibid., p. 149.

93   Cope, ed., *Journals of the Rev. T. L. Hodgson*, p. 182; Eldredge, 'Sources of Conflict', p. 141; Kinsman, 'Hungry Wolves', p. 368; Marion How, 'An Alibi for Mantatisi', *African Studies* 13 (1954), p. 68.

94   Robert Moffat as reported in the *Commercial Advertiser* of 7 Jan. 1824, printed in G. M. Theal, *Records of the Cape Colony* (Cape Town, 1903), XVI, pp. 497–505.

95   Cope, ed., *Journals of the Rev. T. L. Hodgson*, pp. 189–90.

96   Theal, *Basutoland Records*, p. 15.

97   Cope, ed., *Journals of the Rev. T. L. Hodgson*, pp. 254 ff.

98   Ellenberger, *History of the Basuto*, p. 306. Travellers to Aldam on the Sand River can still view the remains of stone huts deserted at this time.

99   See, for example, ibid., pp. 140–1.

100 Lye and Murray, *Transformations*, p. 38. I am inclined to accept the proposition. Sebetwane told David Livingstone in 1854 that he had been at Dithakong. Moletsane's statement of his land claims in the Caledon Valley made in 1852 does not mention Dithakong, but as he was attempting to portray himself as a wronged man, it would have been natural for him to conceal it; statement of Moletsane, Jan. 1852, in Theal, ed., *Basutoland Records*, pp. 517–19.

101 Maggs, *Iron Age Communities*, p. 4.

102 Ellenberger, *History of the Basuto*, p. 165.

103 Lye and Murray, *Transformations*, p. 39; Legassick, 'The Griqua', p. 337.

104 Legassick, 'The Griqua, the Sotho-Tswana and the Missionaries', p. 339.

105 Ibid., p. 367.

106 Arbousset and Daumas, *Narrative*, p. 212.

CHAPTER SIX

'Mantatees', 'Matabele' and 'Fetcani'

Identifying the 'Mantatee'

The events of the terrible year 1823 on the central highveld were poorly understood, even by those who lived through them. The accounts written down by people who heard the tales of survivors made an incredible mish-mash of names and dates. Here, for example, is missionary Robert Moffat's confused account of the people he called 'Mantatees':

> they are from . . . Hambona [land of the Mbo as written on eighteenth- and early nineteenth-century maps], from whence they were driven by two powerful chiefs, Cheeka [Shaka] and Matabele [? this could be a reference to any number of people], whose territories extend from Port Natal to the confines of Delagoa Bay . . . These chiefs . . . [are] able to bring into the field nearly 100,000 fighting men. The Mantatees, on their first eruption, were joined by the Mapootas, a tribe on the sources of the river of the same name [the Maputo; now called the Phongolo]; and, after destroying the Lahogas [Lighoyas, or Taung of the Sand River region], were joined by a tribe of the Macqueans [BaKwena, a totemic name which could have been claimed by many people, including Sebetwane's and Moshweshwe's people], and subsequently, . . . by many of the various conquered nations, who flocked to the same roving standard; carrying devastation, with an overwhelming hand, through a comparatively civilized part of South Africa [Hurutshe and Rolong country]. They were first repulsed by the wary king of the Wankets [Ngwaketse], who fell upon them when their forces were divided, and subsequently by the Bechuanas [the Tlhaping of Kuruman and Dithakong] and Griquas united. . . . Since their repulse at Lattakoo, they have proceeded in an East and S.E. direction, in two divisions, one of which has since met with a second defeat

from the forces of Makabba [Makaba], the king of the Wankets. . . . Their number at a reasonable calculation, exceeds 100,000, which is far greater than was at first supposed. . . . It also appears, in confirmation of a former statement, that there are among them individuals of different colours, from the perfectly white to the deepest dye.[1]

As a result of such muddled accounts, Sotho-speaking people who went looking for work south of the Orange found themselves called 'Mantatees' by everyone, no matter where they came from.[2] They also discovered that Boers and British farmers welcomed them as workers, paying no attention to the laws aimed at prohibiting people from entering the British Zone. (Eventually, in 1828, the British government passed Ordinance 49 which repealed the old laws and allowed people to work in their zone so long as they carried a special 'pass'.)[3] Working for wages – no matter how low – enabled people to learn about horses, guns, money, and the peculiar customs of the Boer farm. As soon as they were able, most returned to their homelands, converting their earnings into cattle (and, occasionally, guns).

Shaka and the Port Natal traders

The learning process worked both ways. Stories of powerful kingdoms and large armies fired the imaginations of people in the British Zone, causing some to seek greener pastures and profits by moving to the heartland. One group headed straight up the coast by sea, aiming to contact King Shaka and gain permission to trade with people in his sphere of influence. First to arrive was a man calling himself Jacob (sometimes John Jacob; perhaps originally Jacot Msimbiti),[4] who had much experience in dealing with Englishmen, for he had grown up among Ngqika's Xhosa people near the British Zone. The British had sentenced him to imprisonment on Robben Island. When the British naval officer W. F. Owen sought an interpreter to help him communicate with people on the lower East African coast, he arranged for Jacob to be released. In 1823 Jacob accompanied two other merchant captains, Francis Farewell and James King, on a reconnaissance of the coast south of St Lucia Bay. When a crewman assaulted him, Jacob left the ship and made his way to Shaka's capital. Soon his command of English and knowledge of affairs along the coast earned him a high position at court. He was on hand to translate when Francis Farewell arrived the following year with a party of British and Khoi men. Shaka allowed the party to settle at the bay they called Port Natal (present-day Durban). Although the king said he would like to send two of his chiefs to Cape Town to learn

148

more about the British and their ways, prospects for trade appeared so poor at that time that only Farewell was left at the end of a few months.[5] The next year Farewell's old associate, James King, turned up with his own party of traders on a small trading vessel – which they promptly managed to wreck at the entrance to the bay.[6]

For the next two and a half years, while a single carpenter struggled to build a replacement boat, the traders depended on the kindness of Shaka and the arrival of passing ships to ply their business. This certainly included trade in ivory, and may very possibly have included clandestine trade in slaves as well. Shaka made presents of cattle to the adventurers, which enabled them to acquire local followings and wives. Within a short time they were acting – and dressing – as though they were minor chiefs.[7] On his part, Shaka planned to enlist them as mercenary gunmen in an attempt to crush his still powerful rival, the Ndwandwe, now under Zwide's son, Sikhunyana.

Mutual misunderstandings plagued their relations from the start. The traders had no knowledge of how properly to *khonza*, or pledge loyalty to a chief. They knew neither their rights nor their responsibilities. They bluffed and blustered their way through their encounters with royalty, pretending that they were great men in their own country. As one of them recalled later, the basic technique was to carry yourself proudly, as though you yourself were a great chief. You did not ask for things; you commanded that they be brought to you. You addressed yourself only to chiefs, and maintained the pretence that whatever you did, you did on the express orders of your own faraway great chief.[8] Nothing short of sending his own messengers to Cape Town would have enabled Shaka to expose the charade. In the meantime, he pumped them for information about the technology, military might and customs of England. In previous years the only source of information about these matters had come from shipwreck survivors. In Shaka's grandfather's time a ship foundered on the coast but none of the survivors spoke a language they could understand. A local chief had acquired a horse and learned to ride it, though no one knew what kind of animal it was.[9] Now Shaka gained at least a second-hand knowledge of British fighting techniques.

One of the traders explained that in a pitched battle, soldiers would form themselves into a square three ranks deep, from which they would fire on the enemy.[10] Seeing how long it took to reload one of the muzzle-loading rifles, some of Shaka's commanders reasoned that by sending a large number of men to charge in a body, they might overcome even this defensive formation (an experiment not destined to be tried until the battle of Ulundi in 1879). Old men recalled in later years how Shaka used to test the efficiency of firearms by ordering the traders to fire at cattle over various distances.

'He was fond of seeing the power of a gun, and his intention was to send a regiment of men to England who there would scatter in all directions in order to ascertain exactly how guns were made, and then return to construct some in Zululand.'[11] Only their guns enabled the traders to escape execution after two of their number ambushed and raped the wife of an important chief. Shaka confronted them with the evidence. According to the law, the whole group must pay with their lives for the crimes committed by any of them. (This the traders would have understood because the same principle was applied by military commanders in the British Zone: 'The crimes were individual, but the punishment was general: the duty of the Commando was to destroy, to burn the habitations, and to seize the cattle; and they did their duty.'[12]) Nonetheless, Shaka eventually issued an extraordinary pardon, on condition that ten of their riflemen accompany an expedition against the chief of the Bheje branch of the Khumalo lineage.[13]

For trade itself, Shaka consistently displayed a soldierly contempt. 'His whole soul was engrossed by war, and he conceived that anything like commerce would enervate his people and unfit them for their military duties.' His eagerness 'for elephant-hunting, and to collect ivory. . . . arose, not for the purposes of commerce, but that he might appropriate it in presents and occasionally exchange it for something ornamental which the Europeans might possess.'[14] The traders, on the other hand, worshipped ivory. Having been lied to on many occasions, Shaka eventually exploded, saying, 'What must I do with you white people! I think I must kill you for you speak falsely even though you swear by God.' These greedy traders, he continued, would say 'anything for the sake of elephants' teeth'.

Shaka seems to have been oblivious to the real object of their other requests that he should put his name to documents granting them the right to land stretching inland from the coast. Land for him was a place to plant crops and graze cattle. Unlike cattle, land had no exchange value. It could not be used to buy cattle, seal marriages or reward *amabutho* for successful campaigns. It cost nothing for Shaka to put his mark on the documents King and Farewell prepared, granting them 'ownership' of large tracts of country in the Port Natal region. Only since about 1822 had he even begun to send fighting forces into that territory. The traders, in contrast, looked on these 'grants' as commodities they might one day cash in should the territory be annexed to the British Zone. Though the British government had told them in 1824 that he could '*not sanction the acquisition of any territorial possession*', he added the words 'without a full communication being made to him of the circumstances' under which land might be offered.[15] In their letters to people in Grahamstown and Cape Town, the men constantly reiterated that Shaka had given them the land. People living in districts where written titles to land could be converted into money expressed surprise

that Shaka could not 'foresee that the admission of a few mercantile adventurers may perhaps lead to the subjugation of his kingdom and posterity'.[16]
Conquest through acquisition of land titles was always on their minds.

For his part, Shaka gained two great things from the troublesome traders
– one visible to the king and the other invisible. The visible reward was
the possibly decisive effect of their rifle fire in the final confrontation with
his oldest enemy, the Ndwandwe, who were lately involved in a succession
crisis. In the spring of 1826, his mixed force of Europeans and *amabutho*
marched north of the Phongolo River and decisively defeated the opposing forces within the space of about an hour and a half. Though King
Sikhunyana himself and a few followers escaped, the grand old names of
Ndwandwe and Mbo would never again send a shudder of fear through the
region.[17] Most of what remained of Sikhunyana's people appear either to
have *khonza*'d Shaka or joined their destinies to Sobhuza's growing power
in the north. A significant number also seem to have joined Soshangane
and Zwangendaba in the Mozambique lowlands.[18]

The invisible reward Shaka reaped from the hospitality he extended to
the traders was the body of written accounts they compiled, accounts which
made his name far more familiar to the world at large than any other king
of the heartland. While Soshangane and Zwangendaba marched back and
forth, subduing vast territories in southern Mozambique, Shaka eclipsed
their fame without moving far from his headquarters in the lower Thukela
River region. The traders, who had a vested interest in representing him as
the greatest conqueror in all the land, served as his propaganda machine,
feeding a steady stream of misleading accounts into the historical record.
For example, following the official Zulu line, one of them dutifully wrote
that Sikhunyana 'had, in his time, been an inhuman tyrant, and had now
received the punishment due him'.[19] Ironically, in the long run the house of
Shaka gained more from the ill-informed scratchings of their pens than any
of them gained from their bogus land grants – which no one ever paid a
cent for.

When at last, in 1828, the carpenter had completed a small ship to take
an embassy consisting of James King, the interpreter, Jacob, and two of
Shaka's trusted chiefs to the British government at Port Elizabeth, it achieved
nothing. The chiefs felt they had been regarded as spies rather than diplo-
mats. Officials refused to treat Jacob as anything other than a disreputable
ex-convict, while King was recognized for what he was: a man trying to
manipulate the embassy in order to achieve his own purpose of having
his land titles recognized. By September of the same year, King was dead
and buried. Some said the cause was dysentery; others said it was cirrhosis
of the liver brought on by heavy drinking.[20] Ignorant to the last of James
King's insignificant status in life, Shaka shed tears at the news of his death.

It would, he said, be a source of great satisfaction to him that 'a white man, and a chief too, lived a long time in my country without molestation from myself or from my people, and that he died a natural death'.

First reports of the Fetcani

Shaka's ambassadors received a less than enthusiastic welcome at Port Elizabeth, primarily because British officials had come to regard Shaka, mistakenly, as the aggressive force who had pushed waves of 'refugees' into their territory. Beginning with Moffat's account of the 'Mantatee' in 1823, the idea that Shaka was behind all the disturbances on the highveld had gained credence among the military men charged with the hopeless task of preventing people from infiltrating the eastern borders of the British Zone. The first reports of strange people making cattle-raids on the Thembu south of the Orange River may have begun to filter through in the latter part of 1822.[21] Soon, Thembu chiefs were gripped by general fear of people they called 'Ficani' or 'Fetcani'. According to the initial reports gathered in May 1825 these Fetcani raiders 'had been driven from their own land by a people of yellow complexion with black beards and long hair' who were 'armed with swords'. The informants added that 'the Ficani were accompanied by their women and children', some 'of their chiefs possess[ed] horses; however they were "not cannibals"'.[22] In other words, the rumour mills of the highveld had fashioned the 'Fetcani' in the same way that the 'Mantatees' had been fashioned – from bits and pieces of unrelated information from sources as widely separated as the slave-raiding fields of Mozambique and the Bergenaar mounted gunmen of the west. According to one Thembu chief then living on the upper Kei River, the 'Fetcani' raids had commenced 'about two years' earlier.

Knowing the distress suffered by people on the highveld during the drought and conflict of 1821–3 (see Chapter 5) makes it is easy to guess the identity of the raiders. They were people of diverse origins – Hlubi, Sotho, Ngwane, Tlokwa, Kwena, Taung and others – seeking cattle to replace those they had lost in the bad years. The Thembu (Xhosa-speaking people who occupied the middle plateaux beyond the mountains, roughly between the Kei and Mtata Rivers) were the closest available source of replacement cattle for the chiefs who had gathered their people together in the Caledon Valley. They lived in one of the most drought-proof regions of southern Africa; on average the rains failed there only about one year out of every ten.[23] Surviving documents indicate that all the important chiefs of the Caledon tried their luck at raiding into Thembu territory.

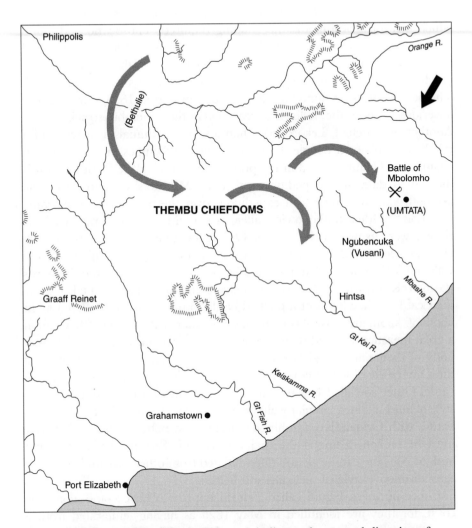

Map 14   Fetcani raids, 1825–8. This map indicates the general direction of
so-called 'Fetcani' cattle-raids. The curved arrows suggest the movements
of people from the Caledon Valley under chiefs Matiwane, Makhetha,
Moshweshwe and Sekonyela. The straight arrow suggests the direction of people
coming down the coast who eventually became known as the Bhaca.

Before surveying the extent and effects of the raids, it is worth making the point that the growth of raiding south of the mountains was more a sign of success than distress. Famine-stricken, weak, hungry and disorganized people could not have undertaken the arduous journeys over difficult terrain which this form of long-distance raiding required. Those who had found water, pasturage and refuge in the Caledon Valley had largely recovered their strength. They sought cattle, not sustenance over the mountains.

Moorosi, one of Moshweshwe's staunch supporters and a man with Thembu relatives, mounted a highly successful raid in 1823, only to suffer a serious reverse the following year when the Thembu struck back.[24] Another Sotho chief, Lekoro, who had lost many animals as a result of a rebellion of his own people, tried to recoup his fortunes in an expedition against the Thembu – and in the process, lost his own life.[25] Although it is difficult to date their expeditions precisely, Moshweshwe and Sekonyela are both known to have sent expeditions over the mountains in the same direction.[26] Other Sotho owing allegiance to Makhetha's branch of the Kwena were likewise active raiders. One of them interviewed in 1826 read-ily acknowledged 'that they were Fetcani'. They had 'always inhabited' the Caledon Valley but 'of late they had been much harassed by the Bastaards [Griqua/Kora] who had repeatedly defeated them in battle and taken away their cattle'. They had lost a pitched battle to the gunmen in 1825 (fought about 30 kilometres east of present-day Wepener[27]). As a result, 'they had in a great measure deserted their former places of residence and . . . the great body of their nation had crossed within two months to the southward of the Orange river' with the intention of purchasing or, if necessary, raiding cattle. Other so-called Fetcani can likewise be identified as Sotho by their style of hut-building: 'circular walls of clay cased with stone'. Tales of pitched battles with Griqua/Kora gunmen feature in so many accounts that they must be reckoned among the major causes of 'Fetcani' raiding.[28] Hlubi and/or Ngwane can be clearly differentiated from other Fetcani because of their distinctive style of speaking and fighting.

Other northern Nguni called Fetcani appear to have come along the coast, for they are identified in May 1825 as having 'emigrated from a great distance northward' and 'unknown' to the Thembu until 'about two years ago'.

Their first assault was upon Vooserine [probably Ngubengcuka, also known as Vusani], a chief near the sea coast, who repulsed them. They then proceeded up the Kay [Kei] river and plundered Hinza [Hintsa], Jalasa [Jalousa] and T'Sambie's [Ndlambe's] people, till these chiefs, combining their forces gave them an overthrow. This compelled them to move further westward when they came upon the Tambookies [a British rendering of Thembu], whom they have completely made their prey. They have driven them from the country they had long occupied beyond the Key [sic] river, plundered them of their cattle and murdered all that fell into their hands. Chei-Chie [sic] has opposed himself three times to them. In the first engagement by taking them by surprise he was successful but in the last two he was so completely defeated that he now lost all heart and his people are so dispirited that they will not again face the invaders. Eight of his relatives, three of whom were his sons, and 240 men, besides women and children, have fallen in these engagements and the quantity of cattle taken is immense. As these people (Infucani) approach the Tambookies fly before them. They (the latter) are now in a country no way adequate to support them, living in wretched huts hastily thrown together of the rudest materials, not even weather-proof. Some have escaped to Jalonsa and Hinza and placed themselves under their protection. The favourite mode of attack of the Inficani (sometimes called Ficani) is by surprising the kraals at night, setting fire to the huts and suffering none to escape. They are extremely bold, always rushing on to close attack and are very swift. Many of them are among the Tambookies, having come a few at a time under the excuse that they were driven away from their own country.[29]

Although it seems that two quite different groups are confused with each other in this document, most likely this particular group of raiders was a heterogeneous group of people mainly from the Wushe and Zelemu lineages. If so, their arrival from the direction of KwaZulu-Natal at the height of the drought of 1823 would have been no surprise. They were neither 'on the run from Shaka' nor were they using the 'new fighting methods' of the Zulu – for they had no *amabutho*.[30] After their chief Madikane (or Madzikane) died in a battle with the Thembu in 1824, they consolidated themselves under his son Ncaphayi (N'Capai) in the Mount Frere region. By the 1830s they were commonly called the Bhaca.

Without descending into further, and very possibly confusing, detail, it will already be apparent that the terms 'Ficani', 'Fetcani' and 'Fetkanie' do not refer to a single ethnic or political group. The words were used generically to describe any group of people raiding the Thembu and Xhosa for about a decade after 1823. No precise meaning or derivation for the words can be guessed nearly two centuries after the event. One contemporary observer asserted that Fetcani was a 'Bushman', a word used to describe 'all wandering tribes who have no settled residence'.[31] Another account translates Fetcanie simply as 'commando'.[32] The words are therefore as vague as 'Matabele', and almost as useless for purposes of historical identification and analysis.

Two quite distinct routes brought the raiders into Thembu territory. One ran down the coast from KwaZulu-Natal. The other ran over the mountains from the Caledon Valley. A great many of the raiders from the Caledon were SeSotho speakers who complained that they themselves had been victimized by Kora/Griqua gunmen. Some of the raiders who spoke northern Nguni languages belonged to Madikane's 'Bhaca' grouping which had made its way along the coast; others were Hlubi and Ngwane from the Caledon. In March 1825 a combined force of Hintsa's Xhosa and Powana's Thembu ventured over the mountains to the north where they suffered a huge defeat at the hands of the 'Fetcani' near Hanglip (about 50 kilometres south of present-day Aliwal North).[33] Six of their great commanders and many soldiers fell in the battle. Who comprised the 'Fetcani' that day cannot be certainly known. Two years later Chief Powana said he had heard from the Fetcani themselves that 'Chaka is driving these people on', but their position indicated clearly that they had come from the Caledon Valley.[34] By 1825 a great deal of mixing between Hlubi, Ngwane, Tlokwa and Sotho had already occurred (see Chapter 5, p. 130), so it may well have been a combined force which won the day. By July 1827 documentary evidence attested to the existence of such forces. A young 'Fetcani' found in the Stormberg mountains related:

> I belong to a tribe on the other side of the Great (Orange) river. Our principal kraal (pointing North East) is distant five days journey from this. Where we cross the Orange river is about half way. Our people consist of two tribes formerly distinct, 'Masutu' [Zulu plural form = amaSutho] and 'Manguana' [amaNgwane]. Our great chiefs are Máhetá [Makhetha] and Máttuaná [Matiwane]. We are very numerous, fought battles with many tribes and beat them all but Chaka's (the Zulus). Chaka beat us some time ago and took our cattle. We heard that the Tambookies [Thembu] had cattle. We sent out Fetcanie [army or, as translated, commando], beat the Tambookies often and took their cattle. We heard of a great chief called Bussana [Vusani, also known as Ngubengcuka]. We are now going to attack him. Our Fetcanie consist of young men, no men having wives and no women accompany it. We purchase our wives and the young men can only get them by fighting and taking cattle to pay for them. We never saw white people, we never heard of them. We are not cannibals. Our property consists in cattle. Chaka took it from us and we will fight and take cattle wherever we can find them.[35]

Here is the clearest possible statement that Matiwane had formally allied himself to Makhetha, legitimate heir to Mohlomi's Sotho kingdom.[36] The reference to many triumphs over the Thembu suggests that the Sotho-Ngwane alliance had been in active operation for some time, perhaps as long ago as the Battle of Hanglip in 1825. The speaker's reference to having beaten everyone but the Zulu indicates that he himself was originally

Ngwane rather than Hlubi or Sotho. For some time thereafter 'Suthu' was treated as a synonym for Fetcani.

Faced with such danger, the Thembu and Xhosa chiefs did not spend much time examining their enemies' pedigree. Their first concern was to move their cattle and followers out of the line of fire. As always, they employed hyperbole to equate the loss of cattle to the loss of everything. After one battle, the defeated chiefs said simply, 'there are no more Thembu'.[37] Chief Galela, having learned in July 1827 that he had lost more than 300 cattle, resolved to take his remaining people and herds into the British Zone.[38] Chief Powana in early 1827 stated that he had been 'reduced to extreme poverty and a state of wretchedness'. A number of his people had deserted to the Xhosa chief Ngqika, and his only help lay in gathering his remaining herds and followers together in the British Zone.[39] By August 1827 virtually all the Thembu chiefs had deserted their homes and were sheltering near Fort Beaufort. Many other minor Xhosa chiefs had joined them, leaving huge areas free for the operation of the Sotho/ Ngwane raiders.

This created a major crisis for the regional British commander, Colonel Henry Somerset. In the first place, the refugees had gathered at the heart of the so-called 'Ceded Territory' which had been seized from Ngqika in 1819 (Chapter 3, p. 66). If they stayed, the intended buffer zone between Boers and the Xhosa would disappear. Furthermore, in simple justice, how could the Thembu be allowed to occupy land which was beyond doubt the ancestral territory of Ngqika's people? Yet when Ngqika proposed moving back into it, Colonel Somerset told him he must stay in 'his own country' and 'attend to its defence'.[40] Meanwhile, two of his principal chiefs and his own son, Maqoma, had seized this opportunity to reoccupy the 'Ceded Territory'.[41] Military patrols sent to locate the 'Fetcani' beyond the Stormberg mountains reported that the territory was 'thickly inhabited' by Boers. This posed a further complication. Though they were beyond the proclaimed boundary of the British Zone, they already suffered 'Fetcani' attacks, and might make a claim for further protection or attempt to repair their losses by attacking Boer farms.[42]

If the Thembu and Xhosa could have been instantly converted into farm workers, the crisis could have been converted into an opportunity, because, after the drought lifted in 1824, there had been continuing calls for labour from Boer and English farmers alike. However, these people came in family groups, armed, organized and clearly intent on maintaining their cultural integrity.[43] Farmers saw them as a threat because they outnumbered them. The favoured method of recruiting farm workers was still to employ individuals – whether captured slaves or 'voluntary' wage-labourers – assimilating them to the rightless, dependant culture of the extended household. Farmers in the British Zone feared people who came in armed groups; they maintained continuous pressure on the government to 'do something' about the 'wandering vagrants'. As one British officer wrote dryly, noting the huge numbers of recently arrived people, 'tho' we wanted servants, this, it must be allowed, is not the best mode of procuring a supply'.[44]

Pushing the Thembu and Ngqika's Xhosa out with military force would have been an act of criminal folly, for they had been recognized allies in the 1819 war against Nxele. Shooting 'refugees' would have raised protests among missionaries and humanitarians back in Britain. And what if the people fought back? The outcome was no foregone conclusion. The only way to move the Thembu and Xhosa out was to clear the land of the 'Fetcani menace'. A conventional commando was out of the question for the whereabouts of the 'enemy' and their herds was unknown. There was no convenient 'spoor' to follow. The headquarters of the opposition lay in what was, for them, unknown territory. One man hoping to 'visit the Ficani' in 1825, said he had been 'informed that a number of curious animals are to be found beyond the Orange river (amongst which the unicorn is said to be)'.[45] Trying to track down the Fetcani in the mountains north of Thembu country would be a wild goose chase. Sending regular cavalry or infantry into those mountains would pose impossible problems of supply. And, in the unlikely event that any Fetcani were found, the cavalry would be unable to charge on such terrain. They themselves might well stumble into an ambush.[46] Alarmed by the dangerous situation, the acting British Governor, Major-General Bourke, decided to make a personal inspection of Fort Beaufort in August 1827. Fortunately for him, by the time he arrived, word came that the 'Fetcani' had 'retreated' north of the Orange River. With the peril removed, he was able to take a tough line on the 'Ceded Territory', telling Ngqika, Powana and the other chiefs that their people must now return to their old lands – apart from those 'inclined to accept' positions of 'service with the colonists'.[47] When Ngqika protested that his country was already too small to pasture all his cattle, and asked for an extension of his border westward to the Kat River, Bourke snapped a peremptory, 'No!'[48]

Against the background of three years of worry that 'Fetcani' raiders 'driven on by Shaka' would push a mass of unwanted Xhosa chiefs into the British Zone, it is easy to imagine the consternation with which General Bourke and his officials greeted news calmly conveyed by James King of the 'Zulu Embassy' to Port Elizabeth. At the very time he left Port Natal, said King, Shaka had been preparing to attack the Mpondo chief Faku, whose capital lay only about a day's journey from King Hintsa's main residence![49] They may well have known King to have been the anonymous author of the account published in a Cape Town paper in July 1826, which proclaimed that when Shaka had succeeded in dealing with Sikhunyana of the Ndwandwe, 'he will not leave a living soul, nor rest until he reaches the white people; he will then be satisfied and enjoy himself with his wives'.[50] No wonder the embassy was treated with such suspicion. King had attempted to invoke the Zulu menace to strengthen his Natal land claim. It had exploded in his face. Too late – much too late – came the message from another disreputable Natal trader claiming (on the basis of no evidence whatsoever) it was not Shaka, but a chief named 'Omsilacosan' who 'drove the Fetcanie' on. The damage had been already been done. The British Government had decided Shaka was a menace, not a potential ally. They believed he had been goaded into the expedition south by the sordid band of adventurers trading at Port Natal.[51]

Mzilikazi and the realignment of politics on the highveld

Chief 'Omsilacosan' – properly spelled Mzilikazi – sprang onto the historical stage like a lion from ambush. He first appears in written records in March 1826, thanks to a conversation between an English missionary and the artful Taung chief Moletsane (Chapter 5, pp. 138–9). Moletsane said he had intended no harm against the missionaries when he attacked their recently established station in 1824. Moreover, he promised to make peace with the Rolong chief, Sefunela, provided that Sefunela would pledge never again to call upon the Bergenaar gunmen for help. Moletsane's overriding concern, however, was an advancing force of 'Matabele' whose language he could not understand, and who were said to be coming, as the 'Mantatees' had come, down the Vaal River.[52] How Mzilikazi got to this point in 1826 has long been a matter of controversy.

He came from the south-eastern lowlands. His father, Matshobane, was head of a Khumalo lineage whose homeland was sandwiched between the Ndwandwe and Zulu spheres of influence at the time Shaka came to power. Mzilikazi must have been a very young man when his father died and Zwide installed him as chief of his lineage. According to one story, Mzilikazi transferred his allegiance to Shaka at some point, and was appointed to command a regiment composed entirely of his own lineage. After one successful campaign, he determined to keep a portion of the cattle he had captured. Shaka replied by slaughtering many of his women at their homes, whereupon Mzilikazi collected a small following of perhaps two to three hundred men and moved swiftly away to the north-west.[53] This must have been some time after the great drought broke, for Mzilikazi later recounted

Map 15   The rise of Mzilikazi, 1825–30. During the period 1825–35, Mzilikazi and a few followers moved onto the highveld and established their dominance over a large territory. Many people welcomed him as a bringer of order and stability after the turmoil of the early 1820s. He organized a highly effective defence against Griqua and Kora raiders.

that he had avoided the 'Mantatee' on his route north and extended his protection over some defeated survivors of the 1823 battle of Dithakong whom he encountered on the highveld.[54] Realistically speaking, Mzilikazi would not have wanted to risk his cattle at any point along the Vaal system before the drought broke in 1824 and planting could be undertaken. His presence was certainly known there by March 1825, because, after Mpangazitha's defeat by Matiwane, his son Mehlomakhulu and a sizeable remnant of Hlubi forces made their way north and pledged their allegiance to Mzilikazi's rising star. These dates can be regarded as reasonably reliable, because, after about a year with Mzilikazi, Mehlomakhulu and his Hlubi stalwarts returned to the Caledon Valley and briefly renewed the contest with Matiwane.[55]

Whether Mzilikazi arrived on the highveld before 1825 is difficult to determine. The few surviving stories are hopelessly at odds with each other. None came from his own lips. It is worth pausing for a moment to dwell on the various accounts and the lessons they teach about the uncertainty of our knowledge of the history of these times. Some stories say that Mzilikazi pushed north and inflicted a huge defeat on the Pedi in about 1822. Although the Pedi have been only briefly mentioned so far in this history (Chapter 2, p. 29; Chapter 4, pp. 74, 99–100), they were an important people, based near the confluence of the Steelpoort and Olifants Rivers. Under their admired chief Thulare (from whose alternative name Moperi they took their name[56]) the Pedi had used their strategic position on the trade route linking the upper Limpopo regions and Delagoa Bay to exercise vast power. As late as 1822 they appear to have extended their domains to include various Kwena groups living in the Magaliesberg mountains.[57] Thulare's death in 1820 – attested to by the solar eclipse of 1820 – was followed by a terrible battle in 1822, in which most of the great king's sons perished.[58] Someone was clearly responsible for such a well-remembered disaster; but was it Mzilikazi? The Pedi would have used the words Ngoni or Matabele to describe their assailants. These, as we have seen, could be applied to a great many different groups.[59] Is it conceivable that Mzilikazi, who could have been no older than twenty-eight at the time, and whose armed following consisted of two or three hundred fighting men, could have inflicted such a defeat on the powerful Pedi? The Zulu chronicler A. T. Bryant guessed that Zwide's Ndwandwe were the culprits.[60] Others, noting that Zwide remained headquartered on the upper Phongolo River, have suggested that Nxaba or one of the other chiefs of the Ndwandwe Diaspora mounted the 1822 attack on the Pedi. After all, Nxaba's route north to the Zimbabwe plateau would have taken his army through Pedi territory. They would have presented an attractive target because their homeland lay in a relatively drought-proof zone.

Some historians who date Mzilikazi's departure from the Zululand region to 1823, say that he simply moved across the eastern Vaal river lands before settling on the Apies River in 1825.[61] Others imagine a much more exciting story in which Mzilikazi for a time followed the footsteps of Soshangane and Zwangendaba into lowland Mozambique. Having done battle with the slavers of that region, he was eventually driven back up onto the highveld and made his way to his Apies River camp.[62] Although this story is based on fragmentary information gathered by a French missionary who visited Mzilikazi in 1832 (but who could not speak his language), something to be said in its favour is that Mzilikazi is known to have kept in touch with other chiefs of the Ndwandwe Diaspora for decades, knowing their movements and counting them among his 'relations'.[63]

A deliberately insulting version of his history told at the Zulu court in 1832 said he was 'a petty chief that left Zindi [Zwide] and has raised himself into importance'.[64]

A much more detailed, though confusing story was told by Mzilikazi's chief councillor in 1835. He stated that Mzilikazi had been driven out of his own country after 'Ziete Kalanga' attacked him and killed his father.[65] After that Mzilikazi stayed with Shaka for only a short period (either 'one month' or 'a few months') before running away in the night. If the name is read as Zwidi kaLanga, and identified entirely with Zwidi, Mzilikazi's departure from the Zulu region would have to have taken place before Zwide's death in 1824 or early 1825.

Another account was collected in 1836 from Nguni and Pedi informants met by French missionaries in the southern highveld.[66] In this version, Mzilikazi moved from his original homeland, not because of Shaka, but because he had been attacked and plundered by a chief called 'Sekognane' or 'Sekongnana'. This name is also close enough to the name of Zwide's son, Sikhunyana (especially as the name might have been spelled by a Frenchman), to excite further interest. It too suggests conflict with the Ndwandwe paramount *after* Zwide's death – perhaps as the result of being on the wrong side in the succession crisis of 1825 – but before Sikhunyana's defeat by Shaka in September or October 1826. That is to say, up until 1825 Mzilikazi may have been still at home in the lowlands. The same account goes on to say that following conflict with various small chieftaincies on the eastern highveld, Mzilikazi was defeated in his attempt to plunder the Pedi. For years, it is said, the Pedi exulted in their triumph, only to find that in 1827 Mzilikazi returned in strength, sacked their chief towns and carried away many of their people. This tale, read in conjunction with oral traditions attesting to a great Pedi defeat in 1822, suggests a solution to a puzzle that has puzzled many historians. Ndebele traditions recount a great defeat at the hands of the Pedi, while the Pedi remember the same encounter as a defeat.[67] The Pedi may have lost to Nxaba in 1822, but triumphed over Mzilikazi later. They could have been the 'powerful nation' said in another story to have checked Mzilikazi's northern progress and turned his steps westward in 1825. Surely if Mzilikazi had been an active military presence on the highveld before that year his name would have been known to so wide-ranging a raider as Moletsane.

Perhaps the wisest course for the historian amidst such uncertainty and contradiction is to suspend judgement about the years before 1825.

Mzilikazi's movements after that year are much more easily traced. He settled down on the Apies River, not far from the present-day city of Pretoria, from whence his influence expanded in all directions. In an era marked by very high levels of imaginative and creative leadership, Mzilikazi stands out as one of the most attractive and effective rulers. As early as 1829 he sent ambassadors to Robert Moffat's missionary station, saying that he wished to learn more of white people's ways and would welcome a visit. When, after a long journey, Moffat arrived at Mzilikazi's capital, he found an athletic man in his early thirties, with a pleasing, soft expression and gentlemanly manners. His voice was 'soft and feminine'. Above all, he was cheerful and good-humoured.[68] An English hunting party who visited him in 1836 found him 'attired in a handsome black leathern mantle; its ample folds, reaching to his heels, well became his tall and manly person; and he looked the very beau ideal of an African chief. He had completely thrown aside that reserve and gravity which in a public assembly he had conceived most becoming, and now appeared in high good humour, joking, laughing, and familiarly pulling our beards, of which the luxuriant growth elicited his admiration and surprise. He frequently asked us how many wives we had, and whether they also had beards.'[69]

Though his body bore the scars of many conflicts, his principal joys were music and the dance. His personal bodyguards sang as they escorted him to and from his morning bath.[70] When Mzilikazi sat in public to deal out justice and hear grievances, the common people sang rather than spoke their feelings.[71] Like Shaka, he loved to lead the dance himself, and was always on the lookout for novelties.[72] As he danced his people watched him closely, aiming 'to imitate as much as possible'.[73] When the Hlubi under Mehlomakhulu appeared before him in 1825, he joyfully welcomed one man who performed a brilliant rendition of the 'Msino', a characteristic Hlubi dance. Mzilikazi first made him a present of a spear and shield. A little later he presented him with a wife – a young woman who had been captured from the Ngwaketse – all because he danced so well.[74] The overwhelming impression gained by those who visited Mzilikazi's kingdom was of order, discipline, bustling towns with laughing, lively people.[75]

Preserving order and security in a land recently emerged from famine and strife required constant vigilance. The kingdom was organized on spatial principles which may seem strange to twenty-first-century eyes. Its human core was remarkably compact, comprising no more than perhaps 20,000 people settled in dense villages within reasonable walking distance of each other.[76] Here most of the women lived and worked. Many of these villages were composed of local people who had accepted the new dispensation and were learning how to be 'Zulu'. Radiating from the dense core were Mzilikazi's cattle stations. Fit and ready *amabutho* maintained themselves in these outlying camps, threshing their own corn and protecting approaches to important pastures.[77] The net spread by these scattered stations extended out as much as 80 to 100 kilometres from the core and constituted the defensive perimeter of the kingdom. Viewed from another angle, the kingdom was an offensive formation, projecting the highly mobile might of some 4000 soldiers.[78] From the safety of the core, explorers, spies and *amabutho* constantly ventured out in search of new cattle to enrich the king, while at the same time keeping a keen eye out for possible dangers. People and chiefs who accepted Mzilikazi's overrule lost many cattle but were allowed to stay where they were. Travellers' reports are unanimous in confirming that people continued to live in what had formerly been independent Kwena and Fokeng villages stretching all the way to the land of the Pedi many hundreds of kilometres to the east.

Understandably, in view of his family's association with the Ndwandwe, he organized his troops on Ndwandwean principles. Advancing to the attack they carried a sheaf of five or six stabbing spears.[79] The younger regiments gloried in their slogan, 'Conquer or Die'. Their feats of bravery bear comparison with any army before or since. A group of six men cut off from the rest of their regiment during a battle with Jan Bloem, Jr's mounted riflemen, 'advanced in warlike attitude and with as much firmness as if there had been at least some chance of successful opposition, and until five of them had fallen under the guns of the invaders, no indications of defeat were evinced'. Only at this point did the one man left standing feel entitled to flee home to tell the tale.[80] On another occasion, Mzilikazi punished three regiments who had wavered before achieving victory, by separating them from their wives and prohibiting all sexual intercourse until they redeemed themselves on the field of battle.[81]

Of course, what looked like order, discipline and bravery to Mzilikazi and his loyal followers, looked like terrifying, unprovoked aggression to those who suffered at his hands. Like other Ndwandwe and Zulu armies, his troops launched attacks at night or early dawn, spreading mayhem with their firebrands and spears. And certainly aggression was a requirement for the expansion of the kingdom from its initial small nucleus. But even in aggression Mzilikazi demonstrated exceptional qualities of diplomacy and finesse. Open warfare was only one of his techniques. It was said that

> the Tswana subjects of Mzilikazi often became his victims through a ruse. The Ndebele would move into the vicinity of a settled village and pretend friendship until the people felt easy. Then, most usually by cover of night, they would surround the village and attack it at dawn when the occupants were not yet alert. After capturing the village, Mzilikazi would usually move [not kill] the older men and women to a distance from their original homes. The younger women and men would be taken to Ndebele kraals where they would be integrated into the ruling elite.[82]

Another account confirms the impression:

> In this way Moselekatse carried his conquests, in the first instance generally cultivating acquaintance and intercourse, then familiarity followed by haughtiness and overbearing conduct; then would follow temptation of cattle allowed to wander in the way of the natives, who also appear to have been easily duped. When such cattle were taken, or other offence given, Moselekatse considered himself the sufferer, with a right to retake his own and punish the aggressors. When any town or towns . . . sued for his friendship and protection, he promptly acceded, immediately sent consuls with the professed object of assuring them of Moselekatse's friendship, and defending them and their property, but in reality to represent their sovereign and be spies on all their transactions. The result was that the warriors of the town were soon called to unite with those of their new ally, and very likely on their first return from the capture of cattle they would seize those of their unconscious assistants on the pretence that they would be safer under the care of Moselekatse.[83]

Those who accepted Mzilikazi as their chief often found an open path to rapid promotion. A Tswana man who had begun adult life as a war captive rose to be a trusted official messenger and interpreter. Not surprisingly he became 'in heart a Zoola and an enthusiastic admirer' of his king.[84] A captive Griqua child related to Mzilikazi's greatest enemies rose to be a commander of a hundred soldiers and ruler of two towns. His young female cousin, Truey David, who had been captured at the same time, was accorded an honoured place among the corps of life-time virgins who attended the king.[85] Within a few years of arriving among the Tswana, Mzilikazi had recruited a regiment of their young men – the Matsetse ('tse-tse flies') – and sent them into battle against the Griqua.

History would eventually decree that Mzilikazi's people would be known to the outside world as 'the Matabele' and their descendants would call themselves Ndebele. Mzilikazi did not use either name. He chose to call his people the Zulu. A vigorous programme of indoctrination underpinned Mzilikazi's campaign to turn captured and recruited men and women into Zulu. Everyone was expected to learn and speak the Zulu language. They were taught how to make their huts of reeds in the lowland fashion. All men had to dress as Zulu, and women were admired for doing so – even though the skimpy costume outraged Tswana concepts of modesty and made naked thighs shiver in the highveld winter.[86] Of course, as Mzilikazi's fame spread, many people of lowland Nguni origin, especially Ngwane and Hlubi, who already knew the language and fashions, sought him out, thus expanding the core group of Nguni lineages.[87] Though Mzilikazi had no need to teach the ideology of obedience to chiefs, he made his capital the stage for a non-stop theatre of absolute rule. It was not all joyful song and dance. Throughout the day people recited his praises: Zulu, the heavens; Nkosi amaNkosi, king of kings; Tlau, the elephant; Tau, the great lion; Bayete, all hail.[88] Execution of wrongdoers was done in public with an eye to maximum impact on spectators. After two of the king's brothers and some of their wives were convicted of treasonable conspiracy, the women were lashed to a tree, strangled with a rope, and then had their eyes gouged from their sockets. The men were impaled on sticks thrust up the anus until they protruded beneath the chin. Then they were left to the vultures.[89]

The advent of this vigorous new force fundamentally altered regional power politics. Decades of internecine conflict and the ravages of Griqua/ Kora plunderers had battered chieftaincies along the length of the Magaliesberg mountains. The desperate assaults of famine-ravished raiders from the plains in 1823 were followed by the much better organized attacks of Sebetwane. (In accordance with the loose usages of the time, he was frequently called a 'Mantatee'.)[90] The visible evidence of these devastations would later, probably unfairly, be blamed on Mzilikazi. He claimed he had given the people of the Magaliesberg peace and security – in exchange for their liberty.[91] Farther to the west, the Hurutshe, whose power had been sapped by an ongoing succession crisis as well as by the loss of herds taken by raiders in 1823, paid tribute to Mzilikazi, worrying all the while that they might be the next to be swallowed up.[92] To the east, the Pedi, who had cherished their own designs on the Magaliesberg, found themselves in 1827 soundly defeated by Mzilikazi's *amabutho*. Not only had they lost vast numbers of their cattle, but many of their people had been recruited as forced labour.[93] Distance proved to be no obstacle to the restless probing of Mzilikazi's lightning cattle-raiders. Before the decade was out, they had struck hard at the Ngwato and the Ngwaketse, taking large numbers of cattle and captive women. Worse still, these weaker chiefs were tempted by the very force of their defeats to seek out Mzilikazi's help in their own local struggles. An Ngwato ambassador was seen at the capital in 1829 simultaneously complaining that his people had been desolated by the king's raiders – and seeking help in retrieving cattle lost to one of their neighbours![94] Who knew what pickings were to be had farther afield? Before 1829 Mzilikazi's scouts had made their way both to Lake Ngami beyond the desert, and to the Zambezi across the Zimbabwe plateau.[95]

The mushrooming growth of Mzilikazi's kingdom critically threatened the ambitions of Sebetwane and his brother-in-law Moletsane (Chapter 5, pp. 136–7). There was simply not room enough in this part of southern Africa for three new, young states aspiring to build their power on cattle captured from other people. During the 1820s Sebetwane remained beyond the reach of Mzilikazi's forces, as he attempted to enrich his forces at the expense of the Ngwaketse and other groups living to the east of the Marico River in what is now Botswana. The Ngwaketse had survived the hard times of 1822–3 in fairly good shape, for when the English missionary Robert Moffat visited them in August 1824 the prosperous kingdom of Makaba II contained an estimated population of 70,000 and many large herds.[96] In a masterly attack, which probably took place in 1825, Sebetwane routed the Ngwaketse, ending in the process the long and illustrious career of King Makaba. The next year, with the help of the guns of English traders, the successor, King Sebego, avenged his father's death in a great battle, which pushed Sebetwane's miscellaneous forces into a search for a new land where their cattle would be safe. This took them over a period of several years through various parts of present-day Botswana. Sometimes they triumphed spectacularly, as when they defeated the Ngwato, seizing large numbers of cattle and forcing the vanquished chiefs to take refuge at Lake Ngami. At other times Sebetwane lost his way in the Kalahari wastes and nearly perished. Eventually he would meet Mzilikazi's *amabutho*, but probably not before the 1830s.[97] Then he would go far away to found an empire.

Moletsane was not so lucky. After huge success in battles against various Hurutshe and Rolong chiefs between 1823 and 1826, he attempted to establish a permanent base at Makwassie (or Matlwase), a little to the north of the Vaal above the place where Bloemhof Dam now creates a lake. In the process he fought and chased out the Rolong chief, Sefunela, after a pitched battle in the picturesque hills of Buisfontein (named for the old Boer adventurer, Coenraad de Buys). Allying himself to a group of Kora (called Links or Lynx Kora after one of their leaders), Moletsane attempted to harness the new technology of firearms to his cause.[98] By 1828 he had fixed his attention on the vast herds of Mzilikazi, staging raids on the outlying cattle posts. In 1829 Mzilikazi hit back, taking much stock and pillaging Moletsane's chief town. As he reeled from this blow, he was hit from the south by Adam Kok's Griqua, and reduced to begging for refuge at the Griqua town of Philippolis.[99] Not long after this he mused regretfully,

'I was once a great man . . . but I have now only about thirty men'. His people, he said, 'are scattered all over the country'. He went on to state, in the characteristic hyperbole of those who had been 'eaten up', that 'the mothers eat their own children'.[100]

It should not be assumed that Moletsane's followers perished in battle. Those who had been with him since the start mostly rejoined the main body of their friends and relations in the Sand River region from whence they had been driven by famine and raiders in 1823.[101] Others sought out more successful chiefs. Moletsane, the man of many faces, had been just one of a number of young chiefs who hoped to become kings by seizing the opportunities open to individuals of talent in the early 1820s. In the days of his victories people eagerly joined him in the hope of winning their own fat cattle and homesteads. When he faltered, they deserted him. Like the other great figures of the time, he had grown in strength by paying no attention to the cultural peculiarities of the people who joined his band. All were welcome: women who were willing to work and men who would follow him bravely into battle. For Moletsane – as for Sekonyela, Sebetwane, Moshweshwe and Mzilikazi – chieftainship and clientship governed the organization of society, not feelings of ethnicity or 'tribalism'.

Did Mzilikazi outdo Moletsane because of superior talent? It is hard to say. Mzilikazi occupied a much superior strategic position during his residence on the Apies River. Hundreds of kilometres of sparsely populated grasslands separated him from Ndwandwe and Zulu enemies. The slavers of Mozambique operated mainly in the Mozambique lowlands, far to the east. To his north lay dry, desolate and disease-ridden wastelands. In contrast, Moletsane was squeezed between Mzilikazi and the Griqua/Kora gunmen. No accommodation short of submission could be made with Mzilikazi. The various Griqua and Kora groups proved to be fickle friends, apt to make an alliance one day and attack the next. The grasslands south of the Vaal and along the Harts ideally suited their mode of attack on horseback. And while they energetically politicked with Tswana chiefs on all sides, they never allowed any but their own people to occupy leadership positions. Like the Boers from whom they had fled – and whose ways they copied – the Afrikaans-speaking Griqua aspired to be a rural aristocracy identified by caste and blood.[102] Moletsane seems for a time to have imagined that he could copy their success as raiders by getting hold of guns and horses. That, however, required that he find something to sell: cattle, captive children, or the labour of his loyal followers. Before he could find the means of embarking on such a revolutionary change in strategy, defeat overwhelmed him.

For their part, the Griqua and Kora leaders recognized by 1828 that the great contest for supremacy on the central highveld now pitted them against

Mzilikazi. They had raided about as far up the Caledon Valley as was possible. The old commando tactic of mounted charges, firing and retreating to load, did not work in mountainous terrain. In contrast, on the wide open plains between the Caledon and the Magaliesberg mountains, horses and guns gave raiders a huge advantage in daylight fighting. By 1827 at the latest, their attacks had extended all the way to the eastern mountains near Pedi country on the Steelpoort and Olifants Rivers. In March of that year, a Zulu cattle-raiding party operating in territory occupied by Sotho-speakers north-west of Delagoa Bay encountered 'yellow people on horses' near 'an immense river or lake' who 'compelled them to return'.[103] These could only have been Griqua/Kora, for slavers operating out of Mozambique could not have come on horseback. Soon the horsemen began to go after Mzilikazi's herds, inviting disaster.

Confrontation and confusion as British commandos seek out the 'Fetcani'

People living in the British Zone learned a little, a very little, of these events through reports picked up from missionaries in the western highveld and from Xhosa chiefs employing the multifarious refugees known as the 'Mfengu' ('hungry people looking for work'; see Chapter 5, p. 130). But so many different kinds of people were called by the names Zulu, Matabele, Mantatees, Mfengu and Fetcani, that the rumour mill merely operated to spread confusion. In May 1828, two disquieting tales spread. One said that the Fetcani were on the move again in Thembu territory. The other said that Shaka was coming to attack the Xhosa.[104] By June it was said that Shaka was leading eight regiments comprising a total of some 20,000 soldiers, and that his goal was to attack Hintsa at the earliest possible opportunity.[105] In distant Cape Town, the British governor and his council hurriedly met to consider options. One possible course of action would be to let the Xhosa and Thembu again fly west to escape the invaders. While it could be argued that this would solve the labour supply problem for English and Boer farmers, wiser heads said 'to turn it to the advantage of the colony seemed impossible as it would be idle to expect that these people would at once fall into the condition of servants or labourers for the colony'. More likely they would roam the country in armed bands harassing people.[106] So, said the governor's men, the Thembu and Xhosa chiefs must co-operate in holding their ground against the anticipated attacks. As an interim measure the governor ordered Major W. B. Dundas to seek out Shaka and attempt to convince him that he should not attack chiefs, 'between whom and the British a good understanding has continued to exist for many years' (ignoring the small matters of the 'clearing' of the Zuurveld, the 1819 war with Nxele and the creation of the 'Ceded Territory').[107]

Ngqika of the Rharhabe Xhosa was naturally surprised to be told that Shaka was marching against him as he had not received the customary prior announcement. Nonetheless, he promised to defend his territory with all the means at his disposal.[108] Likewise, Hintsa, to whom the Ngwane posed no real threat, promised to send troops to join any forthcoming British expedition, probably in the hope of gaining cattle.[109] While Major Dundas hurried north in search of Shaka, the acting governor, Major General Bourke, prepared to conscript a commando from the Boers. He knew that as a matter of course the conscripts would expect to be rewarded in the usual way with booty captured from the 'enemy'. But he fretted that the Boers would be reluctant to participate if word got out that the British government back in London had ordered changes which would give slave-holders less power over their human property. To forestall that possibility he advised his superiors that he would 'delay the promulgation of the amend-ments until a more favourable opportunity'.[110] As always, the need to placate the Boers for military reasons outweighed sympathy for the condition of captive workers.

Though he did not know it, by the time Major Dundas set out in search of Shaka, the Zulu forces were already on their way home. Their target had not been Hintsa or Ngqika, but the herds of Faku, paramount chief of the Mpondo – a people whose independent existence as one of the great coastal powers dated back to at least the seventeenth century (see Chapter 2, p. 23). This was not the first time Shaka's forces had approached Faku's territory. In 1824 a small expeditionary force had met spirited resistance from the Mpondo, before returning home with little in the way of captured cattle to show for their efforts.[111] The attack of July 1828 fared better, in part because Shaka's forces included a party of riflemen led by the Natal trader, Henry Fynn.[112] When Dundas reached Faku's capital, the dispirited chief complained bitterly that he had 'lost all his cattle' and his people 'had nothing to live upon or make clothes of'.[113] Instead of Englishmen coming to his assistance, they had fought in the ranks of his enemy.[114] Although his rage against the English was real enough, Faku was exaggerating his losses in the customary chiefly fashion. His own statement suggests that loss of life in the conflict had been relatively small, though many children had been carried off and many crops destroyed. Other evidence, including oral tradi-tions of the Mpondo, indicates Faku retained most of his royal herds.[115] Shaka had sent messengers after the clash, bearing gifts of cattle which, they said, should be 'received as a token of dependence' upon the Zulu king, signalling that Faku was henceforth 'to be Shaka's friend'.[116]

Major Dundas now turned back towards the Mtata River, intending to visit the Xhosa chief Ngubengcuka (or Vusani). Near the site of the present-day city of Mtata, he ran into a large body of people whom he assumed to be the Zulu. Without pausing to ask questions, he gave the command to open fire, spreading terror on all sides. A junior officer present wrote that it had been 'quite a splendid little fight – shouting and us firing in'; it had been 'THE day of my life'.[117] When the smoke cleared, some seventy people lay dead and Dundas's small force had seized about 25,000 head of cattle. Ominously, 'no prisoners were taken' – in other words, they shot to kill.[118] Although people left alive said they were Ngwane, Dundas persevered in his mistaken view that they were part of the Zulu force that had attacked Faku. To do otherwise would have been to admit that he had mounted an unprovoked attack on innocent people and stolen their cattle. And that was precisely what he had done. He had attacked a body of Ngwane men, women and children who intended to make a new home in the Mtata River Valley.

The raids Matiwane's people had undertaken into Thembu territory with their Sotho allies over the last several years (above, p. 156) had shown them a land of rich pastures which more than rivalled those of the increasingly crowded Caledon Valley where they had lived since 1823 (see Chapter 5, p. 128).[119] Whether they should try the experiment of moving permanently was the subject of lively debate.[120] Many opposed the move, content with the position they had won after the final defeat of Mpangazitha's Hlubi in 1825. Others argued that they had never really made the Caledon their home. Griqua/Kora gunmen blocked access to the lower reaches of the valley. Their neighbours, Sekonyela and Moshweshwe, had grown increasingly powerful since the awful drought years of the early 1820s. Recently, Moshweshwe had pointedly signalled his independence from his nominal tributary relationship with Matiwane by sending an embassy with feathers as a present to Shaka.[121] According to one story, Shaka responded by sending a raiding party to attack Matiwane. According to another story, sons of Mpangazitha invited the Zulu to come and help avenge their father's death. Ngwane traditions remember that Shaka was always alive to possibilities for distant raiding because he kept at his capital a diviner with an ear the size of a shield, which enabled him to hear of faraway events.[122]

Although Zulu traditions are silent on the matter, several Sotho and Ngwane sources attest to a battle fought with Zulu *amabutho* near the present-day town of Ladybrand, perhaps in late 1826 or early 1827.[123] Shaka's half-brother, Dingane, was said to have been in the thick of the battle and to have acquired there one of the four wounds which plagued him for the rest of his life.[124] Matiwane's descendants later recalled using MaNthatisi's trick of dressing women as men in order to scare the Zulu *amabutho* about the size of their army.[125] On another occasion, probably after this inconclusive battle, Matiwane made the mistake of sending his forces against Moshweshwe's stronghold, Thaba Bosiu – most likely in order to punish the Sotho king for his disloyal act of sending tribute to Shaka. The assault failed completely and several great commanders perished as Moshweshwe's forces rolled great boulders down the approaches to the mountain fortress.[126] Yet another factor possibly influencing Matiwane's decision to move was a threatening revival of Hlubi military strength following Hlubi desertions both from his community and from Mzilikazi.[127] While it would be most helpful to know the dates of all these Ngwane setbacks, the sources are too vague to allow them to be sorted out.[128] Perhaps the failed assault on Thaba Bosiu should be dated to late 1827 or early 1828, because Ngwane oral sources imply that the migration to the Mtata River was a direct consequence of that fiasco. It would have made sense to move as after the summer rains of 1828 water levels were low. By July 1828 they had built temporary huts on the Mtata, but apparently not yet planted crops, relying on captured maize fields to supply the main body of old men, women and children.[129] Although it is convenient to refer to Matiwane's following as 'Ngwane', it naturally included numbers of Sotho, Hlubi and other people who joined his ranks in former years.[130] When Xhosa people asked who they were, some said Ngwane, and others that their 'nation was the Makisa' (a word of mysterious provenance; could be Makhetha's).

After three years of sporadic raiding, they certainly would have known that the valley was already occupied, and they would most likely have to fight someone to seize land there. They named Vusani as the chief whose people they expected to expel. They sent messengers to tell him they were coming.[131] What they could not have anticipated was the ferocity of the surprise attacks British forces launched against them. Guns and horses they knew about, if not first-hand, then second-hand, since Griqua/Kora attacks up the Caledon had been common knowledge since 1823 (see Chapter 5, pp. 131–2). Colonel Somerset brought something quite different when, in response to Major Dundas's reports, he moved his force of commando, Xhosa and Thembu troops up to Mbholompo on the Mtata River on 26 August 1828. With no prior announcement, and no attempt at negotiation, Somerset's forces attacked before dawn the next morning with a cavalry charge on the Ngwane huts, accompanied by thud-thud-thudding rounds of cannonfire. When the cavalry and gunfire had done their job of terrifying the ranks of the sleepy Ngwane, the soldiers under Hintsa and Ngubengcuka rushed in to finish off all those who had not already fled screaming. Their reward was the remaining Ngwane herds.

After the 'battle' a British officer who had witnessed the scene declared that 'it was one of the most disgraceful and cold-blooded acts to which the

English soldier had ever been rendered accessory'.[132] The commando forces under Somerset took their pick of the 'widows' and 'orphans' created by their own attack. 'The Burghers', reported Somerset, 'having most kindly offered to take charge of these children to the Colony, I was glad to accede to this proposal, seeing no other way either of conveying them or securing their being taken care of.'[133] While Somerset later made the empty gesture of offering to return women to families who remained in the Mtata area, he was silent on the children. They would spend the rest of their lives working as virtually captive labour on farms. None of this had been done as a response to a threat to anyone in the British Zone. It had all been done to keep the Xhosa people from reoccupying the territories the British had seized from them, and to remove the rumoured 'menaces' of Shaka and the 'Fetcani'.

The catastrophic loss of cattle and military confidence broke the back and the heart of Matiwane's chieftainship. Some of his people stayed on in the Mtata region, making their own accommodations with local chiefs.[134] Many of them were subsequently identified by the catch-all term, Mfengu. A number of other Ngwane ran hundreds of kilometres north and offered their allegiance to Mzilikazi.[135] The news they carried with them ensured that the sound of the cannonfire at Mbholompo would echo in people's imaginations for many years to come. When Mzilikazi first met Robert Moffat only about a year later, he told the missionary he would like to 'have a large gun; that he had heard of such from the Fikani', so that when commandos came against him, 'he might destroy them at once, before they even came in sight'.[136] When he was asked to receive an emissary of the British government in 1835, he said, 'I have heard much of the awful things [meaning cannon] with which the whites are supplied to destroy other people'. He well understood, he said, that the British made war on their neighbours 'for the purpose of acquiring their country and property'.[137]

For their part the Xhosa chiefs professed gratitude for British help in repelling the invaders of their country. They anticipated – mistakenly as it turned out – better relations with their newly discovered ally. Within a few months, the British recommenced expelling people from the self-proclaimed 'Ceded Territory'.

Matiwane himself behaved with becoming nobility. He apologized to Vusani for the invasion and sent him a present of cattle.[138] Then he slunk away back to Zululand by way of the Caledon Valley, a lonely and shattered figure. It is said that as he passed by Moshweshwe's stronghold, his former tributary offered him shelter and an honoured place in the land; one of his wives, in fact, stayed on. But Matiwane trudged on, preferring to lay his bones to rest by the graves of his ancestors.[139]

Even as he walked the news was spreading everywhere that great Shaka, the Zulu king, was dead, murdered by his own brothers on 23 September 1828.

Notes

1   *The South African Commercial Advertiser*, 7 Jan. 1824, reprinted in G. M. Theal, *Records of the Cape Colony* (Cape Town, 1903), XVI, pp. 503–4.

2   George Thompson, *Travels and Adventures in Southern Africa*, ed. V. W. Forbes, 2 vols (Cape Town, 1967), II, p. 115; Alan C. Webster, 'Land Expropriation and Labour Extraction under Cape Colonial Rule' (MA thesis, Rhodes University, 1991), p. 49.

3   Timothy Keegan, *Colonial South Africa and the Origins of the Racial Order* (London, 1996), p. 105.

4   Nathaniel Isaacs, *Travels and Adventures in Eastern Africa*, newly revised and edited by Luis Herman and Percival R. Kirby (Cape Town, 1970), pp. 276–7; Monica Wilson and Leonard Thompson, eds, *Oxford History of South Africa*, 2 vols (Oxford, 1969–71), I , p. 353; *Natal Papers*, I, p. 23. An alternative version of Jacob's background appears in *Records of Natal*, II, p. 197.

5   *Natal Papers*, I, p. 19.

6   John Wright, 'The Dynamics of Power and Conflict in the Thukela-Mzimkhulu Region in the late 18th and early 19th Centuries: a Critical Reconstruction' (PhD thesis, University of the Witwatersrand, 1989), pp. 330, 357.

7   Ibid., p. 336; *Records of Natal*, I, pp. 79–80. ·

8   Adulphe Delegorgue, *Voyage dans l'Afrique Australe*, 2 vols (Paris, 1847), II, p. 460.

9   P. R. Kirby, ed., *Andrew Smith and Natal* (Cape Town, 1955), pp. 60–1.

10   Isaacs, *Travels and Adventures*, p. 53.

11   *JSA*, I, p. 200; testimony of Jantshi.

12   Cowper Rose, *Four Years in Southern Africa* (London, 1829), p. 75.

13   Isaacs, *Travels and Adventures*, pp. 87–91.

14   Ibid., pp. 157–8.

15   *Records of Natal*, II, pp. 28–31; italics as in the original letter. .

16   Thompson, *Travels*, I, p. 174.

17 *Natal Papers*, I, p. 21; Isaacs, *Travels and Adventures*, pp. 45, 60, 71–2; David Hedges, 'Trade and Politics in Southern Mozambique and Zululand in the Eighteenth and Early Nineteenth Centuries' (PhD thesis, University of London, 1978), pp. 201–2. Wright, 'Dynamics of Power', p. 342.

18 John Omer-Cooper, *The Zulu Aftermath* (London, 1966), pp. 57, 64.

19 Isaacs, *Travels and Adventures*, p. 72.

20 *Records of Natal*, II, pp. 56–9, 197, 202–8; Isaacs, *Travels and Adventures*, pp. 136–40, 142.

21 Thompson, *Travels*, I, p. 180.

22 *Records of Natal*, I, pp. 60–2, dispatch of Thomas Pringle, 29 May 1825. The reference to beards and 'swords' strongly suggests the Prazos of Mozambique. Here is a word portrait painted of a Prazo seen at Shaka's court in 1826:

> his hair was long, and covered a great part of his face; he had mustachios, a large beard, a stilletto suspended from his neck, and the other parts of his body concealed by a carosse of hide. This costume, it appears, is common with his nation.

South African Commercial Advertiser, 11 and 18 July 1826, printed in Thompson, *Travels*, II, p. 250.

23 J. B. Peires, *The House of Phalo: A History of the Xhosa People in the Days of their Independence* (Johannesburg, 1981), p. 8.

24 D. Fred. Ellenberger, *History of the Basuto, Ancient and Modern* (London, 1912), pp. 160–4, 191. Moorosi had Thembu relations: J. M . Orpen, *History of the Basutus of South Africa* (Cape Town, 1857), p. 70.

25 T. Arbousset and F. Daumas, *Narrative of an Exploratory Tour to the North-East of the Colony of the Cape of Good Hope*, translated from French by J. C. Brown (first published 1846; reprinted Cape Town, 1968), pp. 92–3.

26 Ellenberger, *History of the Basuto*, pp. 192–3.

27 Andrews to Somerset, 4 Dec. 1826, British Parliamentary Papers, CO 287, pp. 285–303, especially the map on p. 305.

28 Lt W. H. Rogers to Major Forbes, 27 May 1825, in *Records of Natal*, I, p. 59.

29 Ibid., I, pp. 58–9. While this fits very well with other accounts of the 'Bhaca', it also contains a reference to Griqua/Kora attacks, which could hardly have been experienced by the Bhaca. As late as 1837 the Bhaca were still known to the Xhosa as Fetcani, a word one missionary was told meant 'the robber tribe'; see George Cory, ed., *The Diary of the Rev. Francis Owen* (Cape Town, 1926), p. 18.

30 W. D. Hammond-Tooke, *The Tribes of Mount Frere District* (Pretoria, 1955), pp. 10, 32–3, 65, and also *Bhaca Society, a People of the Transkeian Uplands, South*

Africa (Cape Town, 1962), pp. 22–6; J. B. Peires, 'Matiwane's Road to Mbholompo' in Carolyn Hamilton, ed., *The Mfecane Aftermath: Reconstructive Debates in Southern African History* (Johannesburg, 1995), p. 222; Wright, 'Dynamics of Power', pp. 269, 306. Wright describes, p. 303, other groups besides the Bhaca which were penetrating the region at the same time, and could therefore have been called 'Fetcani'.

31   Col. Somerset to R. Plaskett, 2 Jan. 1827 in *Records of Natal*, I, pp. 103–4.

32   W. M. Mackay, July–Aug. 1827, in *Records of Natal*, I, p. 39. For speculations about its meaning in Xhosa, see Peires, 'Matiwane's Road to Mbholompo', p. 237.

33   See map in Document No. 108, Annexure 1, Enclosure 1, *Parliamentary Papers*, Great Britain, CO 2693, p. 795. See also despatch of Thomas Pringle, 29 May 1825 in *Records of Natal*, I, pp. 60–2. It is difficult to pinpoint the battle site, for there was more than one Hanglip. James Wyld's South Africa map of 1842 gives three locations with that name, none of which quite corresponds with the printed sketch map.

34   Interview with Powana, 1827 in *Records of Natal*, I, p. 141.

35   Interview with unidentified man, July 1827, in *Records of Natal*, I, pp. 132–5.

36   Ellenberger in *History of the Basuto*, p. 178, asserts that Matiwane attacked Makhetha and 'absorbed' many of his people sometime in 1827. This does not square with the statement of the Ngwane man taken down in July of that year; for the reason that the statement derives from contemporary documentary evidence, I choose to discount Ellenberger's account. The two might be reconciled to a limited extent by hypothesising that submission and alliance followed a defeat suffered by Makhetha's forces.

37   Somerset to Bourke, 9 Oct. 1826, *Records of Natal*, I, pp. 95–8.

38   Mackay to Plaskett, 26 July 1827 in ibid., I, pp. 457–9.

39   Statement of Powana, ibid., I, pp. 105–6.

40   Somerset to Bourke, 17 Aug. 1827 in *Records of Natal*, I, pp. 124–5.

41   Dundas to Plaskett, 21 Aug. 1827 in *Records of Natal*, I, pp. 129–30.

42   Somerset to Bourke, 9 Oct. 1826 in *Records of Natal*, I, pp. 95–8.

43   See, for example, William Lye, ed., *Andrew Smith's Journal of his Expedition into the Interior of South Africa, 1834–36* (Cape Town, 1975), p. 20.

44   Dundas to Plaskett, 21 Aug. 1827 in *Records of Natal*, I, pp. 129–30.

45   G. Rennie to Major Forbes, May 1825 in *Records of Natal*, I, p. 63.

46   For an appraisal of the difficulties by a trained soldier, see the memorandum of W. M. Mackay, enclosed in Somerset to Bourke, 8 Aug. 1827, in *Records of Natal*, I, pp. 132–5.

47 W. C. van Ryneveld to Landdrost of Somerset, 11 Sept. 1827, in *Records of Natal*, I, p. 145.

48 Address of Major-General Bourke to Gaika and other chiefs assembled at Fort Beaufort, 7 Sept. 1827, in *Records of Natal*, I, pp. 143–4.

49 James King to J. W. van der Riet, Civil Commissioner for Uitenhage, 10 May 1828, in *Records of Natal*, I, p. 156.

50 Reprinted in Thompson, *Travels*, II, p. 249.

51 Notes by the Civil Commissioner of Albany on the statement of John Cane, Oct. 1828, in *Records of Natal*, II, pp. 17–18. See also Bourke to Huskisson, 26 Aug. 1828, in *Records of Natal*, I, pp. 268–9.

52 R. L. Cope, ed., *The Journals of the Rev. T. L. Hodgson* (Johannesburg, 1977), pp. 326–7.

53 D. J. Kotzé, ed., *Letters of the American Missionaries, 1835–1838* (Cape Town, 1950), pp. 132–3. This story was picked up by American missionaries who were newly arrived in South Africa in 1836 (and could not as yet speak any African language). A slightly different version of the story was recorded by the English soldier/hunter, William Harris, who met Mzilikazi in 1836. Harris was told that Matshobane, after having been utterly defeated by an unnamed neighbouring tribe (the Ndwandwe?), took refuge with Shaka. His son, Mzilikazi, attracted Shaka's attention and soon found himself in charge of a large cattle post. Seizing his opportunity, he fled north with a large number of cattle and a number of his people. See William Cornwallis Harris, *The Wild Sports of Southern Africa* (first published 1837; 5th ed. of 1852 reprinted Cape Town, 1963), pp. 39–40.

54 J. P. R. Wallis, ed., *The Matabele Journals of Robert Moffat, 1829–1860*, 2 vols (London, 1945), I, pp. 15–16.

55 R. Kent Rasmussen, *Migrant Kingdom: Mzilikazi's Ndebele in South Africa* (Cape Town, 1978), pp. 54–5.

56 Arbousset and Daumas, *Narrative*, p. 178.

57 Andrew Manson, 'Conflict in the Western Highveld/Southern Kalahari, c. 1750–1820' in Hamilton, ed., *Mfecane Aftermath*, pp. 352–3.

58 M. Wilson and L. Thompson, eds., *Oxford History of South Africa*, 2 vols (Oxford, 1969–71), I, pp. 403–4.

59 The so-called 'Transvaal Ndebele' living south of the Pedi likewise remembered fights with amaNgoni, who may or may not have been Mzilikazi's forces; see Rasmussen, *Migrant Kingdom*, p. 33. For reasons connected more with twentieth-century politics than oral memory, many of the Transvaal Ndebele, whose ancestors had arrived on the highveld centuries before, chose to cherish associations with Mzilikazi; see Peter Delius, 'The Ndzundza Ndebele: Indenture and the Making of Ethnic Identity, 1883–1914', in

P. Bonner, I. Hofmeyr, D. James and T. Lodge, eds, *Holding their Ground: Class, Locality and Culture in 19th and 20th Century South Africa* (Johannesburg, 1989), pp. 228–9.

60 A. T. Bryant, *Olden Times in Zululand and Natal* (first published 1929; reprinted Cape Town, 1965), p. 209.

61 W. F. Lye and C. Murray, *Transformations on the Highveld: The Tswana and Southern Sotho* (Cape Town, 1980), p. 32. James Archbell, who visited Mzilikazi in 1829, was clearly mistaken when he recorded that the chief had been driven out by Shaka in 1817 and immediately proceeded to conquer north-western Tswana people; as reported in J. C. Chase to Lord Goderich, 24 Feb. 1831, in *Records of Natal*, I, pp. 179–82.

62 See Rasmussen, *Migrant Kingdom*, pp. 41–2 for a discussion of the documents on which this story is based: French missionary stories written in 1832, collected in C. Germond, ed., *Chronicles of Basutoland: A Running Commentary on the Events of the Years 1830–1902 by the French Protestant Missionaries in South Africa* (Morija, Lesotho, 1967), pp. 87, 95, 110–11. The single sentence on which the conjecture is based appears in *Journal des Missions Evangéliques* (1833), 8:9 – 'il a même étendu ses conquêtes jusqu'à la côte de Mosambique, où il a repoussé les Portugais, qui avaient fait des tentatives pour s'emparer de son bétail' ('he had even extended his conquests as far as the coast of Mozambique, where he repulsed the Portuguese, who had attempted to seize his cattle').

63 Wallis, ed., *Matabele Journals of Robert Moffat*, I, pp. 103–4.

64 Kirby, ed., *Andrew Smith and Natal*, pp. 86–7.

65 William Lye, ed., *Andrew Smith's Journal*, p. 277.

66 Arbousset and Daumas, *Narrative*, pp. 185–6, 293–4. In the original text, *Relation d'un Voyage d'Exploration* (Paris, 1842), p. 368, the name is spelled 'Sékognané'. The date of the defeat is put at 1822, apparently because the authors wished to connect Mzilikazi to highveld 'devastations' between that year and 1825.

67 See Leonard Thompson's discussion in *Oxford History of South Africa*, I, pp. 403–4.

68 Wallis, ed., *Matabele Journals of Robert Moffat*, I, p. 29.

69 Harris, *The Wild Sports of Southern Africa*, p. 106.

70 Wallis, ed., *Matabele Journals of Robert Moffat*, I, p. 73.

71 Lye, ed., *Andrew Smith's Journal*, p. 239.

72 Isaacs, *Travels and Adventures*, p. 155.

73 Wallis, ed., *Matabele Journals of Robert Moffat*, I, p. 95.

74   Rasmussen, *Migrant Kingdom*, pp. 54–5.

75   Lye, ed., *Andrew Smith's Journal*, p. 214.

76   Rasmussen, *Migrant Kingdom*, pp. 59–60, 91, 95, 101–2.

77   Wallis, ed., *Matabele Journals of Robert Moffat*, I, p. 69.

78   Rasmussen, *Migrant Kingdom*, p. 91.

79   Harris, *The Wild Sports of Southern Africa*, p. 150. Rasmussen, *Migrant Kingdom*, p. 8, rightly dismisses the notion that Mzilikazi borrowed Shaka's 'innovations', noting that 'such ideas must have derived from an older and broader pool of common Northern Nguni practices to which Shaka himself was an heir'. Unlike Shaka's Zulu, Mzilikazi's people were still practising circumcision in the 1830s; *Journal des Missions Evangéliques* 8 (1833), p. 15.

80   Lye, ed., *Andrew Smith's Journal*, p. 219.

81   Wallis, ed., *Matabele Journals of Robert Moffat*, I, p. 69; Lye, ed., *Andrew Smith's Journal*, p. 216.

82   Lye, ed., *Andrew Smith's Journal*, p. 265.

83   Wallis, ed., *Matabele Journals of Robert Moffat*, I, pp. 10–11.

84   Lye, ed., *Andrew Smith's Journal*, p. 202.

85   Wallis, ed., *Matabele Journals of Robert Moffat*, I, pp. 225, 239, 246.

86   Robert Moffat, *Missionary Labours* (London, 1842), p. 511. It was apparently common for the Tswana to call Mzilikazi's people BaMantatote, from the name for naked.

87   The modern Ndebele still count more than sixty names of clans which trace patrilineal descent back to the coastal Nguni; Rasmussen, *Migrant Kingdom*, p. 53.

88   Wallis, ed., *Matabele Journals of Robert Moffat*, I, p. 89.

89   Ibid., I, p. 101.

90   See summary of the journal of the traders, Scoon and Luckie, enclosed in J. C. Chase to Lord Goderich, 24 Feb. 1831, in *Records of Natal*, II, pp. 179–82, where Sebetwane's victory over Makaba is described as Makaba's defeat by 'Mantatees'.

91   As he put it, 'it was the Mantatees and other rascally nations that had made these devastations before he came to the country' in ibid., I, p. 15.

92   Moffat, *Missionary Labours*, p. 516.

93   As related by Pedi informants in 1836; see Arbousset and Daumas, *Narrative*, p. 186.

94   Wallis, ed., *Matabele Journals of Robert Moffat*, I, pp. 17–18.

95 Ibid.

96 Omer-Cooper, *The Zulu Aftermath*, pp. 117–18. The oft-repeated statement that Sebetwane went to the Zambezi in 1824 is based on a misconception first stated in Eugène Casalis, *The Basutos, or Twenty-Three Years in South Africa* (first published 1861; reprinted Cape Town, 1965), p. xix.

97 In 1852 Moletsane gave an account of his career which appears to imply that Msilikazi attacked Sebetwane about the same time he first attacked Moletsane. No reliable dates are given, however, and the statement includes the plainly erroneous statement that in 1852 Sebetwane was still living by Lake Ngami. See statement of Moletsane in Theal, ed., *Basutoland Records*, I, pp. 517–19.

98 Martin Legassick, 'The Griqua, the Sotho-Tswana and the Missionaries, 1780–1840' (PhD thesis, UCLA, 1969), pp. 359–60.

99 Ibid., pp. 421–2; Lye and Murray, *Transformations*, p. 39; Ellenberger, *History of the Basuto*, pp. 173–5, 214.

100 Legassick, 'The Griqua', p. 423.

101 The majority of the so-called Taung of this region had not followed Moletsane, but had reoccupied their old homes, under the chieftainship of Moletsane's uncle Makoana; see Theal, ed., *Basutoland Records*, I, pp. 517–19.

102 Robert Ross, *Adam Kok's Griquas: A Study in the Development of Stratification in History* (Cambridge, 1976), p. 26.

103 Isaacs, *Travels and Adventures*, p. 100. Guessing, A. T. Bryant identifies them as men under Barend Barends; *Olden Times*, pp. 604–5.

104 Major O'Reilly to Somerset, 19 May 1828, in *Records of Natal*, I, p. 161.

105 Methodist missionary W. J. Shrewsbury to Somerset, 12 June 1828 in *Records of Natal*, I, pp. 173–4.

106 Council of Advice Minutes, 21 June 1828, in *Records of Natal*, I, pp. 176–8.

107 J. Bell, Acting Secretary of Government to Maj. Dundas, 21 June, 1828, in *Records of Natal*, I, pp. 180–1.

108 Somerset to Bell, 27 June 1828, in *Records of Natal*, I, p. 184.

109 Peires, *The House of Phalo*, p. 87.

110 Bourke to Huskisson, 29 June 1828, in *Records of Natal*, I, pp. 188–9. The particular law delayed was the so-called 'ameliorative' Ordinance 19; see Keegan, *Colonial South Africa*, p. 111.

111 Timothy Stapleton, ' "Him Who Destroys All": Reassessing the Early Career of Faku, King of the Mpondo, *c.* 1818–1829', *South African Historical Journal* 38 (1998) pp. 60–2.

112 Shrewsbury to Somerset, from Hintsa's capital, 2 July 1818, in *Records of Natal*, I, pp. 203–4.

113 The Natal trader, F. G. Farewell estimated that the Zulu force had taken 'about 60,000 head of cattle'; see Farewell to Dundas, 10 Sept. 1828, in *Records of Natal*, I, pp. 10–12.

114 Dundas to Bourke, 15 Aug. 1828, in *Records of Natal*, I, pp. 271–8.

115 Stapleton, ' "Him Who Destroys All" ', pp. 65–6; Wright, 'Dynamics of Power', p. 290.

116 Dundas to Bourke, 15 Aug. 1828, in *Records of Natal*, I, pp. 271–8.

117 I. Mitford-Barberton, *Comdt. Holden Bowker* (Cape Town, 1970), p. 59.

118 Dundas to Somerset, 1 Aug. 1828, in *Records of Natal*, I, pp. 258–60.

119 While Ngwane participation in raiding the Thembu is not confirmed by documentary evidence before July 1827, their oral traditions clearly state that there had been three years of raiding before the confrontation with the British in 1828; see the reference to 'the third year' in N. J. Van Warmelo, ed., *History of Matiwane and the Amangwane Tribe, as told by Msebenzi to his Kinsman Albert Hlongwane* (Pretoria, 1938), pp. 56, 58.

120 Ibid., 32. While this oral tradition says Matiwane was in favour of the move, a statement collected from the wife of one of his councillors in 1828 stated that 'Captain Mautuana [sic] was desirous of remaining inactive in their present position [on the Caledon] but the people objected to it, stating that they were too numerous and must push forward to get a country.' Of course, after the expedition took a disastrous turn no one would have been rushing forward to take credit for it.

121 Ellenberger, *History of the Basuto*, pp. 37, 170, 200; Eldredge, 'Migration, Conflict, and Leadership in Early 19th Century South Africa: The Case of Matiwane', seminar paper, Dept of History, University of Natal, Durban, 3 Aug. 1994, p. 21.

122 Van Warmelo, ed., *History of Matiwane*, p. 18.

123 Cited in Peires, 'Matiwane's Road to Mbholompo', p. 218n.

124 Arbousset and Daumas, *Narrative*, p. 153.

125 Van Warmelo, ed., *History of Matiwane*, pp. 27–8.

126 Ibid., pp. 38–42. It is difficult to judge the loss of life in this attack because Ngwane messengers said only 'that the army has come to grief and say that So-and-So and So-and-So have died.' When this tale was told and it was reported who had fallen, only the names of princes and men of rank were mentioned, 'for commoners were not counted'.

127   Peires, 'Matiwane's Road to Mbholompo', p. 220. The attempted Hlubi revival was very short-lived. After a failed raid on the Bhaca, most of them joined Sekonyela; see Ellenberger, *History of the Basuto*, p. 180.

128   Ellenberger's *History of the Basuto*, p. 181 dated Matiwane's attack on Thaba Bosiu to July 1827. This is inherently unlikely, given that a document from that month attests to the presence of a large joint Sotho/Ngwane raiding party in Thembu territory that very month (see note 34 above). It cannot be assumed that the raid of July 1827 was part of the mass migration, because Xhosa sources reported the retreat of the 'Fetcanie' and the Ngwane account of the joint raiding party stated clearly that no women and children had accompanied them.

129   Somerset to Bourke, 18 Aug. 1828 and Somerset to Bourke, 23 Aug. 1818, in *Records of Natal*, I, pp. 266, 269–70. For confirmation that the huts were temporary, see Kay, *Travels and Researches in Caffraria* (London, 1833), pp. 329–30. The Ngwane were described as run-down and hungry, despite the huge number of cattle they had brought with them – an indication that they had recently arrived after an arduous journey; see Eldredge, 'Migration, Conflict and Leadership', pp. 41–2.

130   Mpangazitha's son Mehlomakulu said later that his people were with Matiwane on the Mtata. See the account of his visit to the Hlubi Mfengu as related in W. Shaw to A. Stockenstrom, 20 June 1838, in *Records of Natal*, III, p. 313.

131   Somerset to Bourke, 29 Aug. 1828, in *Records of Natal*, II, pp. 88–91.

132   Kay, *Travels and Researches*, pp. 330–1.

133   Van Warmelo, ed., *History of Matiwane*, p. 255. Somerset to Bell, 26 Dec. 1828, in *Records of Natal*, II, p. 66.

134   Ibid., p. 8.

135   Rasmussen, *Migrant Kingdom*, p. 56.

136   Wallis, ed., *The Matabele Journals of Robert Moffat*, I, pp. 27–8.

137   Lye, ed., *Andrew Smith's Journal*, pp. 200, 236.

138   Somerset to Bell, 26 Dec. 1828, in *Records of Natal*, II, p. 66.

139   Ellenberger, *History of the Basuto*, pp. 185–9; Van Warmelo, ed., *History of Matiwane*, p. 72.

CHAPTER SEVEN

Making contact with British authorities; getting guns and missionaries

The year 1828 was a watershed year in southern African history, not just because Shaka died, but because so many other events occurred which appear to mark the end of one era and the beginning of another. For the first time the Xhosa chiefs witnessed the penetration of British troops deep into their territory. The battle of Mbholompo brought Matiwane's career to a close and scattered his followers. In the British Zone the proclamation of Ordinance 50 heightened perceptions of a rift in fundamental values between the colonial farmers and the home government in London. From the Mozambique coast to the Kei River, an arms race commenced as chiefs struggled to match the firepower of Griquas, Natal traders and Boer commandos. This chapter explores the implications of these developments as they worked themselves out during the following six years.

The last days of Shaka

The myths and legends which entwine the figure of Shaka make it hard to see the real man. Both oral traditions and written accounts bear obvious incrustations of vested interest.[1] Some of the most widely circulated stories come from the pens of the early Port Natal traders – at war with each other, greedy for gain, and withholding guilty secrets which they carried to their graves. They grossly exaggerated the extent of their own direct contact with the Zulu king and the court. Historical research has revealed that many of their stories about Shaka were deliberately sensationalized to promote sales of books in Europe. Notwithstanding all these problems, there is enough near-contemporary evidence to suggest that Shaka sat very uneasily upon his throne even after inflicting a crushing defeat on his rival, Sikhunyana, in 1826. His problems were more internal than external, and revolved around the fragile nature of his claim to legitimate kingship. Because they illuminate the structural constraints on rulership in his time, it is worth examining them in some detail.

He could not match the Ndwandwe rulers' long genealogical claims to kingship. Everyone knew the unorthodox route by which he had reached the throne. Good generalship could accumulate herds to reward followers, but popularity won that way lasted only so long as the victories continued. Marrying widely and introducing new women to the *isigodhlo* created alliances with important families, but those alliances likewise created expectations of future rewards which would be hard to meet. Conjuring up help from the departed shades of dynastic ancestors was an important part of every chief's responsibilities. Attempting to exalt them as unseen but powerful supporters of his legitimacy was practically a prerequisite for Shaka's kingship. However, the depth of his ancestry was shallow and his forebears relatively insignificant. Moreover, by prominently associating himself with his father, Senzangakhona, and his father's fathers, he raised troubling issues within his own family. The court was a perpetual hotbed of intrigue. Rivalry among potential successors to chieftainship was a built-in feature of all heartland societies. Senzangakhona had several wives and many sons who might challenge Shaka. Once he bore children of his own, they could be expected to compete among themselves, and perhaps with him. Such things often happened.

Shaka dealt with some of these problems by evasion. He cultivated a vigorous, youthful appearance to conceal any sign of age. He told one of the Natal traders that a king 'must neither have wrinkles, nor grey hairs, as they are both distinguishing marks of disqualification for becoming a monarch of a warlike people . . . it is therefore important that they should conceal these indications so long as they possibly can'. One of the tasks he confided to the 1828 embassy was that they should bring back Maccasar oil, which, he had been told, could turn white hairs black.[2] Another evasion was fatherhood. Every night, it was said, the king slept with 'four of his wives, one on each side and one across the feet and one at the head'.[3] Yet he refused to acknowledge that any of his wives had become pregnant or conceived. Many stories claim that women who did become pregnant were killed. While it is impossible to confirm such stories, this strategy was an obvious way of avoiding the problems posed by potential heirs. For all that, it merely delayed the inevitable day when the succession should be disputed.

Then there were his half-brothers to be considered. The longer Shaka held the throne without heirs, the more their hopes of succession must have risen. The more the name of Senzangakhona was exalted, the more reasonable it seemed that another one of his sons should be the next king. The proper successor should be the son of the king's 'chief wife'. Who that might have been in Senzangakhona's case was very much an open question. Gossips cast aspersions on Shaka's mother, Nandi, even to the extent of doubting the king's legitimate birth. An obvious reason for spreading such stories would be to advance the claims of sons born of other wives. One response to that danger would to glorify his mother. In various ways he did that. She was put in charge of the *isigodhlo*. She was special patron of the *Iziyendane* regiment (see Chapter 4, p. 91). Whether relations between mother and son were really that close was, again, a subject of gossip. She was an independent woman, who even during her husband's lifetime had cohabited with a commoner, by whom she bore a son, Mngadi. On one occasion, Shaka reportedly beat her for failing in her duties as supervisor of the royal household.[4] Yet when she died in August 1827 grief apparently knew no bounds. In one of the most notorious episodes of Shaka's career, scenes of mass hysteria and indiscriminate killing followed her passing.[5] Other, probably less reliable, stories claimed that for a year after her death there were periodical outbursts of similar public grieving – and that all sexual intercourse between husbands and wives was prohibited.

What sense can be made of these stories? Many have argued that Shaka orchestrated the public mourning as a crazed display of personal power. On the available evidence there is no way to measure the extent of the mourning. It was not uncommon for mourning rituals to continue for a year. On the death of the Thembu chief Ngubengcuka, 'all the people, both men and women, shaved their heads and they continued to mourn for the space of one year'. During the same period, it was reported, no belongings could be sold nor cattle parted with, for all property was 'considered unclean'.[6] Similar rituals enacted before ignorant observers at Shaka's court could easily have been misinterpreted and exaggerated. In Nandi's case, while three or four special ceremonies were held over the course of the next year, the intense period of mourning lasted only a month. On 7 September 1827 'the king went with the greater part of his people to a distant forest, to perform the national ceremony of discarding their mourning dress . . . after having duly mourned for the death of royalty. They then proceeded to the river, to perform the customary ablutions. Mourning, after this, was permitted to cease throughout his dominions.'[7] This does not look like a display of tyrannical whimsy. Some light may be shed on the subject by a conversation one of the Natal traders, Nathaniel Isaacs, said he had with Shaka immediately after that event. The king complained that traitors had 'killed all his principal people and his mother' (this may indicate suspicion of witchcraft being used). He needed, he said, to find some place to hide.[8] Perhaps he wondered whether the first scenes of mass grief had been intended by his

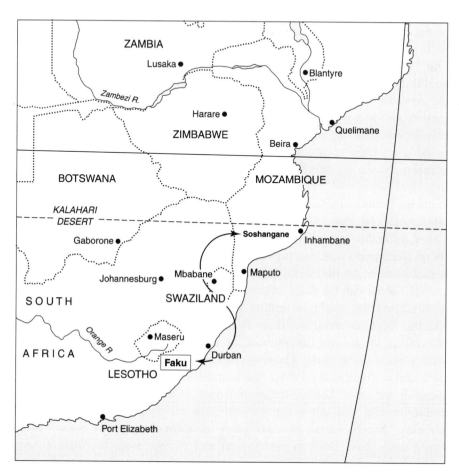

Map 16   Shaka's last campaigns, 1828, versus Faku and Soshangane

enemies to cover their own murderous plots. That we shall never know. What is clear is that the king's mind was in a state of high anxiety.

Arguably, Shaka attempted to bolster his standing among his people with successful military campaigns. Immediately after the first official month of mourning, Isaacs noted, the king 'had frequent consultations with this people on the subject of a projected attack on the tribe of Armampontoes [Faku's Mpondo people] and such tribes as are to the westward of them, until they should reach the possessions of the white people. The warriors were all unanimous in favour of this design.' This is, of course, practically what he did the following year. While the attack on Faku (see Chapter 6, p. 170) was counterproductive in the sense that it raised the 'Zulu menace' in the minds of British commanders, it did result in the capture of significant herds of cattle.[9] It is more difficult to account for Shaka's next move, which was to send a large force to attack Soshangane somewhere in Mozambique. It is said to have comprised 20,000 to 30,000 men, a party commandeered from the Natal traders, as well as herds of cattle to sustain the troops.[10] If the figures are to be believed, this would have been the largest force ever sent to fight more than about 150 kilometres from the capital. The *amabutho* who had participated in the attack on Faku may have had only a few days' rest before setting off to the north. According to one account, they marched to within a few kilometres of Quelimane, which would have represented a march of perhaps 1000 kilometres overland!

That a big expedition against Soshangane was launched seems extremely likely, judging from the number of accounts in which it is mentioned. How far it went, what route it took, who went along and how many returned are all matters for conjecture. All the versions written down in 1828 derived from Port Natal traders.[11] Since some of these may have reasons for wanting to conceal their own presence as mercenary riflemen, they are open to question. One account, delivered by John Cane to an official in the British Zone in October 1828, purports to be a statement made in ignorance of either the expedition's fate or Shaka's murder:

> After Chaka's people returned from the attack upon the Amapondas, they remained only three days at their kraal, when they were sent off in the direction of Delagoa Bay to attack a chief Onchuaguan [Soshangane] with whom they have always been at war. The day before Cane left Port Natal a messenger arrived to inform Chaka that the army had arrived in the vicinity of the nation they intend to attack and that they were then waiting to consume the last of their cattle, Chaka not permitting them to attack any tribe until the whole of their provision is consumed. The Portuguese settlement are friendly towards the tribes of Omchuaguan and have armed them with a few muskets. It is therefore supposed Chaka's army will be defeated.[12]

Another account, from the pen of Francis Farewell, implies that the fate of
the expedition was known well before the day of Shaka's death, and was, in
fact, the reason for his murder:

> Chaka . . . sent a force of about 30,000 fighting men to the Eastward and
> Northward of Mozambique for the express purpose, as it is supposed, of
> weakening his own tribe and exercising upon them more than usual
> brutality. This force marched with provisions only for the advance and
> with orders not to fight until that was expended. The tribe against whom
> they proposed to war, on the advance of the Zoolahs, drove off the whole
> of their cattle and, having surprised and cut to pieces a detached corps of
> about 8,000 Zoolahs, the remaining force was necessitated to retire and
> was subsequently so reduced by famine and casualties that it is said not
> above 10,000 got back to their country.
>
> On hearing of this disaster Chaka ordered the massacre of 2,000 of the
> wives of the defeated army (among whom were those of his own brothers)
> at the rate of 300 per diem. These atrocities at length aroused the revenge
> of the Zoolahs who entered into a conspiracy against the tyrant.[13]

An unidentified Zulu man, who carried Farewell's letter, added his own
oral account of events:

> It appears that the greater part of the force sent by Chaka in the direction
> of Delagoa Bay were destroyed, a portion by the enemy and a larger
> portion by starvation as Chaka would not permit them to take more cattle
> than was sufficient to subsist them till they arrived in the country of the
> people they were sent to attack. On this information being conveyed to
> the Zola[sic] chief he ordered a thousand women to be put to death as an
> expiatory sacrifice, which was partly carried into effect, but the executioners
> having seized some women belonging to his brother, this latter, in concert
> with some other chiefs, rushed upon Chaka and put him to death.[14]

Yet another trader, Henry Fynn, claimed that the conspiracy against Shaka
had been hatched well before any news of the army's fate had been received. Shaka, he said, had been

> killed by his body servant [Mbopho] and Chaka's brothers, Dingarn
> [Dingane] and Amatclangarn [Mhlangana]. Only four or three others
> were in the secret, it had no doubt been some time in contemplation but
> was well managed. While he was sitting with a few of his favorite chiefs his
> servant came with a stick and drove the people away, asking at the same
> time for what they were always bringing false news, and stepping forward
> with a hidden assagai, and Amatclangarn [sic] with another, he was struck
> in the back and only had time to ask: 'What is the matter my father's
> children?'

188

Then there remained one obstacle in the way of the heirs (who are five, as it remains for the nation to decide which of their mothers have the greatest right to her son being king) who were favorable to this project, there being a brother of Chaka's by the same mother who would have opposed them, (perhaps with effect) had the army been at home. They accordingly dispatched him in like manner, took his cattle and sent them to meet the army who were in great stress for supplies, travelling the country without meeting an enemy and afraid to return without cattle to their king. They have now returned, having travelled within a few miles of Quilimaine [sic], some having been killed, being taken by surprise by detachments of the enemy and great numbers by sickness, and the remainder in a starving state.[15]

Eight years after the event, Nathaniel Isaacs wrote that a traitor in their own ranks betrayed the Zulu forces to Soshangane. Facing a well-prepared enemy, the Zulu then won a dubious victory, losing 5000 men in battle and taking no cattle. This, said Isaacs, led to the starvation of another 15,000 later on the return march.[16]

What, if anything, can be made of these accounts? If the traders were attempting to cover some involvement of their own, they failed dismally, because their stories contradict each other on too many points. And why should any of them wish to concoct an easily exposed tale of a total military disaster that never happened? Clinching the case is Shaka's half-brother's statement, recorded eleven years later, that he accompanied that expedition.[17] It is easier to think of reasons why Shaka launched the expedition. If he did fear a conspiracy against him, the best answer would have been a victorious campaign. And what better target could there be than Soshangane, who had been so prominent in the old Ndwandwe coalition and had so obviously prospered in his new home? The best time to launch an attack would have been in winter when the lowland fevers were least dangerous. A great success might revive memories of the glory days of the campaign against Zwide in 1819 and Sikhunyana in 1826. In contrast, sending his army out with the deliberate intention of 'weakening' his own people makes no sense, unless he feared the *amabutho* were in rebellious mood. If they were, then nothing would have been more likely to set off civil war than orders to attack a faraway chief. The army was his greatest strength. The conspirators, if such there were, would be in his own capital, not on the battlefield. Every extant Zulu account of Shaka's murder emphasizes the role of the brothers and places the assassination ahead of the return of the defeated, demoralized army. They could not therefore have been in command of the distant *amabutho*. And they would not, for that reason, have been singled out for punishment for that defeat.

From a common-sense point of view, the military disaster makes a better excuse for the high crime of killing a king than any of the other reasons cited in the early accounts – the excesses of the mourning for Nandi, the rumoured order to kill one hundred women a day, or vague allegations of tyranny and cruelty. Shaka had bought glory by the spear, he must pay for failure by the spear. Whether 2000 or 20,000 died in Mozambique, their loss represented a catastrophe by any historic measure. The efficiency of Shaka's intelligence system was legendary. The news of the defeat would have run to his capital on winged feet. There would have been weeping in every homestead of the kingdom. That outpouring of grief would have been sufficient answer to Shaka's dying question, 'What is the matter, my father's children?'

Isaacs gives a plausible version of the brothers' answer.[18] 'It is the sons of Senzangakhona', they cried, who have killed Shaka to preserve the Zulu nation, the children of our fathers, that they might live in peace and enjoy their homes and families. It is to put an end to endless wars and the mourning of the old woman, Nandi, for whom so many have been put to a cruel death. Their manifesto emphasizes the royal responsibilities of the highborn sons of Senzangakhona, in contrast to the cruel conduct of the son of the mere 'old woman, Nandi'. The reference to endless wars makes a timely reference to the disastrous campaign in Mozambique.

The assassins, Dingane and Mhlangana, now moved quickly to shore up their position. After ceremonies to wash away uncleanness, they had to deal with Nandi's surviving son, Mngadi. Though his father had been a commoner, his mother's rank had sufficed to win him a high position. As he ostentatiously gathered his forces to mourn Shaka, Dingane collected *amabutho* to oppose them. Drawn into a trap, Mngadi died fighting.[19] That killed off the possibility of Nandi's dynasty winning the kingdom; but what of Senzangakhona's? Who would rule, Dingane or Mhlangana? Even before the return of the main army from Mozambique, Dingane struck. Now, of all the sons of Senzangakhona, only Mpande remained as potential challenger. Still a teenager, he wisely waived all claims in favour of his older brother.[20]

Though the succession seemed secure, other serious threats remained. One was the danger of internal rebellion signalled by the defection of Nqetho, heir to the old Qwabe chieftainship which had exchanged freedom for a privileged status in Shaka's kingdom (see Chapter 4, p. 83). He ran south across the Mzimkhulu River with thousands of people from his lineage, taking vast herds of cattle.[21] Dingane's troops chased them, but failed to retake the cattle. Their loss would haunt his thoughts for years to come, not least because of the dangerous example set by a successful revolt.[22] An internal witch-hunt for other possible rebels among Shaka's strong supporters led to a spate of executions.[23]

External dangers also loomed. In November 1828 messengers went out with presents of cattle to the independent rulers who at various times had lost cattle in conflicts with Shaka. They were all invited to attend the coronation of the new king, whenever that should take place. (With rivals out of the way, Dingane could afford to go leisurely through the motions associated with the selection of a new ruler.) The messengers announced that after the coronation, part of the herds taken from them would be returned.[24] The British military posed a more distant threat, but a worrying one, given the carnage at Mbholompo. How could Dingane make contact? He could not have known that Captain R. Aitchison had been dispatched by the governor to discover the true state of matters in Zululand and Port Natal but had scrubbed his mission when he heard the news of Shaka's death. In December, Aitchison met Francis Farewell who carried what he said was a message from Dingane to the effect that they now 'wished to live on friendly terms with every nation and by no means would do anything to displease them'. Aitchison recognized Farewell for the unprincipled schemer he was:

> He certainly does not speak out like an upright honest man and, moreover, he looks very much like a drunkard. I endeavoured to ascertain from him what were the advantages contemplated by an intercourse with this colony but failed in eliciting anything like a satisfactory reply. All he seems to wish is that *he* should be vested by govt with some authority to give him more influence than any other of the settlers and that 10 or 12 families be sent to form a young settlement.[25]

On the basis of his 'land grant', naturally. From other information received, the British commanders concluded that revolts and deaths on the return march from Mozambique had reduced Dingane's effective manpower to about half the size of Shaka's army. He seemed much less of a threat, so the need to visit him appeared less urgent.

At last, in November 1830, Dingane took the initiative, sending a present and a message to the British, which indicated his desire to encourage trade and to obtain a missionary. In the course of time, this would have large consequences.

Trying to make contact through missionaries and gun-runners

Making contact was a prime concern for many other rulers. News of the devastation wrought by the British firepower at Mbholompo in August 1828 had spread rapidly. Chiefs in many different places concluded that establishing relations with this dangerous advancing force was a matter of urgency. They also wanted to find out how to get guns.

Mzilikazi was among the first to act. In March 1829 he sent an *induna* with six oxen to the Hurutshe capital, Karechuenya. Whenever white men should appear, he was to present the oxen and persuade the visitors to accompany him to Mzilikazi's capital. After four months of patient waiting, the envoy found two English ivory traders who jumped at the chance.[26] After conducting trade worth £1800, the traders were told that Mzilikazi wished to have a missionary living in his kingdom. On their return trip they passed on the message to a Methodist missionary, James Archbell, who immediately loaded his wagon and set out. To his very great surprise, he found Mzilikazi well acquainted with the affairs of all southern Africa. The king knew what had recently occurred in Hintsa's Xhosa kingdom, as well as the results of the Zulu raid on Faku. He knew the names of the Port Natal traders and was aware that Dingane would soon be enthroned as Shaka's successor. Mzilikazi assured Archbell that he looked forward to increased trade with the English. While his people had traded for beads with merchants working out of Delagoa Bay, they preferred English-made beads. Above all, he wanted arms and ammunition.

Later in the year Mzilikazi dispatched other messengers with similar instructions to the mission station at Kuruman. This time it was Robert Moffat who, with some trepidation, accepted the invitation to meet the king. Mzilikazi dazzled Moffat, as he had dazzled Archbell, with his vast knowledge of regional affairs. Not only did he know what went on among the Xhosa and Zulu, he had, through the ceaseless activity of his own expeditionary forces, already acquired detailed information about the Lake Ngami region and the Zimbabwe plateau as far north as the Zambezi. Though he turned on all his legendary charm, he had trouble convincing the missionary that the devastation of the Magaliesberg region happened long before his army came on the scene. He said the best thing Moffat could do to promote peace would be to put a stop to Kora and Bergenaar raids. This ever-present danger made the king believe his people would not be safe until they acquired their own firearms. When Moffat suggested that surely Shaka had been the greatest disturber of the peace, Mzilikazi could only partially agree. And far from welcoming the accession of Dingane, he expressed horror at the assassination. 'A king must not be killed,' he said; 'he must not be killed by his own people.' At the conclusion of their conversations, Mzilikazi stressed the importance of regularizing diplomatic communications with the British. 'Tell the white king I wish to live in friendship' and 'let the road to Kuruman remain open'.[27]

Between 1829 and 1833 requests for missionaries proliferated. They should not be taken at face value as requests for religious instruction. People were still secure in their old beliefs. Many of the messages sent to missionaries showed an appreciation for the way that a missionary presence at Kuruman appeared to shield the Tlhaping chiefs Mahura and Mothibi from harm. They would have been aware that as early as 1826 these chiefs had been using firearms and horses in attacks on their enemies.[28] As the Hurutshe regent, Mogkhatla, summed up his situation, 'Without missionaries, we are dead; our enemies press upon us from all sides and we cannot resist them; if, on the other hand, missionaries lived with us they would protect us as they have Mahura. In the old days he was always at war, but since Moffat has been with him, he fears no one.'[29] The Ngwaketse asked for missionaries to come to them at their new home near Lake Ngami. Various groups of Rolong asked for missionaries. Moshweshwe sent a present of cattle to Griqua Town in an effort to buy a missionary.[30]

It was quite impossible for the missionary societies to meet all the needs expressed in these pleading messages. In the first place, they lacked manpower. The Wesleyan Methodist Missionary Society struggled hard to launch a mission to the Rolong under Chief Sefunela. After the first station fell to Moletsane (see Chapter 5, p. 137) the mission moved in 1826 to a place they called Plaatberg on the lower Vaal River.[31] Out of this initiative came the establishment of another mission with Sefunela's erstwhile ally Barend Barends at Boetsap near the Harts River. The London Missionary Society could not afford a single agent to send to Mzilikazi. John Philip, their energetic superintendent at Cape Town, attempted to make up these deficiencies by calling in help from foreigners who broadly shared his religious beliefs: the Paris Evangelical Missionary Society and the American Board of Commissioners for Foreign Missions. Another problem was that Philip's longstanding commitment to Griqua missions created tricky conflicts of interest. Having promoted the Griqua as his best hope for the conversion of all Africa to Christianity, he found it hard to acknowledge their role as regional aggressors, and their continuing close links to Bergenaar and Kora raiders. When, on one occasion, Philip warned against the menace of Mzilikazi by claiming that Mahura was the only Tswana chief he had not subdued, Moffat remarked that it would have been truer to say that Mahura was the only chief the *Griqua and Kora* had not subdued.[32] Most important, Philip could not deliver the most basic demand embodied in the messages he received from chiefs and kings, which was that missionaries should provide official lines of communication to British authorities.

The London Missionary Society was a purely private organization. Neither Moffat nor Philip had the authority to 'tell the white king' anything. Moreover, a succession of governors in Cape Town distrusted Philip and the LMS. Lord Charles Somerset, who governed from 1814 to 1826, thought missions run by British subjects outside the borders of the British

Zone were a constitutional anomaly. He feared that they harboured deserters from military service, escaped slaves and criminals. He knew they regularly evaded his government's laws against the export of firearms.

> To procure firearms and ammunition they must revisit the Colony and bring with them something which will induce the itinerant traders to supply them with these prohibited articles. The consequence is that they plunder the distant tribes and traffic with the booty.[33]

Meanwhile, farmers and traders complained that they were not allowed to leave the British Zone to engage in similar activities. During the 1820s British authorities experimented with various systems to put Griqua trading • on a legal footing, but nothing worked very well. By 1824 they dropped prohibitions which had previously prevented private traders moving outside the British Zone. By 1826 almost anyone with a reasonable excuse could obtain the requisite 'pass'.[34] In a wide land escaping detection was easy. This multiplied sources of firearms for Griqua, Bergenaar and Kora groups, notwithstanding that trade in such items remained illegal.

So, even though Moffat stated the truth when he told Mzilikazi 'the laws of his country' prevented him from selling rifles, the king knew from his own experience that the laws had not prevented Barend Barends, Jan Bloem, Jr, Moletsane, Mahura and others getting guns and ammunition. Distance made it difficult for Mzilikazi to make direct contact with gun-dealers. There was also the problem of money. Trading cattle for guns directly diminished the foundations of his power. Trading ivory was a possibility, but required expeditions to demand tribute or hunt elephants. Rulers situated nearer the British Zone found it much easier to get guns. During the disruptions of the early 1820s many people from the southern highveld found their way to the British Zone and survived by working on farms.[35] They made up the bulk of the misnamed 'Mantatee labourers'. By the end of the decade many had returned to their homes bringing with them cattle, guns, sometimes even horses. Kings like Moshweshwe and Sekonyela re-cognized at once that by tapping this new source of wealth they could meet armed, mounted enemies on their own terms. They sent out messages encouraging people to leave the Cape and return to their homelands. Their chiefly power to manipulate the *mafisa* cattle loan system, allocate grazing lands, and command labour for public purposes enabled both kings to build their armies on new principles. They began to encourage others among their subjects to go to the British Zone for short periods of work. Rewards from this policy came quickly. In 1829 a raid on a Boer farm brought Moshweshwe a horse which he soon learned to ride. Not long afterwards he mastered the rifle. Now he could start confronting the Griqua/Kora raiders on something like equal terms. In 1830, seven years after the first confrontations in the lower Caledon Valley, Moshweshwe's forces met and soundly defeated a combined force led by a prominent Griqua Christian leader, Hendrik Hendriks.[36]

At the ports of Mozambique no restrictions prevented the flow of guns to Soshangane's kingdom. He certainly had guns by the time of Shaka's ill-fated expedition of 1828 and went on to acquire many more as he built up Gasa power.

From such small beginnings sprang an arms race which would continue for decades. It is vitally important to notice at this point that the competition brought people together even as it enabled them to fight each other with more deadly efficiency. Before guns and horses, rulers could supply the basic requirements of existence from the environment around them. Trade brought them goods from faraway places – beads, rare metals, skins, feathers and clothes – luxuries, not necessities. Taking up guns required fundamental changes in the economic system. Shaka could never have hoped to realize his dream of making guns in his own kingdom (see Chapter 6, p. 150). Firearms were improving with frightening speed. As soon as anyone mastered the art of making one kind of gun, a better one appeared somewhere else. Spiral grooves in gun barrels improved accuracy. Expanding bullets killed more people. Revolving chambers and breech-loading rifles cut the time required for reloading. The only way for chiefs to get the right kind of guns and ammunition was to trade for them. Keeping them in good working order required skilled mechanics and access to spare parts. It was no good having just a few guns. Lots were needed, and that meant finding goods or money to trade for them. Once chiefs made the initial decision to go for guns, they were hooked.

With the British prohibiting direct sales from gun-dealers in their zone, the most convenient people to deal with were the very people who had brought them to the heartland in the first place – Griqua, Kora, renegade Boers, contraband gun-runners. Over the next few years deals and alliances between chiefs and old enemies proliferated. Makhetha, Mahura and Moletsane led the way in forming alliances with Griqua/Kora groups. Many more were to follow. Moshweshwe's victory over Hendriks in 1830 was followed by expeditions which captured guns and horses.[37] Sekonyela also made rapid progress in equipping teams of mounted riflemen. The effect of this progress was, paradoxically, to draw more Kora captains up the Caledon Valley where they allied themselves first to one, then another of the region's leading powers. By the early 1830s Gert Taaibosch, Piet Witvoet and the veteran Xhosa raider, Danster (whose followers by then included many Kora horsemen) had made permanent homes in the valley. These owed more to the deals they did with the established chiefs than to their success in battle.

Mzilikazi challenges Griqua/Kora dominance

By 1828 Mzilikazi had come to fear the mounted commandos of Jan Bloem, Jr and Barend Barends as the most persistent raiders of his outlying royal herds. Late in that year his concern grew when Bloem combined his forces with Moletsane and the Links Kora and carried off thousands of cattle.[38] Although Mzilikazi's *amabutho* pursued the retreating commando and retook much of the cattle, he was now wide awake to the threat of an alliance between Sotho/Tswana chiefs and Griqua/Kora captains. This was one of the reasons for his frantic attempt to make contact with missionaries. In July 1829 he demonstrated his ability to penetrate right to the very heart of his enemies' territories when he delivered a knock-out blow to Moletsane's dreams of greatness near the site of present-day Bloemfontein.

Now it was the turn of Barends, Bloem and other captains to fret. For half a century, they, and their fathers before them, had ranged freely from the Orange to the Magaliesberg. Would their dominion now crumble before an army of practically naked, gunless and horseless men? They conceived the issue not just in military but also in moral terms. Barends, wrote Robert Moffat, was 'labouring under an unaccountable delusion' that he was destined to sweep Mzilikazi 'and his gang of blood-guilty warriors from the fine pastures and glens'. Barends was proud of his Afrikaans language and heritage. Whatever others might think of his past record, he looked upon himself as a sincere Christian. He had recently attracted Methodist missionaries to his headquarters of Boetsap on the Harts River.[39] Amazingly, and against all the odds, he succeeded in recruiting a grand coalition to oppose Mzilikazi's ambitions. In June 1831 he marched north at the head of one of the weirdest crusading armies the country had ever seen. Sworn enemies from the old struggles between Hartenaars, Bergenaars and Griqua Town saddled up and rode side by side. From Philippolis (named for missionary superintendent John Philip) came Hendrik Hendriks. From Campbell (named for missionary John Campbell) came Cornelis Kok. At their side ran Tswana spearsmen contributed by a number of chiefs who in former years had done battle with the Griqua and Kora.[40] Estimates of the total number involved vary wildly. Perhaps as many as 2000 set out altogether.[41]

At the moment of truth, the crusaders exchanged dreams of conquest for easy plunder. Finding most of Mzilikazi's fighting men away, they quickly swept off several thousand head of cattle and headed for home. Repeating Jan Bloem's mistake of 1828, they underestimated Mzilikazi's intelligence system. As they slept, not far from the present-day site of Sun City, the king's disciplined *amabutho* found them. Silently they spread a human noose round the unguarded camp, then charged in with the customary clatter of spears on shields.[42] By noon the next day, several hundred lay dead and most of the cattle had been recaptured. Soon Mzilikazi had the satisfaction of watching his victorious troops parade hundreds of captured guns and horses. For years after the site attracted travellers who came to view the 'whitened bones of men and horses, broken guns, and tattered furniture'.[43]

There could hardly have been a clearer demonstration of the superiority of unified command and discipline. Still, Mzilikazi knew he had won a battle, not a war. His people sang with uncharacteristic even-handedness,

> Jan Bloom came with his commando to Kena [at the Vaal]. We came to Kena. The Bastards fell and died at the battle of Kena. We also died at Kena. They fell and we fell at the battle of Kena, therefore we must eat and be fat. . . . The Bastards and Corannas fell upon the Matsetse [regiment]. . . . The Bastards fell and the Matsetse fell. They died. Barend fought against us with the great commando. We fell and died. They died.[44]

When they begged for food at court, they chanted,

> Give us flesh that we may be strong to return the cattle when John Bloom or Barend takes them from us. People who do not eat plenty of flesh are not fat nor in a condition to retake cattle when they are carried away. Corn is not proper food, we must have meat.[45]

Though Mzilikazi now had rifles, he must learn how to take care of them. Though he now had horses, he must learn how to ride, breed and nourish them. If he had not known already that his hold over his neighbours was grounded in fear rather than admiration, he knew now. His spies must be more vigilant than ever. Realizing that those most likely to combine again with Barends and Bloem lay to his west, he moved the core of his kingdom about 200 kilometres in that direction, taking up residence at the head-waters of the Marico River – the very heart of the territory long ruled by Hurutshe chiefs. Mokgathla, the nominal regent of the Hurutshe, had already made his submission to Mzilikazi and was in no position to resist this act which signalled the last step in a gradual process of conquest. Not only was this exceptionally fine country, it opened routes for communication both south towards the British Zone and north to the Zimbabwe plateau. It also made Mzilikazi feel just a little bit safer from cattle-raiders from the south-east. According to some sources, Dingane had recently sent a party to try its luck at pinching cattle from a king whose reputation grew daily.[46]

The ease with which the king moved illustrates the degree to which he and his following had broken free of attachment to place. They showed no disposition to fear the guardians of their enemies' tombs nor cling to the graves of their forebears. A curious tale dating from this time illustrates the point, while at the same time sounding a caution about the perils of the unfamiliar. It seems that a raiding party sent north into Ngwato country found two old women keeping a watch over a covered pot on a lonely hill. One woman fled, but the other kept her vigil, warning that uncovering the pot would spread a deadly sickness across the land. Laughing, the unsuperstitious soldiers removed the cover. Not long after they began to die.[47] Learning to live with diseases endemic to the lowlands to the north was one of the few disadvantages of Mzilikazi's new position. Amid exceptional grazing lands and fine rivers, he could expand his vision of how rich, varied, colourful and disciplined life might be under what he still called Zulu rule – the rule of the heavens.

Though Mzilikazi aspired to absolute rule, eliminating populations had no place in his plan. He was an absorber of people, not a destroyer. Those who had most to fear from him were chiefs who wanted to keep their large herds. Those who could not defeat him tried to put as much distance as possible between them and their nemesis. In the year of his move Mzilikazi launched rapid-fire raids on those whom he suspected of complicity in Barends's great commando, including the most important Kwena, Rolong and Ngwaketse rulers.[48] In the face of this onslaught the Ngwaketse chief moved farther to the west, while many of the Rolong moved south, pinning their hopes for revenge on Barends and Bloem. With their backing, the veteran raiders of the veld were able to continue mounting periodical attacks on Mzilikazi during the next five years.

Perils and profits of dealing with missionaries

If Mzilikazi had known more about missionaries he might have fared better. Nothing in his experience could have prepared him for the men in black. The first arrivals could only speak through interpreters, so there were serious problems in communication. Working out their relationship to the commanders who crushed Matiwane at Mbholompo was extremely difficult. While all the missionaries carried guns and recommendations from the military rulers of the British Zone, their sermons emphasized peace. Like traders, they made presents and exchanged goods. But even as they praised commerce, they absolutely refused to deal in guns or to commit themselves to any future transactions. They claimed to come as teachers, offering useful knowledge about new technology. But most of their talk was of invisible things: people raised from the dead and eternal life in the sky. Their offers to come and live in the country were reassuring. If they really were emissaries of the British government, this was like the familiar practice of having a son of a potentially dangerous enemy living at your court. But unlike a chief's son who would respect your ways, the missionary frankly proposed to live a life apart and to criticize your customs.

Had Mzilikazi been a mind-reader, he would have found even more amazing ideas inside the heads of the missionaries who responded to his invitations.[49] They cast themselves as leading actors in a drama of cosmological dimensions. God, they believed, had chosen them to advance the coming of his kingdom on earth by preaching to people who lived in darkness and sin. When all the peoples of the world had been told how to live morally and to find salvation through faith, God's son would return to reign in glory. The dead would be raised, the righteous exalted to Heaven and the wicked condemned to eternal punishment. Precisely how these mighty forces would direct the individual destinies of the missionaries could not be certainly known. They would see shocking things and face hellish temptations. They must keep a constant watch for signs of God's will. An invitation from a chief might be such a sign. On the other hand, a chief's displeasure might indicate that God wanted them somewhere else. It was never easy to tell. The accounts of their experiences they wrote back to their home countries reflected these fundamental convictions. Everything was painted black and white. Before their coming, the peoples they met lived in a state of misery, war and darkness. Any signs of peace, plenty or happiness were taken as evidence that the missionaries' coming had changed lives. People who welcomed them had been predestined for salvation. Those who thwarted their plans had already been marked out as God's enemies. When, as so often happened, the missionaries' accounts are the oldest written sources, their views tended to get repeated in history books, even by historians with no sympathies for their convictions. The contrasting experiences of Mzilikazi and Moshweshwe illustrate the way missionary chroniclers could make and break reputations.

In 1831, two years after the first visits of Archbell and Moffat, Mzilikazi learned that Samuel Rolland of the Paris Evangelical Missionary Society had arrived in the Marico River Valley to establish a station among the Hurutshe of Mogkhatla. The timing could hardly have been worse. Mzilikazi suspected Mogkhatla of having secretly encouraged Barends's attack a few months earlier. Now black-suited Rolland clattered in, escorted by a caravan of Griqua wagons! It did not take a paranoid mind to work out that Mogkhatla was playing a double game, hoping to use his new missionary connections to escape from the tributary relationship he had recently formed with Mzilikazi.[50] The following year Rolland returned with two young colleagues. They did a little, but not nearly enough, to dispel the king's suspicions that they were in league with his enemies. They sent a message respectfully asking permission to reside in his domain. As proof of their good faith, they warned that Barends was already contemplating a renewed assault. They also sent a gift which, they emphasized, came from the king's 'friend', Robert Moffat.

Mzilikazi tested them by commanding their presence at his own head-quarters (at that time still on the Apies River). They should forget about preaching to his Hurutshe subjects and build their houses near him. Was this God's signal for a change of plans? Or Satan's ploy to divert them from their true errand? Full of suspicion, they decided to send Jean-Pierre Pellissier as their envoy, a young man who had set foot on African soil for the first time in September of the previous year.[51] Mzilikazi rolled out his usual warm welcome. Speaking through an interpreter, he proposed that the missionaries build him a European-style house not far from the place he had selected for the mission. Notwithstanding these professions of good feeling, Pellissier's heart froze as he surveyed the military might deployed around him. His head spun at the sight of more unclothed female flesh than he had ever seen in the whole of his short life. The account he wrote of the three or four days he spent with the king was woven from the threads of his own fears and sexual fantasies. Mzilikazi was, he announced, a rapacious conqueror who inflamed the souls of his warriors by parading naked maidens before them. Those who proved bravest on the field of battle could take their pick from the next batch of captured girls.

No sooner had Pellissier rejoined his comrades than a new message came from the king. All three must come at once and start their mission. Torn between hope and fear, assaulted by a thousand different rumours which they struggled to understand through a haze of imperfect translation, the missionaries panicked. They packed their wagons and ran away to Kuruman. In all likelihood, their flight helped precipitate Mzilikazi's decision to move immediately to Hurutshe territory. Mogkhatla, justifiably fearing that he would be punished for the incident, fled south with a body of his close supporters. Evidently embarrassed by the consequences of their cowardice, the missionaries went looking for the Hurutshe refugees. Their Bible told how the prophet Moses led the children of Israel out of bondage in Egypt. They would redeem their earlier failure by leading this people 'through the desert' to a new home. Yet even this theatrical performance flopped when Mogkhatla decided instead to join his fortunes to Barends's schemes for vengeance.[52]

The power of their pens enabled the French missionaries to hide their own failures behind a lurid portrait of Mzilikazi the merciless destroyer. Not only had Mzilikazi lost another chance to get missionaries, he had suffered a critical setback in his campaign to portray himself as a progres-sive ruler. John Philip translated the gist of Pellissier's crazed report and published it as fact.[53] His pious aim in thus blackening the king's reputation was to rally support for the London Missionary Society's struggling Griqua missions. According to Philip, all of the vast grasslands between Mzilikazi's kingdom and Barends's headquarters at Boetsap had been turned into 'an empty desert'. Already upwards of 20,000 Hurutshe, Tlhaping, and Rolong refugees huddled together under the protection of the Griqua captains. They stood as the last thin line of defence against Mzilikazi's planned assault on the farmlands of the British Zone.

> That it is his intention to seat himself on the borders of the colony is a sentiment he has frequently expressed. By means of the spies he has employed and the information given him by the traders who have visited him, he has an accurate acquaintance with the Griqua country and with the colony, and he says the Griqua country is just such a country as he wished to settle in. He says that the Griquas are his cattle herds and that he will speedily have occasion to ask them for what they are taking care of for him and that he is informed that the colonists have very fine breeds of cattle and very large herds which he desires much to see. . . . The love of power and an insatiable thirst for the name of a conqueror are his darling passions.

Whether consciously or unconsciously Philip was playing on the fears the name of Shaka had evoked in 1828. He conjured up the vision of another threatening conqueror advancing south. Perhaps this one was even greater than Shaka, for his troops were 'numerous beyond any conception we can have of the power of an African chief'. As much as anyone, he helped promote a popular image of Mzilikazi as a monster.

Moshweshwe fared far better in his dealings with missionaries. By accident, he had timed the arrival of his initial embassy to perfection. Just as three fresh French missionaries arrived in South Africa expecting to occupy new stations with Tswana chiefs, they received the terrible news brought by Pellissier and Rolland. Now, in 1833, from a completely unexpected quarter Moshweshwe's ambassadors turned up with an urgent request for a missionary. There was no mistaking the sign – 'the finger of the Eternal was visible, pointing the road we must take'. Here was a heaven-sent opportunity to redeem their colleagues' failure. They hurried up the Caledon Valley to Thaba Bosiu, as determined to find a good ruler in Moshweshwe as Jean-Pierre Pellissier had been to find a bad one in Mzilikazi. They were not disappointed. Moshweshwe hailed them with volleys of riflefire and baskets of food. As the praise singer recited his achievements, he introduced each of his thirty wives. 'My country,' he said, 'is at your disposal. Build, cultivate where you think best. I will regroup my people around you.'[54] To the starry-eyed missionaries Moshweshwe looked 'like a Roman', with his aquiline nose, his oval face and his noble forehead.[55] They hoped he would do for his people what the Emperor Constantine had done for the Roman Empire fifteen centuries before, make Christianity the state religion. If he would be their patron, they would be his scribes, praising his statesmanship and exposing the wicked deeds of his enemies. When Moshweshwe pointed proudly to the rapid progress he was making in adopting new ways – his new European-made suit of clothes, his guns, horses and utensils – Eugène Casalis responded with his own pledge of fidelity. 'We belong to you, to live and die; we are now BaSutu, from this day hence the destinies of your people are entwined with our own.'[56]

Month by month the missionaries wrote Moshweshwe's version of history into their reports. In place of the tough young 'cattle razor' usurping the power which by rights belonged to Makhetha (see Chapter 4, pp. 92–3), they portrayed a legitimate king nobly preserving the historic rights of 'his people'. When they saw him dealing out personal justice by having condemned criminals thrown over cliffs, they praised him for making rape and murder capital offences.[57] They played down his role as a 'Fetcani raider' of Thembu and Xhosa cattle, even though the king was still launching expeditions south over the mountains in 1834.[58] They exalted his courage in standing up to the Kora bandits, who seemed to pose the greatest threat at the time of their arrival. Later, as they learned more about the history of the previous decade, they emphasized Moshweshwe's role in organizing the defence of 'his country' against Sekonyela, Mpangazitha and Matiwane.

It was difficult for them to sift fact from fiction in tales told in a language they were still struggling to master. When they heard of marauding bands 'eating people up', they took the phrase literally and praised Moshweshwe for fighting off cannibals. Perhaps no other single aspect of their writing did so much to distort modern understandings of what went on in the 1820s. They might have guessed from the nursery tales they collected that for generations the bogeyman figure of the cannibal had been used as a metaphor to illustrate the dangers of disorder and disobedience (See Chapter 2, p. 17). They might also have noticed that neither Moshweshwe himself, nor any of the people around him looked back to a time when hunger and danger had led *them* to eat each other. All the alleged 'cannibal bands' were located in wild places among the mountains. A less credulous Frenchman who travelled through southern Africa in the 1830s and 1840s tried his best to find cannibals. Though he heard many tales, he could not locate any. And finding that women and men alike regarded dead bodies with the utmost horror, he observed with heavy irony that by the most remarkable of accidents all the cannibal bands of the region had chosen to live near French missionaries.[59] This only provoked the missionaries to insist more vehemently than ever that cannibals had indeed roamed the land – and had come to prize the taste of human flesh above all other foods.

Horror stories suited the missionaries, because they heightened the contrast between life before and after their coming. Even though they found Moshweshwe's kingdom in a flourishing condition, they wrote as though life had been thoroughly miserable for a decade or more, ever since the drought of the early 1820s set people wandering across the land.[60] Instead of presenting the Caledon in its true colours as a valley of salvation, they pictured it perversely as the place where people suffered most. Their writings are peppered with references to their wagon wheels crunching human bones and grounds strewn with skulls.[61] Ruins, which may have been centuries old, they looked upon as evidence of recent strife. Ignoring the recovery which went rapidly ahead after 1825, the missionaries dated the beginnings of peace and prosperity to their own arrival in 1833. Moshweshwe had no interest in disputing them. He figures as the hero of the French missionaries' history. He is not only rightful king, but also the man who saved the people from invaders and cannibals. In years to come, as more and more people made claims to land on the Caledon, Moshweshwe could count on his French scribes to confirm his version of events.

The great Rolong trek

Methodist missionaries did what French missionaries only dreamed. They led a whole community on a march through the wilderness to a land of plenty. The foundation of this epic had been laid by Chief Sefunela in 1823 when he welcomed two Methodist missionaries to the settlement of Makwassie on the middle Vaal (see above, p. 193 and Chapter 5, p. 137). After attacks by Moletsane, he and a small following of loyal families wandered for nearly two years in search of a permanent home.[62] They finally settled at the place they called Plaatberg near the Vaal River (north of the present-day city of Kimberley). Sefunela found relative peace here by allying himself to Griqua and Kora military leaders. Methodists used that web of alliances to found new stations with people formerly known as conscienceless raiders. One such mission was established with Barend Barends at Boetsap on the Harts River. Methodist backing helped the veteran plunderer to polish up his new-found career as the crusading scourge of Mzilikazi.

As Plaatberg prospered it acted as a magnet for various sections of Tswana-speaking people whose ancestors had not been united since Tau the Lion (see Chapter 2, p. 28 and Chapter 3, p. 53). By the early 1830s local supplies of agricultural land and water could no longer sustain the

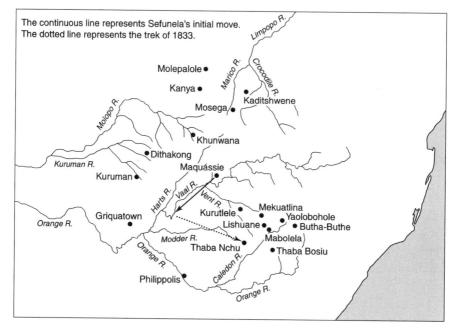

The continuous line represents Sefunela's initial move.
The dotted line represents the trek of 1833.

Molepalole ●
Kanya ●
Mosega ●
Kaditshwene ●
Khunwana ●
● Dithakong
Maquássie ●
Kuruman R.
Kuruman ●
Griquatown ●
Kurutlele ●
Mekuatlina ●
Yaolobohole ●
● Butha-Buthe
Lishuane ●
Orange R.
Modder R.
Mabolela ●
Thaba Nchu ●
● Thaba Bosiu
Philippolis ●
Orange R.
Molopo R.
Marico R.
Crocodile R.
Limpopo R.
Harts R.
Vaal R.
Vent R.
Caledon R.

Map 17   The Rolong Treks. After Chief Sefunela was persuaded to move to
Plaatberg on the Vaal River by Methodist Missionaries, a large population
gathered there. By 1833 it was clear that local resources were insufficient to
sustain the population, so 8–12,000 people trekked to Thaba Nchu.

large population. Attracted by the same reports that encouraged the French evangelists, Methodist missionaries John Edwards and James Archbell made a reconnaissance tour of the Caledon Valley. Moroka, then a candidate to succeed Sefunela as chief, was convinced by their enthusiastic reports – and the prospect of better access to guns and ammunition – to try the hazardous experiment of an overland journey with all his people.[63] In 1833 an estimated 8–12,000 men, women and children gathered their belongings and set off on foot up the Modder River ('Muddy River', more a string of water holes than a flowing stream). This was desolate country where wild animals still ranged in vast herds. People who made the crossing remembered for years afterward how they walked in fear of lions and San poisoned arrows shot from ambush. Somewhat to the east of the spring named for the raider Jan Bloem, Sr – Bloemfontein – they reached the dark hill called Thaba Nchu. There, on 21 May 1833, they called a halt. With the agreement of a local chief and a present to Moshweshwe of seven oxen, one cow, two sheep and a goat, they took possession of about 1200 square kilometres of land.[64] They had already begun to settle down when the French missionaries Arbousset and Casalis passed by the next month on their way to meet Moshweshwe. Within a year or two they had been joined by more Tswana-speaking people and allied groups of Kora and Griqua. Many years of pragmatic co-operation in peace and war had brought old antagonists together. Although the community thus represented the mixing of ethnic populations that had taken place over several decades in all parts of the western highveld, Thaba Nchu soon began to take on a different character. Moroka, who traced his descent back to Tau, accepted the religion preached by the Methodists and consciously propagated the idea that it was his destiny to reunite his people. Soon he had begun to build alliances in the usual fashion through marriages and the exchange of children with his neighbours. Moshweshwe sent him his son, Masupha, who soon became a favourite.[65] Thus the great migration to Thaba Nchu laid the foundation of the BaRolong nation.

Developments in the British Zone

Because the missionaries used Cape Town as their channel for communication back to their homelands, their stories about good kings, bad kings, wars, oppression and cannibals got widely circulated in the British Zone. Never before had there been such a flood of written information. It could not be automatically assumed, however, that British commanders would take missionaries' stories at face value. Most of them looked on missionaries as religious fanatics of low social class and limited education. They tended to echo Governor Somerset's judgement that the Griqua missions were a problem, not an achievement. Philip had recently offended farmers and other employers with his 1828 book, *Researches in South Africa*. This was a scathing, two-volume account of injustice and exploitation. It exposed unfair labour practices, atrocities committed against Khoi and San communities and all the evils of the commando system. The favourable reception accorded to both the book and its author in England created a widespread impression among élite groups that John Philip had caught the ear of important people. The impression was reinforced when Governor Bourke proclaimed Ordinance 50 in 1828 which went some way towards making free persons of Khoi and San descent equal before the law.[66] With many blaming Philip for undue influence, British authorities could not afford to appear to be jumping at his command. They could see plainly enough that his object in promoting the Griqua as a bulwark against Mzilikazi was to secure British annexation and protection of the lands under their control. Surely there was a basic contradiction between Philip's pleas that people of Khoi descent be accorded equal rights south of the Orange, and his project to win the same kind of people a specially privileged position in the north. Still, such a flood of conflicting, confusing and just plain incredible information was now pouring in from missionaries and traders that it seemed necessary to make some concerted effort to find out what was really going on. Was Mzilikazi a threat? Was Philip right about the Griqua? The British need to learn more about affairs outside their zone increased as more and more people moved back and forth across the borders they marked out.

In 1830 an experienced British official, Andries Stockenstrom, had come up to investigate claims that San were being systematically exterminated by Boer and Griqua attacks north of the Orange River. Griqua leaders knew him well. Five years earlier he had helped negotiate an end to hostilities between the Bergenaars and the settled communities under Waterboer and Adam Kok.[67] From the information he could gather it appeared that the centuries-long genocidal war on the San was continuing much as before – and that Griqua commandos were in the thick of it. When asked why they attacked the remaining San, one man replied, 'the Bushmen steal our cattle, we are determined to exterminate them, so that our cattle may graze unmolested day and night'. He excused killing women and children on the grounds that 'the children grow up to mischief and the women breed them'.[68] Such reports did little to foster confidence in Philip's claim that the Griqua stood as a bulwark against aggression. From other information received, Stockenstrom could see that Boers from the south had committed similar atrocities.[69] With or without permission, increasing numbers of Boers were living and travelling among the Griqua, establishing entangling relationships of mutual benefit. As early as 1824 Boers had participated in Bergenaar raids with the object of taking cattle and children.[70]

While Stockenstrom consistently deplored crimes against humanity in a lawless zone of disorderly interaction, he could not hold back the tide of advancing aggression. Indeed, he had helped open the gates. In 1825 as part of an attempt to provide relief to farmers suffering from drought, he had reluctantly issued permits to graze livestock north of the Orange.[71] In May 1829, in a time of renewed drought, he had allowed Boers to contravene regulations forbidding settlement in the 'Ceded Territory' previously established to lessen conflict between Xhosa farmers and their neighbours.[72] By the early 1830s the British had extended the formal boundaries of their zone of occupation to the Orange River and hundreds of Boers had established *de facto* holdings north of that line. Far from opposing these developments, Griqua leaders showed every sign of willingness to 'lease' land and do business with their new neighbours. Every deal concluded put another nail in the coffin of John Philip's hopes for a Griqua state under British sponsorship. The centuries-old trekboer advance toward the heartland had now turned northward. The Griqua would be no better able to halt it than they would be able to play the role Philip fancied for them as a bulwark against Mzilikazi. As the British authorities struggled to hang on to the tattered remnants of the old policy of closed borders, they were being pressured from other quarters to sanction formal schemes of colonization.

Notes

1 On the oral traditions, see Carolyn Hamilton, *Terrific Majesty: The Powers of Shaka Zulu and the Limits of Historical Invention* (Cape Town, 1998), pp. 54–70, 143–50. On the traders' secrets and lies see John Wright, 'The Dynamics of Power and Conflict in the Thukela-Mzimkhulu Region in the late 18th and early 19th Centuries: A Critical Reconstruction' (PhD thesis, University of the Witwatersrand, 1989), pp. 347ff, as well as Julian Cobbing. '"A tainted well": The Objectives, Historical Fantasies and Working methods of James Stuart, with Counter-Argument', *Journal of Natal and Zulu History* 11 (1988), pp. 115–54. For white legends and misperceptions of Shaka, see Dan Wylie, *Savage Delight: White Myths of Shaka* (Pietermaritzburg, 2000).

2 Nathaniel Isaacs, *Travels and Adventures in Eastern Africa* (first published 1836; revised and edited L. Herman and P. R. Kirby, Cape Town, 1970), p. 132. Though the tale has often been scoffed at, it is hard to imagine it being made up by the traders. Its very weirdness bears the ring of truth.

3 Told to Andrew Smith by Zulu informants in 1832; see P. R. Kirby, ed., *Andrew Smith and Natal* (Cape Town, 1955), p. 86.

4 Isaacs, *Travels and Adventures*, p. 73.

5 Wright, 'Dynamics of Power', p. 354.

6 P. R. Kirby, ed., *Andrew Smith and Natal*, p. 123. This was the same chief, 'Vusani', whose land had been threatened by Matiwane's migrating people in 1828.

7 Isaacs, *Travels and Adventures*, p. 108.

8 Ibid., p. 113.

9 Cetshwayo, Shaka's nephew, remembered two campaigns against Faku; Colin Webb and John Wright, eds, *A Zulu King Speaks* (Pietermaritzburg, 1978), pp. 6, 9.

10 Wright, 'Dynamics of Power', p. 368. Mpande told the Boers in 1839 that he had gone on that commando and Cetshwayo confirmed the scale of the attack in remembrances recorded half a century later; Webb and Wright, eds, *A Zulu King Speaks*, p. 7, and interview with Mpande, October 1839, in *Natal Papers*, II, pp. 104–7.

11 One quite ridiculous account that may be dismissed out of hand comes from the pen of A. T. Bryant, writing in 1929; see *Olden Times in Zululand and Natal* (London, 1929), p. 627.

12 Notes on a statement by John Cane, Oct. 1828, in *Records of Natal*, II, pp. 17–18. Cane in other statements refers to previous trips of his own to Delagoa Bay without giving the reasons for them. Was he gathering intelligence for Shaka about Soshangane or was he engaged in trading, perhaps even selling slaves? It is difficult to tell, but Julian Cobbing is certainly justified in raising the slaving question in relation to Cane's journeys; 'Overturning "The Mfecane": A Reply to Elizabeth Eldredge', paper presented to the colloquium, 'The "Mfecane" Aftermath', University of the Witwatersrand, August 1991, p. 37.

13 Enclosed in Cole to Murray, 31 Jan. 1829, in *Records of Natal*, II, pp. 85–8.

14 Statement to D. Campbell, 19 Dec. 1828, in *Records of Natal*, II, pp. 52.

15 H. F. Fynn to Somerset, 28 Nov. 1828, in *Records of Natal*, II, p. 73.

16 Isaacs, *Travels and Adventures*, pp. 172–3.

17 See note 10 above.

18 Isaacs, *Travels and Adventures*, p. 43.

19 Ibid., pp. 161–2.

20 Kirby, ed., *Andrew Smith and Natal*, p. 89.

21 Isaacs to the Governor of the Cape Colony, n.d. (but prior to Dec. 1832), in *Records of Natal*, II, pp. 226–31.

22 Wright, 'Dynamics of Power', pp. 373–5.

23 Farewell to Campbell, 17 Sept. 1829, in *Records of Natal*, I, p. 139.

24 H. Fynn to Somerset, 28 Nov. 1828, *Records of Natal*, II, p. 73.

25 Farewell to Somerset, 15 Dec. 1828, and Aitchison to Bell, 20 Dec. 1828, in *Records of Natal*, II, pp. 49, 64–5.

26 Extracts from the journal of traders Scoon and Luckie, enclosed in J. C. Chase to Lord Goderich, 24 Feb. 1831, in *Records of Natal*, II, pp. 79–82.

27 J. P. R. Wallis, ed., *The Matabele Journals of Robert Moffat, 1829–1860*, 2 vols (London, 1945), I, pp. 15–28.

28 Martin Legassick, 'The Griqua, the Sotho-Tswana and the Missionaries, 1780–1840' (PhD thesis, UCLA, 1969), p. 368.

29 *Journal des Missions Evangéliques* 7 (1832), p. 365; my translation.

30 *Journal des Missions Evangéliques* 8 (1833), pp. 300–1; Eugène Casalis, *The Basutos or Twenty-Three Years in South Africa* (first published 1861; reprinted Cape Town, 1965), p. 71.

31 Margaret Kinsman, '"Hungry Wolves": The Impact of Violence on Rolong Life, 1823–1836' in Carolyn Hamilton, ed., *The Mfecane Aftermath: Reconstructive Debates in Southern African History* (Johannesburg, 1995), pp. 374–5.

32 Quoted in Legassick, 'The Griqua', p. 464n.

33 Somerset to Bathurst, 1817, quoted in ibid., p. 283.

34 *Records of Natal*, II, pp. 177–9; Legassick, 'The Griqua', p. 131.

35 D. Fred. Ellenberger, *History of the Basuto, Ancient and Modern* (London, 1912), p. 159.

36 J. M. Orpen, *History of the Basutus of South Africa* (Cape Town, 1857), p. 7.

37 William Lye and Colin Murray, *Transformations on the Highveld: The Tswana and Southern Sotho* (Cape Town, 1980), p. 50.

38 Legassick, 'The Griqua', pp. 422–3.

39 R. Kent Rasmussen, *Migrant Kingdom: Mzilikazi's Ndebele in South Africa* (Cape Town, 1978), p. 75; R. L. Cope, ed., *The Journals of the Rev. T. L. Hodgson* (Johannesburg, 1977), pp. 375–6.

40 Legassick, 'The Griqua', p. 427; Rasmussen, *Migrant Kingdom*, pp. 74–5.

41 Estimates of the numbers under Barends's command vary from 300 to several thousand.

42 W. C. van Ryneveld to the Secretary to Government, 3 Jan. 1833, in *Records of Natal*, II, pp. 214–19.

43 William C. Harris, *The Wild Sports of Southern Africa* (first published 1837; fifth ed. of 1852 reprinted Cape Town, 1963), p. 193; Adulphe Delegorgue, *Voyage dans l'Afrique Australe*, 2 vols (Paris, 1847), II, p. 348.

44 Wallis, ed., *The Matabele Journals of Robert Moffat*, I, p. 89.

45 W. F. Lye, ed., *Andrew Smith's Journal of his Expedition into the Interior of South Africa/ 1834–36* (Cape Town, 1975), p. 239.

46 Rasmussen, *Migrant Kingdom*, pp. 97–8.

47 Wallis, ed., *The Matabele Journals of Robert Moffat*, I, p. 87.

48 Rasmussen, *Migrant Kingdom*, p. 98.

49 This paragraph attempts to summarize ideas held by agents of the London Missionary Society, the Paris Evangelical Missionary Society and the American Board of Commissioners for Foreign Missions. Not all missionaries would have conceived their work in the same way. For some idea of the diversity of theological positions in this era, see Norman Etherington, *Preachers, Peasants and Politics in Southeast Africa* (London, 1978), pp. 24–46.

50 *Journal des Missions Evangéliques* 7 (1832), pp. 5–26.

51 See Pellissier's account in *Journal des Missions Evangéliques* 8 (1833), pp. 5–22.

52 *Journal des Missions Evangéliques* 8 (1833), pp. 197–208.

53 It first appears as enclosure in Van Ryneveld to the Secretary to Government 3 Jan. 1833, *Records of Natal*, II, pp. 214–19.

54 *Journal des Missions Evangéliques* 9 (1834), p. 9; my translation.

55 Ibid., p. 53.

56 Ibid., pp. 143–5.

57 *Journal des Missions Evangéliques* 10 (1835), p. 41.

58 Orpen, *History of the Basutus*, p. 8. Though the expedition began well, seizing thousands of cattle, by its end Moshweshwe had lost a great many horses and a brother fallen in combat.

59 Delegorgue, *Voyage dans l'Afrique Australe*, II, pp. 543–6. See also Eugène Casalis's rebuttal in *The Basutos*, pp. 19–22.

60 Their own observations that even poor men could afford to present bridewealth of two or three cows plus some sheep and goats, while richer men gave twenty to forty cattle, were ample evidence of relative prosperity; see T. Arbousset and F. Daumas, *Narrative of an Exploratory Tour to the North-East of the Colony of the Cape of Good Hope*, translated from French by J. C. Brown (first published 1846; reprinted Cape Town, 1968), p. 38.

61 See, among many examples, ibid., p. 43.

62 Kinsman, '"Hungry Wolves"', pp. 371–7.

63 Legassick, 'The Griqua', p. 510.

64 S. M. Molema, *Chief Moroka: His Life, His Times, His Country and His People* (Cape Town, n.d.), p. 36; Lye and Murray, *Transformations*, p. 52.

65 G. M. Theal, *Basutoland Records*, I, p. 3.

66 Timothy Keegan, *Colonial South Africa and the Origins of the Racial Order* (London, 1996), pp. 103–6.

67 Legassick, 'The Griqua', p. 316.

68 Ross, *Adam Kok's Griquas*, p. 24.

69 See a later report in Theal, *Basutoland Records*, I, p. 37.

70 Legassick, 'The Griqua', pp. 353–4.

71 Petrus J. van der Merwe, *Die Noordwaartse Beweging van die Boere voor die Groot Trek* (The Hague, 1937), pp. 205–15.

72 Keegan, *Colonial South Africa*, p. 176; A. Stockenstrom to the Secretary to Government, 19 May 1829, in *Records of Natal*, II, pp. 120–1.

CHAPTER EIGHT

Confronting the British threat through diplomacy and war

Dingane had wanted to meet British officials virtually from the time he succeeded Shaka as king of the Zulu. When two Englishmen arrived at his capital in March 1829, hoping to make their way to Delagoa Bay, he made them the princely gift of twelve fat oxen. He was, the Englishmen reported, a very popular king who took a keen interest in their expedition.[1] Like his predecessor, Dingane was misled by the Port Natal traders into thinking they had some official links to authorities in the British Zone. At various times during the year 1830 he talked to them about ways of developing closer relations. Like other rulers, he debated the pros and cons of firearms, wondering about the outcome of a full-scale battle with British troops. He thought his soldiers might have a chance with a surprise attack under cover of darkness. The main problem he foresaw was that the very sound of the firearms would strike terror into their hearts.[2] That made him more deter- mined than ever to teach his own people to use guns in their own defence. To get them, he made the ivory trade a royal monopoly.[3] In other respects he cared more for the joys of peace than the arts of war. Musical composi- tion, poetry, love-making and costume design were his passions. This first- hand description captures something of his commanding presence and complex personality:

> He is tall, at least six feet in height, and admirably, if not symmetrically proportioned. He is well featured, and of great muscular power; of a dark brown complexion, approaching to a bronze colour. Nothing can exceed his piercing and penetrating eye, which he rolls in moments of anger with surprising rapidity, and in the midst of festivities with inconceivable brilliancy. His whole frame seems as if it were knit for war, and every manly exercise; it is flexible, active, and firm. He is reserved, even to the

extreme, and in speaking he seems to weigh every word before he utters it, often displaying an impediment in his speech, although he has not any such imperfection, but from a desire to be distinct and to be understood. He, however, speaks often parabolically, and with more circumlocution than is desirable, until his searching eye has discovered the motives of the individual to whom he may address himself; then he speaks fluently and pointedly, suiting the action to the word. His language is impressive, but more like that of a courtier than a warrior, as he generally discourses on domestic subjects and but little about war. He . . . is very susceptible of any want of respect, when he evinces his displeasure in a tone which cannot be mistaken. He is exceedingly anxious to acquire information, manifests a great desire to be taught himself, and to have his people taught the knowledge of creation; and thus continually expresses a wish to have missionaries settle amongst them. . . . Ambition is very conspicuous in him, and induces him to aim at improvement in those arts of government which may enable him to acquire renown amongst the monarchs of the world. . . . His sensual desires and habitual propensity for corporeal pleasures are unlimited; and a large portion of his time is occupied with his females, either in dancing and singing, or in decorating their persons. His other amusements consist in planting and gathering corn, in which he engages personally to stimulate his people, and in herding his cattle; occasionally also he makes hunting excursions, either in pursuit of the elephant or the buffalo.[4]

After more months passed and still no representatives came from the British governor, Dingane sent his own party to the British Zone. Such a king deserved to be represented by the noblest of embassies, but like Shaka before him, the best he could do was to call on his Xhosa court interpreter Jacob and one of the surviving Port Natal traders, the carpenter John Cane. Though Dingane could not have known it, on a previous visit, Cane had informed the British Commissioner in Grahamstown that the king was 'weak, cruel and capricious'.[5] Now, in December 1830, Cane and Jacob appeared before Colonel Somerset, bearing a gift of ivory along with Dingane's message stating a desire for closer trading relations and a missionary.[6]

They met a predictable reception. Somerset, a foolish pompous man who came from one of the great aristocratic families of Britain, treated Jacob with even less respect than he accorded the low-born Cane. Dingane's present was not acknowledged, nor was any present or message sent back to him.[7] Worse still, John Cane repeated to Somerset the old traders' line that Natal was unpopulated and ripe for settlement. And he mentioned that American ships had begun to call regularly at Port Natal. This led the British Commissioner, Duncan Campbell, to write to the governor recommending annexation of a territory which appeared capable 'of sustaining a more dense population than any other part of Africa'. Another veteran official, Andries Stockenstrom, seconded the proposal, pointing out that if trade in ivory and other goods were diverted from Port Elizabeth to Port Natal, it would lessen income received from taxes imposed on imports and exports in the British Zone.[8] Eventually these considerations moved the governor secretly to commission Andrew Smith, army surgeon and superintendent of the Cape Town Museum, as his emissary to Dingane. He was to pretend to be on a 'scientific' expedition gathering information about plants and animals. His real purpose was to report on the military strength and character of all the rulers along the coast.[9] Smith's embassy did not get under way until January 1832, too late to counter the effect of news Dingane received from Jacob the previous March. John Cane, no doubt fearing to face the king after the failure of his mission, had not even bothered to appear at court.

Jacob, on the other hand, had plenty of information for the king – alarming information. On his way to Grahamstown, Jacob had met a Nwandwe man who, after living for many years among the Xhosa, had decided to offer his allegiance to Dingane. As far as that man was concerned, the king should refuse to deal with the British. The country to the west was now overrun with people from Europe, their houses, their wagons and their horses. War never ceased. Many others would have been glad to join Dingane, only they had heard that the British were planning to attack him too. The invasion, according to Jacob's informant, would begin with a British request for a grant of land. They would put a building on that land, from which they would begin subduing the nation with their witchcraft and their weapons. Already they had been responsible for the death of four great Thembu and Xhosa chiefs – Vusani (Ngubengcuka), Ngqika, Ndlambe and Mdushane. Soon their successors and other leaders would meet to decide what they could do 'to free themselves from the colonial yoke'.[10]

A fair-minded historian has to admit this sketch paints a factual picture of British–Xhosa relations over the previous quarter of a century. Europeans *had* overrun the land. Their fort at Grahamstown *had* been the nerve centre of British military operations. For the last twenty years Methodist missionaries *had* been asking Xhosa chiefs for permission to build houses on their land. Those houses now formed a string of stations extending all the way up to Faku's country. At their religious services they said prayers to heal the sick and bring rain. They openly proclaimed that chiefs who failed to heed their preaching would die and suffer eternal punishment. Who could blame Jacob's informant for connecting that preaching with the deaths of Ngqika and Ndlambe in 1828, Mdushane in 1829 and Vusani in 1830?[11]

A Ndwandwe man living among the Xhosa could not, of course, have been in a position to know that British authorities planned to seek further land grants as a prelude to invading Zulu territory. Most of Jacob's information on that score came from people living in Grahamstown. Soldiers, he said, had asked him what kind of country Dingane ruled. Were the roads good for horses? Did they have many cattle? They told him, 'we shall soon be after you'. John Cane himself had told Jacob that Mr Collis and several Englishmen living in Grahamstown planned to join the traders at Port Natal, 'because the country is much better than their own'. What is more, Colonel Somerset, the terror of the Xhosa chiefs, 'was about to advance with some soldiers' to see Dingane. Jacob supposed that Cane had stayed behind at Port Natal to guide the British force.[12]

Here again, Jacob approached a correct statement of the facts. People in Grahamstown *had* been talking about the economic possibilities of Natal. Saxe Bannister *had* already sought approval for a scheme of colonization based on Farewell's alleged grant from Shaka. James Collis and a new group from Grahamstown *did* arrive at Port Natal in 1831. However, Colonel Somerset was not coming with a detachment of soldiers. Jacob got that wrong. Nor was an immediate conquest in the offing. But there had previously been plans for Captain Aitchison to come with a military escort in 1828 (see Chapter 7, p. 191) and the new expedition led by the army surgeon Andrew Smith was, as we have seen, already in the planning stage.

If Dingane had to face Europeans armed with rifles, an obvious strategic move would be to assemble his own corps of European riflemen. In March 1831 he commanded the Port Natal traders to bring their guns and prepare to help him attack a recalcitrant petty chief.[13] Under the circumstances, a refusal to come would almost certainly be regarded as proof of their complicity in the British invasion plan. When they arrived at the court they found a company of Portuguese riflemen had also answered the call. In an atmosphere heavy with suspicion, the king demanded to know if the rumours about Cane leading a British army were true?[14] When the Port Natal men denied it, the scene was set for a dramatic trial presided over by four of the king's principal advisers. Clearly each of them sided with Jacob. When the traders tried to discredit the story, Jacob steadfastly insisted, 'I am only a child and tell what I have heard.'[15] Dingane himself appeared undecided. Apart from Cane, all the riflemen had shown up and gone, as ordered, on their mercenary expedition against the recalcitrant chief. Proceeding cautiously – he did after all need their rifles – the king withheld judgement on Jacob's story. However, Cane clearly merited punishment for the crime of failing to report the results of the embassy. Dingane then dispatched a company of soldiers with orders to take Cane's cattle and destroy the rest of his property. He tried to make clear to the others that a British invasion would not succeed. If it came, he would not make a stand against horses and artillery. He would disperse his people and cattle throughout the country and fly to a secret refuge until the danger passed.[16] The trader/ mercenaries saw that most of Dingane's circle of advisers was against them. Fearing that what happened to Cane would soon happen to the rest of them, they panicked and ran to the British Zone, some by land, others by sea.

The episode marks a turning point in Zulu attitudes. A few years before, Shaka had debated, in a purely hypothetical way, the possible results of a full-on contest between contrasting military technologies. Jacob's story cast the subject in a darker light. Perhaps for the first time ever, the king and his councillors took something like a bird's-eye view of the heartland. Rising above the age-old competition for cattle, defensible positions and reliable grazing land, they glimpsed in the Xhosa experience a portent of a future contest played for keeps. Since Dingane's accession, the top priorities had been making diplomatic contact with the British Zone, finding a missionary, acquiring guns and perhaps horses. The people Jacob encountered on his return journey to Grahamstown saw treaties, land grants, mission stations, traders, trekboers and British armies as linked chains in a sinister, perhaps irreversible historical process. They suggested what happened three years ago at Mbholompo could happen again and again. They knew well enough how conventionally armed troops would fare in such a fight. Matiwane, who had lost his kingdom in a few hours fighting with British soldiers, had returned to Zululand to tell his woeful tale.

Time passed and a British army did not come. Tensions relaxed and, in March 1832, a genuine envoy from the British government finally met a Zulu king. Smith came as secret agent and left no extended account of his talks with the Zulu king. But he must have done something to quell suspicions of an imminent attack. Among his travelling companions was Henry Fynn, one of the traders who had fled the previous year. Within a few months the whole Port Natal operation was back in business, reinforced by Collis and a party from Grahamstown. Increasingly, their business was gun-running. By pretending to be hunters they could secure the licences required to take arms and ammunition out of the British Zone. Foreign ships also began calling regularly at Port Natal with cargoes known to include firearms.[17] Whether these ships also bought slaves has long been a matter of controversy.[18] By the 1830s all nations but the Portuguese had banned the legal slave trade. Ships flying the flags of other nations caught engaging in the traffic risked losing their ships and having liberated slaves being distributed to employers at Cape Town as 'prizes' – an important source of labour in the British Zone.[19] One way of evading the ban would have been to load a legal cargo at St Helena or some other port, pick up a few slaves at Port Natal and offload them at Delagoa Bay or Madagascar. However, the fitting up of a full-blown slaver would have been too risky for any captain calling at British ports. The evidence of the gruesome trade was notoriously difficult to conceal.[20]

Another source of arms for the Zulu king was Delagoa Bay. In the early 1830s Dingane disputed control of trade to the Bay with the rival kingdoms of Soshangane and Sobhuza. It might be reasonably suspected that he also was drawn into trading slaves – a commodity he could obtain cheaply, though documentation which might reveal the extent of Dingane's dealings in slaves at the Bay has not come to light. In 1833 Zulu forces assaulted the Portuguese fort and killed the governor, though the reason for the attack remains a mystery.[21] It may be guessed that Dingane employed Port Natal mercenaries in this campaign, as he did on many other occasions after the crisis of 1831. If news had got out that they participated in the attack on Delagoa Bay, they risked losing their right to import arms from the British Zone. So they kept very quiet on that subject.

Whatever the traders at Port Natal did during the early 1830s, they did not hunt elephants. The huge beasts survived in significant numbers only in the Mkuzi and Hluhluwe lowlands north of St Lucia Bay and in deep valleys along the southern coast.[22] Port Natal merchants got their ivory by trading, not shooting. It took James Collis only a few weeks in 1832 to buy ivory worth £2000 in British money. Of course he did not pay cash; more likely he paid in guns and ammunition. (Two years later, his trading stock literally exploded in his face, killing several bystanders.[23]) Dingane graphically demonstrated his dependence on the gun-traders in 1833. A company of men sent south to reclaim Zulu royal cattle from the Bhaca chief, Ncaphayi, attacked a Port Natal goods wagon. Other traders, fearing that this was part of a general attack, fired on Dingane's men. When the king ordered all his people to withdraw east of the Thukela River, the traders again panicked and ran away. Instead of celebrating, Dingane sent messengers to reassure them and call them back. As if to show that he no longer suspected them as the advance guard of a British invasion, he ordered the execution of Jacob and several of his important supporters at court.[24]

Dingane would have regretted killing the honest prophet if he could have heard Andrew Smith talking about his kingdom in Cape Town. News of Smith's journeys spread by word of mouth long before he filed his official report.[25] Smith spoke enthusiastically about the advantages of planting a new British colony at Port Natal. He attended a public meeting in January 1834 at which 189 people signed a petition asking the British government to sponsor a settlement there. His written comments on the petition reveal a conqueror's mind at work.[26] Like John Barrow before him (see Chapter 3, p. 59) Smith combined the traits of the doctor, the scientist and the warrior. He was a close observer, an experimenter, a predicter, a classifier of things and people. He boldly imagined using military power to rearrange kingdoms on the map, frustrate the ambitions of Britain's overseas rivals, overthrow rulers, displace communities, make conquered lands pay.

He proposed using Dingane's desire for an alliance with the British to secure the annexation of all the land from Thukela River to Faku's country. Never again could there be a threat that Zulu armies would push Xhosa chiefs towards the lands they had lost to the British in the west. Smith next proposed filling the annexed territory with Boer and British farmers. They would jump at the chance. One such farmer (son of a British-born father and a Boer mother), who had gone with Smith's expedition, exclaimed that he had never seen such fine country. Once British rule was in place he would never want to live anywhere else.[27] As a next step, Smith proposed overthrowing the Zulu king. 'If a military party were to be posted near the Bay I would engage in twelve months after its arrival to be able to dethrone Dingaan by encouraging a rebellion among his own subjects.' From what he had seen in Zululand, Smith concluded that the king was a monstrous tyrant who must be hated by all his people. It could not be expected that a man like Smith would understand that the public executions which occurred every day at Dingane's court were the equivalent of the public hangings which occurred every day in his own country. Smith's sovereign, the British king, killed people indirectly through a complex, seemingly impersonal machine made up of police, judges, jails, and hooded hangmen. When Smith saw a king punishing directly – giving the order and watching the executioner – he could not bear the sight, and concluded wrongly that the sovereign must be hated for his killing in a way that no British king could be hated. Anyway, Smith continued, Dingane was not a young man, and might die soon. If the British were not there, terrible things would happen.

> In such a state of society should the head go nothing but a dreadful
> insurrection could be expected. The remnants of the conquered tribes
> would fly together, a most bloody and terrific war would ensue, one party
> would necessarily [be] subdued and be driven forth in a state of want and
> desperation, wanderers in search of food and enemies ready for attack
> wherever the former was to be found. If it would be desirable to avert such
> occurrences there is no time to be lost, the means are within the grasp of
> the British government.

Otherwise 'the cruel, ambitious and warlike' king Mzilikazi would step in and add to his already powerful empire 'the whole of the inhabitants between Delagoa Bay and Natal'. Or maybe the Americans, whose ships were presently landing guns and ammunition on the coast, might create their own colony.

From a twenty-first-century perspective, it must be said that Jacob Msimbiti observed and prophesied better than Andrew Smith. In 1834 the prospects of grabbing land in Natal excited soldiers, farmers and speculators in the British Zone. The newly appointed governor, Benjamin D'Urban, endorsed the annexation proposal and sent it to his superiors in London, along with Smith's comments. A large party of Boers from the Uitenhage district led by Petrus Uys travelled to Port Natal late in 1834 to make their own assessment of its agricultural prospects. They returned fully determined to migrate with their friends and families.[28] Uys looked on the land with a farmer's rather than a trader's eye. His father had experimented with the breeding of a new kind of sheep, the merino. Unlike the old short-haired sheep bred by generations of trekboers, the merino carried a thick coat of fluffy wool. For twenty years world-wide demand for wool clothing had outpaced supplies. In Australia and the Americas farmers were creating new pastures for sheep at a frantic pace. A similar process was transforming agriculture in the British Zone of South Africa where more and more farmers were replacing their old short-haired sheep with merinos. As the cash value of animals rose, so did the value of the land they grazed. The sight of people selling at high prices land which had been originally acquired for practically nothing promoted a speculative market in land. Even if they had no wool-bearing sheep, speculators hoped to acquire titles to new potential pasture land which looked like rising in value. The traditional method of getting land had been to take it from other people across the border – a process considered as normal and natural as cattle-raiding was in the heartland.

New threats of invasion

The appointment of Benjamin D'Urban as governor in 1834 was routine. Another Major-General. Another veteran of the war against the French. Another one-man band. However, the smooth appearance of continuity was deceptive. D'Urban had been sent by a new British government, elected on a more democratic basis, determined to make big changes. Among its first acts was the abolition of slavery in 1833. At one level, this hardly mattered to people in the heartland. Escaped slaves were now free to travel back to the British Zone, but there had never been many of them; few cared to return to the land of their captivity. At another level, emancipation did matter, because it increased tensions between the landholding elite and their government in the British Zone – tensions that directly and indirectly promoted schemes for invading the heartland itself. Farmers' sense that Ordinance 50 of 1828 aimed to undermine their right to control labour as they wished (see Chapter 7, p. 206) now hardened into an almost paranoid conviction that the British government was controlled by missionaries and humanitarians hostile to their interests. Although the slave-holders were compensated for the loss of their slaves, the money represented only about a third of the estimated cash value of the 'property'. Ironically, the atmosphere of increased liberty emanating from Britain enabled the landholders to express their own discontent more freely and vehemently. When Governor D'Urban changed his Legislative Council to include more representatives of the local élite, the new body devoted itself to devising a new 'vagrancy' ordinance intended to tie workers even more tightly to the farms. They feared that freed slaves would be too free.[29] Newspapers used their freedom to call incessantly for more access to land, more control of labour, more reprisals against Xhosa people who made off with their cattle. As early as February 1834, D'Urban learned that rumours had been circulating for some time about individuals intending to move beyond the boundary line 'with the avowed object of evading the operation of the slave abolition law'. Some intended moving across the Orange. Others contemplated taking 'unoccupied land' between St. John's River and Port Natal, inspired by the 'florid descriptions' of its fertility received 'for some years past from the traders who have travelled that tract of the sea coast'.[30]

Like many earlier governors, D'Urban tried to defuse these discontents by bending over backwards to accommodate them. He announced that he would put a stop to what people called the 'depradations' of Xhosa cattle 'thieves' by negotiating formal treaties with chiefs. It has sometimes been assumed, because he held prior consultations with the London Missionary Society, that his proposed treaty system had a humanitarian bent. This is at best a half-truth. D'Urban's treaty with Andries Waterboer did give the LMS missions in Griqua territory better protection than they had ever previously enjoyed. As 'chief', Waterboer received a personal salary of £100, a school grant, arms and ammunition and some recognition of sovereignty.[31] In contrast, D'Urban's first approach to the Xhosa chiefs was heavy-handed, if not thuggish. In a memorandum dated 6 June 1834, he recorded his dismay at the reports he had received of 'depradations'. He had authorized Colonel Somerset to tell the Xhosa chiefs that the governor was on his way to meet them. The message was to emphasize that

> if I found them acting as enemies they must not expect to be treated as friends, and that I now give them fair warning that I will hold them (the chiefs) responsible for the outrages of any of the people of their respective tribes, which I therefore counsel them to repress since they may assure themselves that if they force me to take measures for their punishment I will not do it by halves but in such a way as they shall long have cause to remember.

His Majesty's <u>unoffending and unaggressing</u> subjects <u>living within the proper boundary</u> of the colony must be protected in their persons and property. This is our first and most imperative duty in their regard and if the Caffres [Xhosa] persist in their marauding, and especially <u>armed</u>, they must be treated like other banditti [robbers] who get themselves shot in the <u>act of theft, plunder</u> and <u>housebreaking</u>, or in the undoubted intention to commit it. . . . [Armed Xhosa] found traversing the country or lurking in the fastnesses afforded by the woods of the Koonap and Fish river districts [north of Grahamstown] will be fired upon.[32]

No humanitarian ever spoke such words. The military mind manifests itself in every phrase: 'force me to take measures for their punishment' and 'I will not do it by halves but in such a way as they shall long have cause to remember'. Chiefs receiving the message would have recognized it as an ultimatum backed by the threat of all-out war. It came on the heels of two years of forced removals from the mountainous regions north of Grahamstown.[33] The chiefs most affected by land losses, Tyhali and Maqoma, would have had particular reason to fear the worst. D'Urban's hard-line stance worried even veteran warriors like Henry Somerset and Grahamstown Civil Commissioner Duncan Campbell. Responding to his call for an expedition beyond the border to 'recover stolen cattle', they urged that it be delayed at least until September. They warned that previous armed commandos like the one mounted against the Ngwane in 1828 had actually given many Xhosa groups an opportunity to *move back* onto their old lands in the British Zone. A selective hit at some chiefs would 'tend rather to perpetuate than to put an end' to tit-for-tat cattle-raiding. Besides, it would take several months to raise a commando from Boers who were struggling with drought conditions. In the end the plan for an immediate commando was dropped, but not before local officials had been told to start planning one.[34] More than likely, rumours of the planned raid would have reached Tyhali, Maqoma and other nearby chiefs, confirming fears of D'Urban's aggressive intentions – and spurring them to discuss countermeasures.

Andrew Smith comes on another secret mission

D'Urban also curried favour with farmers, businessmen and speculators by applauding plans to annex territory at Port Natal and by enthusiastically supporting a new expedition led by Andrew Smith. Its principal aim was to gather information about the more important rulers of the interior,

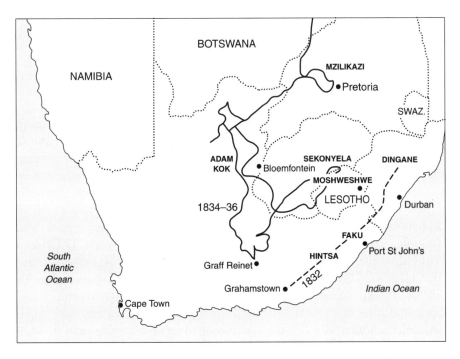

Map 18   Chiefs and Kings who met secret agent Andrew Smith on his
expeditions of 1832 and 1834–6

including Moshweshwe, Sekonyela and Mzilikazi.[35] The expedition set out in July 1834, at the very moment D'Urban's threatening message went to the Xhosa chiefs. Once again Smith posed as a scientific observer, though the kings and chiefs would have had no difficulty penetrating the disguise of the British agent. Never had any of them previously met such a large, elaborately equipped party. Smith came with great tents, splendid wagons, elaborate presents and formidable weaponry. His entourage included newly arrived German missionaries and an escort of soldiers. This could only be the emissary of a great power. The character of Smith himself, however, was hard to read. Was his stiff demeanour a sign of timidity, haughtiness, or just extreme reserve?[36] He lacked the ready smile, the eager handshake, the hearty laugh which made missionaries like Robert Moffat and Eugène Casalis such approachable visitors. All the chiefs would have been astonished at the snap judgements Smith made of their own characters as he wrote each day in his journal. When he talked to Tswana groups trying to scrape a living by working for Boers, he expressed surprise that they looked forward to returning to their own country. This, Smith wrote, proved their brutishness, for only brutes would fail to see the superiority of wage labour over freedom in a land without money.[37] He deplored the large number of independent chiefs in the heartland. It would be much easier for the British to keep the peace if they could be consolidated into a few large nations.[38] He classified everyone into pigeonholes. Some he called 'barbarians', others 'savages'. Some he pronounced 'degraded', others 'half-civilized'. He was confident that skin colour was related to intellectual and moral capacities. People descended from 'white fathers and Coloured mothers', he said, would be deficient in energy and courage.[39] Smith had been strongly influenced by European theories of phrenology which held that personality traits showed up in the shape of people's skulls. Even a person with 'a very trifling degree of physiognomic knowledge' could tell by examining Moshweshwe's head that he was superior to other chiefs.[40]

Smith had looked upon Natal in 1832 as a land fit to be conquered. As he advanced farther into the western highveld he could see that processes of conquest had been at work for half a century and more. A technological conquest spearheaded by guns and horses was driving the hunters he called Bushmen into more and more remote locations. Some of them still fought back with surprise attacks and poisoned arrows, but many had died and others had settled into subservient positions in Griqua, Kora and Tswana communities. A generation earlier, Tswana chiefs had fought the raids of armed horsemen. Now many chiefs had horses and guns of their own. They were as often to be found allied to Jan Bloem, Barends and Kok as opposed to them. Of all the Tlhaping chiefs, only Mahura maintained effective independence and a large following. He owed his relative success to his horses, firearms and alliances with Griqua and Kora leaders. The old Rolong and Hurutshe chieftaincies had fragmented. Individual chiefs who aspired to win back their old pre-eminent positions in the Molopo-Marico region tied their hopes to the dubious schemes of Bloem and Barends to forge a grand alliance against Mzilikazi. Other Rolong had, at least for the moment, chosen to try the Methodist missionary experiment of national renaissance at Thaba Nchu near the Caledon. Thus the cumulative effect of decades of influences emanating from the British Zone (the supplier of arms and ammunition – the end point of long-distance trade in hides, ivory, captured children and animals) had been to break up rather than to build chieftaincies. The ambitious chiefs who aspired to hold on to cattle-based power (Sebego's Ngwaketse, Sebetwane's Kololo, Sechele's Kwena, and the Ngwato) were now concentrated across the upper Limpopo in what is today Botswana. Because everyone he met expressed fear of Mzilikazi, Andrew Smith incorrectly attributed most of the fragmentation he saw to the attacks of that king. He did not see that Mzilikazi regarded himself as the man who restored order by erecting an effective barrier against the mounted raiders.

People greeted Smith with different degrees of enthusiasm, but most were willing to tell their versions of their histories and to seek whatever assistance he could offer.[41] Their perspectives help us piece together a snap-shot of the state of affairs over a great swath of territory lying between Graaf Reinet in the British Zone and the headwaters of the Limpopo River in the north.

In August 1834 few people were on hand to greet him in the desolate country north of Graaf Reinet. Farmers were 'on the *trek*' seeking pastures for their flocks and herds, a good index of land hunger. However, at the tiny village of Colesberg thousands of Boer families and their servants had gathered for a special occasion. The preacher Andrew Murray was about to make one of his rare visits to conduct religious services. The vast gathering showed how much the Boers treasured their faith – and how tenuous was their connection to organized religious networks. A party of Sotho/Tswana-speaking people, who were trudging homeward after a stint of farm work in the British Zone, met Smith north of the Orange River. They complained of being insulted and ill-treated by people who called them 'Kaffirs'. At the same time they appreciated the money they earned. They would have liked to settle in territory closer to wage-earning opportunities, but had been ordered to leave by Griqua. They told Smith what the Boers had told him before, that the Griqua should not be allowed to claim sole ownership of the land they dominated. The resource should be shared.

Naturally enough, this was not the view taken by a Griqua man who met Smith's party as it crossed his farmland. He was surprised to be asked why he was living in a reed hut instead of a stone house. Was Smith not aware, he protested, of the way the lands of his forefathers had been seized by Boers south of the Orange? For the last few years, Boers had been pasturing their flocks in his country and had warned him that if he did not share his land with them, they would come and take it. Why should he build a stone house when at any moment it might be seized? Another Griqua, who had formerly lived in the British Zone, extolled his present situation. Here, he said, he could feel like a man – a sentiment he never experienced in the southland. Griqua at the old LMS mission station, Philippolis, told Smith he picked a bad time to move north, for drought conditions prevailed all the way to Kuruman. If he wanted good pasture and plentiful water for his horses he should head for the Caledon Valley. Even though the notorious Kora raiders Piet Witvoet and Sarel Booi still harassed travellers in those parts, Smith would find the closer he came to Moshweshwe's country, the better the rain and grass would be.

Trekboers had already made that discovery and had been marking out farms in the districts near the present-day town of Wepener. They were overjoyed to see an Englishman and a party of soldiers because they had also heard the rumours that he was coming to inspect the country 'in order to distribute it among the whites'. While they enjoyed certain aspects of life – no taxes and no laws – they would very much prefer to have titles to 'their land' and government officials to protect it. One Boer explained to Smith that he had bought his large farm from 'Bushmen' with a payment of five sheep, but would need his title confirmed if he were ever to sell it.

In October 1834 the French missionary Eugène Casalis gave Smith an even warmer welcome to his station near Moshweshwe. This was his first opportunity to play the part of an intermediary between the king and the representative of a foreign power, a role he knew he must play successfully if he were to satisfy his patron's expectations. Advance information enabled Moshweshwe to receive Smith in a style he supposed would make the best impression. He arrived on horseback dressed like a Boer farmer. After dismounting and shaking hands, the king accepted the offer of a chair, saying 'Good Day' in Dutch. When Smith presented a 'friendship' medal for him to wear in recognition of the visit, Moshweshwe remarked to his entourage that this provided tangible proof of the value of the missionaries he had welcomed into their midst (an indication that many had been doubting it). He listened with evident satisfaction to Smith's account of his tour – until he heard that the British party intended meeting Mzilikazi. Nothing he warned, would be more unwise. The rival king was a treacherous deceiver who professed friendship while secretly planning to do evil. When Smith protested that no one could be more fearsome than Dingane, Moshweshwe replied that Dingane at least had proved his friendship to

British people by welcoming so many to his country. Moshweshwe said that only his mountain-top retreat enabled him to escape unscathed from occasional raids by Mzilikazi's cattle-stealers. Moreover he had heard from reliable sources that Mzilikazi had remarked that a mountain fortress like that would suit him perfectly. Moshweshwe arranged a demonstration to show Smith how Mzilikazi, the man he called 'king of the Matabele', would contrive a surprise attack. He arranged for some of his subjects, formerly of the Hlubi and Ngwane, to advance in a dense formation. On a given signal, many of them rushed out to the right and left till they had completely encircled Smith's party. Then on another signal, all rushed in for the kill, brandishing their stabbing spears. Clearly Moshweshwe did not relish the prospect of a British alliance with the man who now commanded the northern Vaal plains.

Neither did Sekonyela, his great rival across the Caledon, feel very comfortable when Smith came to visit him a few weeks later. He feared with good reason that Moshweshwe and the French missionaries had already poisoned Smith's mind against him. Other missionaries from the Wesleyan Methodist Society had attached themselves to Griqua and Kora groups who had threatened his people. So Sekonyela was no friend to missions.[42] He also lacked Moshweshwe's winning ways and eloquent speeches. Although Smith found Sekonyela's famous mother MaNthatisi an engaging character, he took an instant dislike to the king and spent little time with him. To make sure Sekonyela grasped his people's 'inferiority in respect of weapons', Smith organized a display of artillery. Finding that knowledge of guns had made Sekonyela indifferent to his arsenal, he lit up the night sky with rockets. As men and women screamed and ran in all directions, Smith was at last satisfied he had made his point. Sekonyela confessed that he had changed his opinion about British military strength. Formerly he had thought that Mzilikazi would easily destroy Smith's party. Now he saw 'that with such fire at our command, nothing could injure us'.

Next it was the turn of Moroka, leader of the Rolong exodus from Plaatberg, to greet Smith at Thaba Nchu. The visit suited him, because the question of who was rightful ruler of the Rolong groups gathered there was still undecided. Smith's anxiety to identify and establish regular relationships with all the chiefs and kings he met caused a general meeting, or *pitso*, to be held for the purpose of deciding the question. This enabled Moroka to emerge as the favoured candidate without any divisive open trial of strength. He accepted Smith's 'medal of friendship' as a mark of his new position. He and his councillors unhesitatingly identified the 'Korana' as the principal cause of disturbance in land. Even though some of those very people were present, Moroka spoke of them as unprincipled, predatory, vexatious and irredeemable villains. This strengthened Smith's own view that the British should extend some sort of control over all these territories and end the independence of the raiding communities. When he met the so-called Koranna in person, he was surprised at how smartly they dressed, and how well equipped they were. He took quite a different view, however, of the venerable raiding community headed by Barend Barends. The successful relocation of the Rolong from Plaatberg to Thaba Nchu had led the Methodist missionaries to persuade Barends to make a similar move from the Harts River to the Caledon. One of the leading men of the community, Peter David, told Smith how he had organized a recent expedition up to the territory where the Wilge River flows into the Vaal – a little south of present-day Johannesburg. While Smith believed David's claim that his men had nothing more than hippopotamus-hunting in mind, the modern reader might well suspect that they had hopes of other prey. At any rate, the expedition was attacked by a company of Mzilikazi's soldiers who took away not only seven wagons, oxen and guns, but also Peter David's nephew, William, and his daughter, Truey. All this only served to strengthen Smith's preconceptions about Mzilikazi.

Heavy rains broke the drought and enabled Smith to move out of the Caledon and into the heart of the territory dominated by mission-based Griqua. The wit and wisdom of many of the men who met him strained – but ultimately did not shake – his theories about links between physical appearance and intellectual capacity. Using his 'knowledge of physiognomy' he had been able to identify Peter David as having 'strong marks of being of slave descent' while 'some of his features indicated an alliance of a higher nature'. Back at Philippolis, the Griqua capital, he was amazed to find that the 'low and degraded' people were maintaining schools, a proper courthouse and magistracy, as well as a Legislative Council: the whole apparatus of government deliberately built in imitation of British institutions. He found that Cape Town newspapers were regularly studied so that legal and administrative proceedings could be conducted as they were 'in the *Colonie*'. The secretary to the Legislative Council had recently recommended that members consider adopting the anti-vagrancy law lately discussed at Cape Town. Debate proceeded in a deadly serious fashion until the mover of the motion pointed out that if it passed, the government would have to build a prison large enough to hold all the hundreds of Boer men, women, children and servants who ranged over their pastures in times of drought! Indeed at that very minute lines of their 'vagrant' wagons could be seen at various points along nearby rivers and springs.

If Smith had come over the Orange River expecting to find a wilderness untouched by the laws, economy, technology and culture of the British Zone, he must have been surprised. Wherever he went in the first six months of his expedition, he had found the land and people changed by half a century and more of linkages to the south. There was no 'frontier' that demarcated colonial and non-colonial space. Everywhere he had met people desperate to buy guns, even antique and broken ones. Everywhere he met trade goods, the clothing and the language of people in the British Zone. The intermingling of Boers and Griqua near Philippolis was the visible sign of an historical process which was fast approaching a crisis. The great question was, who would rule a land already penetrated by forces of change whose operations could now be seen to be irreversible?

About this time, late in December 1834, word came that another war had broken out between Xhosa chiefs and their pushy, troublesome neighbours.

The Anglo-Xhosa war of 1834–5

Jacob Msimbiti had heard back in 1832 that the western Xhosa chiefs would soon be gathering to decide what to do about British encroachments on their territory (see above, p. 214). By 1834 there must have been many such discussions, for the British threat grew daily. The territory seized in the wars of 1811 and 1819 now contained more than 30,000 Boer and British settlers and their dependants. They held nearly 7000 horses, over 80,000 head of cattle and 642,000 sheep and goats. The annual export trade from the district amounted to more than £50,000.[43] The Grahamstown papers, which many Xhosa people could read, clamoured for more land and labour. Early in 1833 British soldiers swept through the Macazana and Tyumi River Valleys (near Fort Hare), forcibly removing people and burning their huts and crops.[44] The brunt of these atrocities was borne by the Rharhabe Xhosa, who, since the death of Ngqika in 1829, had looked for protection to his sons Maqoma and Tyhali, and a nearby chief, Nqeno. A particular cause for outrage was the British disregard for chiefs. In defiance of time-honoured custom, they not only seized and imprisoned them, but shot them.[45] As tensions mounted, the young chiefs sounded out other rulers to see what support they might receive should they venture a counter-attack on the British. Hintsa, paramount of the Gcaleka Xhosa, approved retaliation but promised no troops.[46] It appeared possible that disgruntled Khoi who been settled on Xhosa land in the Kat River region might help. The armaments available to Maqoma and Tyhali seemed much better than those employed by Nxele in the 1819 war. For the last several years, the hunger for horses and guns had been as great among the Xhosa as in the Caledon Valley, the western highveld and on the north-east coast. Armaments were purchased with the proceeds of trade and migrant labour. Active gun-runners in the territory included a number of renegade Boer slave-holders, of whom the most notorious was Louis Tregardt.[47] Whether the Xhosa would be able to use guns and horses effectively, only a battle-field trial could show. They were goaded towards such a trial by further British aggression in the spring of 1834. On 17 October, D'Urban ordered Colonel Somerset to clear all Xhosa from land west of the Tyhume River which was earmarked for new farms. Patrols also attacked some of Tyhali's and Nqeno's people.[48] Another insult to chiefly dignity was delivered by a commando which fired on and wounded Tyhali's brother, Xhoxho. On 5 December Somerset delivered an ultimatum to Nqeno, demanding the immediate removal of all his people from the 'Ceded Territory' and within days patrols began rounding people up and driving them east of the Keiskamma.

This seems to have been the last straw, for on 21 December 1834 all the Rharhabe chiefs struck back. Several thousand of their soldiers attacked along the whole frontier of the British Zone. They had learned from Nxele's defeat in 1819 that it was better not to give the chivalrous advance warning they would accord to their other adversaries. Within days they had occu-pied hundreds of farms and seemed poised to take Grahamstown itself. British and Boer farmers ran for their lives. Robert Godlonton, editor of the *Graham's Town Journal* and prominent land speculator, called for total war on what he portrayed as the savage, unprovoked 'eruption of the Kaffir hordes'. In days and years to come, his newspaper published articles imply-ing that huge numbers of innocent people had died in a great conflagration. In fact, in the first wave of attacks, only twenty-five farmers were killed, while – as in 1819 – women and children were unharmed. A number of farmhouses were burned and, naturally, large numbers of animals were seized.[49] The limited nature of the Xhosa war aims was spelled out by Tyhali in a formal message to the governor issued only two weeks after the initial invasion. He, Maqoma and their allies would make peace provided they could retain captured cattle, regain their lost land east of the Fish River and be recompensed for the wounding of Xhoxho. Moreover, they offered to cease hostilities as soon as the British commenced negotiations.[50]

They failed to reckon with D'Urban, who now set out to prove that he did not 'do things by halves'. His commander at Grahamstown, Colonel Somerset, refused to accept the offer of a negotiated peace, claiming that he must await authorization from Cape Town. This bought time, which the British used to marshal their forces. D'Urban hurried to the war zone with an aggressive group of professional warriors. One of the first on the scene was Colonel Harry Smith, another veteran of the war against France in Europe. He brought with him a vast experience of guerrilla warfare in difficult terrain and an unlimited thirst for glory on the battlefield. He dismissed the chiefs' offer of peace out of hand and set about planning to 'punish' them. His attitude paralleled D'Urban's mindset. The object was not merely to win the war, but to inflict the heaviest possible losses so as to 'produce a lasting an impression' on those 'who may survive the war'.[51] The technique, as he summarized it on another occasion, was simple: 'you gallop in and half by force, half by stratagem, pounce upon them and wherever you find them, frighten their wives, lift their cattle, and return home in triumph'. This amounted to a declaration of total war. No distinction would be made between soldiers and civilians. Hunger and terror would be deliberately inflicted on the whole population by burning crops and seizing cattle.

Maqoma, Nqeno and Tyhali knew from the start that the enemy outnumbered them and was far better equipped. At best they might count on a combined force of 10,000 fighting men, few of whom had effective guns and even fewer had horses. Their women could act as spies, but had no battlefield training; the best they could hope to do was to feed themselves and their dependants.[52] On the other side, D'Urban commanded about a thousand full-time professional soldiers, including cavalry and artillery, plus thousands of mounted riflemen brought out on commando. Within four weeks of the onset of the war, Boer forces commanded by the veteran Piet Retief had killed about five times as many Xhosa farmers who had died in the initial attack.[53] In addition, several important Xhosa chiefs took the British side. Phato of the Gqunukhwebe supplied 1200 fighting men. The Thembu chiefs likewise sought recognition as allies. And while Hintsa had offered moral support to the resistance, he maintained an officially neutral stance.

Frustrated in their bid for negotiations, the anti-British coalition turned to a defensive strategy. By February they were withdrawing with their cattle into the Amatola mountains whose rugged terrain suited them and frustrated their enemy. From one point of view, the strategy succeeded brilliantly. Neither cavalry nor infantry could be effectively deployed in the Amatolas. British patrols proceeding single-file on narrow pathways could be ambushed and cut to shreds.[54] On the other hand, the very frustration experienced by the enemy inspired a devastating widening of the war. Harry Smith, who had fought with guerrilla allies in Spain under just such circumstances, could see that the war could not be won quickly – if at all – in the Amatolas. D'Urban demanded a quick, decisive victory. He had been warned by Retief that a commando force could not be maintained in the field for more than two or three months. A long, expensive campaign would be unpopular with his superiors in Britain who had for a long time been trying to cut military expenditures. It could lose him his job. To avoid that disaster he raised the stakes by ordering Hintsa, heir to the Gcaleka chiefs, to mount an attack on the Rharhabe coalition. As a token of his

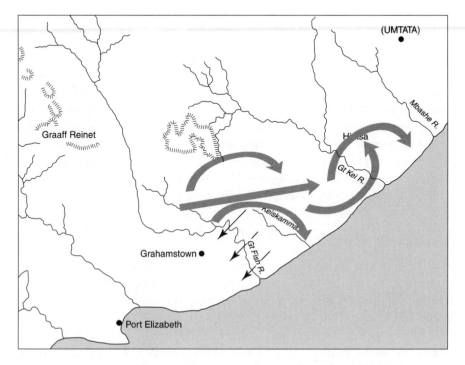

Map 19 The Anglo-Xhosa War of 1834–5. The thin arrows indicate the direction of the Xhosa advance in December 1834. The thick arrows indicate the direction and extent of the massive counter-attack by British army units and colonial commandos.

support Hintsa offered in early February to send 1000 men.[55] But as weeks passed, it became clear that he had no intention of betraying his fellow chiefs. D'Urban used this as an excuse to declare war on him. The British knew it would be far easier to win a war in the open country around Hintsa's capital near the Great Kei River. To justify the campaign, he accused Hintsa of 'masterminding' the whole war. Though he knew it was a lie, he insisted that Hintsa exercised supreme power over all the Xhosa. In pursuit of this new enemy, D'Urban moved the bulk of his forces hundreds of kilometres east where, on 24 April 1835, he finally issued an official declaration of war.[56] This, however, was merely the last act in a drama he had been planning since at least February. The object was to demonize Hintsa in every possible way: to blame him for the whole war and to portray him as a monster. Hintsa knew well enough what was going on and determined not to fight. Three days after the declaration of war he sent four men galloping on horseback to seek a meeting with D'Urban. Contrary to all the laws of war, British as well as Xhosa, they were seized as prisoners. The next day five more men were sent to the British camp with Hintsa's message: 'Why must I die? May I come and ask the reason?'[57] D'Urban replied that he received messages only from the King of England; if Hintsa had something to say, he must come in person. He pledged 'his honour that Hintsa shall return without molestation after the conference'. So the king came and learned that he could have peace if he delivered 2500 cattle and 500 horses within five days and another 28,000 cattle and 500 horses over the course of the coming year. He had to listen while D'Urban berated him for ingratitude. Back in 1828, said the governor, the British had 'saved Hintsa from the Fetcanie' (another lie; see Chapter 6, p. 170). Now the king had sent his forces into the British Zone all 'at once along the whole line from the Winterberg to the sea, wasting all the country with fire and sword, murdering the unprepared and defenceless inhabitants of the farms, pillaging the houses and sweeping off all the cattle, horses, sheep, etc'.[58] Hintsa felt he had no choice but to listen to the lies and insults. On 29 April he agreed to D'Urban's terms and shook hands.[59] And then was astonished to find himself held prisoner.

While this charade of negotiation continued, Hintsa's people did their best to safeguard their cattle. They found their efforts stymied to some extent by so-called 'Fingo' (Mfengu), who took the opportunity of the king's imprisonment to rise up and grab cattle while they could. A great many of these Mfengu were Hlubi, Sotho and Ngwane people who had accompanied Matiwane on his ill-fated migration to the Mtata River in 1828 (see Chapter 6, p. 172). Since that time they had lived in a lowly, largely cattle-less existence under Hintsa's protection. Naturally, Hintsa's people fought the Mfengu's opportunistic rising. Governor D'Urban now achieved new heights of hypocrisy. Forgetting that the Mfengu were the remnants of the 'Fetcani' whom Somerset had attacked in 1828, he threatened to hang Hintsa if he did not 'stop the carnage'. A few days later, Hintsa appears to have made a desperate bid for freedom, though the true facts will probably never be known. D'Urban claimed that the king had been 'shot while trying to escape' by George Southey, son of an English lyric poet.[60] Hintsa's ears were cut off as a trophy. D'Urban must have known that his deceitful and unsoldierly conduct would come to light some time. He and his officers engaged in an elaborate cover-up of the shameful facts, while attempting to cast themselves in the role of the humanitarians who had 'freed the Fingo' slaves. Even though the alleged 'criminal mastermind' behind the Xhosa attack was dead, the war against the dead king's innocent people continued. At D'Urban's urging, Faku came into the war on the British side, sending his seasoned Mpondo troops to attack the Xhosa from the north. Without being asked, in June 1835, Moshweshwe went with two of his sons at the head of a Sotho expeditionary force over the mountains.[61] The ostensible aim was to help their newly acquired British friends, but in other ways it strongly resembled the raids Moshweshwe had been making into that same territory for the last ten years.

Long before peace was declared, D'Urban marked his victory on 14 May 1835. He proclaimed that all the lands between the Keiskamma and Great Kei Rivers would, together with the old 'Ceded Territory', be annexed and named the Province of Queen Adelaide, in honour of the wife of Britain's King William IV. The remainder of the war was occupied with collecting Xhosa cattle, giving English names to places in the annexed territory, and 'bringing out the Fingo'.[62] The first mass exodus took place in May and involved as many as 16,000 people, with at least as many cattle. Seventeen-year-old Theophilus Shepstone, who had grown up among the Xhosa on a mission station and served as D'Urban's staff interpreter, watched the migration, declaring he had never seen 'so many cattle together in all my life'.[63] Whose cattle were they? Conceivably, some may have been seized from Matiwane by Hintsa's troops at the battle of Mbholompo in 1828, now retaken by their owners. But it seems more likely that they consisted of whatever cattle the 'Mfengu' managed to seize. If the Mfengu had possessed so many cattle, they would not have fitted the definition of 'slave' which D'Urban tried to pin on them. The vast number of cattle and horses seized during the campaign marks the war of 1835 as the first which the British fought like heartland chiefs. They hit their enemies where it hurt most by seizing the herds which underpinned their power. Some of these were redistributed to their allies, while others were retained to offset the costs of the war. Meanwhile, D'Urban fought a propaganda war on two fronts. He presented himself to the farmers and townspeople of Grahamstown as a man who warmly endorsed all their views. In May 1835, he told them that 'no two living things more perfectly resemble each other' than the wolf and the Xhosa.[64] To his political masters in London, he bragged that he had managed simultaneously to liberate the 'Fingo slaves' and solve the farmers' labour problems:

> Their subsistence . . . will bring no burthen upon the colony as they have brought with them some 16,000 head of cattle, many herds of goats, with corn and other food, and will immediately commence the culture of the land where they are placed.
>
> This supply of hired servants, and especially for all farming purposes, will be of the greatest benefit to the community for they are well known to be excellent for that purpose.[65]

Godlonton, the fire-breathing editor of the *Graham's Town Journal*, repaid D'Urban by praising him as the best governor of all time. Shifting all the blame for the war on to Hintsa's buried, earless head, enabled D'Urban to lay the basis for peace with the western chiefs who had been his original enemies. They kept their lives and positions by solemnly swearing that they had only obeyed Hintsa's orders. By December 1835 the governor was able to bring an end to hostilities by telling Faku that he could stop attacking the Xhosa.[66]

The war affected people in different ways, depending on their situation. The Xhosa had managed to kill a little over seventy civilians and military on the British side. Over 4000 of their own forces had died.[67] The loss of cattle on the Xhosa side was a disaster which would take years to repair. The land losses appeared on the surface to be equally catastrophic, though in practice the British could not have moved people out of 'Queen Adelaide Province' without reviving warfare and causing an uncontrollable exodus of women, men and children into the British Zone. In 1835 there were an estimated 74,000 people in the conquered territory, plus perhaps another 17,000 classified as 'Fingo'. This represented a population density of about ten times that in the rest of the British Zone.[68] While colonial farmers and speculators salivated at the prospects of new lands, there were no prospects for immediate occupation. Chiefs who had fought on the British side had to be accommodated, as did the 'Fingo'.[69] To keep the peace, the British launched a momentous experiment in government, placing officials as residents in various places with instructions to oversee chiefs in their administration of Xhosa principles of justice. The experiment would evolve over time into what became known as 'Indirect Rule'. The position of the Mfengu in this regime was anomalous because they came under British Rule without established chiefs. A great many of them were Xhosa who had been caught up in the unexpected exodus.[70] Others looked back to Hlubi, Ngwane and Zizi backgrounds. There were enough Hlubi to attract the attention of Mehlomakhulu, the son of Mpangazitha, who had been living under Sekonyela on the Caledon, since deserting Mzilikazi (see Chapter 6, pp. 163, 172). He visited them in 1838.[71] Over time, they developed a community self-consciousness built on a real or imagined northern Nguni origins. Those who did not disappear into the colonial farm work force adapted rapidly to a new life as farmers working on their own behalf, and showed a particular propensity to convert to the Christian religion. Increasing prosperity enhanced their perception of shared origins.

News of the war electrified the Zulu kingdom. It would be gratifying to imagine that Dingane repented many times over his execution of Jacob Msimbiti, the man who had given timely warning. As the king contemplated measures for his own defence, he had, for the first time, the advantage of independent advice, uncontaminated by the lies of the Port Natal traders. About the time the Anglo–Xhosa war began, a man named Allen Gardiner had appeared as if from nowhere, asking permission to come as a missionary. Though he represented no missionary society and had no connections with government, Gardiner appeared to suit the king's needs. He understood military matters, because he had previously been a captain in the British navy – as was evident when he put on his dress uniform. Instead of talking vaguely about 'the white king over the sea', he brought pictures illustrating life at the English court.[72] None of the previous British visitors had shown such sympathetic interest. Gardiner was evidently enchanted. The king was not the 'angry tyrant' he had been led to expect. Everywhere there was laughter, music, poetry and dance. Dingane was a connoisseur of the arts. He had designed the costumes of the women whom he led into the dancing ring 'with much natural grace' and 'no ordinary ease and agility'. The songs chanted were 'chiefly of his own composition', for he had 'a good ear and a correct taste'.

'Are we not', Dingane asked, 'a merry people? What black nations can vie with us? Who among them can dress as we do?' He took a keen interest in European fashion from Gardiner's dress uniform to the sweeping gowns of the women he saw in pictures walking arm in arm with gentlemen of the English court. 'What?' he exclaimed. 'Is this how you walk with women in your country?' The king, who was 'dearly fond of a joke', turned a demonstration of literacy into a contest for the women of his court who would 'not believe that you can do the things that are written down, unless you were present when the directions were noted – but I tell them you can'. Entering into the fun, Gardiner stood outside the fence while his interpreter wrote in pencil the names of several concealed objects. Then the king roared triumphantly as the missionary plucked one after another from its hiding place.

Gardiner, for his part, was appalled to find that the Port Natal traders had built up large cattle holdings as rewards for leading their riflemen on campaigns with the Zulu army. Knowing very well that those same men claimed huge tracts of land, he questioned Dingane closely on the status of the 'grants'. The king acknowledged Shaka's grants of land around Port Natal to Farewell, Fynn and Cane, but said that he had cancelled all but Fynn's grant because of their unfriendly acts. As for the country between the Thukela and Mzimkhulu Rivers, he had permitted them to hunt over that district 'but had never intended that it shall be construed into territorial possession'. Dingane's first impulse was to make Gardiner his agent over those lands, but after further consideration he proposed a new arrangement according to which Gardiner would assume control of a small territory in the vicinity of Port Natal and agree to return outlaws who attempted to escape from his justice. Gardiner could see that this might be the making of his mission, but to accomplish it, he would need some sort of backing from Britain. D'Urban, whose previous plan to annex Natal had been vetoed by his superiors in London, was happy to endorse Gardiner's new plan. With this encouragement, the captain sailed away, after promising Dingane he would return as soon as he had secured support from a missionary society.[73] Understanding at last the dangers posed by men who had talked in the British Zone of unoccupied land ready to be taken, Dingane began moving people over the Thukela to forestall any attempt at conquest. As a first step he proposed settling people in towns and villages along the course of the Mvoti River right up to the Drakensberg mountains.

Far away to the north, Mzilikazi had heard about the Anglo–Xhosa war even before he heard in March 1835 that Andrew Smith was coming to see him. His spies had been to Grahamstown, noted the effects of British artillery, seen that the population there outnumbered his people and warned that 'their soldiers never sleep either by day or by night'.[74] The size of Smith's party would in itself have been enough to frighten him. Fortunately, they had taken the precautions of sending messengers ahead and arranging for the return of cattle the Tlhaping chief Mahura had stolen from him. When the Smith party, reinforced by Robert Moffat, finally arrived in June, Mzilikazi took great pains to lay the groundwork for future good relations. He explained that his people wished to be called Zulu; they hated the name Matabele. He literally threw himself upon Moffat and called him his father. He pointed out that he had taken care to preserve the church the French missionaries had so foolishly forsaken. At a Sunday service conducted during the visit, he ordered that his people should cease all singing and dancing for the rest of the day. He sat decorously on a chair throughout the proceedings, rising when the others did to offer prayers.

When Smith questioned him about the attack on Peter David's party and the capture of his daughter, Mzilikazi did his best to convince him that after a decade of bitter experience he had good reason to suspect all Griqua and Kora bands. Some of David's party had been with Barends in the great commando of 1832. If they wanted their property returned, they could bring an appropriate amount of cattle to exchange in accordance with established custom. Mzilikazi went on to caution Smith that he kept a close eye on anyone going armed on the Vaal plains north of the Maloti mountains. Dingane had sent a commando that way in 1832. From that direction too came raiding parties of the Tlokwa, the people the British called Mantatees, 'always looking out for opportunities to raid and murder'. Mzilikazi had found it necessary, he explained, to retaliate against them with sufficient ferocity to discourage further plundering.

Setting out his hopes for the future, the king wished first of all to have white men living with him as Dingane did. If American missionaries were to come, as Moffat suggested, he had already selected a place for them to live at Mosega. He needed whites primarily to protect himself against Jan Bloem. If he could not acquire some, he would move south to be nearer to Moffat. He would have visited Kuruman in person before this time, had he not feared that his approach with the necessary number of attendants would have been mistaken for a commando. His second requirement was guns. He was willing, indeed eager, to trade ivory to get them. He had practised with the rifles captured from Barends, and was good enough to shoot birds. Nothing would please him better than to have Smith carry out his promise of sending ammunition and a large gun.

The conferences with Smith ended with great shows of friendship and goodwill. Smith presented the king with one of his large tents and a number of masks. Mzilikazi was particularly tickled by this last gift. Nothing of the kind had been seen in his country before. He looked forward to frightening unsuspecting people with the weird European masks. It was further arranged that a group of his chiefs would go with Smith as ambassadors to the governor at Cape Town. Behind all the ostensible camaraderie, however, both sides maintained a cautious, even suspicious view of their possible future relations. Mzilikazi led a dance accompanied by recently composed songs and ferocious gestures. When Smith asked whether this was meant to show how Jan Bloem's next commando would be received, the king said no. It was intended to show how his people would react if the British drove the Xhosa over the mountains, and they came after his cattle. When Smith asked his official guide to show how to reach the sources of the Vaal, the guide wondered aloud whether the real purpose was not to spy out new lands for the British to seize.

Smith for his part made absolutely sure that Mzilikazi's ambassadors understood the lesson of the late war against the Xhosa. After his return home, he wrote that:

> I have let them understand that the white people . . . have been forced to eat up the sons of the late Gaika and kill Hintza. . . . their respect for the govt has been materially increased in the last week by a conversation I had with a Machuana in their presence. . . . He went through the whole affair, pictured the horrible effects of guns and bombs and finished by say[ing] that . . . [even though] they had behaved so badly to the colony, the Governor had taken pity upon them and had given them lands and cattle again. The chiefs could not understand such generosity and declared immediately that . . . nothing ought to have been given them, all ought to have been killed.[75]

As Smith reflected with satisfaction on this healthy show of respect for British power and the crushing defeat inflicted on the Xhosa, there was only one cloud on his horizon. From conversations he had since his return, it appeared that 'a sort of recklessness' had 'got possession of numbers of the Boers'. There was something very like the odour of rebellion in the air.[76]

Notes

1 The travellers, Cowie and Green, ignored warnings not to go to the Bay in fever season and died not long after their arrival. The notes they made of their visit were sent on by the Portuguese commander and are summarized in *Records of Natal*, II, pp. 183–8.

2 Nathaniel Isaacs, *Travels and Adventures in Eastern Africa*, revised and edited L. Herman and P. R. Kirby (Cape Town, 1970), p. 186.

3 Comments of Andrew Smith on a petition seeking annexation of Natal, 6 May 1835, in *Records of Natal*, II, pp. 251–2.

4 Isaacs, *Travels and Adventures*, p. 289.

5 Memorandum of Duncan Campbell, 19 Dec. 1828, in *Records of Natal*, II, p. 52.

6 Campbell to Lt Col. Bell, 26 Dec. 1830 in *Records of Natal*, II, pp. 172–3.

7 Isaacs, *Travels and Adventures*, p. 259.

8 Stockenstrom to the Secretary to Government, 31 Aug. 1831, in *Records of Natal*, II, pp. 208–9.

9 W. F. Lye, ed., *Andrew Smith's Journal of his Expedition into the Interior of South Africa/1834–36* (Cape Town, 1975), pp. 2–4; P. R. Kirby, ed., *Andrew Smith and Natal* (Cape Town, 1955), pp. 1–9.

10 H. F. Fynn to W. R. Thompson, 21 July 1831, in *Records of Natal*, II, pp. 202–8.

11 For the dates see J. B. Peires, *The House of Phalo: A History of the Xhosa People in the Days of their Independence* (Johannesburg, 1981), pp. 49, 83, 86.

12 Isaacs, *Travels and Adventures*, pp. 281–2, citing notes he said he had taken after a conversation with Fynn on 29 May 1831. This is one of the best known stories in Isaacs's book. While historians have doubted Isaacs on many points, the correspondence between this account and Fynn's letter to Thompson of 21 July 1831 (note 10), which Isaacs could not have seen, is very close.

13 Isaacs, *Travels and Adventures*, pp. 256, 261–2, 265–7, 271, 279; D. Campbell to Lt Col. Bell, 12 Aug. 1831, in *Records of Natal*, II, p. 201.

14 Isaacs's account of his part in these events, in *Travels and Adventures*, cannot be trusted. He was well aware that he was suspected of gun-running and other crimes which would have made him liable to punishment in the British Zone.

15 H. F. Fynn to W. R. Thompson, 21 July 1831, in *Records of Natal*, II, pp. 202–8.

16 Statement of W. M. Fynn, made at Bunting mission, Mpondo country, 21 July 1831, in *Records of Natal*, II, pp. 198–200.

17 See statement from a merchant dealing at Uitenhage, 20 July 1831, in *Records of Natal*, II, p. 208. The very vehemence with which Nathaniel Isaacs denies the charge of gun-running in *Travels and Adventures*, p. 256, seems to indicate its truth.

18 Julian Cobbing, 'Grasping the Nettle: The Slave Trade and the Early Zulu', paper presented to the Workshop on Natal and Zululand in the Colonial and Precolonial Periods, University of Natal, Pietermaritzburg, 1990.

19 Christopher Saunders, 'Liberated Africans in the Cape Colony in the First Half of the Nineteenth Century', *International Journal of African Historical Studies* 18 (1985), pp. 223–39.

20 On occasions the reeking slave ships were simply left to rot on the shores of Brazil after unloading their loathsome cargoes.

21 Malyn Newitt, *A History of Mozambique* (London, 1995), pp. 292–3.

22 Elephants could still be found north of St Lucia Bay in the 1840s. A French hunter reported shooting seven elephants in seven days; Adulphe Delegorgue, *Voyage dans l'Afrique Australe*, 2 vols (Paris, 1847), II, p. 2.

23 *Natal Papers*, I, 2: 34–5.

24 Ibid. Other reports say that Dingane permitted John Cane to kill Jacob; see Graham Mackeurtan, *The Cradle Days of Natal (1497–1845)* (London, 1930), p. 167. It may be doubted whether such an extreme departure from usual practice would have been allowed.

25 Kirby, ed., *Andrew Smith and Natal*, pp. 6–7.

26 Dated 6 May 1834, *Records of Natal*, II, pp. 251–2.

27 The man was Hermanus Barry, a Swellendam farmer with an English father and an Afrikaner mother; Timothy Keegan, *Colonial South Africa and the Origins of the Racial Order* (London, 1996), p. 193.

28 A. Gardiner to Governor D'Urban, 24 Nov. 1835, in *Records of Natal*, III, pp. 19–22; Keegan, *Colonial South Africa*, pp. 193–4.

29 The ordinance was passed over D'Urban's objection, but disallowed by the British government in London; see Alan C. Webster, 'Land Expropriation and Labour Extraction under Cape Colonial Rule: The War of 1835 and the "Emancipation of the Fingo"' (MA thesis, Rhodes University, 1991), p. 66.

30 Civil Commissioner for Albany and Somerset to the Acting Secretary to Government, 14 Feb. 1834, *Records of Natal*, II, pp. 241–2.

31 Martin Legassick, 'The Griqua, the Sotho-Tswana and the Missionaries, 1780–1840' (PhD thesis, UCLA, 1969), p. 495.

32 D'Urban memorandum, 6 June 1834, in *Records of Natal*, II, pp. 248–9; D'Urban's own underlining.

33 Webster, 'Land Expropriation', pp. 64, 225.

34 D. Campbell and H. Somerset to the Acting Secretary to Government, 25 July 1834, in *Records of Natal*, II, pp. 270–1.

35 D'Urban to T. Spring Rice, 31 Oct. 1834, in *Records of Natal*, II, p. 234.

36 J. P. R. Wallis, ed., *The Matabele Journals of Robert Moffat, 1829–1860*, 2 vols (London, 1945), I, p. 72.

37 W. F. Lye, ed., *Andrew Smith's Journal*, p. 20.

38 Ibid., pp. 118, 134.

39 Ibid., p. 148.

40 Smith's official report of 1836, printed in G. M. Theal, ed., *Basutoland Records*, p. 9.

41 For the incidents of Smith's journey cited below see, Lye, ed., *Andrew Smith's Journal*, especially pp. 27–31, 33, 35–7, 42, 43–7, 58–64, 74–6, 79–82, 89–92, 116–17, 136–42.

42 Theal, ed., *Basutoland Records,* I, p. 3.

43 Somerset's 'Remarks on the Military Defence of the Eastern Frontier of the Cape Colony', 20 Mar. 1833, in *Records of Natal*, II, pp. 232–5.

44 Webster, 'Land Expropriation', pp. 64–7.

45 Peires, *The House of Phalo*, p. 93.

46 Ibid., p. 108.

47 Ibid., p. 94; Webster, 'Land Expropriation', p. 108. For other evidence of increased volumes of trade, see Kirby, *Andrew Smith and Natal*, pp. 15, 116.

48 Webster, 'Land Expropriation', pp. 68–70.

49 Ibid., p. 75.

50 Peires, *The House of Phalo*, p. 146.

51 Webster, 'Land Expropriation', pp. 95, 183.

52 Peires, *The House of Phalo*, p. 149.

53 Webster, 'Land Expropriation', pp. 93–5.

54 Noël Mostert, *Frontiers: The Epic of South Africa's Creation and the Tragedy of the Xhosa People* (London, 1992), pp. 704–12.

55 Webster, 'Land Expropriation', p. 111.

56 Ibid., pp. 113–14.

57 For eye-witness accounts of Hintsa's messages see the Journal of Theophilus Shepstone, April 1835, Shepstone Papers, volume for the years 1835–49, Natal Archives, Pietermaritzburg. Seventeen-year-old Shepstone, the son of a Methodist missionary, had been chosen as D'Urban's interpreter because of his fluency in the Xhosa language.

58 D'Urban's communication to Hintsa, 29 April 1835 in *Records of Natal*, II, p. 294.

59 Shepstone Journal, April 1835.

60 Peires, *The House of Phalo*, pp. 11–12; Webster, 'Land Expropriation', p. 120.

61 *Journal des Missions Évangéliques* 11 (1836), pp. 23, 140–1; Leonard Thompson, *Survival in Two Worlds: Moshoeshoe of Lesotho, 1786–1870* (Oxford, 1975), p. 83.

62 Shepstone Journal, May 1835.

63 Ruth Gordon, *Shepstone: The Role of the Family in the History of South Africa, 1820–1900* (Cape Town, 1968), p. 88. Pages and pages of Shepstone's journal for 1835 consist of undated descriptions and enumerations of cattle.

64 Webster, 'Land Expropriation', p. 195.

65 D'Urban to the Earl of Aberdeen, Secretary of State, 19 June 1835 in *Records of Natal*, II, pp. 282–93.

66 H. G. Smith to D'Urban, confidential, 15 Dec. 1835, in *Records of Natal*, III, pp. 22–4.

67 Webster, 'Land Expropriation', p. 187.

68 Alan Lester, 'Settlers, the State and Colonial Power: the Colonization of Queen Adelaide Province, 1834–37', *Journal of African History* 39 (1998), pp. 221–46.

69 Shepstone Journal, 4 June 1835.

70 Alan Webster, 'Unmasking the Fingo, the War of 1835 Revisited', in Carolyn Hamilton, ed., *The Mfecane Aftermath: Reconstructive Debates in Southern African History* (Johannesburg, 1995), pp. 261–74.

71 See the account of his visit to the Hlubi Mfengu as related in W. Shaw to A. Stockenstrom, 20 June 1838, *Records of Natal*, III, p. 313.

72 The conversations described in this and the next paragraph are drawn from Gardiner's *Narrative of a Journey to the Zoolu Country in South Africa* (London, 1836), pp. 14, 32–3, 37, 39, 42–3, 52–3, 57, 67–8, 71, 77, 122, 127, 131–4, 151, 161–3, 169–71, 177–80, 213.

73 Gardiner to D'Urban, 24 Nov. 1835, D'Urban to Glenelg, 4 Dec. 1835, and Gardiner to Col. Bell, 13 June 1837, in *Records of Natal*, III, pp. 9–10, 19–22, 178, 186–7.

74 Lye, ed., *Andrew Smith's Journal*, p. 200. For other details of Mzilikazi's reception of Smith cited in this and the following paragraphs, see the same *Journal*, pp. 199–200, 217, 231–2, 236, 238–42, 258; Wallis, ed., *The Matabele Journals of Robert Moffat*, I, pp. 84, 86–9, 92, 96; R. Kent Rasmussen, *Migrant Kingdom: Mzilikazi's Ndebele in South Africa* (Cape Town, 1978), p. 85.

75 Smith, 16 Jan. 1836, in *Records of Natal*, III, pp. 24–5.

76 Ibid.

CHAPTER NINE

The coming of the Boer trekkers, 1836–8

The trekking movement

Within a very short time, what Andrew Smith perceived as a spirit of rebellion among the eastern Boers manifested itself as an invasion of the highveld and Natal. During the years 1836–8 perhaps as many as 8000 people left the British Zone, intending to make permanent homes in the heartland.[1] Although the number involved in this migration was less than the number who had joined the Rolong trek from Plaatberg to Thaba Nchu in 1833 or those who joined Mzilikazi on his progress from the Drakensberg to the north-west, the movement left a more enduring mark on the land. This was mainly because the new wave of invaders came heavily armed. By mid-1837 they counted some 1600 armed and mounted men in their ranks – a fighting force of unprecedented destructive power.[2] They also brought with them a system of land appropriation based on title deeds which enabled them to inscribe territorial claims on maps. When, in later years, those claims were endorsed by British governments, they served as the foundation stones of colonial rule which was to last 150 years.

None of the important regional rulers had prepared to face this menace. Moshweshwe, Sekonyela and Adam Kok felt more secure after Andrew Smith assured them of official British friendship. None of them expected the appearance of Boer forces independent of British control. Mzilikazi had anticipated that defeated Xhosa might flee in his direction, but otherwise he maintained nothing more than his usual defences against Griqua and Kora raids. Dingane, warned by the missionary Allen Gardiner against possible attempts to seize land south of the Thukela River, had begun to settle his people in those districts; but he did not know from what direction the threat might come.

Even after the wagons of trekking Boers had begun to move, the magnitude of the long-term threat was not recognized because the invaders came in small parties rather than regiments. An Afrikaner veld cornet, G. D. Joubert, who had been asked to survey their intentions, reported to the Civil Commissioner of Graaf Reinet in February 1836,

> that they purpose settling somewhere in the neighbourhood of the Portuguese settlement from which they may have their gunpowder, clothing, etc. They are first going as far as the Vaal river, from whence they intend sending out an observatory party. The reason why they leave the colony they state to be because they see no chance of subsisting upon their small farms and as the greater number of them have none at all. I have heard, but do not recollect from whom, that some of them are dissatisfied with the government and laws of the colony, but I do not know whether such is the case for those who have left my ward were highly offended and remonstrated with me for having dashed their names out of my list, and because I informed them that they would no longer be taken to belong to our parish. The greater part or almost every one of those who have for some years been in the habit of wandering over the boundaries but who have desire to remain upon my list still cleave to the government of this colony and have earnestly begged me not to strike their names out of my list or to confound them with those who leave the colony entirely. So that the reports seem exaggerated.
>
> You must not suppose that those people go in a regular band of any considerable number, they go in parties of 2, 3, 4 or 5 families. Some, I hear, take their course over the high country towards Port Natal, others to the Vaal river. Some will remain moving about near the Modder river and sources of the Caledon. I imagine that an entire ruin will soon fall upon these people and those who are not destroyed will return to the colony or near to its boundaries or they will in time become as uncivilised as the heathens.[3]

A typical group consisted of a handful of families travelling together under the leadership of a senior male. These groups tended to be known by the name of their chiefs, i.e., the Cilliers Party, the Bronkhorst Party, the Potgieter Party, etc., even though people with many other surnames were to be found among them. They moved in through territory held by the Griqua, people whom they closely resembled in language, religion and customs. To people living further inland they appeared at first to be just more wagon loads of Griqua families, potentially dangerous because of their predatory proclivities, but a known quantity.

In contrast, people living in the British Zone viewed 'the movement of the emigrant farmers' as a momentous break with the past. This had a lot to do with timing. The wagons began to roll towards the end of the

Anglo–Xhosa war of 1834–5, at a time when the British administration was losing its confidence, cohesion and sense of direction. Elements within the British Parliament who had successfully fought for the abolition of slavery were turning their attention to other violations of human rights. In May 1835 a Select Committee chaired by the anti-slavery champion Thomas Fowell Buxton began to collect evidence about the treatment of 'Aborigines' – the original inhabitants of colonies annexed to the British Empire around the globe. In the course of these hearings, undeniable evidence emerged to show that the Xhosa chiefs had been driven to fight by injustices perpetrated against them. The murder of Hintsa and other atrocities committed in the course of the war also came to light. In the same year a new minister, Lord Glenelg, took charge of Britain's colonial affairs. Like Buxton, Glenelg had close connections to anti-slavery campaigners and was inclined to condemn D'Urban's conduct of the war. He found supporters among his ministerial colleagues appalled by the sheer cost of the war and frightened by the potential expense of annexing and defending 'Queen Adelaide Province'.[4] D'Urban tried to counter his critics by invoking the support of the still powerful military establishment in England, including the Duke of Wellington and King William IV, but this was not enough to stop Lord Glenelg from calling upon him to justify his policies or risk having the annexation of the conquered territories revoked. Glenelg's dispatch landed on D'Urban's desk in March 1836. At about the same time, the governor learned that Glenelg had appointed Andries Stockenstrom as lieutenant governor to take charge of affairs in the eastern section of the British Zone. D'Urban and his soldier clique treated these developments as personal affronts. They fought with every weapon at their disposal to discredit Glenelg and to defend the annexation. Colonel Harry Smith resigned his commission as commander of Queen Adelaide Province, and began firing off letters to his old comrades-in-arms from the Napoleonic wars.[5] The military dissidents had no trouble enlisting support from the landholding élite in the Grahamstown region, chief among them Robert Godlonton, editor of the *Graham's Town Journal*. His newspaper and other voices denounced Lord Glenelg as the tool of mischievous humanitarians and missionaries, especially John Philip of the London Missionary Society who had taken a delegation of Griqua and Xhosa representatives to testify before Buxton's Parliamentary Committee. Even though Lieutenant Governor Stockenstrom was an experienced magistrate raised among Boer farmers (whom he called 'his countrymen'), he too found himself damned as the tool of the missionaries, simply because he had told Buxton's committee that the old system of dealing with cross-border cattle-raiding had proved to be unworkable.

In short, by the middle of 1836 British administration in South Africa teetered on the verge of paralysis. The military men were at odds with their civilian superiors in England. British settlers were at odds with the home government. The governor was actively undermining his lieutenant governor.[6] Consequently, no one in authority took any effective action to halt or control the Boers trekking north across the Orange. On the contrary, the antagonists within the British camp used the trekkers as weapons with which to beat their enemies. Godlonton and his civilian allies claimed that the Boers were so demoralized by Glenelg's reversal of the annexation that they determined to leave a colony negligent of their interests. It was said that when they heard Glenelg had branded them as aggressors, they immediately 'began to prepare for a most extensive abandonment of their native homes, indignant at having insult added to injury'.[7] Having 'shed their blood in defence of the colony', they were thunderstruck to find 'compensation for their losses was withheld'. D'Urban claimed that by revoking his power to operate beyond the official borders, Glenelg had rendered him powerless to pursue the trekkers. Stockenstrom, feeling himself surrounded by enemies, refused to take any action, merely saying in August 1836 that he knew of no law which could stop the movement.[8] The trekkers barged through an open door.

In fact, discussions about moving had begun well before the war, fuelled by Andrew Smith's enthusiastic reports of prospects for agriculture in the hinterland of Port Natal (see Chapter 8, p. 218). Hunting and trading parties who had travelled north of the Orange River spread information about other good grazing lands.[9] As early as February 1834, the Civil Commissioner for Albany and Somerset had reported to the governor that certain individuals contemplated moving out of the British Zone 'with the avowed object of evading the operation of the slave abolition law . . . another scheme . . . is to take possession of the unoccupied land between St. John's river and Natal, of the fertility of which they have been receiving florid descriptions for some years past from the traders who have travelled that tract of the sea coast in their journeys to and from Natal'.[10] Some historians would later interpret these reports and visions as evidence that an organized scheme had been secretly devised by a network of key leaders who were determined to throw off the yoke of British government. Those historians recast simple hunting and trading expeditions of the early 1830s as 'kommissie trekke' (literally, commission treks) designed to spy out land for settlement.[11] Certainly, there was great interest in removing obstacles to emigration, but careful scholarship has demolished the legend of an organized secret conspiracy.[12] Of more immediate importance as an impetus for large numbers to trek was the onset of severe drought in 1836.[13]

The first parties came without fanfare, among them a group headed by Louis Tregardt (or Trichardt), son of a Swedish father and a Boer mother. In 1834 he and thirty Boer families had moved onto grazing land in Hintsa's territory. Most likely, Hintsa had welcomed them as a source of guns and ammunition. Tregardt himself was known to have installed false floorboards in his wagon for the purpose of hiding arms purchased in Grahamstown. He had also gained notoriety for illegally taking slaves outside the British Zone.[14] A patrol guided by one of his own escaped slaves, 'Philis', swooped on Tregardt's settlement at the White Kei River in November 1834 and found a further fourteen slaves. When Colonel Harry Smith offered a reward of 500 cattle for his capture, Tregardt fled, along with a party of about fifty people.[15] For a time he travelled with another sizeable party headed by Johannes van Rensburg. Their goal was the Portuguese stronghold at Delagoa Bay where they would be safe from British prosecution. Not surprisingly, people they met along the way took the Tregardt party to be a band of ivory traders and offered to sell elephant tusks.[16] Finding the way to Delagoa Bay was no easy task. Printed maps of that era gave a misleading impression of the highveld. Anyone reading the Arrowsmith map of 1835, which even the British military relied on, would have been deceived into supposing that Delagoa Bay was only a few days' travel from the upper Vaal River.[17] Tregardt solved some of his problems by engaging a Sotho-speaking man from the Caledon Valley who knew the way to Pedi country in the Steelpoort/Olifant's River region.[18] The daily diary he kept comprehensively refutes notions of a great regional depopulation, for he found flourishing communities and strong chiefs wherever he went.

Some word of Tregardt's adventures eventually filtered back to BaSotho people. It was said that he had gone in search of salt in the territory controlled by the powerful chief, Makopane, whose sphere of influence was the region around the modern town of Potgietersrus. People showed Tregardt the way to a natural salt marsh where he soon filled his wagon. But because he had wandered into tse-tse fly country, his oxen were bitten and died. He secured replacements by threatening inhabitants of a village with death if they refused his request. With the oxen acquired through this act of extortion, he eventually rejoined the rest of his party in the territory of the Pedi paramount chief, Sekwati. In the same territory he encountered two sons of Coenraad de Buys and a pair of 'soldiers' from Delagoa Bay, who could point the way down to the Portuguese fort. No doubt all four were engaged in slaving. Not that this would have bothered Tregardt, whose party included several 'Bushmen children' and two captive BaSotho women. Getting the wagons down the Drakensberg escarpment was no easy business. In the end it was Boer women who spied out the way to begin the descent.[19] When Tregardt reached the lowlands he had reason to regret his plan. He and practically all his party fell ill with malaria and eventually died. The van Rensburg party, who went another way, simply vanished. Their wanderings left few traces on the map; neither party would have been

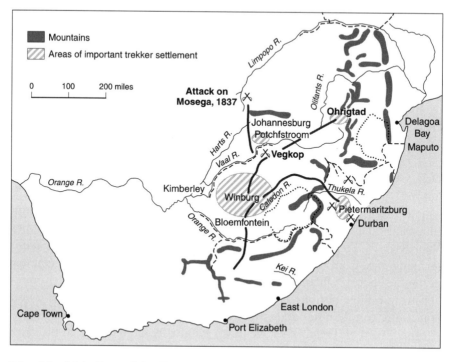

Map 20   Main lines of the Trekker Invasion, 1836–45

remembered today but for the thousands who followed them onto the highveld. Those people would come to treasure the fruitless wanderings of Tregardt and van Rensburg as heroic prefigurings of what was to come.

Many who followed also began with the intention of reaching Portuguese territory, but abandoned their plans when they learned the true facts about the distances they would have to travel and the deadly diseases which could kill them, their cattle and their sheep.[20] The attractions of a land where slavery was legal could not outweigh these perils. Besides, very few of the trekkers had been substantial slave-holders. Their main objective was to find land free for the taking. Once they saw the vast grasslands drained by the Vaal River system, many of them had second thoughts. Here was land enough for all their flocks and herds. Much of it seemed, to their untrained eyes, to be empty apart from antelope, hyenas and lions. They did not share the traditional preference for locating themselves on the sides of hills and mountains. They were happy to live near the bottom of river valleys. They did not understand the spatial organization of large chieftaincies and kingdoms, which clustered settlements and planted fields in favourable locations but projected power over much larger landscapes. On the other hand, the trekkers confidently assumed that their armed commandos would serve them as well on the highveld as they had back in the British Zone.

For their part, many chiefs misunderstood the long-term threats posed by the invaders. Griqua grabbed an opportunity to gain money by leasing land to Boers.[21] They were for some time fooled by professions of friendship, such as those later offered by the trekker commandant, Hendrick Potgieter, who told Griqua leaders, 'We are emigrants together with you . . . who dwell in the same strange land and we desire to be regarded as neither more nor less than your fellow-emigrants, inhabitants of the country, enjoying the same privileges with you.'[22] Other chiefs greeted Boers the way they would greet anyone who asked permission to live in their territory. They welcomed them as new people who would add strength to their chieftainship. Still others sought to enlist the Boers in their schemes to regain lost cattle and territory. Tlhaping, Rolong, Taung and Hurutshe chiefs who had suffered at the hands of Mzilikazi hoped that Boer horses and guns would enable them to build a grand alliance that would succeed where Barend Barends had failed. At Thaba Nchu, headquarters of so many dispossessed, inveterate enemies of Mzilikazi, the trekkers met a warm reception and eager offers of alliance. It seemed a good place to stop and learn the lie of the land. The pattern of future governance was set by parties led by Sarel (or Charl) Cilliers and Hendrick Potgieter who arrived here early in 1836. From long experience of commandos, the trekkers realized that some military order would be required in unknown territory. The sixty-five armed men in the party voted that Potgieter should be their commandant and

Cilliers the deputy. Having secured a position on the Sand River by offering an alliance to the Taung chief, Makwana, the party established a temporary camp. Potgieter and a small party of men set out in May 1836 to find a route to Delagoa Bay. They left the rest of their party encamped in a position which was bound to worry Mzilikazi.

The king had pointedly asked Andrew Smith the year before whether the real purpose of his expedition had been to spy out territory on the tributaries of the Vaal River for settlement by white farmers. Smith had emphatically denied it.[23] On 3 March 1836, Mzilikazi's envoy, Mncumbathe, had concluded a treaty of friendship with Governor D'Urban in Cape Town.[24]

Now, out of the blue, without asking anyone's permission, whole families of white people had appeared in an area where Mzilikazi's intelligence network patrolled constantly, reporting every suspicious movement. Although no record of the king's deliberations survives, it is reasonable to assume that he felt deceived and betrayed. This was not a commando like those mounted by Bloem or Barends. These people came with wagons, women, children. Bags and baggage. Herds and slaves. There could be no doubt that this was an invasion. Of course, according to the rules by which Mzilikazi played, invasions happened. Eleven years before, *he* had been the invader coming with fighting men, herds, women and children. The rules said that the contest between invaders and defenders would be decided on the field of battle. He would not wait for the trekkers to steal his herds. He would strike first.

His regiments attacked Potgieter's camp on 26 August 1836. When the Boer exploring party returned a week later, they found the field littered with corpses and most of the cattle gone.[25] At this point the trekker forces split, some moving well away to the south, while a group of about fifty wagons moved four days' journey south of the Vaal to a place they called Vegkop (south of present-day Heilbron). A few weeks later, in mid-October, Mzilikazi sent a much larger force of perhaps 5000 men under the command of his veteran general, Kaliphi. This time the trekkers were ready. They had drawn about forty-five wagons into the circular formation they called a laager. Thorny branches filled the gaps in the perimeter and heavy hides hung over the wagon canvas, providing further protection against spears.[26] At the centre of the laager a square formed from wagons gave additional protection to women and children. The defending force numbered less than forty trekker men. However, the contest carried a weight disproportionate to the numbers involved. It was the first full-dress battle between an African army and a trekker encampment in defensive formation.

What the outcome might have been had Kaliphi mounted the usual pre-dawn surprise attack is difficult to say. In the event the trekkers had advance warning of the approaching forces from their Tswana and Sotho scouts. A day before he expected to attack, Kaliphi was shocked to see a force of thirty-three mounted Boers riding toward him while he was still about 10 kilometres away from the laager. Confused and contradictory accounts suggest that the trekkers attempted to negotiate peace, using a 'Fingo' interpreter (presumably of Hlubi or Ngwane origin). Kaliphi explained that Mzilikazi alone could countermand his orders. As his forces attempted to surround the horsemen, shots rang out and the first stage of the battle began. The trekkers fought as generations of commandos had fought before them: dismounting, firing volleys, and then riding away to reload.

For Kaliphi, retreat was not an option. He had no choice but to send his men in hot pursuit, all the way to Vegkop. Three hours later, in the full heat of day, his men surrounded the laager and sat down to catch their breath. Staying just out of range of the defenders' musketfire, they seized and slaughtered some cattle, then ate them raw. Next they took off their sandals and heaped them up in a great pile; they would need to be surefooted during the final onslaught. Clad in their battle dress of monkey- and cat-tail kilts, their arms adorned with braided ox-tails, they presented a splendid and terrifying spectacle. At their general's command they seized their kit of throwing and stabbing spears and began to beat rhythmically on their great cowhide shields. Then they ran at the wagons, shouting the name of their king.

Each of the trekker men had taken his place at the front of his wagon, a musket in his hands, and another at his feet, along with a pile of ammunition and a powder-horn. In the face of Kaliphi's thousands, there would be little time available to ram heavy bullets into their muskets. Some of the defenders fired alternate rounds of bullet and shot. Others attempted a faster rate of fire, dropping powder, little bags of shot and shrapnel directly into the muzzles.[27] These sent deadly showers into the massed ranks of their attackers. Many of the boys, servants and women took their place by the wagons, some shooting, others reloading muskets. While some of the attackers hurled spears, others vainly attempted to scale the thornbush barriers between the wagons. Still others tried to crawl between the wheels, only to find Boer women waiting with hatchets to bury in their skulls. The smoke of the dust raised by running feet mingled with the smoke of the musketfire to shroud the battleground in thick haze.

Amazingly, not a single man managed to break into the ring of wagons. The corpses of their comrades mounted till hundreds lay dead. Less than an hour after the first rush at the laager, Kaliphi gave up the struggle and gave the signal to move off. From one point of view the attack had been spectacularly successful, taking some 5–6000 head of cattle and about 41,000 sheep and goats. On the other hand, the disparity in death rates had been frightful. Some 430 of the attackers fell before the musketfire of the Boers, while the 1600 spears thrown had killed two men and wounded fourteen others.[28] Mzilikazi's drive to acquire firearms had begun too late. According to a missionary who witnessed the return of the battered army, 'there was nothing but lamentation heard in the land for weeks on account of those slain in battle'.[29]

Meanwhile, shaken and hungry, the trekkers retreated again to Thaba Nchu. From missionary James Archbell and his wife they got food. From Rolong, Taung, Kora and Hurutshe refugees they got knowledgeable re-inforcements, eager to join another great commando against their old foe. Regaining lost stock was the first priority for the trekkers; without their herds, they were no richer than any other cattleless people on the highveld. Their African allies hoped that a new commando would succeed where the efforts of Barend Barends had failed in earlier years. Mzilikazi's attack had concentrated the trekker forces in one location and shown the need for clear lines of leadership. A men's meeting held in early December 1836 chose Andries Hendrick Potgieter as military commandant and chairman of the *Krygsraad* (Council of War). A separate civil administration headed by a new arrival, Gerrit Maritz, was granted the power to make laws. Under the joint command of Potgieter and Maritz, 107 of the Boer men were ready to ride against Mzilikazi. Riding with them were another forty Griqua horsemen under Peter David and several of Gert Taaibosch's Kora. Sekonyela contributed a few mounted men while the bulk of the foot soldiers comprised Rolong from Thaba Nchu. Their hopes of ever return-ing to their old homelands rested on the success of this expedition. Thus, the great trek of the Rolong people and their Methodist missionaries laid the basis for the first military expedition of the Boers' great trek. With so much expert advice on hand Potgieter and Maritz had no trouble finding their way to Mzilikazi's stronghold.

The allies moved out in January, north along a route taken ten years earlier by Moletsane's Taung, crossing the Vaal at a place still called Kommando Drift, and then proceeding north to Makwassie. There they left their wagons and moved to the Harts River before turning north-east along ways familiar to veterans of Barends's commandos. Their target was the Mosega Valley, the former capital of the Hurutshe chiefs and the place where three American missionary couples had recently reoccupied the build-ings so hurriedly vacated by the French in 1832 (see Chapter 7, p. 200). On the morning of 17 January 1837 the combined force charged into the valley, guns blazing. Apparently, no prior warning had been sent by Mzilikazi's spies. The few able-bodied men who were present had no time to mount an effective defence and the attack soon turned into a massacre.[30] The Rolong/Griqua/Kora/Tlokwa/Trekker forces drove 7000 cattle with them on their return journey to Thaba Nchu. While suffering only a handful of casualties on their side, they had killed perhaps as many as 500 men, women and children. Furthermore, they had persuaded the three American missionary families to join their retreat. Mzilikazi would have no intermediaries to plead his cause in print.

Counting the costs of Vegkop and Mosega: a decisive shift in the spatial deployment of power

The meaning of Vegkop and Mosega extended far beyond the thousand lives snuffed out. In the course of three months the balance of military power between the Limpopo and Orange Rivers changed fundamentally and permanently. For a decade Mzilikazi had dominated the open plains with a spatial deployment of power on the old Ndwandwe model. Until the arrival of the trekkers, the model had proved well-nigh impregnable. The tight cluster of human settlement at the centre of his kingdom occupied a well-watered, diverse and defensible pasture land. The ceaseless movement of his *amabutho* protected cattle stations spread over a much larger territory, ensured that subordinate and conquered chiefs remained true to their allegiance, and kept a lookout for opportunities to raid cattle throughout a still wider sphere of influence extending several hundred kilometres in each direction from the kingdom's heartland. This deployment of power could not be justified on the basis of efficient utilization of pastoral or agricultural resources. It rendered vast tracts of the open plains virtually useless for close human settlement. The only inhabitants of those regions were people with no cattle to lose – poor Tswana and other 'Bushmen' whom Mzilikazi used as spies.

Within the circumference of his extended circle of power, Mzilikazi would admit no independent chiefs or kings. Those who sought to keep their cattle and their independence moved away. This was less a matter of headlong flight than a rational investment policy. Without cattle, no one could be a considerable chief. The Ngwaketse under Sebego had moved off towards Lake Ngami. The so-called Kololo of Sebetwane had moved far north to the Zambezi. The Ngwato of Sekgoma kept a discrete distance between their cattle and Mzilikazi's *amabutho* at their headquarters beyond the Soshong Hills.[31] Such Rolong and Hurutshe chiefs who would not bow to Mzilikazi had moved south of the Vaal with their remaining cattle. Most had temporarily settled at Thaba Nchu. Griqua and Kora raiders had preserved more room to manoeuvre during Mzilikazi's ascendancy. Their horses and guns enabled them to make lightning forays into the king's heartland. However, on no occasion had they succeeded in holding the cattle they seized, so they posed no fundamental threat to Mzilikazi's power base. Vegkop changed the equation by demonstrating that a properly defended laager could withstand a massed daylight assault of *amabutho* in open country. And although the defenders suffered a great loss of herds, the subsequent assault on Mosega showed that in the right circumstances Barends's old plan for a grand commando could take thousands of cattle. Furthermore, the trekkers could see that no one would challenge them on the open plains, provided that they maintained a military organization capable of rapidly mobilizing forces for defence. The key element was the war council or *Krygsraad*, and their most important leaders were military commanders. Their civil institutions remained weak and rudimentary for some time to come.

Mzilikazi understood his changed circumstances. He made no further attacks on the trekkers and devoted all his energies to preserving his herds. There was no time to lose, because the smell of the blood spilled at Vegkop and Mosega attracted a host of predators eager to feast on his wounded kingdom. Griqua and Kora factions temporarily put aside old enmities in an effort to mount a combined commando. In May 1837 a formidable group of fighters met on the Vaal to plan their strategy. Abraham and Cornelis Kok were there. So were Barend Barends and Jan Bloem.[32] By the time they were ready to move in late July, their forces included contingents of Tlhaping and Hurutshe allies. According to the fragmentary accounts which survived they mounted a series of hit and run raids in August which carried off large herds of cattle and killed perhaps as many as a hundred of Mzilikazi's people.

Meanwhile the Zulu king, Dingane, had launched a far more audacious raid. A substantial force including several important *amabutho* left Zululand late in May 1837 and arrived in the Mosega Valley about the beginning of July. They found that Mzilikazi had already withdrawn most of his people and animals towards the lower Marico Valley. After a series of skirmishes in which neither side managed a decisive victory, the Zulu forces at length retired with several thousand head of cattle – some of which were remnants of the herds seized at Vegkop. This campaign and the previous raid of 1832 (see Chapter 7, p. 197; Chapter 8, p. 237) were justly remembered for decades afterward because Zulu armies had never travelled farther under the orders of their king.[33] The reasons can only be guessed. An old man questioned in 1900 recalled that Dingane had told veteran regiments that they could not marry until they put on the head ring. For their head rings they would need 'sinews' from captured cattle.[34] This begs the question, why go so far? Like Shaka's final campaign against Soshangane, such long-distance raids carried obvious risks. Though the winter highveld harboured no deadly fevers, frost and exposure could also kill. During a similar raid against Bhaca chief Ncaphayi in 1831 the angry spirit of Shaka had visited the commanders in their dreams to ask 'what they were doing at such a distance from their own country, since they had killed him, in order that they might enjoy peace and tranquillity'?[35] Among all the reasons that might be advanced to account for the two campaigns against Mzilikazi, the most likely seems to be that the Zulu king felt a constant need to prove his own superiority to competing lords of humankind. One of his official praises included words meaning 'pursue these herds and steal them; the ox of the Zulu is his spear'.[36] Other sources of cattle to reward loyal regiments lay close by, but a successful strike into territory 500 kilometres away from his capital would rank among the greatest military feats of his time. Despite indifferent results on the battlefield, the *amabutho* marched back to Zululand in September 1837 with substantial herds of captured cattle, saying that they had forced Mzilikazi to flee for his life.[37] No South African army would strike so far and return so quickly until late in the twentieth century.

And still Mzilikazi's troubles continued. With the enthusiastic support of Rolong chief Moroka, Hendrik Potgieter led another commando out in October 1837. They caught the king's retreating forces about 80 kilometres north-east of Mosega. In nine days of skirmishing 135 horsemen killed many people and carried away about 7000 cattle, while suffering no casualties on their side. This strike was much more like a conventional Griqua or Kora cattle-raid than the grim February commando. Many of the horsemen belonged to a recently arrived trekker party led by Piet Uys, who had taken no part in the battle of Vegkop and whose intended destination was Natal. They rode for booty, not vengeance. In later years it would be said that the November commando took the north-western highveld 'by right of conquest'.[38] This is pure invention. Neither the Griqua, the Zulu, nor the Boer campaigns had staked out territorial claims in their raids. Each of the invading forces had been assisted by Tswana chiefs who hoped that victory would open the way for them to reclaim the pre-eminent positions they had held before Bloem, Barends and Mzilikazi had disrupted their world. They moved as quickly as possible to repossess their lost lands. They were welcomed back by friends and relatives who had never left the territory and who had thrown off their allegiance to Mzilikazi as soon as his power was broken.

Their late king moved north in search of a safer home. He may have lost as many as 10,000 cattle in the course of the terrible year 1837, but many remained to underpin his power. Their safety was his first concern. Even before Vegkop, rumour said he contemplated moving far to the north where there were people 'who have much cattle and a fine country'. Eventually he made his permanent capital in just such a place: Bulawayo near the Matopos mountains of Zimbabwe, but precisely when he reached that spot is not known. As late as 1844 people of the Magaliesberg ranges still feared his occasional raids, and said that Ndebele outposts were located no more than three or four days' journey north-east of the place where the Marico flows into the Limpopo.[39] Those same people acknowledged no Boer government as their master.

At this point Mzilikazi leaves our story. Historians owe him a great debt, for no other monarch left so much evidence about how rulership on the Ndwandwe model was practised. Mzilikazi's military prowess, cunning, wit and sense of fun ensured that he would not be forgotten. He would not, however, be remembered entirely as he would have wished. It would be his ironic fate to be celebrated as an imitator of Shaka, though he received his lessons in kingship from Zwide, to be cited as a persecutor of missionaries, though he did everything in his power to attract them, and to be known in numerous textbooks as king of the Ndebele, though he wished his people to be called Zulu (see Chapter 6, p. 165).[40] In deference to that wish, the name Ndebele has been avoided to this point. But it is perhaps appropriate to send Mzilikazi off under that banner. When he first appeared on the highveld Tswana-speaking people called him king of the aliens – the 'Matabele'. By the time he had relocated to Zimbabwe, some may have begun to use the Zulu form of that word, Ndebele. On the map sketched by the French hunter and scientist Adulphe Delegorgue in 1845, his name appears by the Limpopo River with the title 'Roy des Ama Débelés', the earliest approximation to King of the Ndebele appearing on any printed page. A stranger again in a strange land, he went on to live another score of years by the Matopos. *Bayete*, Mzilikazi, King of the Ndebele!

The Trekkers advance

Dingane kept close watch on the movements of the Trekker parties. The regiments who straggled home in September 1837 knew that some of the animals they took from Mzilikazi had been taken from the defenders of Vegkop. On their way home Boer horsemen accosted them, demanding the return of the cattle. Like good soldiers, the commanders refused to give them up, saying that they would take them to the king, for he alone had the power to pronounce upon the claim.[41]

What surprised Dingane was not so much the arrival of the Trekkers, but their numbers. The missionary Allen Gardiner had told him in 1835 that the members of the Uys expedition planned to return with 'family and friends', a plan postponed, but not abandoned because of the Anglo–Xhosa war (see Chapter 8, page 219).[42] According to the agreement the king made with Gardiner on 13 July 1835, those people would have been subject to Gardiner's authority, along with the existing white traders and adventurers in Port Natal.[43] That plan received a decisive setback when the British Colonial Secretary, Lord Glenelg, vetoed it along with 'any scheme of colonization' anywhere outside the existing British Zone.[44] This actually increased the dangers presented by potential settlers by removing any check on their activities by British authorities. Not long afterwards, the newly appointed Lieutenant Governor for the Eastern Cape, Andries Stockenstrom, who had in years past been the official mainly concerned with controlling Boer pastoralists grazing north of the Orange, stated frankly and publicly that he had no power to prevent people leaving the colony.[45]

Among those who received this information from Stockenstrom's own hand in September of 1836 was Pieter Retief, a leading Boer, who up until the previous month had been actively discouraging the trekking movement.[46] He had been well known in the Grahamstown area for the previous twenty years. During the first miserable year of British settlement he had made a pile of money selling grain at inflated prices (see Chapter 4, p. 101), a fortune he lost in 1824 when he failed to deliver on a contract to build government offices. Later he held public office as *veld cornet* of the Winterberg district. His inveterate taste for speculation caused him to take a keen interest in the trekking movement, which promised great rewards for those who succeeded in establishing legal title to land. On the other hand, Retief hesitated to risk his life and all his worldly goods on a trek into the jaws of war. A postscript to the letter he received from Stockenstrom mentioned that word had just come of Mzilikazi's attack on the Vaal River trekker encampment. Stockenstrom had anticipated some such catastrophe and commented that those who had encouraged the movement must bear a heavy responsibility. A few weeks later, prospects brightened when Vegkop demonstrated the ability of the wagon laager to withstand a massed attack of disciplined *amabutho*. Within a few days of that news arriving in Grahamstown, Retief announced his intention to trek.[47] Many others made the same decision, now that the path appeared to be safe. Later, in February 1837 Retief listed several reasons for his decision in a letter to the *Graham's Town Journal*.

Retief knew that his letter would be welcomed by the *Graham's Town Journal*, which had already begun to act as a cheering squad for the trekking movement. The editor's hope from the beginning was that the lands occupied by the trekkers would speedily be annexed by Britain.

> this emigration may be made the greatest blessing which has ever yet been experienced in this section of South Africa. Allow the emigrants a due share in the administration of *their own affairs*, and we think that the

influential part of their community will not object to the country being considered and held as a British province, and themselves as subjects of the British crown. *Refuse this concession, and the result may be most disastrous.* We may lose all those commercial advantages which are now presented to us, and may *convert into implacable enemies those who may now be* included in a bond of the warmest alliance.[48]

Members of the English-speaking community in Grahamstown endorsed the sentiment in a ceremony marked by the presentation of a handsome Bible to the departing Uys party in April 1837.[49] Piet Uys (who had been commended by the *Graham's Town Journal* for his military service in the recent war[50]) reciprocated the feeling, writing to Governor D'Urban nearly a year later that he and his whole party continued to regard themselves as 'loyal and devoted subjects'.[51] Such declarations formed part of a calculated campaign to convince the British government in London that all would be well in a united colony if Glenelg's policies were repudiated and D'Urban's reinstituted. Though everyone knew that the Anglo–Xhosa war had inter-rupted plans for immigration, many chose to pretend that Glenelg's con-demnation of the war and D'Urban's annexations precipitated the trekking movement. When trekkers and their sympathizers spoke of a grievance about land, they meant the land which had been handed back to the Xhosa. When they spoke of failure to secure compensation, they meant rewards in land and cattle for the time they had spent in military service. When they spoke about insecurity, they meant the insecurity they felt when they saw Mfengu and other Africans travelling freely about the country instead of being compelled to work for farmers.

Retief played up to these feelings in his highly contrived 'Manifesto', a document which contrasted the insecurity created by Glenelg's policies with the new government which the trekkers would establish – a state which would maintain 'proper relations between master and servant'.[52] He ap-pealed to all the élite landholding class with a blast at 'the unjustifiable odium which has been cast upon us by interested and dishonest persons, under the cloak of religion, whose testimony is believed in England to the exclusion of all evidence in our favour'. Cape Town newspapers reprinted Retief's letter alongside a list of 366 other individuals who had decided to trek, further enhancing the impression of a cause-and-effect relationship between Glenelg's settlement and the trekking movement. In later years many historians would attempt to portray the movement as an act of national self-assertion by Boers in rebellion against British rule. If that were so, Afrikaans-speaking people from all classes and every district of the British Zone would have joined the trek. In fact practically all the trekkers came from the eastern districts; most were people with little or no education or property. If the arrangements for payment of compensation for freed slaves had been a grievance leading to trekking, then it could be anticipated that substantial slave-owners from the western districts would have been prominent among the trekkers. Virtually all of them stayed put. If anti-British feeling underpinned by ethnic solidarity had been a factor, then D'Urban and the haughty military élite would have been excoriated. Instead, the proponents of the trek praised D'Urban, vented their spleen in diatribes against Lord Glenelg in Britain and Stockenstrom, the Afrikaner he had appointed as lieutenant governor.

Piet Retief expected to be acclaimed as paramount leader of the trekker forces and was not disappointed. Almost as soon as his party of a hundred wagons reached the north bank of the Orange in April 1837 he met a deputation inviting him to become both governor and general in place of Maritz and Potgieter.[53] By virtue of education, connections and the offices he had formerly held in the colony, he was the obvious choice. He wielded the power of the pen with great skill. He cast his language in calculated, legalistic phrases, laying the ground work for future land claims while avoiding any step which might antagonize British authorities. His 'Manifesto' specifically mentioned that 'no one shall be held in a state of slavery', because he knew that the British had put a price on Louis Tregardt's head for taking slaves – or 'apprentices' as the ex-slaves were now called – beyond their borders.[54] Knowing that the British had embarked on the experiment of using treaties with independent rulers to dampen tensions, Retief announced that he had concluded treaties of friendship with Moroka, Sekonyela, Moshweshwe and other important chiefs.[55] The Griqua, whose claim to a large, though as yet not precisely defined territory had been recognized in a treaty of 1835, were obvious rivals. If long occupation conferred rights, their claims to the highveld plains were superior to any trekkers'. Retief offered them a treaty of friendship at the same time he denounced their former 'unlawful, murderous, and plundering' raids on Mzilikazi. That king, he said, 'has now alone to do with me, and I will give him sufficient time to decide whether he shall come to me to atone for his atrocious conduct, or whether I am to go to him to punish him for his enormities'.[56] He likewise refused offers of military aid from Moroka and Sekonyela. The obvious purpose was to dissociate himself from the Griqua, Kora, Tswana and Sotho allies who had marched with Potgieter to Mosega. Wiping out the memory of those attacks would aid the trekkers in claiming territory 'by right of conquest'. And by what authority did Retief claim the sole right to deal with Mzilikazi? Because, he told the Christian Griqua, he recognized 'the hand of God in placing me at the head of my countrymen'. There was arrogance aplenty in his assumptions of authority and claims to know what was legal and illegal in a land where no one's law reigned supreme. Retief knew that. His object, however, was not to influence God, but to make impressions on minds in the British Zone. In contrast to rough, unlettered men like Potgieter, he made sure that his words appeared in Dutch and English newspapers as fast as messengers could ride to Grahamstown, Uitenhage, Graaf Reinet and Cape Town.

Retief's propaganda generated rapturous applause from the *Graham's Town Journal*, grim satisfaction among D'Urban's military clique, and consternation among those who hoped that peace and goodwill would end wars and commandos. To the friends of peace, the trekking movement looked like the biggest commando of all time. The question was, how to stop it. The Aborigines Protection Society of London argued that all trekking beyond the frontiers of the British Zone was illegal and a danger to the peace. The damage should be repaired by strict laws forbidding emigration, enforcement of existing laws against taking freed slaves beyond the frontiers, measures to address the just grievances of Boers in the frontier districts, and formation of a confederation of African states under British auspices.[57] What a turnaround. The very people who had encouraged Glenelg to revoke D'Urban's annexations of Xhosa territory and had praised his order forbidding any further annexations, now argued for the umbrella of British authority to be spread over the independent chiefs of the heartland. The missionary John Philip had long advocated precisely such a policy, but by this stage reversing Glenelg's ban on extensions of British authority was beyond the realms of political possibility.[58] The best that could be done was to signal, through the Cape of Good Hope Punishment Act of 1836, that British subjects who committed illegal acts anywhere in Africa south of 25 degrees of latitude would be liable to prosecution in British courts. Since one of those offences was the taking of apprentices beyond the borders, the government asked that word should be sent out that any apprentice in danger of being taken away should seek help from the nearest magistrate. Both measures were little more than pious hopes. How would a Boer servant escape to make a complaint to a distant magistrate? As for the Punishment Act, not a single trekker was convicted of violations.[59] Whatever might be thought in England, in the British Zone the predominant sentiment among the military and civilian élites backed the trekkers as gallant pioneers spearheading a movement which would some day bring all the heartland under their control.

One newspaper claimed that the trek acted as 'a *safety-valve* to the colony', which otherwise might have witnessed rebellions of both English- and Afrikaans-speaking people like those of the English and French which erupted in Canada in 1837. Another advanced, perhaps for the first time, an argument which would be repeated in one form or another for the next 150 years:

What, we ask, has become of the tribes, which once occupied the fertile country where the emigrants now are? Where are all those thousands of inhabitants which once dwelt in the 'fenced cities,' visited only 20 years ago by the missionary Campbell? All, all are swept away, as by 'the besom of destruction!' the country has reverted to an unproductive wilderness – its former populousness is only known as matter of history, or inferred, from the signs of former cultivation, and especially from the human bones which lie so profusely scattered over the whole surface of the land.

Since the Cape has been a British possession not less than 1,000,000 human beings around have perished by their own intestine feuds. They have melted away – not as the consequence of European intercourse, agreeably to the favourite theory – but as the result of the baneful effects of savage life upon the human species. And what have we done to ameliorate this state of things? We answer – nothing. We have looked on with criminal apathy, and while death stalked through the land, we have been indulging ourselves in copious libations of moonshine, – dreaming of unsophisticated nature, or discoursing most sentimentally of the virtues and amiabilities of savage life![60]

Here, in embryo, was the concept later labelled the *mfecane*, alleged to be a period of heartland wars which between 1820 and 1835 killed a million people and depopulated huge areas, leaving them free for the trekkers to settle (see Chapter 12, pp. 331–8). Although the statistics were conjured out of thin air and the argument showed a wilful ignorance of the settlement patterns of heartland peoples, colonial expansionists embraced the concept with enthusiasm. It absolved them from any responsibility for the endless wars on their frontier and wiped the map clean of populations entitled to dispute their right to take new land. It made a fine alibi.[61]

Dingane faces the trekker invasion

But for the war of 1834–5, trekking parties would certainly have moved through Xhosa territory on their way to Port Natal. The British occupation made that impossible for the time being. The only practical alternative route for herds and wagons ran across the highveld. Although a substantial number of trekkers remained committed to going to Natal, the discovery of other possibilities caused many to have second thoughts. At one end of the spectrum was Potgieter, an adventurer in the mould of Coenraad de Buys, Jan Bloem and Louis Tregardt, content with the power his guns and wit could win him in rough contests of raid and trade. At the opposite end were Retief, Maritz and Piet Uys, fixated on the speculative profits to be made from carving land into saleable lots. While Potgieter's eyes gazed north, the others looked for the road down to Natal, where green pastures promised drought-free farming, and whose harbour could be used to export goods without paying duties to British collectors of customs. Retief struggled to achieve unity among the plenitude of trekking parties. Without a unified government there could be no hope of inscribing land titles. For a time in 1837 a semblance of a single government based on 'Nine Articles of Association' agreed near the modern town of Winburg held together before it shattered on the rocks of conflicting ambitions.[62] The parties of Uys, Maritz and Retief wended their separate ways over the mountains into Dingane's kingdom. Meanwhile another game of speculative politics was in progress at Port Natal where Allen Gardiner was seeking vainly to impose his authority on the English and Khoi gun-running, ivory-trading ruffians who had gathered there over the previous six years.

Gardiner had returned to the Port in May 1837 with a commission from the British government to monitor offences committed under the Cape of Good Hope Punishment Act. His power to curb the gun trade rested on moral authority alone. In an attempt to relieve tensions between the Zulu king and the Port Natal settlers, he told Dingane that any refugees from the king's justice who fled to the Port would be promptly returned. For their part, the traders totally rejected his proposals to end their lucrative trade in guns and ammunition.[63] They were, as Dingane and Gardiner clearly saw, playing a double game. On the one hand they supplied firearms and served as auxiliary forces in the king's campaigns, from which they gained handsome rewards in women and cattle. Less than a year before they had sent musketeers to assist a raid on Sobhuza.[64] On the other hand, they knew the Boer trekkers were coming and planned to welcome them. One of their letters printed in the *Graham's Town Journal* on 22 June 1837 acknowledged that 'We hourly expect to hear from the Boers. When they arrive we intend to form an internal government of our own, free from the false measures and wavering policy of the neighbouring colony, and I have no doubt but that every thing will go on smoothly.' Then their land claims would be converted to legal titles.

Dingane's spies kept him informed of these developments. He faced a difficult situation. Gardiner was a useless friend, for he had no army. Moreover, Gardiner had recently forbidden any further trade in guns and ammunition from Port Natal. Dingane, in retaliation, banned *all* trade in November 1837. The missionary Gardiner had recruited from England, Francis Owen of the Church Missionary Society, was worse than useless. Owen sold some gunpowder but refused to give any assistance with guns, even with so small an item as a bullet mould which Dingane hoped might make him less dependent on buying supplies from Port Natal. Moreover, his spies working in Owen's household reported that the missionary called the king a wicked murderer.[65] Other newly arrived missionaries from America had located themselves nearer to Port Natal, far away from the capital, and proved to be equally unwilling to assist with training people to ride and shoot. It was too late for Dingane to fill Port Natal's hinterland with Zulu settlements. The king's forces had brought detailed reports of the contest between Mzilikazi and the Boers. A frontal assault like that mounted by Kaliphi at Vegkop would be very risky. Some other plan would be needed to thwart an alliance between the trekkers and the traders. So the king waited for the inevitable emissaries who would come asking for land.

They were not long in coming. On 19 October 1837 Retief received an enthusiastic welcome to Port Natal. Frank Fynn, Henry Ogle and John Cane – men who owed their lives, property, concubines and cattle to the generosity of the Zulu kings – pledged themselves at a public meeting to join their destinies to the trekkers. They, in turn, were promised that each of the fifty-three English living at the Port would be granted 12,000 acres of the best land in their vicinity.[66] Shortly thereafter Retief sent his first message to Dingane, requesting an interview for the purpose of seeking a land grant. The king replied that he could not discuss the land question until Retief produced a satisfactory explanation of a recent incident in which people claiming to be Boers had raided people 'on the outskirts of my country' and taken many cattle. They wore clothes, rode horses, carried guns and said that one of their parties was on the way to Port Natal. 'It is my wish now,' the king continued,

> that you should shew that you are not guilty of the charge which has been laid against you as I now believe you to be. It is my request that you should retake my cattle and bring them to me; and if possible, send me the thief, and that will take all suspicion away from me, and I will cause you to know that I am your friend. I will then grant you your request. I will give you some men, enough to drive the cattle which you retake to me, which will remove the suspicion that the stolen cattle are in the hands of the Dutch; and I will also give you men whom you may send to make reports to me. If any cattle should be taken besides mine, I request that you will send them to me.[67]

Retief rode to the capital, Mgungundhlovu, in an effort to convince Dingane that the real thieves were Tlokwa men riding with Sekonyela. The king received him with courtesy and a calculated display of Zulu power. Six thousand men danced and several thousand head of royal cattle paraded in formations arranged by colour.[68] Apologizing for the absence of the main body of his army, recently returned from the campaign against Mzilikazi, Dingane showed Retief barracks capable of accommodating 34,000 soldiers.

Retief was impressed as well by the king's huge house whose domed roof was supported by twenty-two columns festooned with beads. The English missionary, Owen, alarmed that Dingane might be about to give Retief the land already granted to Gardiner, asked the king what his intentions were. Dingane replied that the land he would give the Boers was *the land from which his forces had recently expelled Mzilikazi*.[69] Owen then attempted to make sure that Retief also understood the situation. Retief assured the missionary that if the hinterland of Port Natal could not be occupied peacefully, it would not be occupied at all. Retief further agreed that prior to any further negotiations, he would retrieve Dingane's stolen property.

It is possible that Sekonyela's people had taken the cattle. Many of them knew how to ride and shoot. On the other hand, the oral traditions which recall Boers seeking to take cattle from Dingane's forces on their way home from Mzilikazi's country may refer to the incident which so offended the king (above, p. 256). In November Dingane heard that a second attack had been jointly mounted by 'Boers and BaSotho', and dispatched three regiments over the Drakensberg to retaliate.[70] Given the disunity which prevailed among the trekkers, it is entirely possible that some such joint raid took place. Retief's letter, dated 23 October 1837, can be read as an attempt to construct an alibi in advance. He states his belief that Sekonyela, 'committed a daring robbery' with a mounted commando and that he might seek to blame it on the Boers. Retief claims to have seen the Tlokwa king passing his encampment.[71] Whatever the facts, Retief now mounted a theatrical attack on Sekonyela, with whom, it should be remembered, he had recently concluded a treaty of friendship! On 1 January 1838 he reminded Dingane of the Boers' power by recounting the results of the second Potgieter commando raid on Mzilikazi (which, of course, the king already knew about) and announced that he was now riding against Sekonyela. Retief's commando then rode back over the Drakensberg and down the Caledon Valley where he bound his 'friend and ally' Sekonyela in irons and made him confess to the theft of 300 cattle. Retief then demanded delivery of those 300 along with an additional penalty of 400 additional cattle, 70 horses and 30 guns.[72] That is to say, Retief treated the excursion as a typical commando raid, from which extra booty would be taken for distribution among his followers.

How Dingane should respond to Retief on his return was a difficult question. Recent events showed that white people's professions of peace could not be taken at face value. The Anglo–Xhosa war had demonstrated the truth of Jacob Msimbiti's warnings against accepting white farmers as neighbours. The Xhosa king, Hintsa, had believed himself to be an ally of the British, before the soldiers invaded his country, burnt his fields, captured him with trickery and killed him. Mzilikazi's forces had tried and failed in an attempt to overrun a trekker laager which had advance warning of their attack. A treaty of friendship with Retief would be worthless; Dingane's men had seen what happened to Sekonyela. Furthermore, there was an imminent danger that the Natal traders – who had put their firepower at the Zulu king's disposal only a year before in a raid on Sobhuza – were about to join forces with the trekkers. In mid-January 1838 Dingane learned that John Cane had been busy with military preparations. When his messengers asked what was wrong, Cane suggested that all might still be well if the Port Natal settlers were given a clear grant to a strip of coastal land about 30 kilometres wide, between the Thukela and Mkomazi Rivers.[73] Meanwhile, Boer wagons could be seen daily moving down the mountains and camping along the branches of the upper Thukela River even though there had been, as yet, no agreement to admit them as settlers. Taking all these alarming signs into consideration, Dingane decided to hit before he was hit.

On 2 February 1838, he summoned the inexperienced missionary Francis Owen (who had been living at his capital since October of the previous year) and asked him to write a letter to Retief, thanking him for the return of his property and inviting the Boers to join a dance competition at his capital.[74] The Boers should come prepared to show how they danced with their horses, while his people would demonstrate their skill on foot. The next day Retief and his men galloped in, firing their guns in the air and driving the Zulu cattle. For their war dance on horseback they divided into two groups and galloped at each other. After the Zulu men had gone through their routine, the king's messenger approached Retief to demand – as stated in Dingane's original order —the horses and guns taken from Sekonyela. The trekker replied by pointing to the grey hairs on his head and asking, did Dingane take him to be a child? Retief would withhold any further presents pending successful negotiations on the land question. The day of decision was fixed for 6 February.

Early on the morning of that day, as Owen sat reading his Bible, a messenger came from the king to warn him that Boers were about to be killed and that the missionary should not take fright; he was in no danger. The reason for the execution was that the king's spies had learned that the Boers planned to kill him. Across the valley, Owen could see that the final act in the drama was already in progress. Dingane was no more a child than Retief. He explained that the laws of his country did not permit weapons within the royal enclosure. Therefore, the Boers must come unarmed to the ceremony marking their agreement on the land question. After more singing and dancing, the king suddenly shouted the words used at every public execution: '*Bulalali abathakathi*' ('let the criminals be killed').[75] From all sides men rushed forward to seize the Boers and drag them to the hill nearby where they were clubbed to death. Soon the corpses of seventy-one trekkers, thirty of their servants and young Thomas Halstead of Port Natal, who had served as an interpreter, stared with sightless eyes at the heavens from whence the vultures would descend for the feast.

At the same time, ten of Dingane's *amabutho* ran out with orders to attack the trekker parties across the Thukela. They had much better luck than Mzilikazi's men at Vegkop. They caught the enemy encampments unprepared a little before daylight on the morning of 17 February 1838.[76] With no wagon laagers to impede them, they set to work with their death-dealing spears. Eventually some of the trekkers grabbed their muskets and put up a spirited defence. But by the end of the day more than 530 of their number lay dead, while Dingane's regiments had taken an estimated 25,000 head of cattle.[77] From the Zulu perspective this constituted a huge victory, equal to the greatest of Shaka's campaigns. For the trekkers, it was an awful defeat. As yet they had no secure land; now they had lost most of their cattle. In desperation, Gert Maritz took a commando out in hopes of retrieving the herds. Alas, by the time he reached the Thukela River, all the cattle had already been safely driven across and were beyond their grasp. The Boers sat despondent in their saddles, tears streaming down their faces as they raged at the loss of their animals.[78] It was an emotion Dingane understood very well. More commandos would undoubtedly come looking for their herds. The king would be ready for them.

He very much hoped that the Natal traders would not join his enemies and sent them a message specifically asking why none of them had come to see him since the execution of the Boers. The traders' answer was a plundering expedition which went out under the command of John Cane on 13 March.[79] It included a great many men whose chiefs had previously suffered at the hands of Dingane, so it could not be regarded simply as a traders' commando. In the event it never reached Zulu country, having decided instead to attack a tributary chiefdom located south of the Thukela, from whose unoffending people 4000 head of cattle and about 500 women and children were seized.

The next commando from Port Natal attempted to co-ordinate its operations with the trekkers who still remained camped in the up-country grasslands. The trekkers had recently welcomed reinforcements under the command of Piet Uys and Hendrick Potgieter, who had led the second expedition against Mzilikazi the previous November. Four hundred men under their command crossed the Thukela into Zulu country on 6 April. A few days later Cane and Robert Biggar led their mixed armies of musketeers and spearmen out from Port Natal.

Anticipating their arrival, Dingane had dispersed his herds and evacuated people from lands west of his capital. In a basin-like valley not far from his capital, Mgungundhlovu, he deployed some of his *amabutho* as a decoy. They sat calmly on the ground, awaiting the arrival of the horsemen, who had been compelled to enter the valley in single file. The Zulu commanders allowed the trekkers to regroup and to advance to within 20 metres of their serried ranks. Then with a defiant shout they sprang to the attack. As the trekkers opened fire, the Zulu stood for a time, before appearing to run away in panic. The grimly confident horsemen pursued them up narrow gullies in expectation of a speedy victory, only to find the tables turned. Zulu soldiers now rushed in from behind and cut off their retreat. Piet Uys, his son, and many of his men were caught in the trap and died that day. Potgieter, who had held most of his forces back, managed to turn and run away. Shortly thereafter he declared that the Zulu people were too numerous and too strong. He would seek his fortune on the highveld.

Dingane now sent his *amabutho* to punish Port Natal for its disloyalty. They caught the forces of Cane and Biggar on 17 April and scored an even more decisive victory than they won against the Boers. Thirteen of the 17 white men, 10 Khoi men and about 400 of their soldiers died.[80] By the morning of the 24th the Zulu army had reached the ridge overlooking Port Natal, from which they swooped down upon the herds and people of the bay. Thanks to the presence of an armed ship in the harbour, the remaining missionaries managed to make their escape. In a few short weeks the schemes of the traders, the trekkers, the missionaries and hapless Captain Gardiner had all been blasted by the strategic brilliance of the Zulu king and the bravery of his soldiers. Perhaps as many as 40,000 cattle and other animals had been led in triumph to Mgungundhlovu. Dingane had succeeded where Mzilikazi and Hintsa had failed. His gallant *amabutho* had conquered horses and guns. This, however, was no time for celebration. The Zulu had also suffered heavy losses of life. Possibly 1000 men had perished and women's cries of lamentation could be heard in every homestead in the kingdom. Though Potgieter and others had retreated beyond the Drakensberg in fear, the Boers who had suffered the heaviest stock losses refused to leave without their cattle.[81] The womenfolk, in particular, insisted that they had not come so far merely to lose their worldly goods. J. D. Boshof, who spoke to them in June 1838, recorded that it was precisely

the widows and orphans, [who] had the least inclination to return to the Colony. They say, that their means of existence and their oxen have been entirely taken away from them, and in order to get their wagons back to the Colony, not less than 500 oxen and 100 men would be requisite. But now, even supposing they were to return to the Colony, what then? Live on alms? Or to be apprenticed with their children? No! death is more preferable.[82]

They pushed for another commando to be assembled, even if it meant waiting months until conditions were right. It was at this point that Dingane might have opened negotiations, trading the captured trekker cattle for their agreement to leave his country. Instead, he sat tight, hoping to hold on to his gains.

Notes

1 Monica Wilson and Leonard Thompson, eds, *Oxford History of South Africa*, 2 vols (Oxford, 1969–71), I, p. 355.

2 *Natal Papers*, I, p. 91.

3 G. D. Joubert to W. C. Van Rynveld, 25 Feb. 1836 in *Records of Natal*, III, pp. 26–7.

4 These developments are described with incomparable skill, though very old-fashioned language, in John S. Galbraith, *Reluctant Empire, British Policy on the South African Frontier* (Berkeley, 1963), pp. 121–50.

5 Smith to D'Urban, 17 April 1836, in *Records of Natal*, III, pp. 99–109; Galbraith, *Reluctant Empire*, p. 136.

6 Galbraith, *Reluctant Empire*, pp. 140–1.

7 *Natal Papers*, I, p. 39, II, pp. 53–5.

8 Ibid., I, p. 53.

9 Some of these hunting and trading expeditions were later remembered as 'kommissie trek', which gives a misleading impression of a co-ordinated movement planned years in advance.

10 Unsigned letter from Civil Commissioner Campbell to the Acting Secretary to Government, 14 Feb. 1834, in *Records of Natal*, II, pp. 241–2. This was based on earlier reports of mid-January from Resident Magistrate Ziervogel of Somerset; see C. F. J. Muller, *Die Oorsprong van die Groot Trek* (Johannesburg, 1974), pp. 342–3. When the 1836 trek finally got under way, Campbell affirmed that 'I had long anticipated a movement of this kind. The early marriages contracted by the people, the consequent rapid increase of population, their disinclination to procure any other mode of subsistence than that which is obtained by the possession of land, the degradation which is attached to servitude (and which prevails in all countries where slavery has been established), these combined causes rendered a movement such as is now contemplated inevitable when land could no longer be found within the colony'; Campbell to Secretary to Government, 25 March 1836 in *Records of Natal*, III, pp. 27–9.

11 See, for example, Erik Walker, *The Great Trek* (London, 1938), pp. 94–5.

12 The prominent trek leaders Piet Retief and Pieter Uys have both been shown to have had no intention to throw off their allegiance to the British government before 1837; Muller, *Oorsprong van die Groot Trek*, pp. 261–3.

13 Napier to Glenelg, 18 May 1838 refers to 'the almost unprecedented drought of the last two years'; *Records of Natal*, III, pp. 291–5.

14 Muller, *Oorsprong van die Groot Trek*, pp. 337–52; Alan Webster, 'Land Expropriation and Labour Extraction under Cape Colonial Rule: The War of 1835 and the "Emancipation" of the Fingo' (MA thesis, Rhodes University, 1991), p. 108.

15 G. M. Theal, *History of the Boers in South Africa* (London, 1887), pp. 71–2.

16 Claude Fuller, *Louis Tregardt's Trek across the Drakensberg, 1837–1838*, ed. Leo Fouche (Cape Town, 1932), pp. 94, 98, 101, 135, 162.

17 Norman Etherington, 'Genocide by Cartography', paper presented to the Conference of the South African Historical Association, Cape Town, 1999. The version of Arrowsmith's map referred to here was printed in British Parliamentary Papers of June, 1835. A similar map was used by Benjamin D'Urban to note events of the late 1830s; his annotated copy is held by the Royal Geographical Society, London, Map S/D4.

18 T. Arbousset and F. Daumas, *Narrative of an Exploratory Tour to the North-East of the Colony of the Cape of Good Hope*, translated from French by J. C. Brown (first published, 1846; reprinted Cape Town, 1968), pp. 180–3. For other Pedi memories of the Tregardt party see Henri Dehérain, *L'Expansion des Boers au xixe siècle* (Paris, 1905), pp. 113–14.

19 Fuller, *Louis Tregardt's Trek*, p. 98.

20 *Natal Papers*, II, p. 1.

21 Martin Legassick, 'The Griqua, the Sotho-Tswana and the Missionaries, 1780–1840' (PhD thesis, UCLA, 1969), pp. 553–4.

22 Robert Ross, *Adam Kok's Griquas* (Cambridge, 1976), p. 56.

23 P. R. Kirby, ed., *The Diary of Dr. Andrew Smith, 1834–1836*, 2 vols (Cape Town, 1939) II, p. 66.

24 For dates in this section of the chapter I have drawn heavily on Muller, *Oorsprong van die Groot Trek*, pp. 386 ff.

25 *Natal Papers*, II, pp. 71–4.

26 Petrus J. van der Merwe, *Die Matebeles en die Voortrekkers* (Pretoria, 1986), pp. 45–57. The dates of the battle vary in different accounts, though all agree it took place in the second half of October 1836.

27 Ibid., pp. 69–75.

28 Journal of Charl Celliers, translated and printed in John Bird, ed., *Annals of Natal*, 2 vols (first published 1888, reprinted Cape Town, 1965), I, pp. 240–1. Estimates of the exact number killed that day varied; Celliers claimed to have counted 450 enemy dead.

29 R. Kent Rasmussen, *Migrant Kingdom: Mzilikazi's Ndebele in South Africa* (Cape Town, 1978), p. 124.

30 Ibid., p. 125–8.

31 Neil Parsons, 'Khama's Country in Botswana', in R. Palmer and N. Parsons, eds, *The Roots of Rural Poverty in Central and Southern Africa* (London, 1977), pp. 114–15; Thomas Tlou and Alec Campbell, *History of Botswana* (Gaborone, 1984), p. 106.

32 Ibid., p. 130; Legassick, 'The Griqua', p. 551. Ross, *Adam Kok's Griquas*, p. 39; P. Wright to D'Urban, 6 Aug. 1837 in *Records of Natal*, III, pp. 183–5.

33 *JSA*, II, p. 176, III, p. 205, IV, pp. 274, 347.

34 *JSA* IV, p. 274; testimony of Ndukwana.

35 Nathaniel Isaacs, *Travels and Adventures in Eastern Africa*, revised and edited L. Herman and P. R. Kirby (first published 1836; reprinted Cape Town, 1970), p. 193.

36 Arbousset and Daumas, *Narrative*, p. 160.

37 George Cory, ed., *The Diary of the Rev. Francis Owen* (Cape Town, 1926), p. 34; Dingane sent messengers to Port Natal announcing the return of the victorious troops on 17 September 1837.

38 Walker, *Great Trek*, p. 158.

39 Adulphe Delegorgue, *Voyage dans l'Afrique Australe*, 2 vols (Paris, 1847), II, pp. 434–5, 451, 490, 500.

40 So, according to one report, did his son Lobengula; see Rasmussen, *Migrant Kingdom*, p. 238n.

41 *JSA*, IV, pp. 274, 347; testimony of Ndukwana.

42 Gardiner to D'Urban, 24 Nov. 1835, in *Records of Natal*, III, pp. 19–22.

43 *Natal Papers*, I, p. 42.

44 Glenelg to D'Urban, 29 Mar. 1836, *Records of Natal*, III, pp. 30–1.

45 Stockenstrom to Retief, 23 Sept. 1836, in *Natal Papers*, I, p. 55.

46 Muller, *Oorsprong van die Groot Trek*, p. 261.

47 The exact date of Retief's decision is hard to pin down, but it had definitely been made by 12 Nov. 1836; see correspondence in *Records of Natal*, III, pp. 60–8.

48 *Natal Papers*, II, pp. 76–7.

49 Ibid., II, pp. 93–4.

50 Robert Godlonton, *A Narrative of the Irruption of the Kaffir Hordes into the Eastern Province of the Cape of Good Hope, 1834–1835*, 3 vols (first published 1835; reprinted: Cape Town, 1965), III, p. 223.

51 P. L. Uys to D'Urban, 24 Jan. 1838, in *Records of Natal*, III, p. 258.

52 C. F. J. Muller, ed., *Five Hundred Years: A History of South Africa*, 3rd rev. ed. (Pretoria, 1981), p. 161; R. U. Kenney, *Piet Retief, the Dubious Hero* (Cape Town, 1976), pp. 83, 108–9.

53 Walker, *Great Trek*, p. 132.

54 D'Urban to Stockenstrom, 9 Sept. 1836, in *Records of Natal*, III, pp. 90–1.

55 J. A. I. Agar-Hamilton, *The Native Policy of the Voortrekkers* (Cape Town, 1928), p. 20; *Natal Papers*, I, pp. 87–8.

56 See, for example, the references to 'a treaty of peace and amity' in Retief's message to the 'Griqua Captains' of 18 July 1837, enclosed in Retief to the Cape Government, 9 Sept. 1837, in *Natal Papers*, I, pp. 114–15; for Retief's rejection of help from Sotho and Tswana chiefs, see pp. 87–8.

57 Memorial from the Committee of the Aborigines Protection Society, London, 7 Aug. 1838, in *Records of Natal*, III, pp. 246–51.

58 See, for example, Glenelg to D'Urban, 13 Jan. 1839, in *Records of Natal*, IV, pp. 138–9.

59 *Natal Papers*, I, p. 48.

60 Ibid., II, pp. 76–7.

61 Julian Cobbing coined the phrase in 'The Mfecane as Alibi: Thoughts on Dithakong and Mbolompo', *Journal of African History* 29 (1988), pp. 487–519.

62 The most colourful account of the disputes remains Walker, *Great Trek*, pp. 134–44.

63 *Natal Papers*, I, pp. 69, 86–7, 97, 99.

64 Cory, ed., *Diary of Rev. Francis Owen*, p. 134; Graham Mackeurtan, *The Cradle Days of Natal (1497–1845)* (London, 1930), pp. 171, 194–5.

65 Bird *Annals*, I, pp. 335–6, 353; Cory, ed., *Diary of the Rev. Francis Owen*, pp. 40, 58, 64–5, 71–3.

66 Bird, *Annals*, I, p. 370; this, at any rate, was the recollection of Daniel Bezuidenhout, recorded forty years later.

67 *Natal Papers*, I, pp. 131–2. The correspondence was carried on through the medium of English and American missionaries.

68 Cory, ed., *Diary of Rev. Francis Owen*, p. 61: 'He has lately been collecting an immense herd of oxen from distant parts of the country, for no other conceivable motive than to display his wealth to the Dutch.'

69 Ibid., pp. 65–6. Owen conducted these negotiations with Retief in English.

70 Ibid., pp. 70–1.

71 *Natal Papers*, I, p. 126; Cory, ed., *Diary of the Rev. Francis Owen*, p. 100.

72 *Natal Papers*, II, p. 2.

73 Cory, ed., *Diary of the Rev. Francis Owen*, pp. 98–9. It was probably a rumour of this message which led some to believe that Cane had sought to secure his own land claims by telling Dingane that the Boers were in rebellion against the English king, and therefore the Zulu need not fear British intervention. See E. Parker to Major Charters, 20 July 1838 in *Records of Natal*, IV, pp. 28–9. An ingenious, but unprovable variation on this interpretation has been advanced by Adam Kuper in 'The Death of Piet Retief', in *Among the Anthropologists: History and Context in Anthropology* (London, 1999), pp. 191–208.

74 Bird, *Annals*, I, pp. 346–7.

75 Although the literal translation of the words is 'kill the wizards', this should not be taken, as it so often has, to indicate that Dingane regarded Retief and party as evil witches or magicians. Exactly the same words were used even at the execution of petty thieves. See Delegorgue, *Voyage*, II, pp. 51–2, and J. Shooter, *The Kafirs of Natal and the Zulu Country* (London, 1857), p. 141.

76 The trekkers had already given their own names – Blauw Kranz and Bushman's – to the rivers were they camped, and it is by these names that the battles were subsequently known.

77 *Natal Papers*, II, pp. 8–9; Bird, *Annals*, I, pp. 407–8.

78 *Natal Papers*, II, p. 5.

79 Cory, ed., *Diary of the Rev. Francis Owen*, p. 127.

80 *Natal Papers*, II, pp. 14–16.

81 Joubert to Rawstorne, 14 July 1838, in *Records of Natal*, IV, pp. 11–13.

82 Ibid., II, pp. 21–2.

CHAPTER TEN

Adjusting to the presence of new forces in the heartland

Dina's trek

Trekkers had generally ignored prohibitions against taking ex-slaves out of the colony. It had not been practical for most of the so-called 'apprentices' to apply for protection at the widely scattered magistrates' offices.[1] Commanded by their masters to go, they went. When Gerrit van Rooyen's female apprentice tried to buy her freedom, he roared, 'No, I will not allow you to purchase your freedom. No, not for two hundred dollars, and I will let you know that I am your master and not the Special Magistrate.' On the trek, she complained, 'He would tie me to a wagon wheel and beat me until my skin bursted.'[2] In the confusion which followed the Zulu victories, another unwilling servant-trekker found an opportunity to escape. On 24 September 1838 she told her astonishing story to the magistrate at Colesberg.[3] Her name, she said, was Dina. At the beginning of the year 1837 she had informed her master, Matinus Christoffel of Beaufort, that she did not wish to join the trek, but would prefer to go to her mother. When he insisted that he would be taking her daughters, Cornelia and Cotau, she reluctantly agreed to go. The special magistrate lived too far away to be of any help. Her master set off in a family party of six wagons and eventually reached Maritz's camp near the Vaal River. At the time Maritz was ready to move on, Dina's master and mistress were too ill to join him. Fearing that if they remained alone, they would be attacked by cannibals, the party joined Piet Retief on his way over the Drakensberg. At the camps of the upper Thukela, Dina met many other 'apprentices' who had also been illegally dragooned into trekking, though few were so unhappy as she. Her mistress loathed her and her master beat her. Things had not always been so bad. Years before, when her master had been widowed, he had taken Dina as his lover. Her beautiful children were the fruit of their time together. Eventually, however, he married a Boer woman. She and the children were again treated as slaves. As far as she was aware, none of the trekkers had the slightest intention of freeing their 'apprentices'. Before her escape, one of them had offered to buy her youngest daughter. There was no telling what might have become of them had the Zulu not attacked. Dina had heard of the death of Retief from a 'Mantatee' (i.e. a Sotho-speaking man) who had witnessed the execution and managed to escape. This news had caused her master to move closer to the other wagons, though no laager had been formed. Dina seized this opportunity to flee with her daughters into the bush. As they huddled together in the cold night, they heard musketfire and concluded that the camp had been attacked.

Now Dina set out on an even more perilous journey, trying to retrace her steps to her homeland. Thankfully, she had learned a little Xhosa from workers on her master's old farm, so she was able to make herself understood among the people she encountered. Against the odds, she managed to make her way to the Caledon Valley. Everywhere she met kind treatment, even when she stayed at a settlement of 'cannibals'. Terrified that her daughters would be eaten, she would not let them out of her sight, until one of the group explained to her that they did not eat people all the time, only 'every second year'. She appears to have had no inkling that that they were trying to pull her leg rather than to eat it. Their chief, a man named April, told her that many apprentices who had escaped from the trekkers had taken refuge with kings Sekonyela and Moshweshwe. He advised going to Moshweshwe. Dina, however, preferred to press on. By the time she reached the lower Caledon she was among people who spoke her language and could point the way to magistrate Rawstorne's office. What subsequently became of her and her daughters is not known.

While Dina's trek was surely unique, her situation was not. The statement she signed with an 'X' opens a rare window on the experience of the slaves and servants who made up a large percentage of every trekking party.[4] The great movement into the heartland boldly attempted to plant not just Boer families, but a whole way of life in the interior – the elaborate paternalistic farm system that had evolved over centuries under the Dutch East India Company. Whether that attempt would succeed would largely depend, first, on the resistance mounted by African kingdoms, and, second, on the policy adopted by the British government.

Dingane's gamble

Dingane knew he was the strongest power the trekkers had to deal with. Through most of 1838 he waited anxiously to see whether they would manage a counter-attack. The greatest danger was likely to come in the dry winter months (June–September) when river levels dropped. For a time it appeared that a commando would ride against him in July. Gerrit Maritz had seized a cannon from the charred remains of Port Natal, which he hoped would spread terror among the Zulu forces. But as most of the Boer horses were in no condition to undertake a long campaign, the planned invasion was delayed until they could fatten on the spring grasses of October and November.[5] In August Dingane tried a bold experiment of his own. For the first time ever a Zulu force tried an attack in commando fashion on a Boer encampment on the Bushman's River. A force of several hundred men, including a mounted force armed with muskets, swept down at the customary morning hour upon a strong laager of seventy-five Boers equipped with a cannon.[6] Nothing remotely resembling Shaka's mass charge with stabbing spears was undertaken. Instead the Zulu horsemen rode round and round, firing their muskets and hurling long throwing spears. At no time did they bunch together as the Ndebele had done at Vegkop. By nightfall they had taken many cattle and held a great feast within sight of their terrified enemy. Next morning they tried another tack, throwing flaming, grass-wrapped spears at the canvas wagon tops to test their vulnerability to fire. Finding that ineffective, they set fire to all the surrounding dry grasslands, and made off with their plundered stock. Once again the Zulu monarch had shown himself to be the most technologically innovative of all his line.

At the same time that he practised new methods of warfare, Dingane was thinking strategically about fallback plans to ensure the survival of his kingdom and his herds in the event of a major defeat on the battlefield. He would send regiments north across the Phongola River to seize territory from Sobhuza's kingdom. He would then have 'two countries' – in modern terms Zululand and Swaziland. If he lost one to the trekkers, he would still have one to rule over. According to one old Zulu soldier, this meant he was ready to follow the example of Mzilikazi who had 'succeeded in getting two countries'.[7] To put it another way, the success of Mzilikazi, Soshangane, Zwangendaba, Nxaba, Sebetwane and other great chiefs who had saved their power by moving, inspired Dingane to do the same, should the worst come to the worst. Besides, there were opportunities to the north.

The later Ndwandwe diaspora

The leaders of the old Ndwandwe coalition had not done badly since giving up the attempt to destroy Shaka. Most of them became involved in the slave trade, though the details of all their dealings will never be known. Some of

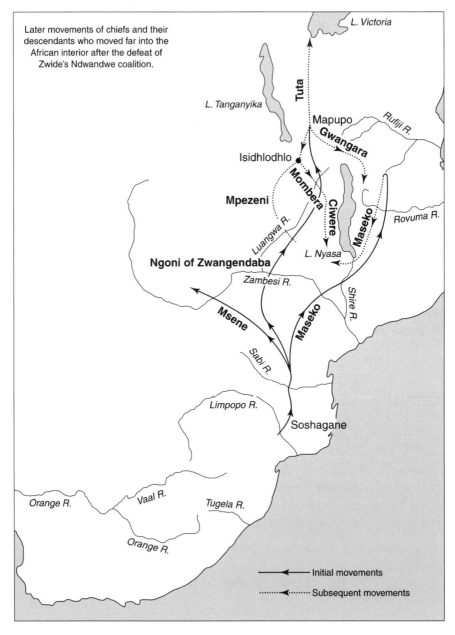

Map 21   Subsequent stages of the Ndwandwe Diaspora
After J. Omer-Cooper, *The Zulu Aftermath* (Longman, 1966), p. 66

Zwide's old comrades in arms moved incredibly long distances, right through the territories most disrupted by the Indian Ocean slave trade as it reached its height in the 1840s and 1850s.[8] Zwangendaba moved up from Mozambique onto the Zimbabwe plateau, and then in about 1835 crossed the Zambezi. By the time of his death in the late 1840s his headquarters lay to the north-west of Lake Malawi and his following were known to their enemies as the Ngoni. Like other migrant chiefs Zwangendaba built a following by incorporating captives and other people from the regions he passed through. Thus, by the time of his death, his people included only a minority from the original south-east African nucleus. An offshoot of the Ngoni later made their way right up to the southern shores of Lake Victoria. Another Ndwandwe offshoot, led by a chief, Ngwane, pursued a similar pilgrimage, eventually becoming known as Maseko, after the son who succeeded Ngwane as leader. They too gained a fearsome reputation throughout what is now south-western Tanzania in the days of its devastation by the slave trade. While the reasons for these movements to East Africa have very little to do with the original break-up of Zwide's coalition, they illustrate the way in which heartland systems of political organization could be adapted to a wide variety of circumstances.

Those who remained in southern Africa also flourished. Sobhuza had created a prosperous kingdom north of the Phongholo which would soon be called Swaziland after his son, Mswati. In his case the perilous struggle to hold his herds and followers involved the incorporation of many Sotho-speaking people, and within a few decades their customs had supplanted many of the old southern usages.[9] Across the Limpopo, Soshangane had done even better. First he had pushed Nxaba out of Mozambique, effectively blasting that chief's dream of founding an enduring kingdom on the Ndwandwe model.[10] By 1838 Soshangane claimed to rule a vast territory stretching from the Limpopo to the Zambezi. His conquest would remain for decades the largest African kingdom in all southern Africa. While retaining a traditional power base founded on control of cattle, he extracted further wealth from tribute and slaving, which enabled him to build an arsenal of firearms.

Dingane's ability to wage war in Mozambique had already been proved by his sack of the Portuguese post at Delagoa Bay in 1833. When Francis Owen on his flight from Port Natal visited the Bay in May 1838, he was told that Zulu regiments were still active in the neighbourhood.[11] If Dingane did move his headquarters north of the Phongola, he could hope to displace both Sobhuza and Soshangane as controller of the coastal trade in slaves, guns, cattle and ivory. If he pulled it off, it would be the last great trek by a whole kingdom. First, however, he would see what the Boer trekkers could do.

The British take a hand

Since 1836, lame-duck governor Benjamin D'Urban and the old military clique had taken perverse delight in each disaster which occurred beyond the borders of the British Zone. In their eyes, Britain's reversal of their aggressive policy on the Xhosa frontier had caused all the trouble, including the trekking movement. They interpreted their orders from London as forbidding them to do anything beyond the official boundaries – a distorted view of affairs echoed by the Grahamstown press and a gang of disappointed land speculators. When ex-slaves like Dina were illegally taken away by their trekking masters, officials wrung their hands in mock sorrow, saying that they had been forbidden to act beyond their jurisdiction. When the news arrived about the battles of Vegkop, Mosega and Blaukranz, they said that under their policies there would have been no trekking, and therefore no battles. Outraged anti-slavery activists in London easily saw through these pretences, and demanded that British officials do something to stop the slaughter. In a petition of August 1838, the Committee of the Aborigines Protection Society requested a stop to 'illegal emigration', enforcement of the treaties of friendship with chiefs and measures to remedy the grievances of Boers in the frontier regions so as to dampen the urge to trek.[12] Moreover, they asked that Britain become the arbiter of all disputes in southern Africa by sponsoring a 'confederation' of chiefs and laying down firm boundaries between kingdoms.

In January 1838 a new governor arrived, George Napier, another old soldier who had the distinction of having lost an arm in battle. While he made it clear that he would adhere to the policy of no annexations (and certainly would not intervene in the affairs of independent kingdoms), he undertook to do what he could to curb abuses perpetrated by the trekkers.[13] In May he sent Gideon Joubert on an expedition to bring back 'apprentices' who had been taken against their will and to gather information on the trekker encampments.[14] Joubert was pleased to find the trekkers willing to give up any apprentices who wished to return to their homeland (forty took up the offer) and was surprised not to hear any of the Boers say even a single 'evil word against the government'.[15] More disturbing was their evident determination to stay put in Natal and settle scores with Dingane. In the hope that a negotiated peace could forestall another calamitous confrontation, Governor Napier dispatched Major Samuel Charters to Port Natal with a company of soldiers in October.[16] The declared purpose was to prevent military supplies from being landed which might be used in more commandos. In addition to the looming contest between the trekkers and the Zulu, Charters faced worrying developments to the south. Thembu and Rharhabe chiefs had sent raiding parties armed with guns against Faku's Mpondo and his Bhaca allies. They were evidently looking for cattle to replace those they had lost to the British in 1835. Faku launched a counter-attack on 9 October, raising the possibility that his forces might drive more Xhosa people into the British Zone. This led Napier to renew the call for an official annexation of Port Natal and its hinterland.[17]

The defence of the Zulu kingdom

Unfortunately, by the time Charters's expeditionary force reached the Port on 4 December, a commando was already moving against Dingane.[18] In a vain effort to stop them, the Major sent a letter warning them not to take 'the law into their own hands' and promising to negotiate with the Zulu king. They ignored this and pressed on in the hope of scoring a decisive victory. Their commandant, Andries Pretorius, was a newly arrived trekker from the old town of Graaf Reinet. Like Retief before him, Pretorius had been captivated by the hope of making a fortune in land speculation. With him came a large number of mounted men from the highveld who had no intention of staying in the lowlands, but were attracted by promises of a share in any booty which might be taken. The unexpected death of Gerrit Maritz in September (from natural causes) removed the only obstacle to Pretorius's election as war commander. With an assorted force of 464 men – Boers, a few English adventurers and some seventy local African forces who knew the country and nourished old grievances against the Zulu king – Pretorius moved through the high country to avoid the swelling waters of the upper Thukela river system. On the morning of 9 December they attempted to summon supernatural assistance:

> On Sunday morning, before Divine service commenced, the chief
> Commandant called together all those who were to perform that service,
> and requested them to propose to the congregation, 'that they should all
> fervently, in spirit and in truth, pray to God for his relief and assistance
> in their struggle with the enemy; that he wanted to make a vow to God
> Almighty (if they all were willing), that should the Lord be pleased to
> grant us the victory, we would raise a House to the memory of His Great
> Name, wherever it should please Him'; and that they should also supplicate
> the aid and assistance of God, to enable them to fulfil their vow, and that
> we would note the day of the victory in a book, to make it known even
> to our latest posterity, in order that it might be celebrated to the honor
> of God.[19]

By 15 December they had established a strong laager on the Ncome River. At dawn next morning the grand army of Zululand ringed their wagons, ready to die for their king and country.

Why Dingane chose to offer battle at the Ncome remains an unsolved puzzle. The last time the kingdom had faced such a threat had been in 1819, when Shaka had retreated far to the south, foreseeing that Zwide's Ndwandwe regiments would be more easily overcome after an exhausting march. It was, however, by no means obvious that this force could be similarly tired out. Their wagons carried ample supplies of food. Their horses would flourish in fresh pasture lands where Zulu lambs were already growing fat.[20] Once beyond the Ncome, no significant obstacle would impede their path to the capital, Mgungundhlovu, and the ancestral graves. It could be that anything less than a full commitment to defence of the sacred places would be unthinkable, particularly after the men had been 'doctored' with war medicines. Or the army may have believed that if they succeeded in overrunning this laager, the 40,000 head of cattle, 300,000 sheep and 3000 horses still held at the trekker encampments would be easy pickings.[21] Perhaps, after his experiment with guns in August, the king believed that he could neutralize the most potent weapons of his enemies. How much detailed information Dingane possessed about the trekker defence of Vegkop is not known. Back in 1830 he had speculated that 'when the white people discharge their muskets, we could go and spear them before they re-loaded'.[22] While this might be true of men firing single slugs, it would not work so easily against men who simply threw powder and shot down the muzzles of their guns so as to vastly increase the speed of firing. In a battle such as Vegkop the scattered shot could work great destruction on the closely packed bodies of an assaulting force. This is what happened at Ncome River on 16 December. The front line of the Zulu advanced on the laager, firing single shots from their own muskets. Behind them came a host of running men, some 9000 or 10,000 in all. When the Boer cannon boomed out from the gates of the laager they did not run as Matiwane's forces had run at Mbholompo. For two hours they maintained their assault, the bodies piling up round the wagon wheels. They had no way of knowing that Pretorius feared he was about to run out of ammunition when he ordered the gates opened for a charge of Boer horsemen. With one-third of the army already fallen, the Zulu generals gave the command to retreat. After three hours of vain pursuit Pretorius called it a day, satisfied with the slaughter done at the place ever after remembered as Blood River.[23]

Dingane now abandoned the strategy of mass assault in favour of a calculated ambush. After deliberately burning his capital to deceive the enemy, he moved the main body of his army to concealed positions among caves and cliffs lying some kilometres to the south. Pretorius found enough valuable items in the charred ruins to justify holding an auction of booty, but remained frustrated in the great aim of his expedition, which was to make up for the losses of cattle the trekkers had suffered in the battles of the last year. When his men went off to look for beasts to plunder, they fell right into the trap the king had set on Christmas Day. Only after five hours of desperate combat on a rocky hillside were they able to fight their way clear. Among their dead was Alexander Biggar, a Port Natal adventurer who had already lost several family members in vain attempts to profit from the war between the trekkers and the Zulu. Vengeance for the deaths of his relatives was certainly on his mind, but so was the hope of seizing the horde of ivory tusks Dingane kept to fund his purchases of guns and ammunition.[24] The bravery shown by the Zulu defenders was strikingly demonstrated by one of their mounted men, who found his horse trapped by a band of Boers. Rather than let them kill him, he plunged his spear into his own heart.

The day had taken a heavy toll on the morale and equipment of the attacking force. Their horses threatened to drop from exhaustion, their ammunition was nearly gone, and they seemed no nearer than ever to capturing any of the royal herds. After some futile attempts to open nego-tiations, Pretorius turned homewards. Had he not succeeded in grabbing 4000–5000 cattle from chiefs living south of the Thukela on their return journey, the expedition would have counted as a failure.[25] Of course, the 3000 Zulu dead at the Blood River counted as military victory – impressive enough to cause the burghers of faraway Graaf Reinet to light bonfires to honour their home-town hero. But as an economic venture Blood River did nothing but spend bullets. One questionable trophy with some potential value did come home with Pretorius. Picking through the bleaching bones and threadbare clothing of Piet Retief and the others who died on the great February day of execution, the Boers claimed to have made a stupendous discovery. Retief's corpse was

> recognized by his clothes, which, although nearly consumed, yet small rags were still attached to his bones, added to which there were other tokens, such as his portmanteau, which was almost also consumed, in which there were several papers, of which some were damaged and rained to pieces; but some were found therein, in as perfect a state as if they had never been exposed to the air; amongst which was also the contract between him and Dingaan, respecting the cession of land, so clean and uninjured, as if it had been written to day. . . .

The words on the paper purported to grant 'Retief and his countrymen' all the land between the Thukela and Mzimvubu Rivers including Port Natal, in gratitude for the return of the cattle Sekonyela had stolen. If the paper was genuine, it did no more than grant what had already been granted several times before going back to the time of Francis Farewell and Shaka. It seems more likely to have been a fraud. Dingane's original demand, written for him by the missionary Francis Owen, had been that Retief bring the cattle in order to clear the Boers of suspicion of involvement in the theft – not as payment for a whole country. The witnesses to this miraculously preserved relic were alleged to be the king and three councillors who signed with an 'X', along with three Boers who died with their commander. The document was dated 4 February 1838, two days before the ceremony which Francis Owen claimed was to finish negotiations. The missionary recorded no meeting on the 4th, and it seems unlikely that Retief collected the king's signature and carefully filed it away minutes before his unexpected death. Fair or fraud, the paper could come in handy in future negotiations with the English, and so the story of its recovery was speedily published in papers throughout the British Zone.

The breaking of the rope

For his part, Dingane could take little satisfaction in the results of the December battles. Though he held his own herds and the previously captured Boer cattle, the human cost had been fearful. More men fell at Blood River than in any Zulu campaign since the ill-advised expedition against Soshangane in 1828. That defeat, as the king would well remember, had helped precipitate the assassination of Shaka. Now, once again, women wailed at every homestead in his kingdom – and, more than likely, his detractors grumbled and plotted round their fires. An immediate attack on the trekkers was out of the question. As months went by the Boer numbers increased, thanks to the news of Blood River and the alleged land grant. While still pondering his strategic plan to shift the kingdom north, Dingane for the first time contemplated serious negotiations for peace. The newly established British commander at Port Natal was more than willing to play the part of intermediary.

From information collected from Zulu men, Major Charters believed that Dingane had been severely shaken by his recent losses and would willingly conclude a peace if Pretorius dropped his demand for full restoration of all captured cattle plus an indemnity.[26] His interviews with trekker leaders, on the other hand, showed them to be in an uncompromising frame of mind. They told him frankly they acknowledged no further allegiance to the British crown and were determined to repair all their losses. Already they were building a village that was to be the headquarters of their government, named Pietermaritzburg in honour of their dead leaders, Pieter Retief and Gerrit Maritz.[27] They would not give Major Charters an immediate commitment to abandon plans for a future expedition against Dingane. A few weeks later Major Henry Jervis, who replaced Charters, sent a message to the king through one of the few surviving old Natal traders, Henry Ogle.[28] In reply, Dingane acknowledged that he was 'on the brink of ruin', and would accept

> any terms the captain of the English may propose for the Boers, that it never was my wish to fight with either. The Boers I never acknowledged nor ever will. The English I always have since Farewell's arrival at Natal. . . . tell Ogle to tell the English captain to write a letter in your presence and not to deceive me for I am now in trouble. Tell the English govt to assist me and send the Boers out of this into their own country.

He would accept a boundary set at the Thukela River and, as evidence of his goodwill, sent back 300 captured Boer horses. In the months to come he sent many more messages assuring Jervis that he would soon have the rest of the Boer property collected, including a large amount of ivory representing the value of cattle that could not be returned. As late as the beginning of August it still appeared that a lasting peace might be concluded, although one which left the trekkers in permanent occupation of land south of the Thukela.[29]

Just seven weeks later news came that the king's brother, Mpande, had thrown off his allegiance. Along with 17,000 followers and huge herds of cattle, he had crossed the Thukela and temporarily settled only a few kilometres north of Port Natal.

The Zulu kingdom had fractured with the force of a thunderbolt because Mpande would not accept Dingane's order to move his followers from the lower Thukela Valley to the upper Mfolozi basin as part of the broader plan to relocate the whole kingdom. Evidently the king had been playing for time during the previous negotiations, hoping to forestall a new attack at the same time as he prepared to seek a new 'country'. He could have expected that internal resistance to his plan would focus on his surviving brother. When Andrew Smith visited the kingdom in 1832, he found that Mpande was 'very popular, and looked upon by the people as the rightful heir to the throne'.[30] His words would carry weight in any discussion of a possible move north, because he had been among those who marched against Soshangane in Mozambique in 1828. It is not surprising that he rejected Dingane's plan. Warned that he might be killed for his opposition, he boldly marched to Port Natal.[31]

This new development spread consternation through the trekker camps. Many viewed it as another one of Dingane's tricks. Boer women, hearing that 25,000 cattle had providentially come within range of their commandos, demanded that the men kill Mpande's people and seize the herds![32] Only after the men pleaded that they would run out of ammunition before they could slay them all did the women agree to the alternative of entering into negotiations. In mid-October a party of about 240 men, including the well-to-do French naturalist, Adulphe Delegorgue, set off for Mpande's headquarters. Fearing at every moment that they might share the fate of Retief, they slept on their guns each night. When they reached their destination, the contrast between their bearing and Mpande's made a striking impression on the Frenchman. Mpande wore

> an ample cloak in the Roman style, with which he draped himself in an eminently noble fashion. . . . The comparison which I was at leisure to make, was to the complete disadvantage of the farmers who surrounded him: great, gangling, long-limbed fellows, with clumsy gestures, awkward bearing, dull faces, faltering speech, gaping mouth, men made to drive oxen and to hold converse with them. Panda was quite different: the large, well-shaped brilliant black eyes were over-shadowed by a jutting brow, surmounted by a high, square forehead on which a few early wrinkles were beginning to show; the nose was not unusual, except for the flaring well-defined nostrils, the mouth was wide with a ready smile expressive of quick comprehension, and the square chin was indicative of strength; in all it was a well-shaped head borne upon a superb body, shining and stout. His bearing was so noble, the limbs so obedient to the will, the gestures so formal, that a Parisian might well have believed that Panda had frequented royal palaces in his youth.

As indeed he had.

The upshot of the meeting was a formal alliance against Dingane. The trekkers believed that in the event of a victory they would regain all their lost stock along with an additional indemnity and even more land. Mpande would be satisfied to inherit the Zulu kingship, provided that he could hold the land he now occupied until his brother was defeated. Immediately following the conclusion of the alliance, Mpande had himself solemnly installed as sovereign, in a ceremony on 27 October 1839, which included the execution of his chief induna, Mpangazitha ka Mncumbata, the traditional sign that a new monarch had assumed the supreme power over the taking of human life.[33] The trekkers held a separate coronation ceremony marked by an exchange of presents, though with customary care for their future land titles, they insisted that none of Mpande's gifts of cattle could be allowed to support any future claim that he had bought the land on which he was now camped (so deeply ingrained was their own habit of claiming that every gift of cattle they presented to a chief represented a land purchase).[34] With these acts of schism people said Mpande had 'broken the rope' which bound the Zulu nation together. The next step would be civil war.

Everything had moved too fast for Dingane. His last hope for survival was the northern migration. That hope began to dissolve when four of his regiments met defeat at the hands of Sobhuza in August. It crumbled for ever when a second campaign in December failed to maintain a position north of the Phongola.[35] This was Mpande's signal to move. On 14 January 1840 Pretorius assembled a commando of nearly 400 mounted men to reinforce the new king's army. In the event, Mpande had no need of re-inforcements. Two messengers brought word on 30 January that Dingane had fled north, hoping to seek refuge with Mzilikazi.[36] The next day Mpande's *amabutho* caught and utterly routed the old king's remaining forces, some of whom changed sides in the course of the contest. Oral tradition says that Sobhuza's men caught and killed Dingane at the Lebombo mountains.[37] The victors took so many cattle that they hardly knew how to drive them. In the end the trekker role in the expedition was limited to shooting out some stragglers who had hidden in caves near the Phongola River. That did not deter them from announcing that following their great victory, they would take 40,000 cattle and pay for the costs of their commando by annexing all the land from the Black Mfolozi River to the Thukela. This truly outrageous claim would have been unthinkable in a world where everyone spoke and wrote a common language. In 1840 it was mere verbal hocus pocus. The real meaning of the campaign was that Mpande was now king in fact, that his southern border was fixed at the Thukela and that he would not further challenge the trekkers in the land they called Natal.

The implications of the settlement extended far beyond the Zulu and the trekkers. Sobhuza had been in touch with Mpande during the campaign and had co-ordinated the movement of his forces.[38] He could now rest assured that the kingdom he had created would survive. Because of the large number of former Ndwandwe who had given him their allegiance, he could count himself among the chief inheritors of Zwide's legacy. Other chiefs had also rushed forward to play a part in Dingane's demise in the hope of restoring the fortunes of their families. The most illustrious of these was Zikhali, son and heir to the great Matiwane, whose hope of founding a kingdom had vanished amid the artillery fire at the battle of Mbholompo in 1828. He had appeared before Pretorius with 250 men in fighting trim on 20 January. Though he gave his name properly as Zikhali ka Matiwane, the trekkers simply called him by his father's name, 'Mattowan'.[39]

Zikhali and the Princess Nomlalati

After the catastrophic Ngwane defeat of 1828, Zikhali had returned with his father to Zululand.[40] Matiwane lived in constant fear that the Zulu king would not permit so great a man to go on living, a fear that proved justified in June 1830 when his execution was ordered.[41] Soon afterwards Dingane sent search parties looking for Zikhali, saying 'whosoever shall find him shall bring him here, for he it is through whom I shall rule'. Zikhali and his followers from the remnants of the Ngwane regarded this as a ploy designed to speed his own death. Remembering that Sobhuza had once given his father twenty heifers when the Ngwane wandered friendless on the highveld, Zikhali crossed the Phongolo to seek refuge with this great king whose reputation grew from day to day. Sobhuza received him with all the honour due to a noble family, hinting that he would find him a suitable great wife. One of the king's daughters, Nomlalati, soon fell desperately in love with Zikhali and made up her mind that she would be that wife. She tricked him into coming to her hut and spending a night in her arms. When Sobhuza learned of the incident, he judged Zikhali guilty of a gross betrayal of trust and made plans to have him killed 'accidentally' during a royal hunt. Warned by a friend, he fled again to Zululand, where Dingane greeted him cordially and gave him a village to govern. All went well until 1836 when Zikhali feigned illness in an attempt to evade the king's order to lead his *amabutho* in the expedition against Mzilikazi. Shortly thereafter he took his people across the Thukela, hoping perhaps, that in the confusion created by the advent of the trekkers, he might find a home again on the slopes of the Drakensberg – the place where his father had stopped in the days of Shaka. Eventually, he did so, but not before going through a series of trials.

The trekkers, who had at first welcomed his help in the grand alliance against Dingane, later accused him of holding back thousands of cattle and ordered him to be held in irons at their capital, Pietermaritzburg.[42] After his release, when he had succeeded in gathering together large numbers of Ngwane people who had moved out of Zululand, he came to the brink of war with a similar group of Hlubi people led by Langalibalele, son of Mthimkulu, who also sought a homeland for his people under the Drakensberg. Many on both sides remembered their wars of the 1820s and longed to settle old scores. Conflict was avoided when Langalibalele's mother, Mntambose, rose majestically in her son's council and demanded that the Ngwane be allowed to pass peacefully on their way. Do you, she thundered, wish my son to find an early grave like his father? No, she would not hear of it.

> Thereupon the chief stood up and said, 'Very well, Queen.' She replied,
> 'Be silent, I tell you, not a word.' Then there stood up the scouts that she
> had sent out. 'You So-and-So, why are you being disrespectful? Don't you
> hear her say that there was not to be another word! She does not want to
> have her son slain.[43]

So war was averted. The Hlubi and Ngwane lived side by side for decades
to come in the shadow of Champagne Castle and Cathedral Peak. For
the Ngwane, 'there was an abundance of corn, and the pumpkins grew
in profusion, there was maize, milk more than the dogs could finish, and
scarcity was no more'.[44] Zikhali was once again a great man, hailed by his
people with the royal salute, 'Bayete'. He won a reputation for wisdom and
justice when he ordered that his men keep the wives they had acquired in
the course of their previous adventures. They had shared the hardships and
could not now be cast off in favour of younger local women on the flimsy
excuse that there had been no proper marriage feast.

> Those wives that marched with my father, wherever the army rested, I saw
> them undo the burdens of grain that they always kept tied up, and the
> corn that we took from Wezi, even now I still drink beer made of it today.
> Wherever the army rested, a woman would go down to the river and grind
> the malt which had sprouted whilst being carried on her head, and the
> beer fermented on her head, and wherever we made a halt, I would see a
> man coming to me saying: Chief, here is some beer made by the wife of
> So-and-So.[45]

It was not long before news of Zikhali's prosperity reached Nomlalati.
Her brother Mswati, who by this time had succeeded Sobhuza as King of
Swaziland, gladly gave his blessing to the union. At her wish, no prior word
was sent to Zikhali. The Swazi king, his sister and the whole grand bridal
party arrived unannounced at Zikhali's great place. As they made their
entrance, dancing the wedding dance, all could see that Nomlalati was
destined to be the mother 'of the chief to come'.

This romantic story illustrates some important consequences of Mpande's
settlement with the trekkers. For the first time in a generation the land of
Natal could be settled by chiefs and people owing no allegiance to the Zulu
monarch. It was not just the Ngwane and Hlubi who staked out territory.
There were also Qwabe, Mbo, Cele, Phakade and many minor chiefs. In
years to come colonial historians would claim they came as 'refugees from
Zulu tyranny'. That interpretation of their migration completely misses the
point. The resettlement of Natal was powered by the ambition of chiefs, not
by the dissatisfaction of ordinary people. Many did not come from Zululand
at all, but were so-called 'Fingo' from Xhosa country and the British Zone,

who sought the land of their ancestors.[46] Once Mpande's treaty with Pretorius removed the threat of Zulu cattle-raids south of Thukela, chiefs realized that Natal was now a place where they could build up herds, and thereby raise the power of their lineage. It was an ironic consequence of the trekkers' treaty that the chiefs succeeded in moving far more people into Natal than all the wagon trains put together. Mpande tried without success to interest the trekkers in making an arrangement which would leave him free to exert authority over those chiefs.[47] The provision in his treaty which forbade him to make war on any other chief without first seeking permission from Pretorius effectively denied him the right to operate in Natal, so the leakage of ambitious chiefs continued. In the course of the next five years the trekker population never climbed above about 5000.[48] During the same period the population governed by the chiefs rose to a figure estimated at 80–100,000.[49] Zikhali was only one of many chiefs to have found a promising country and illustrious wives.

Remarkably, these two treks went on side by side for several years without generating much conflict. This was largely because chiefs and Boers held different ideas about what constituted desirable land. The Boers looked for wide open pasture land with an easy road to Port Natal. This led them to prefer the up-country areas and the broad corridor of elevated land which extends from modern-day Ladysmith via Pietermaritzburg to Durban. They avoided the coastal districts where deep, fast-flowing rivers scored the landscape. They liked to locate farms and villages in broad valleys, close to running water. The chiefs, in contrast, had no need of roads to take their produce to market or to the port. They could make good economic use of broken country, provided the mix of pasturage suited their cattle. Like their ancestors, they valued situations on hillsides which commanded views of the approaches taken by potential enemies and which offered good possibilities for defence.

The short, troubled life of the Republic of Natalia

The Boers were well aware of the problems posed by the parallel black trek to Natal. While they maintained their centuries-old tradition of seeking to tie labour to their farms, the newly established Volksraad (legislature) of the government which called itself the Republic of Natalia decreed in August 1840 that there should not be more than five 'Zulu' families to each 3000-acre farm. The next August the Volksraad passed a second resolution directing that all other chiefs and people should be moved to a designated tract of land south of Mzimvubu River – land to which the trekkers had no claim of any kind and which belonged to Faku's Mpondo kingdom.[50] Though no steps were taken to implement the resolution, it set alarm bells ringing in the British governor's councils. Major Charters's expedition of 1838 had been intended to stop turmoil in Natal from spreading south into Xhosa country. In December 1840 a commando had taken cattle, women and children from Faku's subaltern chief Ncaphayi. Now the Boers proposed pushing tens of thousands of people into an already crowded land. Governor Napier seized on these actions as the pretext for a decisive intervention. In January 1841 he ordered a detachment of troops under Captain T. C. Smith to take all measures necessary to defend Britain's 'faithful ally', Faku.

This action demonstrated the degree to which the governor and the military clique had regained control of policy in the British Zone. The process had begun when Lord Glenelg resigned as British Colonial Secretary early in 1839. His protégé, Stockenstrom, was dismissed as Lieutenant Governor a few months later. The policy of trying to hold a firm boundary between the British Zone and the rest of southern Africa through prohibitions on colonization and treaties with friendly chiefs had collapsed. Thanks to the trekking movement, it no longer had any supporters. Colonial expansionists and land speculators, epitomized by their champion, the *Graham's Town Journal*, had continually denounced it. Senior British army officers in South Africa looked for every opportunity to attack Glenelg and his policies. Anti-slavery and missionary lobbyists changed their minds about Britain's role beyond the borders when it appeared that the policy of disengagement left the trekkers free to fight wars and claim lands wherever they chose to roam. In addition, there was a practical threat to British tax revenue, for if trade from the interior were diverted from Cape Town and Port Elizabeth to Port Natal, less money would be collected in customs duties.[51] As early as 1840 a new colonial secretary, Lord John Russell, stated that he disagreed with Glenelg's opposition to colonial expansion.[52] In September of the same year Russell acknowledged he was 'favourable to the settlement of Port Natal as a British colony'. Although he was 'not prepared to expend large funds to conquer the territory for the emigrant farmers', he would support measures to conciliate the trekkers.[53] This was enough for Napier. He embarked straight away on a scheme to do what his officer corps and the *Graham's Town Journal* had wanted to do from the start – to extend the boundaries of the British Zone to include the lands the trekkers had occupied.

Napier's adoption of that point of view is unsurprising. Every British governor before him had eventually come round to the colonial way of thinking. His conversion took exactly the same course as D'Urban's; it just took a little longer. On a tour of the border districts in 1838, Napier expressed concern at 'the constant and increasing depredations' which Xhosa 'thieves' had perpetrated on colonial farmers.[54] Next he warned Xhosa chiefs – in words like those D'Urban had used in June 1834 (see Chapter 8, p. 220) – that if such incidents recurred they 'must inevitably lead to war' and if he were 'forced to draw the sword, they might rely that I would not sheath it until they were driven, as before, beyond the Bashee'. Soon he was echoing their complaint that people in England were misinformed about the true state of affairs in South Africa.[55] As Napier's conversion proceeded he came to view the trekkers' grievances as entirely justified. Drought, he said, had forced them to seek new pastures.[56] Britain had laid down rules for compensating owners of freed slaves which resulted in most slave-owners receiving less than a third of the fair market value. Surveys of land claimed in remote regions of the British Zone had been carried out in a tardy and slipshod manner, causing many Boers to despair at ever getting legal titles. Some, who feared that they would have to pay twice for title to the same land, decided to trek in search of 'free' land over the border. Finally, Napier agreed with the colonists that a fund of at least £350,000 should be created to compensate all the Boers for losses of time, property and livestock due to their commando service in the 1835 war against the Xhosa.

Like the rest of his circle he did not believe that any but a handful of the trekkers wanted independence from Britain. All that was needed to secure their allegiance was a return to D'Urban's policies. Maybe that might have worked in 1836, but by 1842 much had changed. Something like a spirit of national independence could be detected in many encampments on the highveld and in Natal. People complained that they had been given no assistance and denied the right to import ammunition, even when they were ferociously attacked by Mzilikazi and Dingane.[57] The Volksraad in Pietermaritzburg tried to win support from the Netherlands and flew the Dutch flag.[58] A. H. Potgieter angrily asserted that he did 'not want to subject myself to any Britain nor in justice to any other power in the world'. 'I am', he said, 'no Briton.'[59] The Natal Volksraad claimed the right to be recognized 'a free and independent people' – a right 'so dearly purchased by our blood'. Napier planned to kill these embryonic nationalist sentiments by giving the trekkers what they were most likely to cherish, secure titles to the land they claimed, backed by the full force of British authority.

He had good reason to suspect this would win the day. Much of the work of the Natal Volksraad revolved around land business. Land sales were the chief source of revenue.[60] Land sales had begun at Port Natal in November 1837.[61] Two years later Pietermaritzburg was carved up into town acres and distributed to would-be purchasers by drawing lots. Not content with the 3000-acre farms which had supported most Boer families in the old colony, speculators staked claims to 6000-acre farms. And there was not just one per household; families were laying claim to as many as three farms each.[62] The money value of these claims stood to be multiplied many times if they were guaranteed by the British government.

Napier's problem was convincing the trekkers that he was truly their friend. This was not as easy as it might seem. His excuse for intervening beyond the borders was to protect the interests of chiefs like Faku. Nor could he ignore evidence that the trekkers had illegally retained 'apprentices' and had captured children on their forays into Zululand.[63] For their part, the trekkers feared that any British defence of African interests could threaten their land claims – claims they were prepared to defend by force. The showdown came in 1842 when Napier ordered Captain Smith's force to advance and take control of Port Natal. He did not believe

> that Capt. Smith will meet with the slightest resistance from the people of Port Natal. The great majority of them are anxious to remain in possession of the privileges of British subjects, and if they were only aware that their landed property would be secured to them, I believe that they would long since have signified their willingness to submit. I should mention, that another circumstance which urged me to issue my Proclamation was, my having received information of an intention on the part of the Boers, to turn the natives out of their gardens and take possession of them themselves.[64]

His plan did not take account of the fighting spirit of the Boer women, who once again feared a loss of all they had struggled for.[65] They did not cower before the British any more than the Zulu. Under their goading Pretorius decided to take an aggressive attitude, sending Captain Smith a protest against the occupation and declaring that his people were free subjects owing allegiance to the Netherlands and Belgium. Smith was no more impressed than a bugler in his regiment who ridiculed Pretorius as a pompous blowhard with 'a belly on him like the bass drum'.[66] On his own authority Smith decided to attack the Boer camp at Congella on the moonlit night of 23 May 1842.

Smith's plan was to march along the beach and rendezvous with a boat whose small cannon would rake the enemy lines while his forces overran the camp.[67] Everything that could go wrong did go wrong. His marching forces were clearly visible in the moonlight, making easy targets for Boer marksmen hidden in the thick bush. The gunboat did not arrive on schedule, and by the time it did appear, confusion already reigned in the British ranks due to a rush of Boer oxen. The battle finished in an inglorious rout as Smith's men slogged back to headquarters through the incoming tide. By the time the fiasco finished, Smith counted thirty-four of his men dead, six missing and another sixty-three wounded. Three days later the Boers used the small cannon they had captured to take further ground, leaving Smith besieged in his own fort. Several of the Boer men marvelled that God had given them the victory as he had delivered Moses from Pharaoh, by sending the sea to engulf the enemy.

For the first time in the nineteenth century a battle had been fought pitting British against Boers – a momentous event. But, as would often happen in the future, the inevitable consequence of an initial victory was eventual defeat. Once his men had come under fire, Governor Napier needed no permission from his superiors to mount a counter-attack. The first relieving ship anchored off Port Natal on 25 June, carrying a detachment of soldiers under the command of Lieutenant Colonel A. J. Cloete and Major W. J. D'Urban. Napier probably hoped such appointments would help smooth the way to a peaceful settlement. Cloete came from an old Cape Peninsula family and could speak to Pretorius in his own language. D'Urban was the son of the man whom the Natal Volksraad a few months before had called 'the best Governor we ever had'.[68] Major D'Urban actually went so far as to say it 'was a distasteful duty' to 'have to fight against men who had done such good service under Sir Benjamin' in the Xhosa war. Napier's orders ran in the same spirit. Provided that the trekkers returned captured property, reaffirmed their allegiance to the Queen of England and refrained from making war on local chiefs, their Volksraad could continue to govern and collect revenue, pending a permanent decision on the future government of Natal. However, too much water had already flowed under the bridge for these conditions to be accepted without a fight. Pretorius and his associates still believed in the fantasy that the government of Holland would come to their rescue, and therefore determined to resist the British advance. With big naval guns to cover their advance Cloete and D'Urban had little difficulty in taking Port Natal. They had come just in time for their besieged comrades at the fort. Captain Smith had eaten a roasted crow for breakfast on the morning he was relieved.

Within a few weeks the British force had advanced to Pietermaritzburg where, on 15 July 1842, the Volksraad made their submission to the Queen's authority. A general amnesty was issued to all but four of the 'rebels'.[69] There were handshakes all round. The events underlined more than ever before the British double standard in South Africa. When Governors D'Urban and Napier wrote to Xhosa chiefs who were their 'friends and allies' they warned that in the event of any misconduct they 'would not proceed by half-measures'. When they went to war against those same 'friends and allies', they killed chiefs, captured women and children, burned crops and spread general mayhem. When the Natal trekkers killed and wounded a hundred British soldiers and brought Captain Smith's men to the verge of starvation, the British made a speedy peace and issued a general amnesty. Although Mpande and Natal chiefs both offered to assist the British, Cloete refused 'to adopt the degrading process of enlisting the savage in our cause'.[70] Even more conciliatory gestures were made the next year when the colonel's brother Henry Cloete came back to Natal as Commissioner charged with completing arrangements for annexation of the territory (proclaimed 12 May 1843). Cloete took the Boers' side against those they accused of stealing their cattle. He proceeded to confirm British titles to most of the farms claimed by the trekkers, even those which had never been occupied, on the pretext that the unsettled state of the country had made it difficult to occupy many districts.[71] He also backed their claims to the triangle of territory between the upper Thukela and Buffalo Rivers, known as the Klip River District. Cloete took quite a different line with the chiefs, however, insisting that they were simply refugees with no enforceable land rights. He recommended that Boer claimants be given titles to 760 farms, comprising some 2.1 million acres, and the chiefs be granted nothing. Another 8.5 million acres were to be reserved for future immigrants from Europe.[72] It is a familiar story. In this, as in every previous annexation in South Africa, British governors and their agents made it their priority to appease the Boers, whose muskets and horses they would need in the event of hostilities with chiefs.

This time, however, there were many who refused to be appeased. Pretorius had not been included in the general amnesty and could only escape punishment by fleeing north across the Drakensberg, the line at which commissioner Cloete had set the interior boundary of British Natal. Others reacted badly when they learned that the new authority would not permit 'any distinction of persons or disqualification founded on mere distinction of colour, origin, language or creed'. They had learned it was possible to survive outside the British Zone without such policies. Rather than accept them many preferred to trek across the mountains with Pretorius. Another group who refused to be reconciled were the Boer women of Pietermaritzburg led by Mrs Erasmus Smit, who interrupted Commissioner Cloete's meeting with the all-male Volksraad on 8 August 1843. After inviting him to the neighbouring courtroom, the women locked the doors and made the Commissioner listen for two hours to their grievances. They argued that their sufferings and contribution to the trekker war effort ought to entitle them to vote in elections for the proposed Legislative Council. When Cloete told them that the vote for women could not be granted because it would humiliate their husbands, they vowed they would walk barefoot over the mountains rather than submit to British authority.[73]

Many historians have viewed these strong expressions of feeling as evidence of the motives behind the trekking movement. However, if desires for liberty in general had been the cause, then people would have trekked from *every* part of the British Zone – not just from the eastern districts. The sentiments expressed in 1843 were the consequence, not the cause of the trek. Time would show that the spirit of independence was a genie which would be hard to put back in the bottle. It remained to be seen whether the British would follow up their annexation of Natal with a similar attempt to impose their will on trekker settlements on the highveld.

New warlords in the northern highveld

Many of the considerations which caused Napier to intervene in Natal also applied on the highveld. The advent of the trekkers disturbed the peace and altered the balance of power. The struggle against Mzilikazi had killed thousands of people and was followed up by plundering expeditions which captured cattle and children. Some of the chiefs who felt threatened by the trekkers believed that the treaties of friendship they concluded with Andrew Smith in 1835 would protect them against encroachments on their lands. Missionaries and the Aborigines Protection Society were pressuring the British government to do something on the highveld as well as in Natal.

On the other hand, there were many reasons for Napier to think twice before making any move north of the Orange. There was no access by sea permitting the easy landing of troops as had been done at Port Natal. The pattern of trekker interaction with chiefs was not a simple matter of invasion on one side and resistance on the other. Many different groups and individuals allied themselves with the trekkers in order to promote their own interests. Griqua landowners had been making money by leasing grazing land to Boers even before the trekking movement began. They happily leased many more thousands of acres after 1836. Some Griqua leaders had joined in the commandos against Mzilikazi. So had Hurutshe and Rolong chiefs who hoped to re-establish their former predominance in the Marico River basin. All along the Caledon Valley, too, competing chiefs courted the assistance of trekkers in struggles against old rivals. After forty to fifty years experience of mounted men and guns, there was no initial reason to think that the newcomers differed greatly from the Kora and Griqua.

The land was vast, so vast that in most places the trekker encampments were mere dots on the map.[74] After the defeat and withdrawal of Mzilikazi they scattered in several directions. Like the Kora and the Griqua they gathered round particular leaders, each of whom jealously guarded his independence from all other authority. They tended to call their chief villages after themselves. The impact of their presence varied, depending on the activities they pursued. Those who trekked north of the Vaal River mostly adopted the trading/raiding/hunting lifestyle of their Griqua and

Kora forerunners. The most restlessly active and ambitious of their number was A. H. Potgieter, an adventurer in the mould of Coenraad de Buys. In his very first expedition to the north-eastern highveld he made contact with De Buys's sons, who later became his partners. The pole star of his trekking career was the road to Delagoa Bay (Chapter 9, pp. 246–7). His commando raids against Mzilikazi had opened his eyes to the potential of the old trading route running from the Marico/Molopo region to the coastal ports of Mozambique. The obvious advantage of this east–west road to the sea was that there were no troublesome British regulations or duties. Ivory and hides still brought good prices and the slave trade remained legal at Portuguese stations. In fact, the volume of slave exports in the 1840s and 1850s was at least as great as in the 1820s and 1830s.[75] Muscling into this trade required alliances with strategically located chiefs who soon came to know Potgieter as 'Ndeleka'.[76] As his reputation grew other trekkers began calling him 'king of the blacks'.[77] And with good reason, for he had learned in the 1836 commandos that promises to share out captured cattle could buy loyal service from brave soldiers. Again and again he recruited men from the allies who had first marched with him against Mzilikazi. In 1843 he took Rolong men from Thaba Nchu in a renewed attack on the Ndebele. In 1846 and 1847 he used a similar force in raids on the eastern highveld and Mozambique.[78]

Potgieter's involvement in slave-trading probably began very soon after his arrival on the highveld.[79] His western headquarters were the Magaliesberg mountains and the village of Potchefstroom. From this region a small-scale trade in captured children sprang up which supplied southern Boer farms with *inboekeling* (apprentices) – just as a generation earlier children had been supplied from this region to the British Zone by Griqua and Kora.[80] By 1845 Potgieter had established an eastern outpost at the new village of Andries Ohrigstad on the edge of the Drakensberg escarpment. It was probably he who showed up at Delagoa Bay in 1844 leading a party of twenty-four well-armed Boers and 300 slaves for sale.[81] His cherished goal was still to find a fly-free route to Delagoa. By the 1840s he was also working with the Portuguese adventurer João Albasini, who commanded a private army and a retinue of 500 slaves.[82]

In the eastern region the slave trade was directed mainly at supplying Brazil and Madagascar. During the 1840s Soshangane's Gaza kingdom held the dominant strategic position in the lowlands between the Portuguese ports and the northern Drakensberg, but many other chiefs managed to get a share of the action. The trade was not simply concerned with slaves; guns, ammunition, ivory and cattle were also important. Newly installed King Mswati of Swaziland was one of many who relied on the trade to Delagoa Bay to provide him with guns.[83] He welcomed the opportunity to forge an

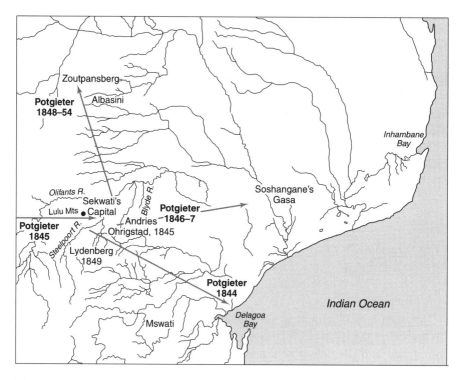

Map 22 'King of the blacks': Potgieter, his allies and his ventures, 1844–54

alliance with Potgieter and the Ohrigstad community of trekkers. Sekwati, who commanded a much diminished Pedi kingdom after the death of his father, Thulare, and who had lost many cattle to Mzilikazi, greeted Potgieter with an offer to 'be his dog'.[84] This was mere manner of speaking, for he sought nothing less than to restore his father's legacy. Within a few years the initial amity had given way to open warfare. In 1846 Potgieter's African mercenaries combined with Michael de Buys and succeeded in carrying off 8000 of Sekwati's cattle.[85]

Potgieter, Mswati and Sekwati all aspired to control the region south of Ohrigstad because it was here that the fly-free high country made its closest approach to Delagoa Bay. Potgieter's preference was simply to claim the territory and hold it by force, but the majority of trekkers at Ohrigstad thought it wiser to pay tribute to Mswati who was clearly the strongest power in the region. They sent him 100 cattle, and with the usual care for future title claims, secured his 'X' on a document written in Dutch, ceding to them 'all the territory conquered by Sobhuza, and extending northward from Ohrigstad to the Olifants River, and along its course to the boundary of Delagoa Bay . . . westwards to the Elands River as far as the 26th parallel, eastwards to the junction of the Crocodile and the Komati, and southwards to the Crocodile'.[86] If this were made good it would guarantee control over the key territory through which trade was funnelled from the highveld to the Bay. But, as Potgieter understood, Mswati's 'X' on paper was worthless unless backed by force. Even as his fellow Ohrigstaders put their faith in Mswati, Potgieter was once again justifying his nickname, 'king of the blacks', by lending his mercenary gunmen to aid a Zulu raid on Mswati's people.[87]

He made an even more audacious attempt to capture vital trade routes in 1846 and 1847. With a force of 238 men he set out to find a reliable route to the port of Inhambane. Not surprisingly his army ran straight into Soshangane's *amabutho* and fought an inconclusive battle in which Potgieter lost about sixty of his black soldiers. The only evidence for this encounter comes from two letters Potgieter wrote to a Dutch trader and it has created great puzzlement for historians. P. J. van der Merwe could not imagine why Potgieter should want to open a stock road through tse-tse fly country to Inhambane. Van der Merwe therefore decided that Potgieter was trying to cover up the real reason for his expedition: a renewed attack on Mzilikazi in his new home north of the Limpopo.[88] However, the letters make perfect sense if the 'Matebele' mentioned in Potgieter's letters are identified as Soshangane's soldiers. This would suggest that the true object of the failed expedition was an attempt to break Soshangane's stranglehold on the trade of slaves and ivory to Inhambane.[89] With that hope dashed Potgieter moved his base yet again, up to the Zoutpansberg range near the Limpopo where he co-ordinated slaving and hunting activities with Albasini and Michael de Buys. The trio supplemented their income by demanding tribute on subordinate chiefs through a levy called the *opgaaf*. This could take the form of cattle, trading goods or labour service.[90] As the Portuguese slave trade began to wind down after 1850, the ivory trade came to play a larger part in the northern economy. Despite reiterated trekker prohibitions against the gun trade, large numbers of African sharpshooters were recruited to step up the slaughter of elephants. The culture of the gun spread farther and farther afield.[91]

Without Potgieter, the village of Ohrigstad struggled to survive. Threats from their neighbours caused them to live in fear of attack, as the ruins of their walled fort still attest. The mosquito proved in the end to be an even deadlier enemy than either Sekwati or Mswati. Malaria forced the trekkers to move away to Lydenburg in 1849. With their threat removed, Sekwati succeeded in building a Pedi kingdom which surpassed the remembered glories of his father. The key elements in his success were: construction of a strongly fortified village at Thaba-Mosego in the Lulu mountains (near present-day Sekhukhune); renewed involvement in ivory hunting and trade to Delagoa Bay, through which guns were acquired in significant numbers;[92] and rebuilding his own royal herds, partly through astute marriages of his daughters to chiefs who recognized his paramountcy.[93]

It seems more than likely that through his relations and contacts in the Caledon Valley he had learned the secrets of state-building on Moshweshwe's principles.[94] In 1847 he withstood a raid launched by Mpande, but conciliated the Zulu king through the same annual tribute of ostrich feathers that Moshweshwe practised. By the 1850s Sekwati was sending young men to the faraway British Zone where their earnings as migrant labours enabled them to purchase guns and ammunition.[95] The trekkers could no longer call Sekwati their dog and would eventually be forced to recognize his independence through a formal treaty (1857).

Thus, by the late 1840s the northern highveld in many ways resembled the southern and western highveld in the 1820s. Hunters, raiders and slavers freely roamed a land where might made right. With their superior guns and equipment, trekkers quickly displaced the Griqua and Kora as the most feared raiding bands. Trekkers and chiefs joined together in mutually advantageous warfare. The only significant difference between Potgieter and men like Barends or Jan Bloem was that Potgieter inscribed his grotesque land claims on paper, just in case they might prove useful in the future.[96] The truth was, however, that the northern trekkers truly ruled only in a few small districts, divided by distance, personal antagonism and religious affiliation. They agreed on one thing in 1844, that in time of peril Hendrik Potgieter should be their War Commander.[97]

In the north-west, as in Natal and the eastern highveld, the paradoxical result of the advent of the trekkers was to open opportunities for chiefs and commoners to resettle lands which had been unsafe for cattle-keepers in the days of Mzilikazi's greatness. When Adulphe Delegorgue made his way from Natal to the Magaliesberg in 1843, he was surprised to find Sotho-speaking people everywhere – living proof that the country had not been 'depopulated by Zulu warfare'.[98] Many in the Marico and Magaliesberg districts were people who previously acknowledged Mzilikazi but chose to remain in their ancestral homes rather than move across the Limpopo. Another significant group comprised about 3000 BaRolong people who reversed the direction of their previous trek (Chapter 7, p. 203) and slowly made their way back to the Mafeking area. Their descendants would for decades to come remember the early trekkers as benefactors rather than enemies.[99] Many of the Hurutshe would also have liked to return to their former headquarters in the splendid Mosega basin, but continued activity by Mzilikazi's patrols and the potential power of the Boers made them wary. The district remained an eerily quiet no man's land throughout the early 1840s.[100]

A new economy and struggles for land on the southern highveld

South of the Vaal River, a different economy and society developed in the 1840s. The first trekboers to cross the Orange River were seeking little more than grazing for their cattle and sheep. Even when thousands more joined them in 1836, few thought of doing more than following the lifestyle of their forebears. By 1840, however, a new factor came into play. Demand for wool to supply textile factories in Britain led to a world-wide boom in wooled sheep production. South African farmers moved quickly to take advantage of this unprecedented opportunity. In 1836 about 373,000 pounds of wool were exported. By 1839 this figure had jumped to 586,000 pounds. Three years later it nearly trebled again and by 1848 it stood at 3,671,000 pounds. Some of the best potential sheep country in all southern Africa lay between the Vaal and Caledon Rivers, which now became a zone of intense competition.[101]

In the west where rain was unreliable, sheep needed permanent springs and water holes. Trekkers got access to some of these by making deals with Griqua farmers who had a pretty fair idea of the nature of the transactions.[102] In other cases, people who still measured power through ownership of cattle rather than land were enticed into signing away valuable land for practically nothing. One farmer claimed to have paid five sheep for a valuable farm in the lower Caledon region.[103] Another ploy was to persuade chiefs to sell land they did not own. Makwana, who claimed to be the rightful chief of the Taung, 'sold' to the trekkers a gigantic tract of land between the Vet and Vaal Rivers. While this was indeed his people's patrimony, he had not occupied the area for a long time; his 'sale' intensely annoyed his more famous nephew, Moletsane, who had hoped to re-establish Taung dominance in the old territory.[104]

Such tricks could not be played in the upper Caledon Valley where missionaries advised important chiefs in all matters concerned with writing. It might have been supposed that the trekkers would avoid a district so densely settled, so well defended and so fiercely contested. What drew them to the Caledon were reliable water, a route to Natal, good grazing and the best horse-breeding country on the highveld.[105] The presence of so many independent chiefs with overlapping land claims actually assisted their efforts to gain a foothold because each could be played off against the others. Most of the trekkers were no more scrupulous in their dealings with Caledon chiefs than Piet Retief had been when he betrayed his 'friend and ally' Sekonyela in order to curry favour with Dingane. Matters were further complicated by the presence of competing groups of missionaries – Methodist and French Evangelical – each siding with the chiefs they relied on for support. As rivalries and claims multiplied in the early 1840s every aspirant group tried to defend its case by writing letters to the British governor in Cape Town. As Governor Napier had been charged with the task of preventing the trekkers from perpetrating injustices against the chiefs who had concluded treaties of friendship in the 1830s, he had the opportunity to initiate another dramatic British intervention.

Notes

1   Governor Napier claimed that with only 1500 troops to guard his frontier, it was impossible to stop apprentices being taken; Napier to Glenelg, 21 Sept. 1838 in *Records of Natal*, IV, pp. 36–7.

2   Sworn Statement of Roos, 1838 in *Records of Natal*, III, pp. 305–6.

3   Statement of Dina, to Special Justice Rawstorne, 24 Sept. 1838 in *Records of Natal*, IV, pp. 41–3. For Rawstorne's background, see Robert Ross, *Adam Kok's Griquas* (Cambridge, 1976), p. 40.

4   F. Rawstorne to Secretary to Government, 25 Aug. 1838, in *Records of Natal*, IV, pp. 23–5.

5   G. D. Joubert to F. Rawstorne, 14 July 1838, in *Records of Natal*, IV, pp. 11–13.

6   *Natal Papers*, II, pp. 27–8; Eric Walker, *The Great Trek* (London, 1938), pp. 176–8.

7   Statements of Ndukwana 15 and 17 Sept. 1900, *JSA*, IV, pp. 276, 279. These oral memories are in remarkable agreement with the most important surviving written evidence of Dingane's intentions, in July 1838, which reports that the king, 'to secure his cattle', sent them into the territory of Sobhuza. The same document reported that Sobhuza's forces had repelled the invasion, killing many men and taking possession of many of these cattle; Letter of Revd. Palmer, 11 July 1838, forwarded to the Cape Government by W. Fynn, in *Records of Natal*, IV, pp. 15–16. This accords with Ndukwana's statement of 23 Dec. 1901, if the date of the reported clash with Sobhuza's forces is advanced to 1838, rather than being fixed at the time of Mpande's defection in 1839; see *JSA*, IV, p. 345.

8   John Omer-Cooper, *The Zulu Aftermath* (London, 1966), pp. 64–85.

9   Philip Bonner, *Kings, Commoners and Concessionaires* (Cambridge, 1982), pp. 24–34.

10 Malyn Newitt, *A History of Mozambique* (London, 1995), pp. 260–2.

11 George Cory, ed., *The Diary of the Rev. Francis Owen* (Cape Town, 1926), pp. 139–40. This passage, however, appears in places to confuse Dingane with Soshangane.

12 *Records of Natal*, III, pp. 246–51.

13 John S. Galbraith, *Reluctant Empire, British Policy on the South African Frontier* (Berkeley, 1963), pp. 142, 144, 183–4.

14 Eric Walker, *History of South Africa* (London, 1965), p. 207.

15 Joubert to Rawstorne, 14 July 1838, in *Records of Natal*, IV, pp. 11–13.

16 Napier to Glenelg, 16 Oct. 1838, in *Records of Natal*, IV, pp. 47–8.

17 W. Fynn to Acting Secretary to the Lieutenant Governor, 18 Oct. 1838; and Napier to Glenelg, 20 Nov. 1838, in *Records of Natal*, IV, pp. 56–7, 70–5.

18 John Bird, ed., *Annals of Natal*, 2 vols (first published 1888, reprinted Cape Town, 1965), I, pp. 433–6.

19 'Journal of the Expedition of the emigrant Farmers . . . kept by an Emigrant Mr. J. G. Bantjes', in *Natal Papers*, II, pp. 56–9.

20 The Boer invaders marvelled at the size of the Zulu sheep and lambs, 'such as no one had ever seen before in respect of largeness and fatness'; see the 'Journal of the Expedition of the emigrant farmers under their chief Commandant A. P. W. Pretorius . . . in the months of November and December, 1838' in *Natal Papers*, II, pp. 56–9.

21 Manfred Nathan, *The Voortrekkers of South Africa* (London, 1937), p. 237.

22 Nathaniel Isaacs, *Travels and Adventures in Eastern Africa*, newly revised and edited, L. Herman and P. R. Kirby (Cape Town, 1970), p. 186.

23 *Natal Papers*, II, pp. 56–9, 69–70.

24 Bird, *Annals of Natal*, I, p. 552.

25 Charters, notes of interview with C. P. Landman, 14 Jan. 1839, in *Records of Natal*, IV, pp. 483–9.

26 T. Shepstone to Charters, 7 Jan. 1839, in *Records of Natal*, IV, pp. 168–9.

27 Bird, *Annals of Natal*, I, pp. 530–1.

28 Jervis to Napier, 27 Mar. 1839 in *Records of Natal*, IV, pp. 221–7.

29 Jervis to Napier, 28 July 1839, in *Records of Natal*, IV, pp. 254–64.

30 P. R. Kirby, ed., *Andrew Smith and Natal* (Cape Town, 1955), p. 89.

31 Transcript of interview with Mpande, 15 Oct. 1839, in *Natal Papers*, II, pp. 104–7.

32 Adulphe Delegorgue, *Travels in Southern Africa: Vol. 1*, translated from French by Fleur Webb (Pietermaritzburg, 1990), pp. 82–9.

33 Ibid., p. 354n. Mpangazitha was a high-ranking Ndwandwe defector to Shaka's rule. There are two versions of his death. One ascribes it to a regiment disgruntled at the new order of things. I prefer the account according to which Mpande himself ordered the execution because it parallels the death of the chief induna, Masiphula, at the coronation of Cetshwayo in 1873. See Norman Etherington, Review of Carolyn Hamilton, *Terrific Majesty* in *South African Historical Journal* 39 (1999), pp. 228–35; and *JSA*, I, p. 102, II, p. 216, and III, p. 237.

34 *Natal Papers*, II, pp. 108–9.

35 Henry Cloete, *Five Lectures on the Emigration of the Dutch Farmers from the Colony of the Cape of Good Hope and their Settlement in the District of Natal* (Cape Town, 1856), p. 97. Oral tradition confirms this account; see testimony of Ndukwana, 16 Sept. 1900 in *JSA*, IV, pp. 276–7.

36 Ibid., II, pp. 121–8.

37 Testimony of Mtsahpi, 3 April 1918, *JSA*, IV, p. 68.

38 *Natal Papers*, II, p. 120.

39 Ibid., pp. 120, 128.

40 The following account draws heavily on N. J. Van Warmelo, ed., *History of Matiwane and the Amangwane Tribe, as told by Msebenzi to his kinsman Albert Hlongwane* (Pretoria, 1938), pp. 74–152.

41 For the date of the execution see H. F. Fynn to Bell, 16 June 1830, in *Records of Natal*, II, pp. 159–60. The reasons for Dingane's fear of Matiwane are obscure. It is, however, certain that Dingane regarded the Ngwane chief as a dangerous man. When the simple-minded missionary Francis Owen tried to preach to Dingane about heaven and hell, the king responded by saying, 'I and my people believe that there is only one God – I am that God. We believe there is only one place to which all good people go, this is Zulu land – we believe there is one place where all bad people go, there said he, pointing to a rocky hill in the distance [presumably the place of execution]. There is hell, where all my wicked people go. The Chief who lives there is Umatiwane, the head of the Amagwane. I put him to death and made him the devil chief of all wicked people who die. You see then, there are but two chiefs in this country, matiwain [sic] and myself, I am the great chief – the God of the living, Umatiwane is the great chief of the wicked'; Cory, ed., *Diary of Francis Owen*, p. 174.

42 *Natal Papers*, II, pp. 128–9.

43 Van Warmelo, ed., *History of Matiwane and the Amangwane*, p. 126. This was not the only time she intervened in matters of great importance; John Wright and Andrew Manson, *The Hlubi Chiefdom in Zululand-Natal* (Ladysmith, Natal, 1983), pp. 11, 28.

44 Ibid., p. 144.

45 Ibid., p. 142.

46 Norman Etherington, *Preachers, Peasants and Politics in Southeast Africa* (London, 1978), pp. 90, 105.

47 See the negotiations with Mpande's messenger, Nongalaza, June 1840, in *Natal Papers*, II, p. 141.

48 Nathan, *The Voortrekkers*, p. 237.

49 Bird, *Annals of Natal*, II, p. 311.

50 E. H. Brookes and C. de B. Webb, *A History of Natal* (Pietermaritzburg, 1965), pp. 37–8.

51 Andries Stockenstrom recognized the threat back in 1831; see Stockenstrom to Secretary to Government, 31 Aug. 1831, in *Records of Natal*, II, pp. 208–9.

52 Chase, *Natal Papers*, II, pp. 150–2.

53 Bird, *Annals of Natal*, I, p. 613.

54 Address to the Legislative Council, 10 Nov. 1838 in *Natal Papers*, II, pp. 48–9.

55 Napier, reply to the Memorial from Port Elizabeth, 26 Oct. 1840 in ibid., II, pp. 150–2.

56 Napier to Glenelg, 18 May 1838 in *Records of Natal*, III, pp. 291–5.

57 Address of the Volksraad to Napier, 21 Feb. 1842, in *Natal Papers*, II, pp. 198–205.

58 Cloete, *Five Lectures*, pp. 123–4.

59 A. Du Toit and H. Giliomee, eds, *Afrikaner Political Thought, Analysis and Documents* (Cape Town, 1983), p. 217.

60 Norman Etherington, 'Old Wine in New Bottles: The Persistence of Narrative Structures in the Historiography of the Mfecane and the Great Trek' in Carolyn Hamilton, ed., *The Mfecane Aftermath: Reconstructive Debates in Southern African History* (Johannesburg, 1995), p. 47.

61 Graham Mackeurtan, *The Cradle Days of Natal (1497–1845)* (London, 1930), p. 211.

62 Walker, *The Great Trek*, p. 249.

63 The trekkers admitted the charge, but put up the time-honoured excuse:

> The Zoola children, who, after the war, fell into our hands as orphans, who were brought to us by their parents, who had been robbed of all their cattle by Dingaan, lest they should perish from starvation, are indentured here by the Landdrosts, – the boys until they shall attain the age of 25, and the girls that of 21 years; and the Landdrosts have been directed to watch with a vigilant eye that no fraud be practised in this respect.

See Commandant Lombard's statement of 10 Feb. 1841, in *Natal Papers*, II, pp. 162–73. Nor was this the only instance in which children were taken. French missionary Samuel Rolland wrote in 1839 that 'many times have I through the telescope seen a small party of Boers driving those poor children along the road like a flock of sheep before their horses'; Rolland to Stockenstrom, 28 Nov. 1839 in Theal, ed., *Basutoland Records*, I, pp. 38–40.

64 Napier, address to the Legislative Council, 19 Jan. 1842, in *Natal Papers*, II, pp. 195–6.

65 Adulphe Delegorgue, *Voyage dans l'Afrique Australe*, 2 vols (Paris, 1847), II, p. 67.

66 From the journal of bugler Joseph Brown, 27th Regiment, May 1842, in *Natal Papers*, II, p. 211.

67 Capt. J. C. Smith to Col. Hare, Lt Gov. of Eastern Cape, 25 May 1842 in *Natal Papers*, II, pp. 215, 218; Delegorgue, *Voyage*, II, p. 78.

68 George M. Theal, *History of South Africa* (4th ed. of 1915; reprinted Cape Town, 1964), VI, pp. 428–36; Volksraad to Governor Napier, 21 Feb. 1842, in *Natal Papers*, II, pp. 198–205.

69 *Natal Papers*, II, p. 230.

70 A. J. Cloete to Napier, 4 July 1842, in ibid. Interestingly, Cloete had previous contact with Zulu officials, as he had been responsible for arranging the return of Shaka's embassy in 1828; Cloete to Bell, 7 Aug. 1828, in *Records of Natal*, I, p. 255.

71 Walker, *The Great Trek*, p. 305.

72 This injustice provoked a rare outburst against Cloete's ignorance and incompetence from the twentieth-century missionary-historian A. T. Bryant, a man who was generally tolerant of white supremacists. 'The injustice of all this', he wrote, 'is so glaringly apparent that one must wonder how any self-respecting Englishman can ever dare to raise his head again and look the world in the eyes without shame'; see *Olden Times in Zululand and Natal* (first published 1929, reprinted Cape Town, 1965), p. 230.

73 Mackeurtan, *Cradle Days of Natal*, p. 287; Theal, *History of South Africa*, VI, pp. 450–1.

74 A good example of how small those dots could appear is William C. Harris's hand-drawn 1837 map, 'Country North East of the Cape Colony shewing the relative positions of the Emigrant farmers & Native Tribes'; South Africa S/Div. 8, Royal Geographical Society, London. This map formed the basis for the less satisfactory map which appeared in his *Wild Sports of Southern Africa* (first published 1837; fifth ed. of 1852 reprinted Cape Town, 1963).

75 Newitt, *History of Mozambique*, p. 270.

76 A version of his name, Hendrik; P. J. van der Merwe, *Die Matebeles en die Voortrekkers* (Pretoria, 1986), p. 360.

77 Delegorgue, *Voyage*, II, p. 337 (in French, 'roi des Caffres').

78 William F. Lye and Colin Murray, *Transformations on the Highveld: The Tswana and Southern Sotho* (Cape Town, 1980), p. 55; S. M. Molema, *Chief Moroka: His Life, His Times, His Country and His People* (Cape Town, 1951), p. 62.

79 Letter of the trekker P. Zietsman, 5 Jan. 1841, in *Natal Papers*, II, pp. 164–5.

80 Fred Morton, 'Captive Labor in the Western Transvaal after the Sand River Convention' in E. A. Eldredge and F. Morton, eds, *Slavery in South Africa: Captive Labor on the Dutch Frontier* (Boulder, 1994), pp. 168–9.

81 Mabel V. Jackson, *European Powers and South-east Africa* (London, 1942), p. 207.

82 Roger Wagner, 'Zoutpansberg: The Dynamics of a Hunting Frontier, 1848–67' in S. Marks and A. Atmore, eds, *Economy and Society in Pre-Industrial South Africa* (London, 1980), pp. 321, 324, 332.

83 For a measured appraisal of the growing importance of trade and slaves in Mswati's realm, see Philip Bonner, 'Classes, the Mode of Production and the State in Pre-colonial Swaziland' in Marks and Atmore, eds, *Economy and Society*, pp. 96–7.

84   Nathan, *The Voortrekkers*, p. 326.

85   See the statement of Sekwati's messengers to Major Warden, 30 Oct. 1846 in G. M. Theal, *History of the Boers in South Africa* (first published 1887, reprinted Cape Town, 1973), pp. 233n.; Molema, *Chief Moroka*, p. 62.

86   Nathan, *The Voortrekkers*, p. 327.

87   Potgieter denied the charge, but both Zulu and Swazi witnesses agreed on its essential truth; van der Merwe, *Die Matebeles en die Voortrekkers*, p. 353. See also Cetshwayo's memories of raids against Sekwati and Mswati, in Colin Webb and John Wright, eds, *A Zulu King Speaks* (Pietermaritzburg, 1978), p. 15.

88   van der Merwe, *Die Matebeles en die Voortrekkers*, pp. 354–6.

89   Jackson, *European Powers*, pp. 208–10. While local officials showed some enthusiasm for dealing with the Boers, the Portuguese government in Lisbon refused to antagonize the British by openly allowing their ports to be used to evade British customs charges levied in Natal, Port Elizabeth and Cape Town. They even contemplated attacking Boer settlements.

90   Jan C. A. Boyens, '"Black Ivory": The Indenture System and Slavery in Zoutpansberg, 1848–1869', in Eldredge and Morton, eds, *Slavery in South Africa*, pp. 195–6.

91   Boyens, 'Black Ivory', pp. 330–1.

92   T. Arbousset and F. Daumas, *Narrative of an Exploratory Tour to the North-East of the Colony of the Cape of Good Hope*, translated from French by J. C. Brown (first published 1846, reprinted Cape Town, 1968), pp. 179–80.

93   H. O. Mönnig, *The Pedi* (Pretoria, 1967), p. 20.

94   Sekwati's messengers told H. D. Warden in 1846 that 'Sequati has heard that the Boers do not molest Moroko, Moshesh, and other chiefs, because they are in alliance with [the British] Government. Sequati therefore wishes to be placed on the same footing'; Theal, *History of the Boers*, p. 234n.

95   Mönnig, *The Pedi*, p. 24; Peter Delius, 'Migrant Labour and the Pedi, 1840–1880' in Marks and Atmore, eds, *Economy and Society*, p. 296.

96   Some were based on dubious 'purchases'; others were claimed by 'right of conquest'. See Nathan, *Voortrekkers*, p. 322; Molema, *Chief Moroka*, p. 46; Lye and Murray, *Transformations*, p. 60.

97   Ross, *Adam Kok's Griquas*, p. 55.

98   Delegorgue, *Voyage*, II, pp. 323–5.

99   Molema, *Chief Moroka*, pp. 61–2; see also Sol Plaatje's novel, *Mhudi* (first published 1930, republished Oxford, 1978), pp. 114–15. For further evidence of mutually beneficial relations between the Thaba Nchu Rolong and the

trekkers, see James Backhouse's comments in Theal, ed., *Basutoland Records*, I, pp. 34–5.

100 As Francis Owen discovered when he tried to revive his missionary career by re-opening the station previously abandoned by French and American evangelists. He could not persuade Hurutshe chiefs that the area was yet safe, and he too gave up the effort in 1841; Cory, ed., *Diary of Francis Owen*, pp. 146–54. Adulphe Delegorgue encountered no trekker farms in the western Magaliesberg in 1843, though he did find the Boers active in the ivory trade; he was told by several chiefs that Mzilikazi's regiments were still active raiders in the region; see *Voyage*, II, pp. 405, 434–5, 451.

101 Tony Kirk, 'The Cape Economy and the Expropriation of the Kat River Settlement, 1846–53', in Marks and Atmore, eds, *Economy and Society*, p. 229; Monica Cole, *South Africa* (London, 1962), pp. 106–8, 240–2; Ross, *Adam Kok's Griquas*, pp. 66–9.

102 Report of J. Boshof, June 1838, in Chase, *Natal Papers*, II, p. 29; Martin Legassick, 'The Griqua, the Sotho-Tswana and the Missionaries, 1780–1840 (PhD thesis, UCLA, 1969), pp. 553–4; Ross, *Adam Kok's Griquas*, pp. 32–3.

103 W. F. Lye, ed., *Andrew Smith's Journal of his Expedition into the Interior of South Africa/1834–36* (Cape Town, 1975), p. 44.

104 Arbousset and Daumas, *Narrative*, p. 210; Molema, *Chief Moroka*, p. 46; statement of Moletsane, Jan. 1852, in Theal, *Basutoland Records*, I, pp. 517–19.

105 Theal, *Basutoland Records*, II, pp. 44–6.

CHAPTER 11

British officials intervene on the highveld

New rules and treaties for the Caledon Valley

The first scene of the last act of the great heartland drama was now about to be played out where eagles keep their soaring watch for prey by the Maloti mountains – a few days' walk from Harrismith where this book began. The forces which had swept over southern Africa over the past generation sucked into the vortex of the Caledon Valley a remarkable array of characters who had played leading roles in the previous scenes. Sekonyela, son of MaNthatisi, thrived, more powerful than ever – hated by missionaries but still adept at attracting followers. Living among his people and in other parts of the valley were remnants of the Hlubi and Ngwane groups who had followed Mpangazitha and Matiwane to glory and catastrophe. Barend Barends, ancient terror of the western highveld, had moved to the village of Lishuani, though Peter David now commanded the remnants of his following, people still happy to be known as Bastards.[1] A trio of the Kora leaders – Gert Taaibosch, Gert Lynx and Piet Witvoet, alias 'Wicked Pi' – lived in more or less neighbourly peace with people who had formerly had cause to dread their very names. So did old Nzwane, alias Danster, son of Rharhabe, the Xhosa raider who had brought the first firearms to the valley. Moletsane, the man of many faces, survived under Moshweshwe's protection, still scheming to rebuild a Taung kingdom stretching beyond the Sand River. Moroka, chosen chief of the Rolong at Thaba Nchu was there, showing signs that he would adopt the religion of the Methodist missionaries who had accompanied his people on their great trek. Missionaries – British, French and German – had by this time planted themselves near all the major chiefs of the region.

High up in his old fortress of Thaba Bosiu the 'cattle razor', Moshweshwe, prospered beyond his youthful dreams. All southern Africa now knew him as the 'Basuto' king and his greatness far outshone any of his ancestors. His elder sons were now grown up and associated in all his empire-building enterprises.[2] Younger sons were being educated at British schools in Cape Town. With wealth built up through loans of cattle and thousands of armed, mounted men at his disposal, he was probably the strongest military power north of the Orange River. Though he still cherished dreams of controlling all the valley and the high country as far as Thembu territory, Moshweshwe had long since ceased to play the audacious cattle-raider. He gloried in his reputation as a wise statesman and had no desire to force a contest with the trekkers whose numbers grew day by day. They were nonetheless a worrying presence, plotting with his enemies and claiming land on the basis of dubious payments. By the early 1840s there were nearly 500 Boer families settled in the valley.[3] Through the medium of the French missionaries, Moshweshwe protested to Governor Napier that he had freely assented to the trekkers passing through his territory but absolutely denied their right to settle down.[4]

The British action in Natal alerted everyone to the possibility that this unpredictable but potentially dangerous power might take a hand in events. But it was far from certain that British intervention would work to the disadvantage of the trekker land-grabbers. The loudest calls for British help came from people who were, perhaps, the least entitled to it. Griquas under Hendrik Hendriks, Adam Kok and Andries Waterboer had for years been encouraging Boers to trek into their land. They also had welcomed many Khoi from the Kat River district who had joined the trekking movement.[5] The expansion of trekking after 1836 put money in Griqua pockets but the long leases that many of them granted threatened the survival of the Griqua as an independent people. John Philip and the London Missionary Society still clung to their vision of the Griqua as God's chosen agents for the conversion of Africa to Christianity. They had far more Calvinist ministers and lay preachers among them than the trekkers.[6] Philip's letters, along with those of Moshweshwe and the French missionaries, helped prompt Governor Napier to proclaim in September 1842 that Britain's queen would 'regard with the liveliest indignation any attempt upon the part of any of her subjects, to molest, invade, or injure' the people of any chief.[7] A few weeks later a group of trekkers tested Napier's resolve by claiming a large tract of Griqua land on behalf of their Volksraad. The British judge who went to investigate this remarkable move pronounced the trekkers guilty of violating the Cape of Good Hope Punishment Act and promptly extended the protection of the British government over all the Griqua lands. While Napier hastily denied that the judgment amounted to annexation, he acknowledged that more such incidents would occur unless his government took action. In 1843 Adam Kok and Moshweshwe gladly accepted Napier's offer of formal treaties making them responsible for maintaining order in their territories and returning any fugitives from British justice for punishment by colonial courts.[8]

The question was, what lands belonged to Kok and Moshweshwe? Trekkers indignantly rejected Kok's power to rule them. Moroka and Sekonyela saw Napier's treaty as an audacious attempt to put the whole upper Caledon region under the BaSotho king. Through letters written for them by Methodist missionaries they asserted their land rights. By the time Lieutenant General Peregrine Maitland replaced Napier as governor in 1844 there had already been several clashes between trekkers and Griqua, as well as between the competing chiefs of the Caledon. Moshweshwe was told by one Boer that if he tried to interfere in trekker affairs he should 'expect to be received with loaded muskets'.[9]

Demonstrating beyond question that governors had been freed from the old constraints on action beyond their borders, Maitland in 1845 led a detachment of troops across the Orange and attempted to impose his own ideas of how to resolve disputes about land. Showing no comprehension that attempts over the last seventy years to end disputes by drawing boundary lines had comprehensively failed, Maitland got out his map and drew lines. He divided Griqua territory into two districts. One was pronounced to be 'inalienable' land; as trekker leases expired, they would revert to Griqua ownership. In the other district, Griqua could continue to lease land. As Griqua and trekker concepts of ownership were more or less the same, this might have been workable had there been proper surveys and a land court capable of resolving disputes. All Maitland provided was a British resident to be stationed at Jan Bloem's old headquarters, Bloemfontein. Many of the leases already granted had years to run, so no separation of Griqua and trekkers was achieved. In a similar exercise that same year Maitland concluded a treaty with Faku, the Mpondo paramount, which assigned to him all the land between the Mtata and Mzimkhulu Rivers between the sea and the mountains.

Maitland's attempt to delineate power relations in the Caledon Valley by drawing boundary lines was doomed from the start. Chiefs ruled by virtue of the people who acknowledged their authority, not by virtue of the land they occupied. The governor's lines reflected the very different historical development of England where great lords wielded power through their rights to extract tribute from people who lived on 'their land'. From the time Major H. D. Warden took up his post as resident at Bloemfontein in January 1846, his office was flooded with missionaries' letters asserting the land claims of competing chiefs. He possessed neither the training nor the imagination the job demanded. More than twenty years' service as an army officer in the border districts of the British Zone had given him the typical prejudices of his class and profession. Back in 1826 he had crossed the Orange in search of information about the 'Fetcani' raiders.[10] He had assisted Colonel Somerset in the campaign against Matiwane in 1828 and had spearheaded assaults on Xhosa chiefs in the 1835 invasion. Like the rest of the British officer clique he had learned to value Boer commandos as friends and allies. A strong recommendation from Benjamin D'Urban helped him get the job as resident. For better or for worse, this was the man whom chiefs would have to win to their side if they were to hold their positions on the Caledon. A remarkable gathering of chiefs on 10 March 1846, which included Moshweshwe, Sekonyela, Moroka, Moletsane and Peter David, told Warden that they could not agree on their respective claims.[11] If boundaries must be drawn, he would have to draw them. Every stroke of the resident's pen was bound to offend someone. But before he had even begun to draw his lines, an apparently trivial incident that same week in March was about to plunge Britain into another war with the Xhosa and lead to even more dramatic interventions on the highveld.

The 'War of the Axe' and the return of Harry Smith

A man named Tsili, who had been accused of stealing an axe from the trading post of Fort Beaufort on the British frontier, was handcuffed to two other prisoners and marched off toward Grahamstown for trial. Although his chief, Tola, was but a minor ruler, he knew that obligations binding chiefs to their people ran in both directions.[12] After the British had refused to give up his man, on 16 March Tola organized a rescue party which audaciously rushed in, cut the prisoner free – by hacking off the hand of the man to whom he was handcuffed – and dashed away into the bush. Colonel John Hare, who had succeeded Stockenstrom as Lieutenant Governor with responsibility for the eastern section of the British Zone, regarded this as an opportunity to demonstrate his power. Hare was a soldier of the dreary old school who believed that the only reason the British had trouble with 'cattle thieves' was that they were too lenient with the Xhosa chiefs. Cheering him on were the covetous Grahamstown land speculators, whose zeal for annexations had been spurred by the demand for new land to pasture sheep. In 1844 Hare had sent a punitive expedition into Xhosa territory which, he wrote, 'had all the effects I desired of striking terror into our troublesome and deceitful neighbours and forcing them to a compliance with my just and reasonable demands'.[13] By 1846 those same neighbours were suffering through another horrendous drought. Hare had recently outraged all the chiefs by ordering a new fort to be built on the left bank of the Keiskamma River in what every treaty had declared to be the territory of Sandile, descendant of Rharhabe. Now Hare was demanding that Tola be caught and brought to him for punishment. When Sandile refused, Hare declared war for the sole object of 'teaching him a lesson'.

At first it was the British who had the lesson. Like Moshweshwe, Sekonyela and Dingane, the Xhosa chiefs had been acquiring horses and guns. The wool boom in the British Zone had greatly expanded opportunities for Xhosa men to earn money to buy them. By 1846 an estimated 7000 armed and mounted men backed by several thousand more traditionally equipped soldiers were ready to meet the British threat.[14] In the first major engagement they managed to cut one of the invaders' wagon trains of baggage and supplies. Soon it was the village of Grahamstown that feared invasion. Much had changed since 1819, however. Reoccupying the lost lands of the Zuurveld could only be achieved by driving all British forces into the sea, a task that was far beyond the capacities of the disunited chiefs. The most they could hope for was to wear down the British will to fight on. At each renewed assault they harried the supply lines and tried to avoid pitched battles in open country. By September they announced that they were willing to make peace on the basis of the established borders. To their dismay the British would not accept the offer, demanding instead an unconditional surrender and evacuation of all land west of the Kei River.[15]

The great problem the chiefs faced was not the British war machine – which repeatedly spluttered and faltered – but the British war culture. Neither the officers nor the governors would make peace until they had scored something that could be called a decisive victory. In 1836 Lord Glenelg had challenged the war culture with his order countermanding D'Urban's annexations (Chapter 9, p. 245). This time there was no Glenelg to force a settlement. Important sectors of public opinion in England were saying that colonists in South Africa, Canada, Australia and New Zealand should be allowed to run their own affairs – even if that meant invasions, massacres and dispossession like those the Americans regularly inflicted on their 'Indians'.[16] Benjamin D'Urban was no longer scorned, but sought out for his 'wise counsel' on South African affairs. Politicians of both major parties bemoaned the expense of the latest South African war even as they sent more money and supplies to 'teach a lesson'. The same tendency to demand unconditional victory infected all the élite classes of the British Zone. Andries Stockenstrom came out of retirement to lead a Boer commando; his plan was to push beyond the Kei and strike at Sarhili who had assumed Hintsa's mantle as paramount of the Gcaleka Xhosa.[17] John Philip supported the war and hoped it would bring all the Xhosa under British rule. Henry Calderwood resigned from the Methodist Missionary Society in order to serve the war effort. White men who differed on every other question united in the opinion that the war must be prosecuted until it was 'won'. The *Cape Frontier Times* demanded war be made on 'huts and gardens. Let all these be burned down and destroyed. Let there be no ploughing, sowing or reaping.'[18] The British governor obliged, seeing no alternative to 'devastating their country, destroying their kraals, crops and cattle and letting them finally understand that, cost what it may, they must be humbled and subdued'.[19] Knowing that chiefs' power still depended on their cattle, British patrols shot cattle and left them to rot when it was impractical to capture them. The burning, devastating and destroying went on, month after pointless month.

Time and again the chiefs tried to make the British accept their surrender. Each time the offer was rejected because they had not been 'sufficiently humbled'. After their offer of September was turned down, they tried a new tactic, refusing to fight when challenged. Instead they sat down before the attacking soldiers, inviting them to shoot unresisting men.[20] Towards the end of 1846 the drought broke and the land was inundated with water. British troops sloshed in misery through an unfamiliar land and yet they still would not accept a settlement. The next year they made the capture of Sandile the object which alone might bring peace. Remembering Hintsa's fate, Sandile would not give himself up until, in October 1847, he was tricked into thinking that the British had agreed to negotiate with him. Instead he was seized and held captive. And even that did not end the war. Peace only came when a new governor substituted the theatre of humiliation for humiliation on the battlefield.

The new man wore the familiar face of Harry Smith: D'Urban's faithful subordinate in 1835, the man who had Hintsa 'shot while trying to escape', the man who had resigned in 1836 as a protest against Glenelg's policies. He had left South Africa in 1840 as plain Colonel Smith. He now returned as Major-General Sir Harry Smith, promoted, decorated and idolized for victories he had won fighting Sikhs on the north-west frontier of British India. His dual appointment – Governor of the Cape Colony and High Commissioner for South Africa – acknowledged that with the creation of Natal there was now more than a single British zone of occupation in southern Africa. Before leaving England Smith had assured his superiors that he would bring the long expensive war to a close, cut costs and bring peace to the land.[21] His real objectives were to bring about the final triumph of D'Urban's policy for the Xhosa and to reconcile the trekkers to British rule by giving them practically everything they wanted. Soon after his arrival he made a triumphal progress to Port Elizabeth, released Sandile and called the other principal chiefs to meet him on 7 January 1848 in the heart of the territory D'Urban had a decade before proclaimed as Queen Adelaide Province. After annexing all the territory west of the Keiskamma River, Smith announced that the chiefs would remain on their lands but would henceforth be governed by his appointed agents. All former treaties were abolished; the newly annexed territory would be called 'British Kaffraria'. The old 'Ceded Territory' would again be made over to colonial farmers. Then Smith made each chief in turn come forward to kiss his boot. The humiliation and the subduing was accomplished. Four weeks later he annexed all the territory bounded by the Drakensberg mountains in the east, the Vaal River in the north and the Orange River to the south.

Harry Smith inscribes a new order on the highveld

No one, not Tau the Lion nor Mzilikazi nor Barends nor Bloem nor Moshweshwe nor even Potgieter, had ever claimed such dominion. When Smith sat down to explain the reasons for acting without authority, he pleaded the precedent of British governors in India:

> My position has been analogous to that of every Governor General who has proceeded to India. All have been fully impressed with the weakness of that Policy which extended . . . possessions, and yet, few, if any, especially the men of more gifted talents, have ever resigned their Government without having done that, which however greatly to be condemned by the theory of Policy, circumstances demanded and imperatively imposed upon them.[22]

That is to say, he made his huge claim in order to prove himself a great man of gifted talents. At the same time, it must be said that he truly thought his huge gamble would succeed and future generations would bless his name. His guiding belief, which all the men of his type had shared since 1836, was that the trekkers were good people who would never have turned against British rule if Glenelg had not reversed D'Urban's wise policies. He argued that aside from a handful 'who style themselves Patriots', the bulk of the emigrants were loyal subjects who longed to get secure land titles and government support for their churches. In his eyes even the outlaw Andries Pretorius was 'a shrewd sensible man'.[23] After travelling from Bloemfontein via the trekker capital of Winburg and over the Drakensberg to Natal, Smith declared that the country was ideal grazing country where 'no native is to be seen; nor for many years, if ever, has it ever been inhabited by one'. This signified that Smith would see only what he wanted to see.

What he most wanted to see was trekkers on his side, as they had been in the old days. One of his first acts was to confirm Boers in possession of all their leases in Griqua territory, not just for forty years, but for ever. When Griqua leaders protested that this was contrary to the 1845 treaty, Smith simply said, 'Damn the treaty.'[24] Not only did Smith forgive Pretorius for his former disloyalty, he offered him a place on the land commission he established to investigate the status of land claims in Natal. At the same time he issued a proclamation guaranteeing all white farmers grants of 6000 acres.[25] He was genuinely surprised when Pretorius and many others ignored this confirmation of land titles and crossed the mountains in an effort to preserve their independence. Next it was the turn of Pretorius to be surprised when the chiefs and Boers of the highveld failed to rally round his flag. On 14 February 1848 he met Moshweshwe's sons, Letsie and Nehemiah, demanding that they abrogate their treaty with the British.[26] Being told that the king would not see him, Pretorius saddled up and angrily declared that Moshweshwe 'is no longer my friend. I will have the great chief Panda for my ally.' That was even more unlikely; as long ago as 1842, the Zulu king had offered to assist the British in their assault on Port Natal. Sekonyela proved equally unwilling to provide soldiers to Pretorius, though he did promise to prevent Moshweshwe from riding to the assistance of the British. In the end Pretorius could find only about 400 trekker horsemen to join his challenge to Harry Smith's annexation.[27] In July 1848 they overwhelmed Warden's post at Bloemfontein, but had no hope of withstanding the superior forces which rode against them under the personal command of Harry Smith in August. They were caught, beaten and forty-nine of them killed at a place called Boomplaats (south-east of present-day Jagersfontein). Pretorius retreated north over the Vaal and Harry Smith took charge of the territory he called the Orange River Sovereignty.

Almost immediately settlers, both English and Boers, rushed to claim grazing land. Land speculators made their headquarters at the village of Bloemfontein.[28] They applauded every new tract of land taken from chiefs, and howled at the unfairness of any attempt to shield the ancient inhabitants from their thirst for land to serve the wool boom. Within the space of a few months, a single farm might change hands several times, each time at a more inflated price. The biggest problem for the speculators was getting the land surveyors to keep up with them. John Orpen, one of the surveyors who witnessed those mad days, wrote that 'land was, at that time, being given away right and left, or sold at public sales for £20 for a farm'.[29] So great was the demand that he and his fellow surveyors asked to be paid in farms rather than cash. On the open plains where no significant cattle-owning chiefs took the risk of locating, the land rush caused only minor problems. The great difficulties occurred in the Caledon Valley which both chiefs and speculators recognized as the most valuable land in the Sovereignty. According to the treaty of 1843 all the upper valley was confided to the care of Moshweshwe, but from the very beginning it was plain that he would be challenged.

His most formidable opponent turned out to be the man from whom he had once expected most friendship. Early in 1847, British Resident Henry Warden had declared that Moshweshwe had a clear right to claim both sides of the Caledon River from Thaba Bosiu almost all the way to Bloemfontein.[30] However, as time went on, Warden changed his mind, partly because he relied on calling out Boer commandos in times of emergency, and partly because of the insistent pressure of the Methodist missionaries who had established stations among nearly all of Moshweshwe's most determined enemies. Unlike the French missionaries, the Methodists spoke his language; what is more the brother-in-law of their superintendent worked in his office. After the 1848 annexation, Warden stayed on as the chief British agent in the Orange River Sovereignty. Soon he was recommending more land sales in the lower Caledon for the reason that most of the old trekkers now 'believe Sir Harry is a true friend to the Boers'.[31] By 13 April 1849 he had clearly shifted his position on Moshweshwe's claims, telling Smith that the king 'is disposed to give . . . some trouble regarding boundary lines'. Urged on by the French missionaries his people 'continue to encroach on lands occupied by the farmers'; 'the Boers in that part of the country are in consequence restless and discontented'. Each new attempt to draw firm boundary lines was less favourable to Moshweshwe – and just as ineffective in ending disputes.

Chiefs increasingly took matters into their own hands. Sekonyela, though persistently underestimated and disliked by the British, used his considerable military power to resist advances by Moshweshwe's sons and to raid for cattle.[32] Moletsane complained to Warden of attacks by Kora, Tlokwa and 'Matabele' (Thembu from over the mountains). The old Kora raider Carolus Baatje complained in his turn that Basuto raids were ruining the 'Bastards of Plaatberg'. Many Boers had adopted a more subtle technique of asking chiefs for permission to share access to springs and then building houses. Later, when they complained to Warden that their stock was being stolen, the resident decreed that no chief's people could locate nearer than one half-hour's walk from a Boer house, effectively transferring the spring to Boer ownership. Some of the most serious clashes pitted Moroka's Rolong of Thaba Nchu against the forces of Moshweshwe and his ally, Moletsane. In November 1850 Warden had begun to think about marching against them to recapture the Rolong 'stolen' cattle. The force he proposed to assemble bore a striking and ironic resemblance to the forces that Barend Barends led against Mzilikazi in 1831 and Potgieter commanded in 1836:

300 of Adam Kok's Griqua
150 of Waterboer's Griqua
200 of Gert Taaibosch's Kora
1000 of Moroka's Rolong
300 Boers
600 of Sekonyela's Tlokwa
a 'large contingent' of Jan Bloem's men.

Warden's attempt to bring his idea of British order to the highveld had ended in his conversion to the old highveld way of warfare.

The end of Harry Smith

The same month that Warden was preparing to fight Moshweshwe, Harry Smith teetered on the edge of a new debacle in the on-again, off-again war against the Xhosa chiefs. The cause was a breakdown in the experimental settlement imposed after the War of the Axe. In the reconquered territory Smith built a strong network of forts and then tried ruling the people by using their own chiefs as British agents. While nothing of this kind had previously been attempted in Africa, a system built along similar lines prevailed in British India. From the start Smith disregarded problems, insisting that the majority of the people are 'most happy under our rule'.[33] That pretence was difficult to maintain during the summer of 1849–50 when drought once again parched the land. Chiefs grumbled that their government salaries gave them too little resources with which to rule. Rumour said that prophets were stirring up discontent with forecasts of stupendous events which would convulse the land. In an effort to conciliate the chiefs and calm the people, Harry Smith summoned a meeting at the fort of King Williams Town on 26 October 1850. Remembering how he had been tricked into captivity during the last war, Sandile refused to come. This 'disobedience' was the pretext Smith had been looking for to depose the most powerful and independent-minded of the chiefs.

In a last-ditch effort to keep the peace, Sandile's own mother, Sutu, widow of Ngqika, visited a nearby mission station to ask why the English wanted war. When she was told that people were disobedient, she replied that 'you have taken away all my power; you take away the power of the chiefs, and then you find fault with us for not keeping the people in order'.[34] On 24 December 1850 Harry Smith sent an expeditionary force into the

Amatola mountains with orders to seek out Sandile. The governor who had promised his superiors that he would end war and cut expenditure had started another war, one that would rage on until 1853 and cost Britain more millions. Even Smith's own Khoi soldiers joined the enemy after they were pushed from land at Kat River.

The repercussions of the conflict were felt almost immediately on the other side of the mountains; thousands of Thembu families tried to safeguard their lives and cattle by trekking north. Abandoning their differences for the moment, a joint British/Boer/Basuto force assembled to push these innocent refugees back across the Orange, along with other Thembu people who had been living in Moshweshwe's territory for years.[35] Warden next tried, too late, to curb the arms race in the Sovereignty by forbidding the sale of firearms and ammunition to 'any Native chief' as well as to the subjects of those chiefs. With a recklessness born of desperation Harry Smith now endorsed the plan for an attack on Moshweshwe, writing to Warden on 9 June 1851 that it was time to 'come to the point'. 'If you have force attack him at once if necessary.'[36] Warden duly proclaimed Moletsane and Moshweshwe to be 'enemies of the Queen' and called out his troops.

Moshweshwe could hardly believe the injustice of these proceedings. No one in the valley had been a more faithful friend to the fickle British. Unlike Sekonyela, he had not allied himself to the trekkers. He had been the first to welcome Christian missionaries to the Caledon. In 1835, 1846 and 1851 he had offered to help the British fight the Xhosa.[37] He had been the first to agree to Harry Smith's proposition that he accept British paramountcy. Now he was called an enemy of the Queen. He would have been even more amazed could he have heard Harry Smith's lying allegations that the king had allied himself to Sandile and that the most deserving candidate to be paramount chief in the Caledon was the Rolong leader Moroka, by virtue of his 'hereditary descent'![38] Nonetheless, Moshweshwe held his fire until Warden's forces attacked Viervoet, stronghold of his ally Moletsane, on 30 June 1851. Very few Boers turned up for the commando, so Warden had to rely on his Griqua, Kora, Tlokwa and Rolong auxiliaries. No sooner had they taken Moletsane's stronghold and started plundering than they were routed by a combined force of Taung, Kora and BaSotho forces under the command of Moshweshwe's son Molapo.[39] All things considered, it was an even more humiliating defeat than Warden had suffered at the hands of Pretorius in 1848. Moshweshwe quickly followed up his victory by filling conquered land with people and preparing for yet another assault on Sekonyela. Warden's call for reinforcements from Natal was answered by two *amabutho* (probably composed of Hlubi and Ngwane) led by English officers. Their arrival added to the confusion, for they were soon raiding cattle from the very people they were supposed to be defending.[40]

The news of the Xhosa war and Warden's defeat drove the British government in England to the verge of distraction. Harry Smith had comprehensively failed to deliver on all his promises. He had done things he ought not to have done, and not done those things he ought to have done, so his days as governor were numbered. The spectacle of Warden leading an African army into battle while the Boers stayed at home was particularly galling, because Smith's plan for the Orange River Sovereignty had relied on winning Boer support through generous support for their land claims. Now Warden was writing that many Boers preferred Moshweshwe's rule to his own.[41] Two special commissioners, Major William Hogge and Charles Mostyn Owen were sent from London to investigate the affairs of the Sovereignty. Both had previous South African experience and hence shared the usual prejudices in favour of Boers and against chiefs. They reported that between the Caledon Valley and the Vaal the Sovereignty was a flourishing district worth retaining as a British possession. Already something like 10,000 British and Boer settlers had infiltrated the land. Bloemfontein, Winburg and Harrismith were prosperous and growing villages. The commissioners viewed trekker settlements beyond the Vaal with suspicion and recommended that the British government renounce all claims to jurisdiction north of the river. This was sealed by an agreement signed at the Sand River on 17 January 1852 with Andries Pretorius, who had been authorized by the *Krygsraad* (war council) of trekker communities north of the Vaal to represent their interests. (Characteristically, Potgieter took no part in the proceedings.) Henceforth their territory would be known as the Transvaal.

Despite the commissioners' recommendation that the Sovereignty be retained as a British colony, the Secretary of State for Colonies, Lord Grey, was losing faith in the venture. In September 1851 he warned Harry Smith that if the white settlers could not support the government of the Sovereignty there was no reason to keep it.[42] Four weeks later he wrote again announcing that 'the ultimate abandonment of the Orange Sovereignty should be a settled point in our policy'. Smith must have known that his own recall could only be a matter of time. In January 1852, he was replaced by Lieutenant General George Cathcart, personal choice of the Duke of Wellington who had commanded him at the battle of Waterloo in 1815.[43] Cathcart was to be the last of his generation to govern in South Africa and he exemplified its guiding principles. Though he came with clear instructions to wind up the experiment in ruling the highveld, he was determined to go out with a bang.

Warden told him that Moshweshwe and Moletsane must be 'humbled'.[44] He agreed that so far the chiefs had not received 'a sufficient impression as to the power of the British nation'.[45] As Moshweshwe was the 'centre of aggregation', had committed 'depradations' and did not sufficiently appreciate the force used in the latest war against the Xhosa chiefs, it followed that he must be subdued, overawed, humbled and taught a lesson. Parroting all the cliches of the British war culture, Cathcart led 2000 men to the Caledon at the end of November 1852 'to restore an adequate respect for the power and means of the British Government'. He made no effort to understand the rights and wrongs of the situation, dismissing the statements made by Moshweshwe, Moroka, Moletsane and the other chiefs as 'political frauds' concocted by missionaries. He simply told Moshweshwe on 15 December 1852 that he must deliver 10,000 cattle within three days 'to save yourself and your people from ruin'.

The startled king told Cathcart he had no hope of complying so quickly for most of his own herds were loaned out and widely scattered.[46] Confiscating the property of his subjects would be unthinkable. Very well, said the general, there shall be war, to which the king answered, 'Do not talk of war, for, however anxious I may be to avoid it, you know that a dog when beaten will show his teeth.' Three days later his sons brought in 3500 cattle. Cathcart put them aside as part payment for the expenses of his expedition and ordered his forces to attack. Both the king and his people were outraged at this disregard for the customary courtesies of negotiations, and prepared to give Cathcart the same uncomfortable reception others had met when they assaulted Thaba Bosiu. Six thousand horsemen in disciplined cavalry formations met the assault on 20 December and turned it back, inflicting heavy casualties in the process, though the British seized thousands of cattle.[47] However, as Commissioner Owen was quick to tell his commander, the BaSotho could rightly claim the victory:

> In . . . attempting to enforce the payment of the penalty imposed upon
> Moshesh . . . the British Troops have been resisted by a large Basuto force,
> have retired with severe loss, leaving upwards of 40 men on the field with
> most of their arms, accoutrements, and horses, which . . . will be paraded
> as trophies of their power . . . besides an officer taken prisoner and
> afterwards, as there is too good reason to believe, butchered, – while
> Thaba Bosigo [sic], Moshesh's stronghold, has not been reached, nor has
> the amount of the original penalty been captured . . . [The BaSotho have
> not been] either humbled or overcome, they having followed and kept up a
> heavy fire upon the Troops to their encampments last night, and retaken
> part of the Cattle.[48]

In this single engagement Moshweshwe proved himself to be the greatest heartland war leader of his generation. No one before him – not Mzilikazi, nor Dingane, nor even the tenacious Xhosa generals – had marshalled armed and mounted forces on an open battlefield and carried the day. It is difficult to say what Cathcart would have done next had Moshweshwe not demonstrated that his diplomacy matched his generalship. The very evening of his victory he dictated a message which opened the way for a face-saving compromise.

> As the object for which you have come is to have a compensation for Boers, I beg you will be satisfied with what you have taken. I entreat peace from you, – you have shown your power, – you have chastised, – let it be enough, I pray you; and let me no longer be considered an enemy to the Queen.[49]

With palpable relief, Cathcart replied that those 'were the words of a great chief. . . . I have taken the fine by force, and I am satisfied. I am not angry with your people for fighting in defence of their property.' A few days later he commended the 'bravery and discipline' of the king's troops who had done 'as well as any Cossacks [a Russian cavalry corps] and I have had plenty to do with them'.[50]

The High Commissioner continued his theatrical performance by leading the captured cattle to Boer villages and telling the bemused burghers that henceforth they must guard their own property 'according to the commando system'. And with that Cathcart departed, leading his troops back over the Orange. The British would not appear again with such forces until 1877. A year later, on 23 February 1854, Britain surrendered control of Harry Smith's ill-fated Orange River Sovereignty to a group of English and Boer 'representatives', who shortly thereafter brought into existence an independent nation called the Orange Free State. In order to make doubly sure that Britain would escape further entanglements of the kind which ruined Henry Warden, the government cancelled all treaties with chiefs north of the Orange.[51]

With his customary sagacity, Moshweshwe was the first to grasp the implications of Britain's withdrawal. Even before the signing of the Bloemfontein convention, in October 1853 he capitalized on his triumph over Cathcart to send his forces into battle against his oldest enemies: Sekonyela and the various Griqua and Kora captains who had tried to make their homes in the Caledon.[52] With one ruthless strike, he swept them all away and at last reigned alone in the richest agricultural region of all the highveld. The people who had followed the defeated chiefs made their customary submission to the victor. Whether their ancestors had called themselves Nguni, Hlubi, Ngwane, Tlokwa, Fokeng or Kwena, they would henceforth all be known as BaSotho. Only Moroka and his Rolong at Thaba Nchu – protected by their alliance with the Boers – remained as a reminder of the many chiefs who had tried to find prosperity and security by trekking into that coveted territory.

Conclusion

To dismiss all Harry Smith's doings as farce and failure – as many historians have done – seriously underestimates the consequences of his short-lived bid to establish British supremacy in the heartland. Before his intervention the scattered trekker communities depended, like their predecessors the Griqua, on the force of arms to maintain their position. Smith's importance lay not in the relatively puny power of his sword but in the might of his energetic pen. He marked out tract after tract of land to be surveyed into neat rectangles of saleable merchandise. He secured the trekkers' farms in up-country Natal, in Griqualand and the Orange River Sovereignty. Not all of the original claimants stayed on those properties, but the security of the titles attracted a host of new settlers who would never have taken their chances with Retief, Pretorius or Potgieter. Their numbers ensured that white-dominated states would survive for a long time to come. The secure titles also accelerated the advance of the wool boom in the southern highveld, guaranteeing that the newly created Orange Free State would have the revenue required to support its government and the military forces needed to confront mighty Moshweshwe.

Because most of the ordinary settlers who followed the trekkers into the Sovereignty came from the Cape, they brought that colony's distinctive pattern of farm labour and social organization to the highveld. More women like Dina were dragged to faraway places, bearing their masters' children along with the burdens of domestic labour, while the official wives commanded the house and raised the sons who would inherit the farms. Children of the servants grew up on the land, tied to the land, unable to move without a signed pass from the master. And when there were not enough children and servants, more kidnapped children could always be bought through the illicit labour trade across the unpatrolled border at the Vaal. The implications of the export of this system to the heartland were enormous and would endure right through the twentieth century,

> from the Cape to the White Highlands of Kenya. This was, of course, only one possible model for colonial agricultural exploitation, in contrast, for instance, to the plantations of much of the colonial world or the family farms of New England. Moreover, it was a specific historical construction. It was developed in the Cape Colony during the first two centuries of European colonial rule and then extended further and further north. It was in fact the specific form that gentry domination of the rural economy took.[53]

With the larger strokes of his pen, Harry Smith helped complete the inscription of a map of southern Africa whose outlines are still visible even in

an era when many old names are being overwritten by new ones. The Free
State was distinguished in the north from the Transvaal, in the south-east
from Natal and in the south-west from the Cape Colony. The line he drew
across the ancient Xhosa homeland at the Kei River still survives in the
common parlance which distinguishes Transkei from Ciskei. The busy pens
of Smith's subordinate map-makers erased Tswana, Sotho and Nguni names
of rivers, hills and mountains. In their place they wrote the repetitive and
simple Afrikaans names by which places had been marked out by passing
Griqua and trekker bands: Mooi Rivier, Spionkop, Olifants Rivier, Plaatberg,
Modder Rivier, Sand Rivier, Driefontein – tediously repeated labels which
still confound and confuse travellers and historians. Smith had indeed proved
himself to be 'the true friend of the Boers'. In the days of D'Urban's gover-
norship, he and the rest of the military clique had joined the English press
and their land-speculator cronies in welcoming each advance of the trekkers.
Under Smith's High Commissionership the trekkers' precarious claim to
have conquered other people's land was written onto maps which were
read and respected all round the world.

That does not mean that the conquest had happened. Powerful chiefs and
kings still held the best well-watered defensible positions where agriculture
could be practised alongside pastoralism. After eighty years of continual
struggle against the unrelenting cupidity of their western neighbours, the
courage and military skill of Xhosa people had preserved an amazingly large
portion of their original lands. Faku held his ground and had strengthened
his hold on the territory beginning to be known as Pondoland. Though Natal
was now a British colony, great chiefs like Zikhali, Phakade and Langalibalele
had taken up enviable positions in land unsuited to settler agriculture.
Mpande still watched over the graves of his brother Shaka and his father
Senzangakhona in the country everyone now called Zululand. To the north
and north-east of Mpande the residue of the old Ndwandwe power was concentrated in the kingdoms of Swaziland and Gasa. Between the Vaal and the
Limpopo, many powerful chiefs disputed the exaggerated claims of the little
bands of trekker-adventurers who settled among them. The greatest of these
was Sekwati, a man who took Moshweshwe as his model and who achieved
comparable success in building a modern military power capable of thrashing
Boer commandos. In the north-west Hurutshe, Rolong and Fokeng chiefs
had reoccupied old lands in and around the Magaliesberg hills. For them
the 'South African Republic' and 'the Transvaal' were not even names, let
alone a government. Men such as Potgieter, 'king of the blacks', and Pretorius
with the 'belly like the bass drum' would have to settle their differences with
each other before they could aspire to the status of a nation. As it happened,
neither lived long enough. They died within a few months of each other in
1854, each leaving ruthless, capable sons who would carry on the struggle.

Just as Mpande, Moshweshwe, Sekonyela, Makhasane, Faku, Zikhali, Soshangane, Mzilikazi, Adam Kok and Moroka outlived the trekker leaders, the institution of chieftainship lived on. In some ways it seemed little changed. It still rested on control of cattle which in turn controlled the productive and reproductive powers of women. It was still hedged about by awe-inspiring ritual, medicines, magic and the omnipresent influence of ancestors. However, south of the Limpopo chiefs were now limited in significant ways. Movement was constricted. Chiefs found it difficult to preserve their herds by moving beyond the reach of their enemies, unless they chose to follow Mzilikazi, Zwangendaba, Sebetwane and Soshangane in search of suitable country in northern Mozambique, on the Zimbabwe plateau or beyond the great Zambezi. It was likewise difficult to mount long-distance raids on the old grand scale. Without new supplies of cattle to reward brave *amabutho*, new ways had to be found to sustain the power of the state. Chiefs on good agricultural land near the white people's towns and villages could raise cash by selling grain. Some of the most powerful rulers copied Moshweshwe and changed the way they mobilized the labour of young men. Instead of recruiting teenage boys to the regiments, they sent them off to work for wages in distant places such as the Cape Colony and Natal. With that money youths could buy the cattle they once would have borrowed or captured; they could also help arm their rulers with modern weapons. More conservative leaders like Mpande resisted the temptation to export their young, hoping to find enough raiding opportunities in northern campaigns to make up for the lost raiding fields of the highveld and the southern coastal regions. Even this was not enough to satisfy Mpande's ambitious sons; his reward for having many children was to see them fight each other. In 1854 two of them, Cetshwayo and Mbuyazi, had already formed their own factions and were preparing to challenge each other for the right to succeed to the throne.

Over the next generation lines of labour trekkers moving between the rural strongholds of their rulers and the ports, plantations and mines run by white men became a common sight across the heartland. Whether these would continue to sustain the old chiefs or become so many ruinous pathways to proletarianization would depend on how well the strongest rulers succeeded in maintaining their independence from the political and economic forces at work all around them. In the short run, military power would be as important as lines drawn on the map in fixing the boundaries between independent chiefdoms and the realm of real estate auctions. This was pretty well understood by the time the Bloemfontein Convention brought the great Boer trek to an end. John Orpen had done so well out of his surveying work that he decided stay on in the town of Harrismith, which kept its name even after the inglorious departure of the vainglorious Sir

Harry. He even served for a time as the town's representative in the Free State Volksraad. Surveying could still be perilous work. One day on the side of the great mountain whose updrafts send eagles soaring over Harrismith Orpen had a close encounter with a lion. On another occasion he was surveying in the nearby district of Witsie's Hoek, where a typically mixed assortment of Sotho and Nguni people still occupied most of the land lately held by the fearless raider Witzi, one of Moshweshwe's less reputable allies, he found

It was rather ticklish work to survey these farms occupied by people who, no doubt, were strongly averse to this work [of preparing their land for sale]. I took no particular notice of them though I had to camp near, and often among them, but I went on quietly with the survey, including the putting up of big beacons. One day all my white calico flags were stolen. Next day I painted my name in red oil paint on a fresh supply – partly to spoil the calico and partly to make the natives fearful of witchcraft hurting them. This seemed to succeed. One day, a commando of Wietzie's people mounted and armed came up and surrounded me for several hours as I was riding from one beacon to another and taking observations. I laughed at them and went on with my work quietly and so got through the work and, besides, made a fair military map of the whole of Wietzie's Hoek which was of use in a subsequent campaign and in various ways.[54]

There would be many 'subsequent campaigns'. In those wars the Zulu, Pedi, Gasa and BaSotho armies would do much better than expected, and inflict severe defeats on their British, Boer and Portuguese enemies. But that is another story.

Notes

1 *Basutoland Records*, I, pp. 51, 108–9; William Cornwallis Harris, *The Wild Sports of Southern Africa* (first published 1837; fifth ed. reprinted Cape Town, 1963), pp. 119–20; T. Arbousset and F. Daumas, *Narrative of an Exploratory Tour to the North-East of the Colony of the Cape of Good Hope*, translated from French by John C . Brown (first published 1846; reprinted Cape Town, 1968), pp. 210, 226.

2 Leonard Thompson, *Survival in Two Worlds; Moshoeshoe of Lesotho, 1786–1870* (Oxford, 1975), p. 87.

3 *Basutoland Records*, I, p. 108.

4 Casalis to Lieutenant Governor, 16 Oct. 1844, in *Basutoland Records*, I, p. 81.

5 Robert Ross, *Adam Kok's Griquas* (Cambridge, 1976), p. 43.

6 Martin Legassick, 'The Griqua, the Sotho-Tswana and the Missionaries, 1780–1840' (PhD thesis, UCLA, 1969), p. 533.

7 *Natal Papers*, II, pp. 255–64; Thompson, *Survival in Two Worlds*, p. 121.

8 Monica Wilson and Leonard Thompson, eds, *Oxford History of South Africa*, 2 vols (Oxford, 1969), II, pp. 415–16.

9 *Basutoland Records*, I, p. 86.

10 Warden to Secretary to High Commissioner, 13 April 1849, in *Basutoland Records*, I, pp. 115, 117, 231; Warden to Somerset, 7 Sept. 1828, in *Records of Natal*, II, pp. 5–6; Alan Webster, 'Land Expropriation and Labour Extraction under Cape Colonial Rule' (MA thesis, Rhodes University, 1991), pp. 116–17. John Philip had advised that too many treaties would only confuse matters, therefore the only treaties should be with Moshweshwe and Kok; *Basutoland Records*, I, p. 46.

11 *Basutoland Records*, I, pp. 119–20.

12 J. B. Peires, *The House of Phalo: A History of the Xhosa People in the Days of their Independence* (Johannesburg, 1981), pp. 130, 134.

13 John S. Galbraith, *Reluctant Empire, British Policy on the South African Frontier* (Berkeley, 1963), p. 167.

14 Ibid., 171; Noël Mostert, *Frontiers: The Epic of South Africa's Creation and the Tragedy of the Xhosa People* (London, 1992), pp. 869–90.

15 Peires, *House of Phalo*, p. 151.

16 Galbraith, *Reluctant Empire*, pp. 174–5, 216, 248–9.

17 Mostert, *Frontiers*, p. 901–2.

18 Quoted in Peires, *House of Phalo*, p.155.

19 Quoted in Mostert, *Frontiers*, p. 923.

20 Mostert, *Frontiers*, pp. 903, 904, 921, 927.

21 Ibid., pp. 928–35; Galbraith, *Reluctant Empire*, pp. 220–6.

22 *Basutoland Records*, I, pp. 159–65.

23 Galbraith, *Reluctant Empire*, p. 231.

24 Ross, *Adam Kok's Griquas*, pp. 64, 81.

25 Galbraith, *Reluctant Empire*, p. 231.

26 Warden to the Secretary to the High Commissioner, 24 Feb. 1848, in *Basutoland Records*, I, p. 168. J. M. Orpen, *History of the Basutos of South Africa* (Cape Town, 1857), p. 34; Thompson, *Survival in Two Worlds*, pp. 142–3. The argument sometimes advanced, that Pretorius held Mpande in check, is not backed by

any credible evidence; for one version of it see C. J. Uys, *In the Era of Shepstone* (Lovedale, 1933) pp. 32–3.

27 Galbraith, *Reluctant Empire*, pp. 232–3.

28 Warden to Smith, 18 Aug. 1850, in *Basutoland Records*, I, p. 315; Ross, *Adam Kok's Griquas*, pp. 66–9.

29 J. M. Orpen, *Reminiscences of Life in South Africa* (vol. I originally published 1908, vol. II compiled from newspaper articles; reprinted as two volumes in one, Cape Town, 1964), p. 51.

30 Ibid., pp. 26–7, 78; *Basutoland Records*, I, pp. 147–8.

31 *Basutoland Records*, I, p. 276.

32 Warden to Smith, 11 Aug. 1850, in ibid., p. 314; see also pp. 256, 341 as well as Orpen, *History of the Basutus*, pp. 59–60.

33 Galbraith, *Reluctant Empire*, p. 246–7.

34 Quoted in Mostert, *Frontiers*, p. 1010.

35 *Basutoland Records*, pp. 352, 360–4.

36 Orpen, *History of the Basutus*, pp. 70, 80; *Basutoland Records*, I, p. 410.

37 *Basutoland Records*, I, pp. 223–3; Orpen, *History of the Basutus*, pp. 29–30; E. Casalis, *The Basutos or Twenty-Three Years in South Africa* (first published 1861, reprinted Cape Town, 1965), pp. 63–4.

38 Smith to Warden, 17 June 1852 in *Basutoland Records*, I, p. 402; Thompson, *Survival in Two Worlds*, p. 154.

39 *Basutoland Records*, I, pp. 421–7.

40 *Basutoland Records*, I, pp. 428, 477, 584.

41 Warden to Secretary to High Commissioner, 14 July 1851, in *Basutoland Records*, I, p. 428.

42 Grey to Smith, 15 Sept. and 21 Oct. 1851, ibid., I, pp. 445–8, 463.

43 Eric Walker, ed., *Cambridge History of the British Empire, Vol. VIII: South Africa, Rhodesia and the High Commission Territories*, 2nd edn (Cambridge, 1963), p. 356.

44 Warden to Hogge, 2 Feb. 1852, in *Basutoland Records*, I, p. 534.

45 Cathcart to Secretary of State for Colonies, 14 Nov. 1852, and Cathcart to the British Resident, 2 Sept. 1852, in *Basutoland Records*, I, pp. 587, 604–8,

46 Report of Cathcart's interview with Moshweshwe, 15 Dec., 1852 and Memorandum relative to Cattle received, 19 Dec. 1852, in *Basutoland Records*, I, pp. 618–22.

47 Thompson, *Survival in Two Worlds*, pp. 161–3.

48 Owen to Cathcart, 21 Dec. 1852, in *Basutoland Records*, I, pp. 628.

49 Moshweshwe to Cathcart, 20 Dec. 1852, and Cathcart to Moshweshwe, 21 Dec. 1852 in *Basutoland Records*, I, p. 627.

50 *Basutoland Records*, I, pp. 632–5.

51 Wilson and Thompson, eds, *Oxford History of South Africa*, I, pp. 422–4.

52 Thompson, *Survival in Two Worlds*, pp. 165–6.

53 Robert Ross, *Beyond the Pale: Essays on the History of Colonial South Africa* (Johannesburg, 1994), pp. 48–9.

54 Orpen, *Reminiscences*, I, p. 66; on Witzi see *Basutoland Records*, I, pp. 398, 498–9.

CHAPTER 12

Legacies

Readers whose interest lies mainly in the story of southern Africa in the era of great treks may close the book. Those who are interested in the way *the past* is converted into *history* may want to read on. In the late twentieth century the artificiality of history became an intellectual cliché, as though people had for the very first time discovered that all the hustle of daily activity in millions of individual lives cannot be condensed to a chronological story of 'what actually happened'. Those who have tried to tell 'true' stories about the past have always known that the project is no more practical than persuading witnesses to agree about what happened in a bar-room brawl. The historian's craft consists precisely of using disparate accounts to weed out bad evidence from better evidence and making hard decisions about what is important and what is not. Historians have also always been aware that some things which must have happened have to be consigned to the realm of speculation because no evidence survives to be tested by the canons of historical research. Indeed, for the conscientious historian, the rigorous sifting of evidence is more important than the story-telling. Writers of fiction are permitted to imagine without limits. Historians are required to make their imaginings stand up to the tests required by the traditions of their trade. The *art* of history consists in telling stories which, while not contradicting the available evidence, make narrative sense by filling in the inevitable gaps. The resulting history will always reflect the personal tastes, beliefs and prejudices of the individual historian. This has been the case with histories of early nineteenth-century southern Africa since people began to write them. A particularly noteworthy feature of those histories is that so many of the main lines of story-telling, explanation and analysis appeared in print while the events recounted in this book were happening. Without pretending to be a full historiographical essay, this chapter briefly traces the way a few highly influential stories were taken up and repeated in subsequent eras, even when they lacked supporting evidence. It argues that it is time to throw some of them out.

The erroneous but enduring idea that the Zulu kingdom was an entirely new and enormously destructive force

An early and still valuable collection of documents compiled by John Centilivres Chase was published by Robert Godlonton as *The Natal Papers* in 1843. Chase and Godlonton were at the centre of the nest of land speculators who clamoured for annexation of territories held by the Xhosa and the Zulu.[1] Chase had convened the meeting held in Cape Town in 1833 to discuss formation of a formal British settlement at Port Natal and had been active in promoting labour migration. On page 20 he gave an account of the history of the Zulu monarchy said to have been communicated by the adventurer, Henry Francis Fynn, to Major Charters, who led the British expeditionary force to Port Natal in 1838:[2]

> In the year 1780 a chief of the name of Tingeswio ruled over the Umtetwa tribe, and inhabited the country to the eastward of the Toghela River. He is represented as intelligent, warlike, and enlightened far beyond what might have been expected from a barbarian. He opened a trade with the Portuguese, bartering ivory and oxen for beads and brass. He divided his army into regiments according to the color of their shields; and he subjugated all the neighboring tribes, and amongst these the Zulus, then under the chieftainship of Senzengakona, and not exceeding 2000 people. One of the women belonging to the last-mentioned chief gave birth to a son, named Chaka, who, as he grew up, shewed himself possessed of such energy of character and such warlike qualities, that Tingeswio took him under his protection, instructed him in the art of war, and gave him a command in his army. On the death of Senzengakona, Umfugas, the legal heir, succeeded to his authority; but his reign was brief, for he was soon assassinated by Chaka, who, not having sufficient scope for his ambition in the command of a small tribe, found means to alienate the army from their allegiance to his benefactor, Tingeswio, whom he attacked, made prisoner, and put to death. Chaka then possessed himself of supreme authority over all the tribes which had owed allegiance to Tingeswio, and united them into one nation, under the name of Zulus. As soon as the chief found himself firmly seated in his authority; he bestowed his whole care in disciplining his army; he substituted the short, stabbing assegai for the long

missile weapon used by the other Kafirs, by which means he entirely changed the mode of warfare, causing his men to close immediately with their forces, and fight them hand to hand.

He carried his victorious arms west as far as St. John's River, and east to De la Goa Bay, putting to death all whom he could overtake, and driving the fugitives to seek for refuge, and food in distant lands, leaving the countries which he passed over a solitude and waste. Chaka may be termed the South African Attila: and it is estimated that not less than 1,000,000 human beings were destroyed by him.

This thumbnail sketch incorporates several tales destined to live on: Dingiswayo the wise ruler who built his kingdom on trade and invented a new type of army; the emergence of Shaka who fostered a more ruthless form of warfare and united many 'tribes'; and the assertion that a million people died as a result of Shaka's conquests. No supporting evidence was offered for these assertions apart from the word of Fynn, who only arrived in Natal in 1824, long after the death of Dingiswayo. The date 1780 could only have been a wild guess. While a careful reading will show that Fynn does not credit Shaka with the invention of the short, stabbing spear – only the requirement that his soldiers use no other weapon – the story laid the basis for countless future tales of Shaka's military genius. The figure of a million dead, based on no evidence at all, received even wider circulation. For example, Hannah Arendt's hugely influential twentieth-century treatise on *The Origins of Totalitarianism* cited it as evidence of genocidal violence in Africa.[3]

Fynn's narrative of Zulu history was partly a product of obvious self-interest. By the time he told his story to Major Charters he was the only surviving member of the Port Natal traders to possess a credible claim to a large tract of land. He stood to gain by promoting the idea that Shaka's wars had swept away all the original inhabitants of the lands south of the Thukela. Other aspects of Fynn's narrative reflect his constrained field of vision. He spent very little time at the Zulu court and conducted most of his activities south of Port Natal. He knew the Nwandwe to be a formidable military power, but had no idea that their line of kings extended far back into the past. He knew little or nothing about the chiefdoms and kingdoms which lay north of the Phongola River. He correctly called attention to the way the emergence of the new kingdom of the Zulu upset previous power relationships, but was wrong to imply that the Zulu was a new kind of kingdom. However, it was not until the last third of the twentieth century that historical scholarship began to demonstrate that numerous other large kingdoms predated both Dingiswayo and Shaka. Until that time, historian after historian adopted Fynn's perspective – one that made the Zulu loom so large as to completely overshadow all rivals from the Great Fish River to the Zambezi.

By 1825 Thembu chiefs were complaining of raids by people they called Ficani or Fetcani (see Chapter 6, p. 152) who came from north of the mountains. While the word has an uncertain derivation it was originally used to refer to any aggressive movement or 'commando' composed of unknown people. As late as the 1830s it was being applied to Tswana groups who had moved south of the Orange to escape Kora and Griqua attacks.[4] It was still being applied to the 'Bhaca' chieftainship in Faku's territory in 1841.[5] From the time they first heard of Fetcani attacks British officials feared that they would drive Xhosa and Thembu into their zone. Through the reports of Port Natal traders they learned of Shaka's power and jumped to the conclusion that it was the Zulu king who had 'driven the Fetcanie on', even though other hypotheses were available.[6] The notion of people being 'driven south' towards their territory became an *idée fixe* in the minds of the British military. It was probably attractive at a psychological level because it directed attention away from their own aggression which was the fundamental source of turmoil among the Xhosa. Even after the initial mystery concerning the identity of Matiwane's combined Ngwane and Sotho forces at Mbholompo had been cleared up, some officials continued to assert that Shaka had sent forces against the Xhosa chiefs in 1828.[7] This gave birth to a myth that Shaka's campaigns created an enduring antipathy between Zulu and Xhosa people, even though the only attack he ever made south of the Mzimvubu was directed solely at Faku's cattle. In the course of time, the idea of the Zulu kingdom as an explosive force that drove other chiefs fleeing in all directions came to be applied to all southeastern Africa up the Zambezi and beyond. The Zulu, who only ever scored two notable victories against white opponents, were exalted as invincible warriors above the Xhosa chiefs who could claim many more successes in their resistance to Boer and British aggression.

Later Zulu kings found much to admire in this version of history. Portraying Shaka as the great conqueror who founded a new kind of state helped erase the inconvenient memory of the Ndwandwe and kindred groups whose pedigree extended back for generations and whose political organization probably supplied the model for Dingiswayo's and Shaka's statebuilding projects. Mpande on one occasion expressed delight at a gift of wild vegetables from one of Sikhunyana's daughters. Only people such as her father, whom Shaka had driven away, would have to eat wild food, he said. Mpande went on, boasting that 'we drove Sikhunyana far away; we drove Mzilikazi far away; and we drove Nxaba ka Mbekane far away'.[8] It is conceivable that the real object of Dingane's quixotic, unsuccessful raids against Mzilikazi and Soshangane was to prove that no one could hide from the Zulu king. Through a stroke of luck, the Zulu version of history received massive support in Natal from colonial officials who formed their opinions about the past on the basis of interviews with old men in their neighbourhood. One of these officials, James Stuart, interviewed hundreds of men in the Zulu language over a period of several decades, compiling a massive collection later to be translated into English and published as *The James Stuart Archive*. Before their publication these papers were consulted by the missionary A. T. Bryant and provided much of the material for his influential book, *Olden Times in Zululand and Natal* (first edition, 1929).[9] Even those of Stuart's interviewees who hated Shaka agreed with the colonial writers in rating him the most powerful and important of southern African kings. It is difficult for historians to cut the Zulu kings down to size, because they are so much better documented than most other African leaders.

Stories of the *'lifaqane'* in the Caledon Valley and emergence of the concept of the *'mfecane'*

One of the very few leaders to rival Shaka's fame was Moshweshwe, founding king of Lesotho. French missionaries did him the service A. T. Bryant performed for the Zulu, compiling over the course of many decades a huge written archive based on the oral testimony of Moshweshwe, his subjects, descendants and allies. Because his realm eventually came under the control of British administrators, his version of history also captured the attention of colonial officials – though none equalled the energy of Stuart in Natal. The French missionaries had found a success with Moshweshwe that had been denied them elsewhere (see Chapter 7, pp. 201–3) and repaid the favour by celebrating his wise statesmanship. Despite the wealth of evidence attesting to his skill and daring as a war leader, they presented the king as a pacific statesman who only resorted to force when his people were attacked. They inserted themselves into the scenario as God's messengers who brought the message of peace to a land convulsed by savage struggles.[10] The broad outlines of this story can be read in various mission magazines and tracts in the 1830s. However, the land struggles which followed Napier's and Warden's attempts to inscribe boundary lines in the Caledon made history-writing a practical necessity. Every chief tried to follow Moshweshwe's example by having missionaries put their version of history on paper. By 1883, most of these written statements had been edited by George McCall Theal and published as part of the *Basutoland Records*.

General Cathcart was to some extent justified when he dismissed them all as 'political frauds' concocted by missionaries. They are filled with contradictions and confusions of places, names and dates. On the other hand, they provide the nearest thing to a chronicle of events in the Caledon by the people who lived through them. None could claim that their ancestors held undisturbed primeval ownership of any tract of land. The best any of them could do was to claim to have arrived earlier than others. Because they composed their accounts for judgement by British officials, they could be expected to suppress information about their own aggression and to emphasize the aggression committed against them. The result was that every leader from Moshweshwe down to Gert Taaibosch posed as the victim of other people's violence, having been driven to take refuge in this magnificent territory. They elaborated and embellished stories of cannibalism.[11] They glossed over the fact that their mountain fortresses were seized from people already living on them. None claimed to have gone to the Caledon to take advantage of opportunities for raiding in the valley or across the mountains into Thembu and Xhosa territory. Taken together these accounts present a paradox. On the one hand the Caledon Valley is described as a territory devastated by violence in which huge numbers of people lost their lives and some were driven to cannibalism. On the other hand, the region is shown to have attracted a large population who by the 1830s possessed enviable herds, flocks and horses along with large numbers of firearms. Had the conflicts of the early 1820s really been as horrendous as most of the accounts suggest, such a leap forward in material prosperity would have been impossible. It would at the very least require a comprehensive and convincing explanation. In the absence of such an explanation the historian must choose between the two pictures. As the prosperous times in the Caledon were reported in documents composed by living witnesses and the alleged disasters of the 1820s rely on hearsay evidence recorded later, the judicious historian will surmise that losses of life in the bad times were greatly exaggerated. Adulphe Delegorgue arrived at this conclusion in the 1840s when he could find no evidence for cannibalism being practised anywhere except in the accounts of French missionaries. His sarcastic observation was that in all southern Africa, cannibals were only to be found in the vicinity of the mission stations of Morija, Motito, Thaba Nchu and Thaba Bossiu.[12] It is much easier to agree with Delegorgue than with the missionary D. F. Ellenberger, who proffered the following quite fantastic calculation of death by digestion in the Caledon Valley alone.

Let us estimate the number of cannibals at a minimum, say 4,000. Say each one ate one person a month, and we arrive at the total of 48,000 persons eaten during one year; and during the six worst years, between 1822 and 1828, at the appalling figure of 288,000 devoured by their fellows. If we allow for those eaten during subsequent years, it is easy to arrive at a total of 300,000.[13]

As his estimate for the whole Sotho population between the Orange River and the Magaliesberg hills in 1800 was 448,700, this means he believed that 40 per cent were eaten by cannibals!

More recently Elizabeth Eldredge has produced convincing reasons for drastically scaling down estimates of lives lost in the wars of the 1820s.[14] She observes that the first clash between Matiwane and Moshweshwe was remembered as a major battle because some 3000 cattle were taken, while the actual death toll appears to have been only four men killed. When we consider that all the great chiefs aside from Mpangazitha survived the bad times, Eldredge's case appears very strong.

Nonetheless, for a century and a half, most histories reprinted the legend of devastation, depopulation and cannibalism in the Caledon. They also presented a sequence of events said to have caused this disaster, which ran roughly as follows: Shaka attacked Matiwane who attacked Mpangazitha who attacked Sekonyela, who attacked Moshweshwe, thus setting off a chain-reaction of war which spread mayhem in all directions. The time of troubles itself was eventually given a name in BaSotho histories: *lifaqane*, whose meaning is variously given as 'time of crushing', 'time of uprooting', 'time of migration by whole communities', to name but a few. As the word has now disappeared from common speech and survives only in the histories, it is impossible to reach agreement on a single definition. What matters most is the way the term was gradually assimilated to the word Fetcani, which was used by Thembu and Xhosa people in the 1820s to describe the raiders who entered their territory from over the Drakensberg and across the Mzimvubu River. The conflation of the two terms eventually resulted in the coinage of a new term toward the end of the nineteenth century: *mfecane*, used to refer to a period of warfare said to have convulsed all of southern Africa.

In this way, the self-interested tales told by competitors for rights to land in Natal and the little world of the Caledon Valley were inflated into a grand narrative which was applied to all the heartland from the coast of Mozambique to the Kei River and from the Drakensberg to the Zambezi. George McCall Theal began to gain recognition as South Africa's first professional historian in the 1880s through his publication of a collection of documents, *Basutoland Records* (1883), and *History of the Boers in South Africa* (1887). With this background, it was not surprising that he should view the history of all southern Africa from the perspective of the southern highveld. In the *History of the Boers* he calculated the 'destruction of human beings in what is now the Lesuto, and in the north-east of the present Free State ... at three hundred thousand' and 'on the other side of the mountains at least half a million'. He followed this estimate with a telling comment: 'Compared with this, the total loss of human life, occasioned by all the wars in

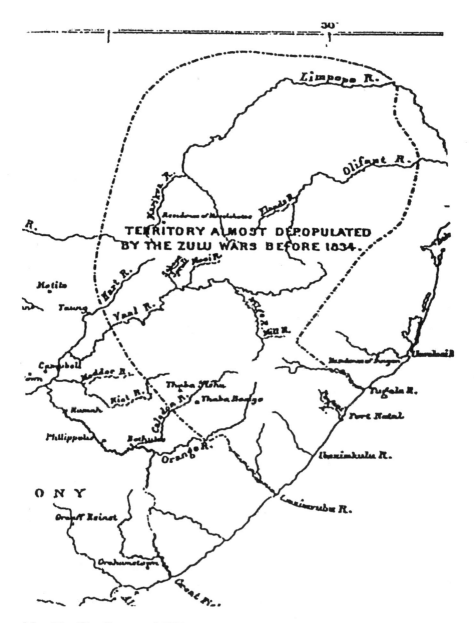

Map 23   Theal's map of 1891
Source: G. M. Theal, *History of South Africa* (London: Swansonnenchein, 1891)

South Africa in which Europeans have engaged since first they set foot in the country, sinks into insignificance.'[15] He repeated that sentence word for word four years later in his *History of South Africa*, but without citing any evidence expanded his calculation of lives lost during the period 1810–34 in the entire heartland region to 'nearer two millions'.[16] This leap of (bad) faith changed the tales told by Caledon land claimants into an excuse for Boer and British aggression: whatever the commandos and cannons had done, Shaka and Mzilikazi had done far more in the way of killing. Theal included a map purporting to show 'Territory almost depopulated by the Zulu Wars Before 1834' which included all the highveld and Natal. He obviously chose the date 1834 with care to suggest that when the trekkers set out into the interior they were entering a land which had already been practically emptied of people. This transformed the Caledon *lifaqane*, which had been used to justify African land claims, into a much larger phenomenon for the purpose of justifying claims to the whole region.[17]

Further refinement of the mfecane concept

In 1928 another historian, Eric Walker, first used the term *Mfecane* to denote a period of ceaseless warfare throughout the entire region shown on Theal's map. 'For fifteen years or so before D'Urban's arrival,' he wrote, '"pandemonium had raged" among the Bantu of South-eastern Africa.' The whole heartland was a 'whirling mass of tribesmen'.[18] No one knows precisely where Walker picked up the term; it does not appear in any pre-existing dictionary of the Zulu or Xhosa languages. He may have invented it after seeing a definition of *lifaqane* attributed to Neamiah Moshweshwe:

> The word Lifaqane is of Seteble origin, and denotes a state of migration. It is used here as describing the struggles of wandering tribes accompanied by their families, flocks, and herds, as distinct from the ordinary expeditions of inter-tribal warfare in which as a rule only the fighting men took part.

The reference to the foreign origin might have inspired Walker or one of his acquaintances to invent a Zulu version of the word, though none was to be found in any dictionary. Whatever the derivation, for the next sixty years virtually all historians accepted that there had been such a thing as the *mfecane* though many questioned Theal's huge estimate of the numbers of people who perished. Eventually, the word was Sotho-ized in some books, and written as *difaqane*, adding further to the confusion, but cementing the underlying idea as one of the foundation stones of regional histories.

Historians clung to the concept of the *mfecane* even after most of their profession had ceased to use it as a justification for Boer and British seizures of land. In some books the *mfecane* becomes a thing in itself, a dark monster moving across the landscape: 'By 1825 the *Difaqane* had passed beyond the Southern Sotho, but it continued to plague the Tswana for another few years.'[19]

In a landmark book, *The Zulu Aftermath* (1966), John Omer-Cooper turned the idea upside down and hailed the *mfecane* as evidence of African abilities to invent new ways of warfare and new kinds of states.[20] Drawing heavily on Bryant's *Olden Times in Zululand and Natal* and Ellenberger's *History of the Basuto*, Omer-Cooper accepted the idea that Shaka launched a 'revolution in Bantu Africa' characterized by a new state structure and a series of military innovations. He employed that assumption over and over again.[21] The Swazi, he said, used 'the system of military organisation which developed as a result of contact with the Zulu'. Soshangane 'employed the age-regiment system and Zulu fighting methods'. Zwangendaba 'drilled his followers in Zulu fighting tactics'. Mzilikazi triumphed because of 'military discipline and Zulu fighting techniques'.

Only in the 1980s did the concept of the *mfecane* come under attack in a series of critical papers by Julian Cobbing, who mercilessly exposed the flaws in logic and evidence used by historians to blame (or credit) the rise of the Zulu kingdom for setting off a 'chain reaction' of violence.[22] Cobbing's critique made it impossible to sustain the idea of the *mfecane* as a 'Zulu aftermath'. However, the door remained open for those who wanted to retain *mfecane* as a label for a period of violence and state-creation lasting from about 1810 to 1830. Cobbing himself assisted the retention of this residual *mfecane* by insisting that the motor of political change in the heartland during that period was aggression associated with Griqua raids in the west and slaving from the Mozambique coast in the east. He saw the Zulu, Ndwandwe, Gasa, Basotho and other states arising as 'defensive formations' responding to threats from slave-raiders which then were drawn into that very trade. This book has gone beyond Cobbing, arguing against the unsubstantiated assumption that no large states appeared before the nineteenth century. On the contrary, such states are known to have existed in the north-west, in the Limpopo Valley, on the Zimbabwe plateau and along the Indian Ocean coast.[23] All the essential building blocks required to build such states, especially the control of production and reproduction based on cattle holding, had existed for centuries. There may have been many such states, but once they collapsed, their successors would have used their control of official remembering to suppress memories of their predecessors. This book has further argued that the Zulu was a new kingdom (but not a new type of kingdom) which copied the political and military institutions of the much older Ndwandwe kingdom; there were no 'new fighting methods' aside from Shaka's ban on using throwing spears in combat (an innovation which no one copied). Finally, this book finds no credible evidence to support the assertion that the kind of conflicts observed in the Caledon Valley convulsed all south-eastern Africa. Any theory which tries to link external violence, whether of slavers or commandos or Griqua, to the emergence of larger states must of necessity explain why those forces *broke up* states on the western highveld and along the British frontier. It is impossible to quantify deaths due to warfare in the heartland in the early nineteenth century and there is no solid basis on which to compare them with mortality rates in previous eras. All Europeans had a tendency to magnify deaths in battle because in their own wars the principal aim was to inflict maximum casualties on the enemy. The principal aim of heartland chiefs was to capture cattle, not kill people. Modern scholars should take note of the discrepancy and hesitate before dismissing any conflict as 'a mere cattle-raid'.

One of the least noticed flaws in the *mfecane* concept, one that had been present from the very beginning, was acceptance of the idea that the vast open grasslands of the heartland were cleared of people by the violence that allegedly erupted at the dawn of the nineteenth century. Most probably the open country had never been home to many people apart from cattleless so-called Bushmen. Rainfall and water were too unreliable. It was hard to protect herds of cattle, which is why reports of vast herds, hippopotami, lions and hyena still abound in travellers' accounts of the western and central highveld as late as the 1830s. Like other parts of the continent, south-eastern Africa remained relatively under-populated until the twentieth century.[24] Archaeological investigation has shown that chiefs preferred to locate their people mostly east of the 500mm annual rainfall line and above the 1500 meter contour which is similarly associated with uncertain rainfall.[25] 'The important settlements tend[ed] to be on or beside mountains or hills.'[26] While proximity to rivers could be important, settlements were rarely located on rivers, because of the potential damage of flooding. The explanation for the famous horseshoe-shaped configuration of twentieth-century 'Bantustans' in South Africa is not that Africans were pushed into them, but that through stubborn resistance chiefs managed to hold sections of the lands they regarded as best suited to an economy based on mixed farming and pastoralism.[27] The earliest proponents of the *mfecane* concept blamed Shaka and Mzilikazi for depopulating land which had never carried many people, because it suited their purposes to emphasize alleged 'savage depredations'.

Thus, the historians who have suggested that the *mfecane* be dropped from our vocabulary present a convincing case. Dan Wylie correctly observes that the *mfecane* 'is fundamentally, and essentially no more than a rhetorical construction – or, more accurately, an abstraction arising from a rhetorics of violence'.[28] There is no evidence – and it is unlikely that evidence will ever be found – to substantiate the proposition that all southeastern Africa was caught up in a storm of violence. The documented conflicts in the north-west, the Caledon Valley, and the hinterland of Delagoa Bay cannot in themselves justify the use of the umbrella term *mfecane*. The idea that those conflicts can be separated from disruptive forces emanating from the British Zone and the Mozambique coast is unrealistic. For all these reasons, this book has avoided speaking of the *mfecane*.

The 'Movement of the Emigrant Farmers' becomes 'The Great Trek'

While the basic stereotypes of Shaka the innovator/destroyer and of the *mfecane* were widespread among literate observers by the 1830s, the idea of the trekking movement as a national awakening of the Afrikaner people only emerged late in the nineteenth century. Mzilikazi and Dingane found it difficult to distinguish the trekkers from Griqua, Kora, or other invaders who came on horses wearing European clothes and carrying guns. Neither did the Griqua leaders Adam Kok and Waterboer initially differentiate the Boers who had been coming over the Orange in search of good pasturage since the late 1820s from the trekking parties who came in 1836. British colonists wished the trekkers Godspeed, loading them up with memorials, Bibles and offers of help. The British military élite agreed with the editor of the *Graham's Town Journal* when he blamed the trekking movement on philanthropists in England and the misguided policies of Lord Glenelg. No one at the time remarked on antagonism between individual Boers and Britons. No one blamed British officials in South Africa for pursuing discriminatory policies towards the Afrikaans-speaking population. The Natal Volksraad itself pronounced Benjamin D'Urban to have been 'the best governor we ever had'. An English-language newspaper expressed the hope that 'this emigration may be the greatest blessing which has ever yet been experienced in this section of South Africa'.[29] By which was meant the speedy annexation of the territory occupied by the trekkers.

Sir Harry Smith's grand plan was grounded on his presumption that the trekkers would revert to being good British subjects once they saw he was reinstituting the policies of his old commander, D'Urban. Henry Cloete, who was both a British official and a member of one of the élite Afrikaner families of the Cape Peninsula, acted as a propagandist for Harry Smith's administration when he delivered 'Three Lectures on the Emigration of the Dutch Farmers from the Colony of the Cape of Good Hope' in Pietermaritzburg in 1852.[30] Virtually every historic occurrence emphasized in later interpretations of the trekking movement was announced in those lectures to an enthusiastic audience which included many people who had taken part in the events of which he spoke. He began by conjuring up a mythic past he claimed existed in 1813 when the Cape enjoyed peace and prosperity under the best of administrations. 'A small military force, under the command of my never to be forgotten brother-in-law, Col. Graham' had cleared the Zuurveld of all Xhosa farmers; wise laws maintained proper relationships between masters and servants. Into this paradise came the 'illiterate and prejudiced' missionaries Read and Van der Kemp who laid mischievous charges and instigated a rebellion of farmers, several of whom were hanged at Slagter's Nek in 1815.

Cloete claimed to know 'from personal interviews with several of the descendants of those who were then executed, that these events which I have now detailed, have left in their minds a far more indelible impression than even their losses by the . . . wars, or the abolition of slavery'. Even in Natal Cloete said he had more than once heard the words 'We can never forget Slachters Nek'.[31] His account continued by blaming missionaries for establishing stations where people could live in idleness rather than working for Boers. Labour problems were further compounded by the poor compensation offered when slavery was abolished. He himself had received only £47 for a slave previously valued at £500. Even as these grievances were mounting, frontier problems were exacerbated by Shaka who, having depopulated Natal, 'drove the remnant of all these tribes, under the name of Fetcanee' upon the Xhosa, causing them to increase their thefts of Boer cattle and eventually to launch the 1834–5 war. Meanwhile Andrew Smith's expedition had demonstrated the economic potential of Natal. When the annexations of D'Urban, 'without compare the best Governor with which the Cape Colony has ever been favoured', were reversed by Lord Glenelg, Boers concerned about land, labour and security determined on an 'Exodus'.

Although later writers put their own individual twists on Cloete's story, they preserved its basic elements from generation to generation.[32] In Cloete's eyes the trek resulted from correctable mistakes in policy. Tough labour laws, a firm policy on the frontier and conciliatory gestures would restore the lost subjects to their allegiance. Cloete regarded the trekkers as people, not *a people*. The move toward regarding the trek as an expression of 'a nation's will' began in the minds of some individual trekkers as they discovered their ability to survive without protection from the British government and came to view their land claims as a heritage purchased by their battles and hardships. When, in 1839, the *Graham's Town Journal* published the outline of the scheme promoted by Chase and Bannister to make Natal a British colony, the Natal Volksraad solemnly protested that they 'bought their land by their blood, guided by God, after having been driven from their own country by the taunts, ridicule and robbery' of African 'vagabonds'.[33] During the 1860s and 1870s such feelings grew in the Transvaal republic and the Orange Free State, as the new governments developed a sense of separate identity. This was not yet, however, a sense of an overarching Boer or Afrikaner identity. Only when a failed British attempt at annexing the Transvaal in the years 1877–82 caused an outpouring of fellow-feeling among many Afrikaans-speaking communities in the Cape Colony did a true spirit of nationalism emerge.[34] That spirit strengthened during the years leading up to the Anglo-Boer War of 1899–1902. It was during these years that what Cloete's generation had called the 'movement of the Emigrant Farmers' began to be called the Great Trek, and the trekkers, Voortrekkers.[35] The word Voortrekker was especially significant because it denoted a vanguard of those who went ahead where others would follow. By this process the trek of a few thousand individuals was transmuted into a movement of the whole 'Afrikaner nation', including the majority who stayed in the Cape Colony. In the same way the core events of Cloete's story were exalted to the status of milestones on the route to nationhood.

English-speaking writers were surprisingly quick to adopt the phrases Great Trek and Voortrekkers, though the attitudes they expressed on these subjects varied widely. At one end of the spectrum, the trekkers were accepted as worthy representatives of pioneering European 'civilization'. Novels such as Rider Haggard's *Swallow* (1899) and a series of films in later years celebrated their nobility and their hardships.[36] The split between the Afrikaners and British colonists was seen as an unfortunate development which needed to be repaired. This attitude represented something of a continuation of the earlier military/colonial voices calling for conciliatory policies which would bring Boers back into the fold. At the other end of the spectrum, the existence of the Afrikaners as a nation or 'race' was accepted, but they were regarded as a rather peculiar people. Many who favoured the British side in the second Anglo-Boer War were drawn to the idea that the trekkers perpetuated a 'seventeenth-century' way of life at odds with modernity. People of liberal political or religious tendencies looked on the Great Trek as a tragedy which gave a narrow-minded, reactionary white oligarchy control of all the highveld's human and material wealth.

André du Toit has traced this strand of opinion back to the Victorian missionary David Livingstone, who believed that the trekkers suffered from the delusion that they were God's chosen people, divinely ordained to rule over their new-found land of milk and honey.[37] What is at stake here is not the religiosity of the trekkers, but the propositions that their convictions were grounded in Calvinist theology and that Afrikaners viewed themselves as a chosen people. Their religious zeal was probably exaggerated in an effort to counter the charges made by missionary critics, but many surviving documents evidence the trekkers' frequent allusions to the Bible and the parallels they drew between their experiences and those of the ancient Israelites – witness their thankfulness that God had caused the waves to engulf Major Smith's ill-fated assault on the Congella camp in 1842 (see Chapter 10, p. 292) However, it is hard to find any evidence that this sense of God's protection was a heritage of Calvinism or that the trekkers regarded themselves as a divinely inspired vanguard of a nation. Such beliefs only developed later in connection with the rise of Afrikaner nationalism.

For much of the twentieth century regimes dedicated to the survival and advancement of Afrikaner nationalism ruled South Africa. They commemorated 'The Great Trek' in public festivals, holidays, statues and monuments throughout the land. An imaginative journalist and master publicist, Gustav Preller, wrote extensive popular histories and helped make films about the Voortrekkers.[38] He immediately grasped the way the *mfecane* concept could be married to his narratives of Afrikaner civilization versus African savagery. 'The Boers had converted, in the short period of four years, into a peaceful land full of promise this howling wilderness in which before only the Zulu assagai and beasts of prey held sway.'[39] He had little or no knowledge of previous heartland history, but had no hesitancy about making it up. One of his books identified Mzilikazi as 'one of Dingane's chief men' and made Shaka an omnipresent mass murderer:[40]

> In the Zoutpansberg, Lydenburg and the Drakensberg his armies drove the
> survivors of more than one tribe into cannibalism. There was, indeed,
> hardly a square mile of what is now Natal, that had not been drenched
> with the blood of men, women and children, belonging to weaker tribes
> that had been put to the assegai.

It was not enough that land had been emptied to clear land fit for Voortrekker farms. Preller regretted that the job of extermination had stopped short of the goal: 'if Pretorius and Kruger in the north had eradicated the Ndebele and Venda and the English had done likewise to the Zulus and Basothos in the south – how much sorrow and suffering and adversity would they not have saved their own nation'.[41] The huge Voortrekker monument standing on the outskirts of Pretoria embodies the nationalists' chosen image of their putative forbears. Its iconography completely rejects the notion of the trekkers as backward rustics. An official guide explains:

> [At the gate] assegaais [sic] represent the power of Dingane, who sought to
> block the path of civilisation. . . .

343

[a statue of mother and child] symbolises the civilisation and Christianity that were maintained and developed by the women during the Great Trek.

Black wildebeest: symbolise Dingane's warriors, but also the barbarism that yielded to civilisation.

Triangular Cornice: Around the top of the Monument is a cornice in a zig-zag pattern. This symbolises fertility. The civilisation brought by the Voortrekkers must grow. . . .

The floor of the Hall of Heroes is lined with ever-widening rings of marble . . . which represents ripples after a stone has been cast into the water, becomes progressively wider until it fills the entire building. It symbolises the diffusion of the spirit of sacrifice that was generated by the Voortrekkers, and that eventually spread throughout the entire country . . . Flame: symbolises the flame of civilisation in South Africa.[42]

The theme is continued on the panels of the historical frieze that lines the interior. The Voortrekkers, immaculately groomed and dressed, leave the Cape Colony with herds and fancy Bibles. The land they enter is anything but empty. To possess it they must go into battle (the men wearing coats and ties, the women their best frocks) against countless 'savage' and deceitful enemies.

Although the sun still sends a shaft of light streaming through a hole in the roof each 16 December on the anniversary of the Battle of Blood River, the monument receives few visitors these days. Other public remembrances of the trek have been even more neglected since democracy came to South Africa.[43] Afrikaner nationalism, always a doomed project because of its minority base of support, teeters on the verge of extinction. With it dies the loaded narrative embodied in the terms Great Trek and Voortrekkers – which is one reason why those terms do not figure in this history. The trek of 1836–40 was only one of many treks undertaken by people following different leaders, speaking different tongues, honouring different ancestors, and seeking different homelands. It has no special claim to be called Great.

Forgetting chieftainship, inventing tribes

Apart from a few individuals affiliated with Christian missions, people of the heartland took no part in formulating the historic narratives of Zulu hegemony, the *mfecane* and the Great Trek. Different conventions informed their oral rememberings and few of those recollections were written down. This creates great difficulties for anyone wishing to visualize the early nineteenth century as African people experienced it. Accounts written by people raised in European cultural milieux embody deep-seated assumptions about political and social organization. Europeans conceived their own ancient history in terms of 'tribes', for example, the 'Germanic tribes' described by the Roman historian Tacitus. By the nineteenth century the notion of a tribe carried undertones of incipient nationalism. The English traced their ancestry to 'Anglo-Saxon tribes', the French to 'the Gauls', the Scandinavians to 'Vikings'. They remembered the 'tribal migrations' of Wends, Goths, Visigoths and Vandals. In their own age the spirit of nationalism permeated intellectual life. The tendency to see history in terms of tribes who were separate 'peoples' was all but irresistible. So they spoke of the 'Kaffir tribes', the Zulu tribe, the Basuto tribe and so forth. This led them to misunderstand profoundly the nature of the relationship between chiefs and their followers. Ordinary people did not give themselves ethnic labels. A person who *khonza'd* Shaka (who pledged their allegiance to him) became one of Shaka's people. Most people called their groups by the names of the chiefs they followed. As chiefs' fortunes rose and fell so did the numbers of their followers. The *James Stuart Archive* of Zulu testimony is filled with instances of people leaving one chief and joining another. Some authors have taken this as evidence of the disturbed nature of the times: 'in these circumstances to use the name of traditional clans to identify the wandering hordes becomes meaningless'.[44] But the near universality of the practice of identifying with one's chief or the chief's ancestor, claiming to be 'MaNtathisis' or 'Baraputsas' or 'Gasas' or 'Machobanes' or 'Soshanganes' argues against that hypothesis. The kings of the people now called Swazi, called themselves in succession by the names of their kings Ngwane, Sobhuza and Mswati. Perversely, in the few cases which feature chiefs trying to give their people new names, European observers tried to obliterate them. So Mzilikazi's 'Zulu' had to become 'Matabele' and the 'Bastards', Griqua. Anyone who studies old maps is instantly struck by the plethora of unfamiliar 'tribal' names. Again, this has been used in support of the mistaken concept of a pervasive *mfecane* obliterating settled 'tribes'.

This book has tried to emphasize the enormous importance of chieftainship and the virtual absence of ethnic feeling in the heartland during the early nineteenth century, but it has been uphill work because of further developments in European intellectual life. In the late nineteenth century the discipline of anthropology began to emerge, heavily influenced by nationalist assumptions about 'peoples'. Peoples were said to be distinguished by special ways of thinking, physical appearance, language, customs, marriage patterns and kinship linkages. As anthropology gained respectability the 'tribes' of South Africa were represented as a myriad of individual cultures, each one embodying a mental world of its own. Succeeding governments of South Africa employed anthropologists to compile 'ethnographies' of all the tribes. The idea of social organization grounded in shifting allegiances to chiefly families was obliterated and replaced by the notion of many different cultures who happened to be led by chiefs. The damage done by this 'creation of tribalism' cannot be over-stressed.[45] Land was assigned on the basis of putative cultural identities. Stereotypical representations of cultural differences worked their way into every nook and cranny of European writing, both fact and fiction. Eventually many people came to accept these stereotypes as authentic representations of the communities to which they belonged. And even when people knew them to be false, they saw their political utility in certain situations.

The anachronistic ascription of ethnic identities to the groupings which nineteenth-century Europeans called tribes caused otherwise careful historians to misinterpret the moves undertaken by chiefs in pursuit of power as 'migrations of people'. Schematic maps drawn to represent the so-called *mfecane* assigned ethnic labels to chiefs and used arrows to suggest wholesale migrations by ethnically homogenous communities. The 'Tlokwa' move down the Caledon; the 'Ndebele' move to the Magaliesberg; Moletsane's 'Taung' attack Makwassie, the 'Kololo' move beyond the Zambezi, etc. This practice reflects old European ideas of tribal migrations but misrepresents the historical experience of heartland peoples whose allegiances were constantly shifting – had probably always been shifting as far back as memory could recall. While this history has occasionally slipped into speaking in the misleading ethnic terminology, as in discussions of the 'Rolong Trek', it has tried to preach the lesson that in future anyone wanting to understand movements of people in the early nineteenth century must think in terms of chiefly families and followers, not 'peoples'. Only then will we have a proper conception of the many different great treks whose stories retain their power to fire the human imagination.

Notes

1 *Natal Papers*; P. R. Kirby, *Andrew Smith and Natal* (Cape Town, 1955), p. 145; John Wright, 'The Dynamics of Power and Conflict in the Thukela-Mzimkhulu Region in the late 18th and early 19th Centuries: A Critical Reconstruction' (PhD thesis, University of the Witwatersrand, 1989), pp. 69–70; Alan C. Webster, 'Land Expropriation and Labour Extraction under Cape Colonial Rule: The War of 1835 and the "Emancipation of the Fingo"' (MA thesis, Rhodes University, 1991), p. 159.

2 Apart from the figure of one million dead, several elements of Fynn's communication to Charters also appear in information he gave Andrew Smith in 1832; see Kirby, *Andrew Smith and Natal*, pp. 42–6.

3 Hannah Arendt, *The Origins of Totalitarianism* (London, 1973), p. 192. The citation has not changed through many editions since first publication in 1951.

4 Statement of William Hartley, 29 June 1833 in *Records of Natal*, II, pp. 223–4.

5 *Natal Papers*, II, pp. 159.

6 Christopher Saunders, 'Pre-Cobbing Mfecane Historiography', in Carolyn Hamilton, ed., *The Mfecane Aftermath: Reconstructive Debates in Southern African History* (Johannesburg, 1995), p. 24.

7 Henry Cloete, *Five Lectures on the Emigration of the Dutch Farmers from the Colony of Good Hope* (Cape Town, 1856), p. 59.

8 Statement of Mandhlakazi, 7 Jan. 1921, in *JSA*, II, p. 188; see also *JSA*, II, pp. 230 and III, p. 45.

9 For a critical appraisal of Bryant's work, see Wright, 'Dynamics of Power', especially pp. 96–9.

10 Other missionaries practised the same pious deception. See John Edwards's description of his pioneer journey to a new station in a wagon whose wheels crushed skulls as it went; *Reminiscences of the Early Life and Missionary Labours of the Rev. John Edwards* (Grahamstown, 1883), p. 56.

11 Moshweshwe to the Secretary to Government, 15 May 1845, in *Basutoland Records*, I, p. 82; Leonard Thompson, *Survival in Two Worlds: Moshoeshoe of Lesotho, 1786–1870* (Oxford, 1975), pp. 128–32.

12 Adulphe Delegorgue, *Voyage dans l'Afrique Australe*, 2 vols (Paris, 1847) II, pp. 543–6.

13 D. Fred. Ellenberger, *History of the Basuto, Ancient and Modern* (London, 1912), pp. 225, 303. A similar silly calculation was made by Methodist John Ayliff who reckoned that 'Shaka killed 690,000 Fingo'; see Webster's critique in 'Land Expropriation', p. 19.

14 Elizabeth Eldredge, 'Migration, Conflict and Leadership in Early 19th Century South Africa. The Case of Matiwane', seminar paper, Dept of History, University of Natal, Durban, 3 August 1994.

15 George M. Theal, *History of the Boers in South Africa* (first published 1887, reprinted Cape Town, 1973), p. 34. On Theal's career see Christopher Saunders, *The Making of the South African Past* (Cape Town, 1988), pp. 9–29.

16 Julian Cobbing, 'The Mfecane as Alibi: Thoughts on Dithakong and Mbolompo', *Journal of African History* 29 (1988), p. 315; Saunders, 'Pre-Cobbing Mfecane Historiography', p. 23. On Theal's map see Saunders, *Making of the South African Past*, p. 41.

17 John Wright puts the case in a slightly different way, arguing that Theal's importance consisted in taking the Natal stereotype of Shaka's devastations

and attaching it to the whole tableau of South African history as a first cause; 'Dynamics of Power', p. 77.

18 Eric Walker, *A History of Southern Africa* (first published 1928; London, 1962), pp. 175–6. However, Walker dismissed Theal's claims of 'depopulation'.

19 William Lye and Colin Murray, *Transformations on the Highveld: The Tswana and Southern Sotho* (Cape Town, 1980), p. 38.

20 John D. Omer-Cooper, *The Zulu Aftermath: A Nineteenth-Century Revolution in Bantu Africa* (London, 1966). According to John Wright, 'Dynamics of Power', p. 87, Omer-Cooper 'standardized' the meaning of the *mfecane* 'and projected it into general usage'.

21 Ibid., pp. 51, 59, 64, 131.

22 Many of these unfortunately remained unpublished: 'The Case against the Mfecane', seminar paper presented at Centre for African Studies, University of Cape Town, 1983; 'Jettisoning the Mfecane (with *Perestroika*)', paper presented at Africa Studies Institute, University of the Witwatersrand, 1988; 'Grasping the Nettle: The Slave Trade and the Early Zulu', paper presented at Workshop on Natal and Zululand in the Colonial and Precolonial Periods, University of Natal, Pietermaritzburg, 1990; and 'Overturning "The Mfecane"': a Reply to Elizabeth Eldredge', paper presented to Colloquium on the Mfecane Aftermath, University of the Witwatersrand, 1991.

23 As Malyn Newitt notes in his *History of Mozambique* (London, 1995), p. 257.

24 A proposition convincingly documented by John Iliffe in *The African Poor: A History* (Cambridge, 1987) and *Africans: The History of a Continent* (Cambridge, 1995).

25 T. M. O'C. Maggs, *Iron Age Communities of the Southern Highveld* (Pietermaritzburg, 1976), pp. 31, 193, 306.

26 Ibid., p. 31.

27 See, for example, the map of Bantustans in Leonard Thompson, *Politics in the Republic of South Africa* (Boston, 1976), p. 42.

28 Dan Wylie, *Savage Delights: White Myths of Shaka* (Pietermaritzburg, 2000), p. 194.

29 Volksraad to Napier, 21 Feb. 1842 in *Natal Papers*, II, pp. 198–205; see also II, p. 93.

30 After the incorporation of two further lectures carrying the story through to 1843, Cloete published his *Five Lectures*.

31 Ibid., pp. 7, 18–25, 32–3, 38, 47, 59, 61, 65, 73–75. Cloete used the old Dutch spelling of *slachter*. Floris Van Jaarsveld, who knew Cloete's work, inexplicably wrote that 'it was approximately in 1868 only when British pressure on the North was mounting, that Slagtersnek was "discovered"'; *The Afrikaner's Interpretation of*

South African History (Cape Town, 1964), p. 56. The mistake is repeated in Ken Smith, *The Changing Past* (Johannesburg, 1988), p. 60.

32 There is a large literature on this subject. For a sample of opinions see: Norman Etherington, 'The Great Trek in Relation to the Mfecane: A Reassessment', *South African Historical Journal* 25 (1991), pp. 3–21; Van Jaarsveld, *The Afrikaner's Interpretation*; Smith, *The Changing Past*, pp. 18–102; W. A. De Klerk, *The Puritans in Africa* (London, 1975).

33 Memorial of G. P. Kemp and others, 11 Nov. 1839, in *Natal Papers*, II, pp. 112–14.

34 Floris A. Van Jaarsveld, *Die Ontwaking van die Afrikaanse Nationale Bewussyn 1868–1881* (Johannesburg, 1957), published in English as *The Awakening of Afrikaner Nationalism* (Cape Town, 1961).

35 Leonard Thompson, *The Political Mythology of Apartheid* (New Haven, 1985), p. 173.

36 Edwin Hees, 'South Africa – Cinema – History. The Voortrekkers on Film: From Preller to Pornography', paper presented at the S.A. Cultural History Conference, Two Centuries of British Influence in South Africa (1795–1995), held in Pretoria, 29–30 June 1995. At the time of writing the text could be found at the website, http://www.und.ac.za/und/ccms/articles/voortrek.htm.

37 André du Toit, 'No Chosen People: The Myth of the Calvinist Origins of Afrikaner Nationalism and Racial Ideology', *American Historical Review* 88 (1983), pp. 920–52.

38 Isabel Hofmeyr, 'Popularizing History: The Case of Gustav Preller', *Journal of African History* 29 (1988), pp. 521–35.

39 Gustav Preller, *Day-Dawn in South Africa* (Pretoria, 1938), p. 200.

40 Ibid., pp. 175, 179.

41 Quoted in Isabel Hofmeyr, *'We Spend our Years as a Tale that is Told'*: Oral *Historical Narrative in a South African Chiefdom* (London, 1993), p. 151.

42 Riana Heymans, *The Voortrekker Monument, Pretoria* (Pretoria, 1986).

43 Albert Grundlingh and Hilary Sapire, 'From Feverish Festival to Repetitive Ritual? The Changing Fortunes of Great Trek Mythology in an Industrialising South Africa, 1938–1988', *South African Historical Journal* 21 (1989), pp. 19–37.

44 William Lye and Colin Murray, *Transformations on the Highveld: The Tswana and Southern Sotho* (Cape Town, 1980), p. 35.

45 See Leroy Vail, ed., *The Creation of Tribalism in Southern Africa* (Berkeley, 1989).

FURTHER READING

P. Bonner, P. I. Hofmeyr, D. James and T. Lodge, eds. *Holding their Ground: Class, Locality and Culture in 19th and 20th Century South Africa* (Johannesburg, 1989).

Cobbing, Julian. 'The Mfecane as Alibi: Thoughts on Dithakong and Mbolompo', *Journal of African History* 29 (1988), pp. 487–519.

Omer-Cooper, John. *The Zulu Aftermath* (London, 1966).

Crais, Clifton. *White Supremacy and Black Resistance in Pre-Industrial South Africa: The Making of the Colonial Order in the Eastern Cape, 1770–1865* (Cambridge, 1992).

Delius, Peter. *The Land Belongs to Us: The Pedi Polity, the Boers and the British in the Nineteenth-century Transvaal* (London, 1984).

Eldredge, E. A. and Morton, F., eds. *Slavery in South Africa: Captive Labor on the Dutch Frontier* (Boulder, 1994).

Etherington, Norman. *Preachers, Peasants and Politics in Southeast Africa* (London, 1978).

Galbraith, John S. *Reluctant Empire* (Berkeley, 1963).

Hamilton, Carolyn. *Terrific Majesty, The Powers of Shaka Zulu and the Limits of Historical Invention* (Cape Town, 1998).

Hamilton, Carolyn, ed. *The Mfecane Aftermath, Reconstructive Debates in Southern African History* (Johannesburg, 1995).

Keegan, Timothy. *Colonial South Africa and the Origins of the Racial Order* (London, 1996).

Lye, William F., ed. *Andrew Smith's Journal of his expedition into the interior of South Africa, 1834–36* (Cape Town, 1975).

Lye, William F. and Colin Murray. *Transformations on the Highveld: The Tswana and Southern Sotho* (Cape Town, 1980).

Marks, Shula and Atmore, Anthony, eds. *Economy and Society in Pre-industrial South Africa* (London, 1980).

Maclennan, Ben. *A Proper Degree of Terror: John Graham and the Cape's Eastern Frontier* (Johannesburg, 1986).

Mostert, Noël. *Frontiers, the Epic of South Africa's Creation and the Tragedy of the Xhosa People* (London, 1992).

Muller, C. F. J. *Die Oorsprong van die Groot Trek* (Johannesburg, 1974).

Newitt, Malyn. *A History of Mozambique* (London, 1995).

Parsons, Neil. 'Khama's Country in Botswana', in R. Palmer and N. Parsons, eds., *The Roots of Rural Poverty in Central and Southern Africa* (London, 1977).

Peires, Jeff B. *The House of Phalo: A History of the Xhosa People in the Days of their Independence* (Johannesburg, 1981).

Rasmussen, R. Kent. *Migrant Kingdom: Mzilikazi's Ndebele in South Africa* (Cape Town, 1978).

Ross, Robert. *Adam Kok's Griquas: A Study in the Devleopment of Stratification in History* (Cambridge, 1976).

Ross, Robert. *Beyond the Pale: Essays on the History of Colonial South Africa* (Johannesburg, 1994).

Stapleton, Timothy. '"Him Who Destroys All": Reassessing the Early Career of Faku, King of the Mpondo, *c.* 1818–29', *South African Historical Journal* 38 (1998).

Thompson, Leonard. *Survival in Two Worlds: Moshoeshoe of Lesotho, 1786–1870* (Oxford, 1975).

Vail, Leroy, ed. *The Creation of Tribalism in Southern Africa* (Berkeley, 1989).

van der Merwe, Petrus, J. *Die Noordwaartse Beweging van die Boere voor die Groot Trek* (The Hague, 1937).

van der Merwe, Petrus, J. *Die Matebeles en die Voortrekkers* (Pretoria, 1986).

Walker, Erik. *The Great Trek* (London, 1938).

Wilson, Monica and Leonard Thompson, eds. *Oxford History of South Africa*, 2 vols (London, 1969–71), Vol. I.

Wright, John B. and Colin de B. Webb, eds. *The James Stuart Archive of Recorded Oral Evidence Relating to the History of the Zulu and Neighbouring Peoples*, 5 vols (Pietermaritzburg, 1976–2001).

Wylie, Dan. *Savage Delight: White Myths of Shaka* (Pietermaritzburg, 2000).

INDEX